WAVES OF DECOLONIZATION

NEW AMERICANISTS

A Series Edited by Donald E. Pease

WAVES OF DECOLONIZATION

Discourses of Race and

Hemispheric Citizenship in Cuba,

Mexico, and the United States

DAVID LUIS-BROWN

DUKE UNIVERSITY PRESS

Durham and London 2008

© 2008 Duke University Press
All rights reserved
Printed in the United States of America
on acid-free paper ∞
Designed by Jennifer Hill
Typeset in Minion Pro
by Keystone Typesetting, Inc.

*Library of Congress
Cataloging-in-Publication Data
appear on the last printed
page of this book.*

CONTENTS

ACKNOWLEDGMENTS

◑ In describing the process of writing this book to my nonacademic friends, I liken it to the craft of candle dipping. Just as a candle gains its shape through the process of repeatedly dipping the wick in hot wax, so these chapters came into being through a long process of research and writing, conversations in and out of the classroom, travel, and help from other scholars.

I am grateful to all those who generously added the hues of their own thinking to this project. Susan Gillman has been the best possible mentor and an invariably stimulating intellectual interlocutor. Norma Klahn shared her comprehensive knowledge of Latin American history and literature. José Saldívar's impassioned teaching and writing have inspired my hemispheric approach to cultural production. I am extremely grateful to George Lipsitz for his comments on an earlier draft of this book—they provided an invaluable compass to me through the final revisions; to Beth Freeman for meeting with me at an early stage in the publication process; and to Robert Gross—who came to my aid at a crucial moment—for his suggestions for revision. For their comments on chapters or parts of chapters, many thanks go to Chris Breu, Johnnella Butler, John González, Gwen Kirkpatrick, Vibeke Laroi, Francine Masiello, Julio Ramos, Roger Rouse, Roz Spafford, and the late Gene Ulansky and to my graduate school buddies Stuart Christie and Chris Shinn. Cathy Rigsby, the executive editor of *American Literature*, and the anonymous readers for the journal provided suggestions for editing and revising an earlier version of chapter 1 that was published as an article. I would also like to thank Judy Frank, my thesis advisor at Amherst College, and Robert Gooding-Williams, Robert Gross, George Kateb, Barry O'Connell, Andrew Parker, and Robert Thurman for their inspirational teaching before my graduate career began. Thanks as well to Dickson Bruce and Raúl Fernández at Irvine and to Michael Cowan and Lourdes Martínez-Echazabal at Santa Cruz for teaching courses that proved important to my career.

I am grateful to several sources for their financial support. Two two-year fellowships allowed me to research and finalize the manuscript. A University of California Predoctoral Humanities Fellowship provided me with two years of full support for graduate study. And a University of California President's Postdoctoral Fellowship gave me the opportunity to finish a draft of the manuscript as I began work on a new book project. Fortunately for me, Sara Johnson's time as a postdoctoral fellow at Berkeley overlapped with mine; I enjoyed talking with her about all things Cuban. Other fellowships that supported my research and writing included two Amherst College John Woodruff Simpson fellowships for graduate study; a University of California at Santa Cruz Literature Department qualifying examination fellowship and dissertation quarter fellowship; a University of California Humanities Research Institute Fellowship to participate in the residential research group "The Cultures of the Americas and the Narratives of Globalization," convened by Gwen Kirkpatrick. I am grateful to the participants in the Humanities Research Institute who helped to make my time in Irvine productive and enjoyable: Leo Chávez, Beth Marchant, Sergio de la Mora, Francine Masiello, Roger Rouse, and Josefina "Fina" Saldaña. My friends from the Los Angeles area also kept me going: "Little" Luis Camacho and his daughter Alexis, Michael Matteucci, Buddy Méndez, Casey Nagel, and Anita Weston. Casey deserves special mention for spending hours helping me to solve computer and software problems. Finally, a National Endowment for the Humanities Summer Institute Fellowship allowed me to participate in "The Americas of José Martí" institute at the University of South Florida in Tampa and at the Centro de Estudios Martianos in Havana, Cuba. I'd like to thank Jossianna Arroyo, Laura Lomas, and Elliott Young for their camaraderie in Tampa and Havana and Ivan Schulman for having led the institute.

Nahum Chandler's work on W. E. B. Du Bois has been the greatest gift to me, and I was delighted to finally meet him while we were both working short stints in the Department of Comparative Literature at the University of California at Davis. Many thanks to Neil Larsen for his interest in my work and his advice. The final stretch of revisions of this book took place as I worked at Lafayette College. I would like to thank all of my colleagues there, but especially Paul Cefalu, Bianca Falbo, Tori Langland, Alix Ohlin, Beth Seetch, Andrea Smith, and Lee Upton. I would also like to thank my new colleagues at the University of Miami for welcoming me and for helping to make my transition run so smoothly.

Publishing with Duke University Press has been a dream come true, especially because the two anonymous readers of the manuscript were so helpful in their suggestions for revision. I would also like to thank my editors at Duke, Sharon Parks Torian and Reynolds Smith, for all of their work in making this book a reality, as well as the rest of the staff at the press.

Finally, I would like to thank my family for their emotional and financial support: the late Tina (Puccinelli) Acerbi, my *nonni* (Italian-American dialect for grandmother); Brenda and Donal Brown, my parents; my sister Paula, her husband, John, and their children Erin and Evan; the late "Uncle" Al Minetti, my godfather, who was like a grandfather to me; my son Dante, my daughter Sofia, and my life partner and wife, Tina. In tribute to Tina I can do no better than to agree wholeheartedly with my mother-in-law, who tells me that even if my travails as a graduate student and professor haven't made me rich, I've been "livin' on love!" My in-laws have been wonderful: Connie and Frank Prado, their children, especially Mark Luis, and their many grandchildren. And *un abrazo fuerte* goes to the late Warren Kolodny, my best friend from college and a consummate "*cronopio*" to boot.

A shorter version of chapter 1 appeared as "'White Slaves' and the 'Arrogant *Mestiza*': Reconfiguring Whiteness in *The Squatter and the Don* and *Ramona*," in *American Literature* 69.4 (December 1997): 813–39, copyright 1997 by Duke University Press.

Introduction

Wave on wave, each with increasing virulence, is dashing this new religion of whiteness on the shore of our time.
—W. E. B. DU BOIS, "The Souls of White Folk," *Darkwater* (1920)

The colony has continued to survive within the republic.
—JOSÉ MARTÍ, "Nuestra América" ("Our America," 1891)

THE "WORLD ASPECT" OF THE "COLOR LINE" IN "TIME AND SPACE": DU BOIS'S CHALLENGE TO AMERICAN STUDIES

In *The Souls of Black Folk* (1903), W. E. B. Du Bois writes, "The problem of the twentieth century is the problem of the color line,—the relation of the darker to the lighter races of men in Asia and Africa, in America and the islands of the sea."[1] The lesser-known second clause of Du Bois's most famous pronouncement pushes the color line beyond the United States, sketching out a global approach. What would the disciplines of American studies and American literature look like if scholars were to use the global color line in order to transform their fields into comparative, transnational endeavors?

Du Bois offers one possible answer in "Of the Dawn of Freedom" in *Souls*, which begins with this formulation of the problem of the color line. Du Bois's assessment of the Freedmen's Bureau's efforts to enfranchise African Americans following the Civil War concludes, "Despite compromise, war, and struggle, the Negro is not free" (*S* 239). Nominal freedom, we learn, is not a solution but rather a chronic problem: "Thus Negro suffrage ended a civil war by beginning a race feud," Du Bois writes (*S* 238). By beginning this chapter with his theory of the color line, Du Bois transforms the meanings of what is usually regarded as a chapter in U.S. history: it now appears as part of a broader series of fortifications and adjustments of the global color line. Therefore the defeat of Reconstruction is not just a blow to U.S. democracy, but a loss felt by democratic movements across the world. Here Du Bois's technique is not to turn African Americans into figures of the universal but rather to magnify their significance as a test of global democracy. Equally important, Du Bois's method is to take the *conclusion* of the Civil War period—the ostensible attainment of African American freedom in Reconstruction—as the *beginning* of inquiry, as itself a problem for both investigation and activism. If the discourse of freedom/emancipation is the North's proposed resolution for slavery, a "second slavery" of inequality emerges that Reconstruction attempts to resolve with a discourse of racial equality (*S* 220). In his own post-Reconstruction moment, Du Bois attempts to build on and refine that discourse of racial equality in *Souls*. He presents a two-pronged method of analysis, expanding outward from the United States along the cross-national "color line" and straddling the bounds of conventional historical periods in order to show that despite the fact that such periods appear to be finished, they are characterized by problems that extend into our present in altered form.

In order to understand the full implications of the color line as a methodology of periodization and transnational analysis, one needs to look beyond *Souls*, which mainly focuses on the United States, to his lesser-known texts. In an earlier speech, "The Present Outlook for the Dark Races of Mankind" (1900), in which Du Bois introduces the color line concept to the African American intellectuals gathered at the third annual meeting of the American Negro Academy, he states, "It is my purpose to consider with you the problem of the color line not simply as a national and personal question but rather in its larger world aspect in time and space."[2] Time and space. Even in his earliest formulation of the color line, Du Bois emphasizes its connection not only with space, but also with time, confirming the two-pronged character of the color line as a methodology.

In this speech, the "world aspect" of the color line, somewhat implicit in "Of the Dawn of Freedom," comes to the fore, as Du Bois assesses the history of colonial conflict and racial strife in Africa, Asia, and Latin America. Du Bois devotes special attention to U.S. imperial ambition in Latin America and the Pacific:

> Most significant of all at this period is the fact that the colored population of our land is, through the new imperial policy, about to be doubled by our

own ownership of Porto Rico, and Hawaii, our protectorate of Cuba, and conquest of the Philippines. This is for us and for the nation the greatest event since the Civil War and demands attention and action on our part. What is to be our attitude toward these new lands and toward the masses of dark men and women who inhabit them? Manifestly it must be an attitude of deepest sympathy and strongest alliance. ("PO" 53)

Du Bois argues that U.S. imperialist expansion is the "most significant" development along the global color line since the Civil War, thereby linking domestic civil rights struggles to anti-imperialism. Furthermore, in what is his boldest claim, Du Bois argues that numerous "colored" populations subjected to the "new imperial policy" have become de facto members of the U.S., if not yet de jure citizens, and therefore African Americans should forge alliances with them. One result for intellectual inquiry is that if for many scholars U.S. history can be viewed as an exclusively national story, such is not the case for Du Bois. More specifically, Du Bois figures the extension of U.S. empire in the Spanish-American-Cuban War of 1898 as *the* defining event for African Americans. Here is a second result of Du Bois's emphasis on the importance of 1898: it calls on African Americans to forge a political identity that goes beyond their particular ethnic identity.

As Du Bois states to the audience of black intellectuals, "I freely acknowledge that in the red heat of a burning social problem like this, when each of us feels the bitter sting of proscription, it is a difficult thing to place one's self at that larger point of view and ask with the cold eye of the historian and social philosopher: What part is the color line destined to play in the twentieth century? And yet this is the task I have laid out for you this evening, and one which you must take up for yourselves; for, after all, the secret of social progress is wide and thorough understanding of the social forces which move and modify your age" ("PO" 47). Du Bois's challenge to the American Negro Academy—and, by extension, to today's American studies—is to adopt "that larger point of view" and pay attention to the plight of those "dark races" who face U.S. imperialism.

More broadly, this "larger point of view" calls for a rethinking of both the geographical bounds of U.S. American history and culture and their chronology, linking and decentering the U.S.-based periods of slavery, Civil War, and Reconstruction with a broader formulation, the global color line, a chronotope, or figure of the interrelations of time and space, for histories of racism, imperialism, and decolonization.[3] I would argue that the term *decolonization* captures Du Bois's focus on the dual temporal and spatial significance of thinking from the perspective of the color line. Here I understand decolonization to entail the intellectual activist project of assailing the antidemocratic policies of imperialism along the global color line and developing new and more egalitarian societies. The color line's "world aspect in time" emerges in the ways in which it reshapes our sense of history and the future by naming *avant la lettre* the *longue durèe* of decolonization, a term coined in 1932. The color line's "world aspect in . . . space" is evident in the series of racial divisions that Du Bois explores. The notion of the color line presents conceptual difficulties because it traces and traverses national boundaries, but it also presents new opportunities because it suggests the need for linking domestic civil rights movements to struggles against imperialism.

WAVES OF DECOLONIZATION AS A METHODOLOGY FOR COMPARATIVE CULTURAL ANALYSIS

In this book I map the Du Boisian color line onto what Du Bois terms "the new imperial policy" of the United States in the years preceding and following 1898 to call our attention to the crucial role of the Americas in narratives of imperialism and decolonization. Taking up Du Bois's challenge to consider the color line in its "world aspect," this book explores how writer-activists in the United States, Cuba, and Mexico defined their local struggles in relation to broader hemispheric movements against imperialism and racial oppression in the 1880s and 1920s and thus to varying degrees promoted or rejected decolonization.[4] The cross-national scope of their own writing, expressed in their commitment to interethnic and transnational alliances, requires us to reevaluate ethnic and national histories of culture by linking them in a comparative analysis that crosses national, linguistic, and ethnic boundaries. On the one hand, these writers suggest that an analysis of imperialism and neocolonialism sheds light on the significance of domestic racial inequalities. On the other hand, their writings on race need to be viewed as investigating and contributing to the cross-national cultural currents of what would come to be known as decolonization. My use of decolonization as an analytical frame attempts to account for the transnational scope of their analysis and practice in the unconventional context of the Americas rather than in the better-known sites of Africa and Asia.[5] Mary Louise Pratt has argued that "the Americas have remained almost entirely off the map of the colonial discourse movement and colonial studies in general" owing to the hemisphere's differing "chronology with respect to colonization and decolonization."[6] She goes on to make a case for the inclusion of the Americas within histories of decolonization. This book is my attempt to construct just such a chronology of decolonization in the Americas.

Such a chronology of decolonization does not need to coincide with formal independence movements because decolonization posits the cultural as necessarily political, as integral to struggles for social equality, as in the call of the Cuban independence leader José Martí to get "Spain out of our habits" and in the Mexican anthropologist Manuel Gamio's call for a "mental revolution" to remedy the shortcomings of the Mexican Revolution.[7] In these accounts, the attainment of independence for the nation-state sets in motion a lengthier process of decolonization in which the transformation of culture plays a key role.

A more elaborate theory of how cultural transformations can foster social change was devised by Gamio's contemporary, the Italian Marxist Antonio Gramsci, who argued, " 'popular beliefs' and similar ideas are themselves material forces."[8] In Gramsci's theory of hegemony, such "popular beliefs" form the foundation for cross-class coalitions opposing the dominant order. Gramsci's theory of hegemony focuses on the ways in which a ruling order is constituted not only through the use of military or police force, but also by the organization of a collective political will across differences of class and region.[9] Those who consent to a particular mode of rule form part of the hegemonic bloc, or the ruling cross-class coalition. However, in constituting subjects as political actors, no hegemony exhausts all political potential, as Raymond Williams has reminded us.[10] A variety of subjects develop emergent understandings that can be used to create cross-class coalitions opposed to the status quo. These coalitions are counter-hegemonic because they form alternative ruling blocs with the aim of wresting control from the dominant. Thus in Gramsci's theory of hegemony, as in decolonization, culture is a "material force" that plays a central role in shaping possibilities for political action and alliance.

It is no mistake that Gramsci devised his concept of hegemony through careful attention to the processes of decolonization in the Americas. He developed his theory of hegemony through a comparative historical reflection that focused in part on "the *Kulturkampf* of Calles in Mexico."[11] By correctly locating the Mexican president Plutarco Calles (1924–28) within the *Kulturkampf*, or cultural war, of the anticlerical Mexican state against the power of the Catholic Church, Gramsci implicitly identifies some of the considerable institutional and ideological obstacles to decolonization in Mexico and emphasizes the arduous cultural work that hegemony requires.[12] What better illustration of the "war of position"—the cultural conflict that takes place when military confrontation is not desired or is ineffective—could Gramsci find than Gamio's "mental revolution" and what Calles called the "psychological revolution" in Mexico?[13]

By identifying continuities among writers who with Du Bois sought to forge the "coming unities" among the racially oppressed of different nations, decolonization provides a theoretical model that builds on the Gramscian theory of hegemonic coalition building. It does so by emphasizing the postcolonial contexts that Gramsci's theory of hegemony mentions in passing, linking a wide variety of U.S. writer-activists to those in Cuba and Mexico through discursive and institutional commonalities— links that these writers forged among themselves as well.

Such commonalities come into focus through my examination of a set of literary and social scientific genres that crosses national borders: sentimentalism, folk primitivism, and ethnography. In general terms, sentimentalist discourses focus on sympathetic responses to the victimization of besieged or oppressed groups in order to create moral resolutions of collective dilemmas. Primitivist discourses create an opposition between so-called primitive peoples and those deemed civilized or modern, usually making the case that either one or the other is a superior form of life. Finally, ethnography, or writing about culture after an experience of participant observation, emerges with the professionalization of anthropology in the early twentieth century. These modes of writing are most often viewed in isolation from one another, separated into distinct periods and disciplines, rather than linked. Scholars have generally associated them with racial divisions and hierarchies and only recently have begun to point toward their simultaneous, if contradictory, use in the projects of affiliation and collectivity that are proper to decolonization.

One reason for the persistent association of sentimentalism, primitivism, and 1920s ethnography with racial hierarchies is that the history of ideas has failed to explore the ways in which these discourses both conflicted and coincided with social movements.[14] Mexican *indigenismo*, Cuban *negrismo*, and the New Negro movement in the United States drew on discourses of primitivism and ethnography. At the same time, those discourses intersected with two social movements constructing anticolonial collectivities: Pan-Africanism,[15] movements of solidarity among African and diasporic peoples; and *latinoamericanismo*,[16] varied efforts by the lettered elite to construct a unified Latin American identity across divisions of class and ethnicity. Thus the widely accepted view that primitivism promotes demeaning representations of nonwhite peoples obscures its concurrent and competing uses in articulating struggles for self-determination. In other words, the widespread emphasis on the ways in which primitivist discourses freeze the darker peoples in an inert past—the temporal component of the chronotope of primitivism—has led to the relative neglect of the ways in which primitivism is part of a larger project of forging links among the darker peoples, setting blueprints for inquiry, association, and activism along the color line—the spatial component of the chronotope of primitivism. Decolonization movements utilize discourses of primitivism in forging ties across national, ethnic, and linguistic lines, as occurred in the considerable crossover among the New Negro (Harlem Renaissance), Mexican indigenismo, and Cuban negrismo movements of the 1920s.

The evolving meanings of equality appear in readings of texts within two waves of decolonization, the first in the 1880s and 1890s, the second in the 1920s.[17] The two waves of decolonization in this book roughly coincide with the age of Pan-Americanism, an institutional and ideological project defined by U.S. efforts to gain economic and political control over Latin America. Pan-Americanism began with the First International Conference of American States in Washington, D.C., in 1889 and concluded, at least for the purposes of this book, with the Seventh Pan-American Conference in Montevideo, Uruguay, in 1933, where the United States agreed to a policy of nonintervention in Latin America, inaugurating the age of the so-called Good Neighbor under Franklin D. Roosevelt, which actually extended U.S. neocolonial control over Latin America.[18] These waves are also shaped by four decisive wars: the Mexican-American War (1846–48), in which the United States annexed half of Mexico, the war for Cuban Independence (1895–98), which ironically paved the way for U.S. neocolonial rule under the terms of the Platt Amendment (1903), the Mexican Revolution (1910–17), and World War I (1914–18).[19] Here is an overview of the hemisphere's differing chronology of imperialism and decolonization.

Exploring the aftermaths of independence, when there is a protracted struggle over what sorts of egalitarian projects constitute decolonization, I take Mexico and Cuba as geopolitical focal points for my comparative project because of their long-standing centrality to the history of U.S.

imperialism—both were objects of U.S. annexationist designs from the early nineteenth century.[20] And I have chosen the period of the 1880s through the 1920s because the Mexican War and the Spanish-American-Cuban War and their aftermaths marked a historical peak of U.S. imperialism, or what Du Bois calls the "new imperial policy." Indeed, the periodization of waves of decolonization directs attention less to specific wars in the Americas than to the *longue durée* following them.

RESTLESS UNIVERSALISMS: "THE DARKER WORLD THAT WATCHES" IN DU BOIS AND UNSATISFIED LIBERTY IN MARTÍ

As the first epigraph to this introduction suggests, my chronology of waves of decolonization grows out of Du Bois's investigation of "wave on wave . . . of whiteness" in *Darkwater* (1920) and other writings between the world wars, in which he applies the color line methodology to keep pace with the evolving realities of imperialism and neocolonialism. During his first years as editor of *The Crisis*, Du Bois worked to counter the U.S. government's self-serving narrative of "making the world safe for democracy," exposing the use of this phrase in attempts to solidify and extend the leading role of the United States among the imperial powers of the day.[21] He did so by turning his body of writings on waves of whiteness into a resource for antiracist and anti-imperialist activists.

To read Du Bois's writings from this period is to encounter what seems to be an anticolonial encyclopedia, one that is defined by Du Bois's dizzyingly profuse references to the plights of a variety of darker peoples across the globe, ranging from outrages in the Congo and the exploitation of Chinese coolies to antiblack riots in East St. Louis.[22] How Du Bois's analysis of "waves of whiteness" serves as a model of decolonizing writing and writing decolonization can be seen in the perspective Du Bois adopts in *Darkwater*. He begins *Darkwater* by articulating the perspective of the racialized subject, shaped by the ur-event or recurring event (the "twice-told tale" in *Souls*) of the formation and maintenance of the color line—this is by no means a neutral or objective history.[23] Du Bois's "veiled corner," his marginalization by race, affords him a privileged view of "the human scene" that allows him to perceive it in "illuminating ways"—he will go on to claim a "singular clairvoyance" (*DW* 483, 507). More specifically, the theme of "second-sight" in *Souls* now becomes literalized as "the darker world that watches." The point of view of "the darker world that watches" is what molds historical events in *Darkwater* (*DW* 507).

Indeed, the autobiographical chapter "The Shadow of Years" addresses the formation of a subject who is racialized in such a way as to perceive the need to look beyond race. This chapter sets the stage for the broader conception of "the darker world that watches" and the stinging indictment of white colonialism and World War I in the second chapter, "The Souls of White Folk." In writing of his first travels to Europe in "Of the Shadow of Years," Du Bois focuses on his emerging sense that Negro identity was not a racial essence but rather a political aspiration: "The unity beneath all life clutched me. I was not less fanatically a Negro, but 'Negro' meant a greater, broader sense of humanity and world-fellowship. I felt myself standing, not against the world, but simply against American narrowness and color prejudice, with the greater, finer world at my back urging me on" (*DW* 491). Here, the specific meaning of "Negro," once illuminated by "the unity beneath all life" itself paradoxically takes on the features of the universal: " 'Negro' meant a greater, broader sense of humanity and world-fellowship." Du Bois's strategy is to argue that because the particular ("Negro") embodies what the false universal (whiteness) attempts to exclude or deny even as it produces it as a problem ("the problem of the color line"), the particular holds the key to the truly universal.[24]

In the chapter "The Souls of White Folk" in *Darkwater*, Du Bois explains how the phrase "wave on wave . . . of whiteness" names the structures that oppress the darker peoples along the color line. He equates waves of whiteness with a belief in white racial superiority. Race thinking, Du Bois argues, has created a rift in the Enlightenment vision of a "Universal Man": "up into the eighteenth century we were hammering our national manikins into one, great, Universal Man, with fine frenzy which ignored color and race even more than birth" (*DW* 498). Even as the "hammering" suggests that Enlightenment universalism sought to violently force divergent phenomena into a single mold, Du Bois implicitly portrays national citizenship as a potentially valid egalitarian project. Indeed, in another chapter of *Darkwater*, "Of the Ruling of Men," Du Bois writes that the Enlightenment "Philosophy of Democracy" held that "if All ruled they would rule for All and thus Universal Good was sought through Universal suffrage" (*DW* 550). Du Bois regards the Enlightenment as a democratic legacy we must claim in order to oppose recurring waves of racism.

The waves of whiteness replace the rule of all by all with a competing project of nationalism as racial contest and empire, the rule of some by others: "Wave on wave, each with increasing virulence, is dashing this new religion of whiteness on the shores of our time" (DW 498). Thus waves of whiteness consist in myriad expressions of white racial violence that thwart the ideals of democracy. Whiteness becomes a "tragedy" when, inevitably, "the black man begins to dispute the white man's title to certain alleged bequests of the Fathers in wage and position, authority and training; and when his attitude toward charity is sullen anger rather than humble jollity" (DW 499). In this book I historicize the "dispute [of] the white man's title" as waves of decolonization in which the darker peoples and imperial subjects contest their exclusion from citizenship rights.

The chapter "Of Work and Wealth" frames one particular wave of whiteness—the antiblack riots in East St. Louis in 1917—as part of a global, "ethical question": "How we may justly distribute the world's goods to satisfy the necessary wants of the mass of men?" (DW 533). The answer provided by whites in East St. Louis—the exclusion of blacks from unions paired with vicious antiblack riots—reveals that whiteness is a false universalism that shrinks the category of the human. Those who insist on human rights must first admit how the human has itself paradoxically been used as an exclusionary category: "What we must decide sometime is who are to be considered 'men' " (DW 534). In other words, racial antagonism is the chief contradiction of the U.S. labor movement and, more broadly, of democracy. Until that contradiction is resolved, the category of the human ("the human scene" or "Universal Man") will remain inadequate as the supposed subject of universal emancipation, and so-called human rights will uphold white racial domination.

Addressing issues of class will not magically solve such racial inequalities. But the addressing of racial inequalities will prepare the way for a more thorough resolution of class contradictions. As Du Bois insists, "These disinherited darker peoples must either share in the future industrial democracy or overturn the world" (DW 534). Here is the utility of universalism for antiracist and decolonization movements: it sets up expectations of self-governance that can lead to uprisings when not met. Indeed, Du Bois views World War I as "the prelude" to "that fight for freedom, which black and brown and yellow men must and will make unless their oppression and humiliation and insult at the hands of the White World cease" (DW 507). Thus to the extent that Du Bois can be said to endorse universalism, he proposes a restless universalism that (1) adopts the perspective of the particular in order to engage in a critique of false claims of democracy for all and (2) exposes the ways in which universalist claims set the agenda for a painstaking resolution of competing claims. I would argue that decolonization requires the perspective and strategy of a restless universalism—it calls for "engaging the universals," in Dipesh Chakrabarty's terms, but with the aim of exposing their inadequacy from the perspective of the "darker world that watches."[25] Following Du Bois's restless universalism, I set out in this book to show how the "darker world that watches" characterizes the possibilities of critique and action against waves of whiteness. The interrelated concepts of the color line, "the darker world that watches" and the dual notions of "wave on wave . . . of whiteness" and waves of decolonization can serve to orient projects of comparative scholarship on decolonization and imperialism.

Both epigraphs to this introduction, Du Bois's on waves of whiteness and Martí's on the colony continuing to survive in the republic, address the persistence of oppressive structures in the midst of liberatory movements and the paradoxically elusive egalitarianism of universalisms such as the ideal of democracy for all. Martí thinks through democracy's unfulfilled promise in relation to the keyword of liberty in his writings from the 1880s and 1890s. His writings on the contested character of liberty can serve to unpack the critique contained within the phrase "the colony continues to live in the republic" by demonstrating that the concepts that undergird the republic are fraught with pitfalls. In the *crónica* (chronicle) "The Celebration of the Statue of Liberty" (1887), Martí describes the festivities that took place in New York City in honor of the unveiling of the Statue of Liberty in 1886. Because of the essay's incisive critique of the related concepts of liberty and democracy, it deserves to take its place alongside the much-anthologized "Our America" (which is now included in the *Heath Anthology of American Literature*) as one of the most frequently taught texts by Martí.

"The Celebration of the Statue of Liberty" is pervaded by Martí's presence as both an observer of the celebration and an unusually passionate participant in struggles for liberty. As a journalist, Martí observes the throngs of people crowding the piers of New York harbor trying to spot the new Statue of Liberty. As an activist, Martí is a participant-observer in the sense that his own demands for liberty for Cuba led the Spanish colonial government to send him into exile. So this crónica takes a privileged place in the corpus of Martí's writings because it provides him with the opportunity of reflecting critically on what is perhaps the central ideal that has shaped him as a writer-activist. He writes about liberty in a counter-intuitive and impassioned manner, exposing the paradox at the heart of the concept: "It is terrible to speak of you, Liberty, for those who don't have you. Those who have you, oh Liberty, don't know you. Those who don't have you should not speak of you, but conquer you. . . . Liberty, it is your hour of arrival!" (1764).[26] Those who "have" liberty but do not "know it" are content with freedom and are blind to its inherently elusive character. In "Nuestra América" ("Our America," 1891), the essay from which the above epigraph is taken, Martí writes of the danger that Latin American independence could lead to a regime change but not to a change in the manner of ruling: "The problem of independence did not lie in a change of forms but in a change of spirit."[27] Similarly, in the celebration of the Statue of Liberty that Martí observes for his readership of *La Nación* in Buenos Aires, there is a spectacle of freedom achieved and democracy triumphant. But from Martí's viewpoint, the Statue of Liberty is a highly contested figure.

Indeed, Martí viewed France's gift of the statue to the United States as an occasion for the meeting of two powers with strikingly different visions and uses of liberty: "selfish and scheming in the United States, and in France generous and expansive" ("Fiestas" 1766). Even if Martí idealizes the republican legacy of France, he rightly disputes the spectacle's implicit projection of a universally accessible and uniform liberty. Rather than liberty for all, there is liberty for some—paradoxically, republican universalism ends up serving particular interests, as in Du Bois's discussion of the exclusionary uses of the category of the human.

Martí fleshes out this contrast between the French and U.S. republics' conceptions of liberty through various references to central events in the struggles to attain democracy in the Americas. Martí refers to the Mexican War in a description of the celebration at Madison Square, next to which the president's parade will pass, noting the irony of celebrating liberty in a square that features "the impious monument that records the inglorious victory of the North Americans over Mexico" ("Fiestas" 1777). Here Martí's emphatic negation of the U.S. claim to glory in the Mexican War—which he drives home with the pairing of the adjectives "impious" and "in-glorious"—demonstrates that the U.S. conception of liberty is rife with contradictions. As Martí puts it in a later essay in which he outlines the philosophy of the coming Cuban War for Independence, countries frequently invoke freedom in justifying its suppression elsewhere. The United

States is particularly guilty, Martí suggests, of "the attempt to prevail in the name of freedom by means of ruthless actions in which the rights of others to freedom's methods and guarantees are set aside."[28] Martí's critique of the United States for invoking the name of freedom in order to ruthlessly "set aside" the rights of others to freedom is still relevant today, in the context of the ongoing U.S. war on Iraq.

In the Statue of Liberty essay, Martí shows that this setting aside of freedom takes place within the United States as well, with regard to those whom Martí terms "los oprimidos" (the oppressed) ("Fiestas" 1770). Of the throngs of immigrants who crowd the piers during the celebration, Martí writes, "Look at them run to the piers, joyous like the shipwrecked who believe that they see a life-saving sail, where they can spot the statue! They are the most miserable, who are afraid of the populous streets and of the clean people." ("Fiestas" 1770). For these immigrants, Martí suggests, liberty can offer only false hopes of salvation—they remain shipwrecked on the shore, gazing longingly at a liberty that remains remote. That is why they share the paradoxical position that defines liberty: they are at their most joyous when they see the Statue of Liberty precisely because they are most miserable in their everyday lives. There is considerable historical irony in the fact that the Statue of Liberty would later come to be celebrated in the United States as a figure that embraced immigrants, rather than giving them false hopes, as in Martí's critique. Turning to African Americans, another marginalized population, Martí writes that the Marquis de Lafayette, "not satisfied" with the nominal liberty attained by the U.S. American Revolution, asked Congress to free "his brothers the blacks" ("Fiestas" 1776–77). To Martí, the Marquis de Lafayette's proposed extension of liberty to blacks serves as a model of fraternity and expanded freedom for his own revolution and exposes the racial contradictions of what passes for U.S. liberty.

Rather than viewing the failures of the United States to extend the fruits of liberty to the oppressed as aberrations, Martí uses them to define liberty in the abstract as he surveys the scene at the harbor and addresses the statue:

Man grows: look how he no longer fits in churches and chooses the sky as the only temple worthy of covering his deity! But you, O marvel, you grow at the same pace of man; and the armies, and the whole city and the boats adorned with bunting that will celebrate you reach up to your feet veiled by the fog . . . when the spirit of the storm, wrapped up in lightning, strikes across the cloud-blackened sky. You are right, Liberty, to reveal yourself to the world on a dark day, because you still can't be satisfied with yourself! And you, heart without celebration, sing the celebration! ("Fiestas" 1765)

Martí portrays the statue itself, shrouded by clouds, as embodying the inherently unsatisfied character of liberty that Lafayette exposed in relation to the U.S. American Revolution's creed of liberty that was restricted to whites. Here, in a somewhat different guise, is the restless universalism evident in Du Bois's writings.

In "The Celebration of the Statue of Liberty," Martí suggests that *freedom* may be the most dangerous word there is because it is so vulnerable to betrayal, but also one that is still necessary because it holds so much promise. A complacent freedom, a freedom unmodified, must be feared, suggests Martí, who calls for "*true* freedoms" and a "*genuine* and *vigorous* freedom" in order to shore up an "endangered freedom" ("WA" 139, 143). In his reports on the so-called "land of the free," Martí, the revolutionary, takes the U.S. American Revolution to task: for Martí, the revolution betrayed in the United States must lead to the revolution realized in Latin America.

In the writings of Martí, liberty is implicitly a chronotope in that those who think they have liberty believe its "hour of arrival" is in the past and present. Those who don't have liberty are those from the margins—immigrants and blacks in the United States and the colonized abroad—who work toward its future realization. In terms of time, conflicting narratives of liberty work to either rationalize the status quo or require social change. In terms of space, the center proclaims a liberty triumphant, while the marginalized and the oppressed constitute its contradiction and its promise. Martí gains critical purchase on the concept of liberty by bringing together elements of its chronotope that have been assigned separate geographic and temporal spaces—the complacent and unsatisfied liberties.

Martí calls attention to the contradictions of the ideal of liberty through two key moves. First, he simultaneously calls attention to the plight of the "oppressed" within the United States and, implicitly, in colonies outside the United States. Second, he tests the claim that liberty was triumphant in 1887 by comparing that moment to the achievements and limits of the French and American revolutions a century earlier as well as to the more recent Ten Years' War in Cuba. Thus in their examinations of the possibilities of freedom, Du Bois and Martí both follow the chronotopic methodology of decolonization: in terms of space they bring together groups in the

United States and abroad that have been denied the fruits of liberty; in terms of time they present a foreshortened, telescopic vision of major historical events, dramatizing the "unsatisfied" character of liberty that sets the stage for coming "fight[s] for freedom" by the darker peoples and the colonized (*DW* 507).

I explore in these pages the many restless universalisms that either link or delink discourses of universalism and narratives of decolonization in the discourses of sentimentalism, indigenismo, ethnography, negrismo, and the New Negro. Sentimentalism is typically a discourse of human rights that mobilizes universal human affect—"ye feel the same sorrow!" (Stowe) —to encourage readers to redress the denial of rights based on race. However, in *The Squatter and the Don* (1885), by María Amparo Ruiz de Burton, sentimentalism does not even aspire to a universal reach. Instead, it is used to expand whiteness to include the elite of a previously excluded ethnic group while maintaining a host of other racial inequalities. And even in its universalist variants, sentimentalism stops short of endorsing the essential components of decolonization—self-rule, full equality, and an end to exploitation. Indeed, Helen Hunt Jackson's *Ramona* (1884) works to establish the humanity of Indians, and even imagines the possibility of an anti-imperialist war waged by Indians and Mexicans against the United States, but is untroubled by the exploitation of Indians' labor.

The paired discourses of *indigenismo* (Indian reform) and *mestizaje* (racial mixing) in Mexican postrevolutionary nationalism resulted in another limited and contradictory universalism, in this case achieved through the "incorporation" of Indians into citizenship—a process that was normally imagined to necessitate their "deindianization" (Guillermo Bonfil Batalla's term)—but there were important dissenting currents. Gamio, one of the primary theorists of mestizaje and indigenismo, advocated and achieved some of the most radical social transformations of the postrevolutionary era, including land reform, in the early 1920s. And Felipe Carrillo Puerto's socialist government in the Yucatán (1922–24) went to even greater lengths, drawing on both Marxist and anarchist theory and on the practical experiences of the U.S. Socialist Party and Soviet Union in devising a socialist program adequate to the needs of the Mayan Indians and the rest of the heterogeneous population of Mexico's Yucatán, enacting programs of land redistribution as well as social organizations called *ligas de resistencia* (resistance leagues) and *ligas de feministas* (feminist leagues) that drew increasing numbers of peasants, Indians, and women into the political pro-

cess. Carrillo Puerto's eclectic socialism for the Yucatán constitutes a restless
universalism that modifies socialist theory to account for local specificities
and the racial contradictions of modernity. Miguel Angel Menéndez, who
wrote his novel *Nayar* (1940) at a time when the sorts of radical reforms
proposed by Gamio and Carrillo Puerto gained momentum in the administration of the Mexican president Lázaro Cardenas (1934–40), opposes
such radical reformism in favor of a more conservative, state-centered
program of mestizaje. Against the radical feminism of Carrillo Puerto's
ligas de feministas, Menéndez counterposes a portrayal of two adulterous
women whom he puts in their places; against the attempts to foster indigenous autonomy in Gamio's applied anthropology and in Carrillo Puerto's
ligas de resistencia, Menéndez suggests the need for federal intervention to
alter indigenous systems of rule and thereby supposedly preserve the rights
of the individual in indigenous communities. While Gamio and Carrillo
Puerto sought to decolonize the incomplete universalism of revolutionary
nationalism through an insistence on the rights of oppressed and exploited
groups of Indians and *campesinos* (farmworkers), Menéndez turns against
decolonization in the name of the competing, ostensible universalism of
individual rights—a conception that would ironically strengthen the cen-
tralized state at the cost of the autonomy of indigenous groups.

Ethnography is a social scientific practice of writing culture that re-
placed the earlier evolutionary scheme of a universal progression from
savagery to civilization with an exploration of multiple cultures and civilizations that were no longer hierarchically arranged. Because in the practice
of ethnography all cultures are considered to be unique, culture can no
longer be the site of a universality conceived of as singular, but instead a
universality established through the plurality of cultures, all of which are
viewed as equally valid. More specifically, in Gamio's *Mexican Immigration
to the United States* (1930) and *The Mexican Immigrant: His Life Story* (1931)
and in Zora Neale Hurston's *Mules and Men* (1935) and *Their Eyes Were
Watching God* (1937) shared cultural practices and vocabularies among
Latin American and African American migrant and immigrant workers
serve to cut across ethnic and racial particularisms and create broader
unities in the face of a racially hostile United States: the discourse of *la raza*
among Latin American immigrants and the conception of African Americans as a racially mixed and racially heterogeneous "mingled people" in
Hurston.

In the Cuban negrismo movement, Jesús Masdeu's novel *La raza triste*

(The Sad Race, 1924) portrays the turn away from universalism toward racism in the ostensibly independent neocolonial Cuba. The Afro-Cuban writer Nicolás Guillén later concurs with this assessment, arguing in 1929 that Cuba has taken the "road towards Harlem," leading toward U.S.-style racial segregation and oppression. As in Masdeu, in the New Negro movement representations of the failures of universalism abound. In the writings of Langston Hughes and Claude McKay, Africans in the diaspora respond by staking claim to separate enclaves in which they can achieve a modicum of self-rule and elude the forces of racial oppression. But they also claim solidarity with black and brown peoples in other parts of the hemisphere, exposing the intertwined character of race and imperialism in Hughes's concept of the "white shadows" of U.S. neocolonialism in the Haiti of 1932 and in McKay's description in his novel *Home to Harlem* (1928) of the "black and brown hybrids and mongrels" along the color line who are exploited in the "pits" of "that grand business called civilization." Both strategies stand as an indictment of failed universalisms but also suggest the possibility of revitalized universalisms that address the problems of race, empire, and class. In sum, narratives of decolonization adopt a skeptical stance toward universalist claims, even as they modify those universalisms to make them adequate to the needs of fully realizing nationalist, antiracist, and egalitarian aims.

THE CHRONOTOPE OF DECOLONIZATION AND DISCOURSES OF HEMISPHERIC CITIZENSHIP

In their writings on key historical events, Du Bois and Martí construct history as a story of successive waves of decolonization and democratization. This book follows suit in adopting their chronotope of decolonization as a methodology for cultural analysis. As Mikhail Bakhtin writes, chronotopes "are the organizing centers for the fundamental narrative events of the novel."[29] Similarly, in the narrative of this book, the chronotope of decolonization tells stories of struggles for democracy that tend to bring together certain distant moments in time and to tie together disparate spaces, crossing national, linguistic, and ethnic boundaries.

My analysis begins in the late nineteenth century in order to call into question the widespread insistence on the novelty of twentieth-century culture—evident in the widely circulating use of the terms *new* and *renaissance* to describe cultural events in Harlem and Mexico in the 1920s. I have found that discourses from the nineteenth century persist in these movements, including appeals to romantic racialism in all three countries and evolutionary discourse in Mexico.[30] My account thus differs from other studies that have assumed, rather than proven, a stark contrast between nineteenth- and twentieth-century cultural discourses. For instance, scholars of representations of Indians in Mexico have sharply delineated between the exoticist tendencies of nineteenth-century narratives of *indianismo* and the reformist impulse of twentieth-century indigenismo, despite the fact that the most astute scholars have found exoticism and reformism to be present in both centuries.[31] The study of Pan-Africanism has made a similarly spurious distinction between proto-pan-Africanism (usually written with a lowercase p), denoting nineteenth-century "cultural" movements, and the Pan-Africanism proper of twentieth-century "political" movements (the Pan-African Congresses)—a distinction clearly untenable if one views culture as itself political.[32] I have found that such stark distinctions fail to hold up under scrutiny: two of the most prominent nationalists in 1920s Mexico, Gamio and José Vasconcelos, indulged in exoticism by viewing Mexican Indians as more sexually and emotionally liberated than acculturated *mestizos*. Their thinking consists of an uneasy combination of reformism, a romanticization of indigenous life, and a neoevolutionary belief that indigenous acculturation to a supposedly civilized Mexican mainstream is necessary and irreversible (see my comparison of these two figures in chapter 3). In the U.S. context, the Chicago School sociologist Robert E. Park argued in 1918 that the Negro was the "lady among the races," thereby perpetuating the nineteenth-century discourse of romantic racialism, which associated blacks and women alike with what most white men allegedly lack: Christian morality and reverence paired with deeply felt emotions and artistic sensibilities (for a discussion of romantic racialism in a different context, see chapter 1).[33]

Just as twentieth-century discourses of race did not fully purge themselves of their nineteenth-century antecedents, so decolonization could not attain the pure state of freedom implied in its name. Decolonization in the Americas has proceeded unevenly and has been marked by a great degree of paradox. If the postrevolutionary Mexican nationalism of Vasconcelos and Gamio relied in part on a celebration of ancient indigenous civilization and art and adopted a defiant attitude toward U.S. imperialism, Mexican nationalism did not refuse U.S. funding: Gamio's archaeological project to restore Chichén Itzá was funded by the Carnegie Institute, one of the principal funding sources of U.S. State Department Pan-Americanist initiatives.[34] Moreover, Gamio saw no irony in describing his project of indigenismo as a continuation of colonialism, as suggested by his phrase "The New Conquest," the title of his article in the *Survey Graphic* (1924) special edition on Mexican nationalism, the magazine that would later publish the celebrated *New Negro* collection edited by Alain Locke.[35] Ironically, Gamio's imperialist view that the inhabitants of the Valley of Teotihuacán belong to a "backward civilization" underwrites his efforts to undo the legacies of colonialism through his project of anthropology as social reform.[36]

Moreover, Gamio and Vasconcelos viewed imperialism as exterior to Mexico, associating it with the United States, yet relied on the idiom of empire themselves: Vasconcelos used the same eugenic discourses that rationalized the sterilization of poor, nonwhite peoples in the United States and Latin America in the 1920s.[37] Paradoxes of this sort led Bonfil Batalla, writing before the Zapatista uprising in Chiapas in 1994, to argue that there has been a continuing history of colonialism and racism in Mexico that has resulted in the exploitation of Indians and the suppression of democracy.[38] Here again Martí's "colony [that] has continued to survive in the republic" is visible.[39]

While decolonization reveals the limitations of nationalist movements, its transnational focus sets in relief the varied and sustained efforts of writer-activists to narrate and practice an alternative form of citizenship—hemispheric citizenship. Discourses of hemispheric citizenship mark a more encouraging continuity between the nineteenth century and the twentieth. Those who practice hemispheric citizenship work to turn critical perspectives on U.S. imperialism in Latin America to the political advantage of the oppressed in both regions, as in Du Bois's "attitude of deepest sympathy and strongest alliance" toward the "colored" populations absorbed by the U.S. empire following 1898, and Martí's critique of the tendency of the United States to invoke freedom so as to "set aside" freedom for Latin Americans. Dissenting U.S. citizens, for instance, can use the political and material privileges afforded by U.S. citizenship to oppose neocolonialism and therefore support the restoration of a range of rights to the inhabitants of affected countries.[40] By transgressing the traditional national bounds of citizenship, discourses of hemispheric citizenship put into practice the restless universalisms of Du Bois and Martí.

In order to understand how discourses of hemispheric citizenship dispute imperialism, one must first understand how imperialism and neo-colonialism adversely affect citizenship rights. Imperialism and neocolo-nialism strip subject populations of their citizenship rights, to varying degrees.[41] In the most extreme examples of neocolonial rule, the popula-tion faces a condition of "dominance without hegemony": dissent runs up against the full deployment of state violence, as during the Gerardo Ma-chado dictatorship in Cuba (1925–33).[42] While U.S. neocolonialism created a situation of dominance *without* hegemony in Cuba, it maintained domi-nance *through* hegemony domestically, leaving open avenues of dissent. In such situations of dominance through hegemony, discourses of hemi-spheric citizenship originating in the neocolonial power can represent neocolonial subjects in both the artistic and the political sense of the word, advocating on their behalf. The protests against the U.S. occupation of Haiti (1915–34) offer a somewhat different version of discourses of hemi-spheric citizenship, one in which migrants or exiles utilize the possibilities of dissent in what Martí called "the belly of the beast." In both cases, there is a gray zone of citizenship in which U.S. imperialism denies rights and dissenters reassert rights on a hemispheric scale. The locus of the insistence on the restoration of rights has shifted away from the states under imperial rule and toward the U.S. neocolonial center that is running the show.

Imperial subjects thus face a specific predicament with regard to their citizenship rights. Because imperialism strips subject populations of rights, a vacuum forms in the political and cultural representation of those groups —they are rendered "half stateless," to borrow the term Hannah Arendt used to describe refugees in Europe following World War I.[43] Much like the refugees who flooded Europe at that time, minorities and imperial subjects often suffer from "the deprivation of a place in the world which makes opinions significant and actions effective," and in that sense they are often "rightless" as well ("Decline" 176).

While Arendt writes over a generation removed from World War I and focuses on refugees *within* Europe, in the 1920s Du Bois writes about prob-lems stemming from "the rule of aliens" and the effects of stripping the darker peoples of citizenship in their own countries and *outside* of Europe, in Africa, Asia, and the Americas—this denial of citizenship rights defines the Du Boisian color line.[44] Arendt seeks to undermine the classic opposi-tion between citizen and alien in discourses of modern rights—and to point out the failed universalism of national citizenship rights—by arguing that "stateless persons" are "the most symptomatic group in contemporary politics" and that human rights discourse is the neglected "stepchild" of political thought ("Decline" 157, 173). By contrast, Du Bois undermines the citizen-alien opposition by terming the imperial powers themselves aliens, thereby reconstruing the "problem" (a keyword in Du Bois's thought) as not a matter of victimized peoples, but rather one of aggressor states. Moreover, in an age of experimentation with supranational institutions such as the League of Nations, Du Bois attempts to apply discourses of citizenship to the darker peoples across the world.

These dual problems that define the color line for Du Bois—the "rule of aliens" and rightlessness—can be productively reframed as a dilemma of transnational citizenship: if processes of citizenship are traditionally considered to take place within a given nation, what happens to discourses of citizenship when an imperial state has usurped another country's sovereignty? Du Bois's writings can be viewed as a resource for a host of writers from a range of disciplines—anthropology, history, law, literature, philosophy, political science, and sociology—who are working to define the potential of what Etienne Balibar has recently termed "transnational citizenship."[45]

How have scholars of citizenship traditionally defined their object of study? And how have they of late dramatically revised understandings of their field? If the phrase *hemispheric citizenship* sounds like a contradiction in terms, that is because citizenship has traditionally been associated with legal and political rights promised within the space of a single nation-state. But in the context of the geographically "stretched out" character of social relations under imperialism and neocolonialism, citizenship acquires new meanings.[46] Conventional definitions have indeed viewed the nation-state as the principal agent in practices of citizenship. The most influential conception, "ascriptive citizenship," holds that "citizenship is the quality or status that the state . . . confers on individuals" (*WP* 182). Although this particular definition is state-centered and construes citizens themselves as relatively passive recipients of citizenship, there is quite a bit of latitude in many conceptions of citizenship. As J. G. A. Pocock has argued, the modern notion of rights mediates between two dominant models of citizenship in classical European political thought: on the one hand, the Gaian emphasis on discipline and, on the other hand, the Aristotelian emphasis on personal freedom.[47] Current understandings of citizenship still span the distance between these two bedrock notions, replaying the tension in discourses of race between racial identity as a state of being and racial identity as bound up in certain political perspectives and aspirations. Linda Bosniak has similarly listed three main understandings of citizenship that constitute quite a broad definition: (1) "membership in a political community," (2) "active engagement in the life of a polity," and (3) "an experience of identity and solidarity."[48]

All three senses of citizenship have engaged the attention of scholars who have been working to define what some term "cultural citizenship." Renato Rosaldo defines "cultural citizenship" as being concerned with "how concerned parties conceive, say, equity and well-being" or "full citizenship."[49] Cultural citizenship moves away from conceiving citizenship as primarily consisting in duties to the nation-state and moves toward a definition of the citizen as taking a proactive role in the polity: shaping political communities rather than being defined by them and creating new forms of identity and affiliation. This proactive conception of citizenship lends itself to the evolving work on what scholars have variously termed postnational, transnational, denationalized, global, and flexible citizenship, all of which recognize that practices of citizenship "exceed the boundaries and jurisdiction of the territorial nation-state" ("Denationalizing" 241).[50] Such transnational practices of citizenship differ greatly in terms of political efficacy. Transnational citizenship, Bosniak argues, is "least plausible when we speak of citizenship as legal status" and most convincing when citizenship is viewed "as a form of political activity" ("Denationalizing" 241–42).

What was the Du Boisian idiom for transnational citizenship? First, Du Bois frequently employs discourses of citizenship in his writings of the 1910s and 1920s. In an article in *The Crisis* in 1918, he adopts the precise wording of President Woodrow Wilson's call for full women's citizenship and applies it to "black fellow citizens": "Shall we admit them only to a partnership of suffering and sacrifice and toil, and not to a partnership of privilege and right?"[51] Here Du Bois shrewdly builds on the political momentum for women's rights, implying that the expansion of rights can be applied to other groups as well. As a scholar of citizenship has written, "Historically, citizenship and its rights and privileges have expanded in waves, with changes in how the national public is defined in relation to class, gender and age"; Du Bois adds the racially subordinated to the list of those who should possess rights.[52]

Second, Du Bois also frequently spoke of rights and allegiances that cut across national boundaries. He regarded the rights of blacks in Africa, in the United States, and elsewhere in the diaspora as "entwined" with those of other peoples: "The narrow confines of the modern world entwine our interests with those of other peoples. We desire to see freedom and real national independence in Egypt, in China and India. We demand the cessation of the interference of the United States in the affairs of Central and South America."[53] The metaphor of the entwined rights of the darker peoples suggests that they are distinct but also dependent on one another; they gain strength by being bound together, and they weaken if unraveled.[54] For Du Bois, therefore, mindful of a racist climate across the globe, the full citizenship rights of nonwhites can be gained only through a collective, transnational struggle: "The world-fight for black rights is on!" he writes in 1919.[55]

Given such entwined interests among the darker peoples, Du Bois recognizes certain ethical imperatives to act on behalf of those who lack political power as a result of racism and colonialism. To those who "deny self-government to educated men," Du Bois writes, "we complain, but not simply or primarily for ourselves, more especially for the millions of our fellows, blood of our blood and flesh of our flesh who have not even what we have—the power to complain against monstrous wrong, the power to see and know the source of our oppression."[56] Here the Pan-African "we" acts as the eyes, ears, and even voice of those who lack "the power to complain." This "we" includes people in many social positions, including Du Bois himself as an intellectual, the "darker races" assembled to hear his address at the Pan-African Congress of London in 1921, as well as the broadly multiethnic, heavily African American readership of *The Crisis*.

If Du Bois's statements of entwined fates and rights and their prescriptions to act can be considered practices of citizenship, then these practices are surely not rooted in any one nation-state. And they are too broad and interethnic to be termed diasporic or Pan-African citizenship. How, then, does one name these denationalized citizenship practices?

Perhaps Du Bois's own preferred term "the darker races" best approximates the anticolonial, antiracist political community he is trying to assemble in order to dismantle the color line and its discrepancies of citizenship. Scholars of Du Bois are most conversant with the Pan-African subset of the "darker races." But there is another, lesser-known body of writings in which Du Bois addresses the specific plight of populations subjected to U.S. racism and imperialism—in 1920, as if to follow through on "The Present Outlook for the Dark Races of Mankind" (1900), Du Bois refers to "the other Americas," that is, Latin America and the Caribbean.[57] Writing in *The Crisis* in 1926, Du Bois assigns a strategic importance to "the other Americas" in laying bare the hypocrisy of the U.S. ploy of using supranational institutions such as the League of Nations to further its image as a defender of democracy and to conceal its imperialism: "If America can go into the World Court and League of Nations with her hands red in the blood of Haiti and her pockets filled with the loot of Nicaragua, she will be free for further imperialism in Central and South America."[58] In 1926, U.S. imperialism was in full throttle in Latin America and the Caribbean and was responsible, to varying degrees and through differing methods, for depriving the citizens of these regions of rights.

In exposing the hypocrisy of U.S. democracy in 1926, Du Bois mentions two countries: Haiti and Nicaragua. In Haiti, the United States was entering the eleventh year of a bloodily repressive and notoriously racist military occupation that had begun in 1915. Du Bois was one of the very first African Americans to publicly condemn the U.S. occupation of Haiti (1915–35). In a letter to President Wilson in 1915, Du Bois writes, "I am so deeply disturbed over the situation in Hayti and the action of the United States that I venture to address you."[59] Years later, in 1921, in another letter to a president, this time Warren Harding, Du Bois writes that alongside U.S. Negroes' demands for voting rights and to be free of insult, they call for "FREEDOM FOR OUR BROTHERS IN HAITI."[60] In Nicaragua, a peasant revolt headed by Augusto César Sandino erupted in 1926 against a U.S.-installed regime that had depleted the national treasury, fueled the growth of U.S. finance by privatizing key industries, and suppressed dissent by hosting the U.S. Marines.[61] Thus Du Bois combines demands for African American citizenship rights and opposition to imperialism, especially U.S. imperialism in the Caribbean and Latin America, as part of a single political stance that opposes the U.S. disfranchisement of "darker peoples," whether at home or abroad. The history of protests against the U.S. occupation of Haiti reveals that Du Bois spearheaded and publicized protests against the occupation and found himself swept forward and even left behind by those protests.[62] Writer-activists provide points of entry into the activism that characterized practices of hemispheric citizenship but by no means exhaust such activism. Du Bois's colleague James Weldon Johnson, a poet and novelist and the field secretary of the National Association for the Advancement of Colored People (NAACP) beginning in 1916, initially argued that U.S. intervention in Haiti was necessary to rectify Haiti's continuing political upheavals.[63] But Johnson followed Du Bois's lead and turned critical of the occupation in 1918, when U.S. rule required Haiti to accept "an unpopular constitution."[64] In 1920, Johnson went on a fact-finding trip to Haiti that was funded by the Republican Party. Upon his return to New York, Johnson publicized the plight of Haiti in a four-part series of articles in the *Nation*.

The subsequent organizing against the U.S. occupation exemplifies the practical side of discourses of hemispheric citizenship, bringing together African Americans, Haitian immigrants and nationalists, and white activists. Johnson founded the Haiti–Santo Domingo Independence Society in order to press for the withdrawal of U.S. troops from those countries. He also played a role in forging an alliance between the NAACP and the Patriotic Union of Haiti, a resistance group modeled after the NAACP ("Response" 132–33; *Taking* 191). The Haitian nationalist Sténio Vincent, a leader of the Patriotic Union, frequently availed himself of the NAACP's offer to provide him with office space at its New York headquarters. Vincent and the Haitian immigrant community staged a demonstration against the visit of the Haitian president Louis Borno to the United States in 1925. The NAACP also entered into a coalition with white organizations such as the Popular Government League and the Foreign Policy Association to oppose the intervention ("Response" 133, 138–39). By the mid-1920s, black churches and black women's clubs spoke out against the occupation, as did black political groups like the International Council of Women of the Darker Races, the National Colored Republican Conference of 1924, and the Communist-leaning American Negro Labor Conference of 1925; interracial groups like the Women's International League for Peace and Freedom and the Workers' Communist Party also voiced their opposition ("Response" 137; *Taking* 266, 267–69). These and other organizations engaged in practices of hemispheric citizenship in order to restore the citizenship rights denied to Haitians under U.S. imperial rule.

Discourses of hemispheric citizenship bring to light the contested gray zones of citizenship within social spheres of the United States, Mexico, and Cuba that have been partly denationalized due to U.S. imperialism.[65] These gray zones of citizenship play a central role in the cultural texts examined in this book: Jackson's Ramona forges an allegiance with U.S. Indians and Mexican nationals in opposition to the racial politics of U.S. expansionism; Ruiz de Burton, having forfeited her Mexican citizenship for U.S. citizenship, advocates on behalf of regions and marginalized groups that she believes were victimized by U.S. imperialism; Martí wages an organizational and ideological battle for Cuban and Puerto Rican independence while based in New York; Du Bois condemns the U.S. military occupation of Haiti and its puppet regimes in Nicaragua and Cuba and hails the Mexican Revolution as an important battle in the coming "fight for freedom" by darker peoples; the white radical journalist Carleton Beals and Hughes articulate critiques of U.S. neocolonialism in the 1920s through their travels to Latin America; Gamio engages in advocacy on behalf of Mexican immigrants to the United States while working at the University of Chicago; and Hurston writes about the lives of African American migrant laborers in the South. Thus discourses of hemispheric citizenship expanded the "self" in self-determination beyond the borders of the nation, turning a transnationalism against the imperial state.

The paradoxical history of Pan-Americanism shows how alternative practices of hemispheric citizenship negotiated within and against institutional efforts to forge hemispheric unity on the terms of U.S. business interests. An examination of the history of competing efforts to claim the mantle of Pan-Americanism reveals some of the political stakes of hemispheric citizenship as well as its grounding in a host of social movements. The history of Pan-Americanism also demonstrates the potential pitfalls as well as the promise of hemispheric Americas studies.

Movements claiming the title of Pan-Americanism have both promoted U.S. business interests at the expense of the majority of Latin Americans and critiqued U.S. state policy. Those critics familiar with its intended use by the U.S. government to serve business interests have associated Pan-Americanism with a "stifling dependence upon imperialism," and there is much evidence to support this claim.[66] The so-called father of Pan-Americanism, U.S. Secretary of State James G. Blaine, was also a leading proponent of Manifest Destiny.[67] Blaine convened the First International Conference of American States in Washington, D.C., in 1889 with the aim of setting in motion the U.S. "annexation by trade" of Latin America.[68] The term *Pan-Americanism* was coined at this conference. In 1895, Secretary of State Richard Olney further infuriated Latin Americans when he declared that the United States was "practically sovereign" in the Americas.[69] These Pan-Americanist projects articulate the flexible, expanded sovereignty of U.S. imperialism that would set the scene for discourses of hemispheric citizenship.

Yet the common conflation of Pan-Americanism and U.S. imperialism is overly reductive for two reasons. First, the aims of U.S. policy have varied considerably over time. The history of Pan-Americanism usually begins with Blaine's conference in 1889 and the founding of the Pan-American Union in 1910, spans the various Pan-American conferences of the 1920s, and touches on President Franklin D. Roosevelt's misnamed Good Neighbor Policy of 1933, on the founding of the Organization of American States in 1948, on President John F. Kennedy's Alliance for Progress in 1960, which founded the Inter-American Development Bank, and on the passage of the North American Free Trade Agreement (NAFTA) in 1992. The term *Inter-American* begins to displace the even more vexed term *Pan-American* with the foundation of the Organization of American States.[70]

Second, conventional accounts of the history of Pan-Americanism are incomplete because they ignore the ways in which U.S. and Latin American citizens resisted the U.S. State Department's narrative of hemispheric relations, often by appropriating the term *Pan-Americanism* for their own purposes. Hemispheric citizenship was perhaps practiced most fully in the various Pan-American and Inter-American social movements that emerged within, alongside, and in outright opposition to the U.S.-initiated, state-sponsored versions of Pan-Americanism that promoted the interests of U.S. capital. These social movements created what Gamio called "un verdadero panamericanismo" (a true Pan-Americanism), and their aim was to meet the needs of a variety of social groups from Latin America and the United States, including labor and feminism, rather than to serve U.S. business elites.[71]

These social movements included the Inter-American Committee of Jurists, which condemned U.S. interventionism in Latin America in 1927, the Pan-American Federation of Labor, and Latin American state representatives who spoke out against U.S. interventionism in the Pan-American Conferences themselves, as in the Fifth Pan-American Conference in Santiago, Chile, in 1923.[72] Prominent among these opponents to U.S.-initiated Pan-Americanism were women's organizations, among them the Pan-American Conference of Women, founded in 1922 to promote women's suffrage throughout the hemisphere; and the Inter-American Commission of Women at the Sixth International Conference of American States in Havana in 1928.[73] The members of this commission demonstrated against the U.S. occupation of Nicaragua and protested the conference's dismissal of representatives of the Haitian government-in-exile.[74] Latin American women occupied leadership positions in these organizations: for example,

Elena Torres, a Trotskyite socialist from Mexico, was vice president of the Pan-American Conference of Women. Thus despite its efforts, the U.S. State Department never succeeded in putting a lid on the tendency of Pan-Americanism to generate contradictory meanings and practices. As newcomers to the long-standing practice of hemispheric citizenship, scholars currently engaged in a comparative study of the Americas participate in varied efforts to establish new modes of inquiry and association in the hemisphere.

This book examines the unfolding narratives of decolonization in the United States, Mexico, and Cuba by attending to the shaping of culture through the interplay among regional and national factors and transnational forces of capital, culture, migration, and travel. Chapter 1, " 'White Slaves' and the 'Arrogant *Mestiza*': Reconfiguring Whiteness in *The Squatter and the Don* and *Ramona*," focuses on narratives of struggle for social position within the racialized social hierarchy of 1870s California in the aftermath of the Mexican-American War. In Ruiz de Burton's *Squatter* (1885) and Jackson's *Ramona* (1884), elite *Californios* and unpropertied Indians exploit the shifting definitions of white identity, reconfiguring its bounds and meanings in order to endorse, modify, and at times even oppose the terms of U.S. imperial citizenship. Using the generic mode of the sentimental melodrama, which allegorically unites differing national constituencies through marriage and homosocial bonds, Ruiz de Burton and Jackson construct critiques of social relations in the Californian borderlands, shaped by the legacy of past Spanish imperialism and reconstituted within contemporary U.S. imperialism. For both writers the intertwined discourses and histories of U.S. slavery (antislavery sentimentalism) and the Mexican-American War (U.S. imperialism) meant that devising a discourse of hemispheric citizenship on U.S. soil would necessarily involve exploring conflicting perspectives on the rights of redress by groups construed as victimized: blacks, Indians, and Mexicans in Jackson and the Californios and the white South in Ruiz de Burton. While *Ramona* sympathizes with Mexicans and Indians as the victims of U.S. empire and thus constructs a decolonizing discourse of hemispheric citizenship—albeit a contradictory one—*The Squatter and the Don* rejects the struggles of African Americans and Indians for land and rights in staking a claim for Californios and naturalized Mexicans to be considered a part of the white South and granted the rights due to faithful U.S. imperial citizens.

Ruiz de Burton and Jackson remain within certain limits of sentimentalist antislavery discourse (à la Alexander Kinmont and Harriet Beecher Stowe) in that they construe oppressed groups as *victims*. To be sure, Jackson's *Ramona* calls for the recognition of the personhood of people of color and for their freedom. But the sentimental insistence on personhood rights relies on the readers' acceptance of racially different groups in the discourse of romantic racialism; and racial difference is an unreliable foundation for insisting on full citizenship in an age when it is so often used to deny rights. Similarly, Martí (in "The Charleston Earthquake," 1886) and Du Bois (in *The Souls of Black Folk*, 1903) deploy the romantic racialist discourse of racial gifts and assert black superiority in the limited realms of "communion with Nature" and "loyalty" (Martí) and "simple faith and reverence" (Du Bois). However, both also work toward disputing racial difference as a valid category, retooling sentimentalism so as to recognize what Du Bois called the "entwined" character of rights in the shadow of empire (for white and black Cubans and Puerto Ricans in Martí and for the "darker peoples" in Du Bois).

Despite considerable differences in circumstances, tactics, and aims, the War of 1898 shapes the careers of both Martí (proleptically) and Du Bois (in retrospect). Martí died on the battlefield in 1895 in the War for Cuban Independence and therefore helped to create 1898, understood as the clash of Cuban independence advocates, Spanish colonialists, and U.S. imperialists. Martí and Du Bois constructed "1898" as a historical moment that marked the dual ascendance of the United States as an imperial power and practices of hemispheric and diasporic citizenship that sought to critique and undermine the U.S. empire. Chapter 2, " 'The Coming Unities' in 'Our America': Decolonization and Anticolonial Messianism in Martí, Du Bois, and the Santa de Cabora," argues that Martí and Du Bois expanded the meaning of decolonization through a politics of transnational and interracial alliance that defines practices of hemispheric and diasporic citizenship. Martí included Afro-Cubans in a broad, egalitarian, Latin Americanist social agenda, which he termed "Our *América*." In his writings from *The Souls of Black Folk* (1903) to *Darkwater* (1920) and *Dark Princess* (1928), Du Bois increasingly focused not only on conflicts along racial color lines, but also on economic and gender inequalities, a stance captured in his phrase "the coming unities."

Thus although Martí and Du Bois have been considered founders of Cuban and black nationalisms, they also devised forms of identification that cut across racial and national divides: *latinoamericanismo* in Martí and

Pan-Africanism in Du Bois, both of which deploy anticolonial and racial messianist discourses. Anticolonial messianist discourse consists of a variety of movements that galvanized resistance to colonialism with rapt visions of the oppressed prevailing over the oppressors. Anticolonial messianism in Du Bois and Martí registers in the realm of high culture the global proliferation of messianic rebellions among colonized peoples, such as that coalescing around the figure of Teresa Urrea, the "Mexican messiah" of the 1890s, whose life is the topic of Brianda Domecq's *La insólita historia de la Santa de Cabora* (*The Unusual Story of the Saint of Cabora*, 1990). Urrea was a young *mestiza* woman whom the Indians of northern Mexico believed to be a saint. She became the figurehead of their rebellions against the Porfirio Díaz dictatorship, which prioritized the needs of foreign capital over those of indigenous groups in Mexico. Urrea engaged in a "paper revolution" against the Díaz dictatorship with a fellow journalist in the borderlands of Texas, Arizona, and California. Like Martí and Du Bois, Urrea was a figure who was as much a product of the movements she joined as the "author" of her life and texts. Whereas Martí and Du Bois wrote anticolonial messianist texts, the Santa de Cabora became an anticolonial messianist text herself, one created to a great extent by the speeches, rumors, and belief systems of Mayo and Yaqui Indians of northern Mexico. Just as important, Urrea offers a third model of interethnic alliance as a practice of hemispheric citizenship in the shadow of empire, one that effaces the role of the putatively heroic intellectual-activist in favor of a collectively authored messianic text. Martí, Du Bois, and Urrea construct messianic figures as the imagined redemption of events of the past, particularly 1848 and 1898.

Chapter 3, "Transnationalisms against the State: Contesting Neocolonialism in the Harlem Renaissance, Cuban *Negrismo*, and Mexican *Indigenismo*," maps cross-fertilizations among these three nationalisms, all of which were constituted through representations of racially subordinated groups. By reassessing the relationship between these nationalisms and the vexed category of primitivism and suggesting a more fine-tuned view of the varied political uses of primitivist discourses in the 1920s, this chapter provides a way of viewing these nationalisms as deploying a popular transnational discourse to keep pace with the shifting cross-national formations of U.S. neocolonialism in Cuba, Haiti, and Mexico. Two sets of test cases on the use of primitivist discourses as modes of sociopolitical critique bear out the benefits of viewing the Harlem Renaissance in a transnational frame. First, in texts written while they were traveling in Latin America, Beals and

Hughes practiced hemispheric citizenship by constructing broad alliances among the poor and racially and politically oppressed. Second, I examine novels emerging within and responding to the three nationalisms, situating them within broader cross-national sociopolitical formations: McKay's *Home to Harlem* (United States, 1928); Menéndez's *Nayar* (Mexico, 1940); and Masdeu's *La raza triste* (Cuba, 1924). Both sentimentalist romantic racialism (chapters 1 and 2) and primitivist discourse (chapter 3) evolve from discourses of fixed racial identity (which are vulnerable to assertions of the inferiority of nonwhite groups) to discourses of political identity that articulate historical affinities among the darker peoples in discourses of diasporic and hemispheric citizenship.

In an age when differing forms of national self-determination rights were proclaimed in President Wilson's Fourteen Points (1918) and by the Fourth Congress of the Communist International (1922), the emancipatory potential of the term *self-determination* was often diminished by its bifurcation into two components: national independence in an age of imperialism and popular sovereignty.[75] But the subcultural groups that demanded self-determination in the United States, Mexico, and Cuba in the 1920s bound together the two sometimes mutually exclusive components of self-determination, insisting on combining national independence for the colonized with the political enfranchisement of subordinated groups and classes in a politics of decolonization.

Chapter 4, "Rising Tides of Color: Ethnography and Theories of Race and Migration in Boas, Park, Gamio, and Hurston," redirects and extends the mapping of New World nationalisms and primitivisms in chapter 3 by focusing on a shared institutional and intellectual frame for the Harlem Renaissance and Mexican indigenismo: Boasian anthropology and the Chicago School of Sociology. Franz Boas played a crucial role in providing intellectual and institutional underpinnings for both the Harlem Renaissance and Mexican indigenismo. In the United States, he delivered a series of lectures on the Negro Problem, including one at the 1906 commencement of Du Bois' own Atlanta University, where he exhorted African American graduates to aspire to the same greatness that their ancestors achieved in Egypt.[76] He later served as Zora Neale Hurston's mentor at Columbia University. And in Mexico, he cofounded the International School of American Archaeology and Ethnology in 1910, which provided Mexican nationalists with evidence of the artistic and scientific achievements of pre-Columbian indigenous civilizations with the unearthing of Chichén Itzá and Teotihuacán. The Chicago School similarly made waves in both sites. Robert E. Park, the most prominent Chicago School sociologist, trained two of the main players in the Harlem Renaissance, E. Franklin Frazier and Charles S. Johnson. And Robert Redfield, a student of both Boas and Park, joined the Mexican-born Boasians Gamio and Anita Brenner in the circle of the most prominent anthropologists working in Mexico in the 1920s. Boas's attack on evolutionary notions of the primitive in the 1910s and 1920s ushered in a new era of respect for so-called primitive cultures as alternative rather than inferior forms of civilization and a corresponding new methodology in anthropology: the participant-observation of ethnography. But even if the shift from race to culture in the social scientific theories of Boas and Park cleared the space for such auto-ethnographers as Gamio and Hurston, who drew on the energies of nonwhite nationalisms, there was no inevitable connection between the new ethnography of the 1920s and decolonization.

The most effective way of exploring the extent to which Gamio and Hurston contributed to the egalitarian projects of decolonization by working within anthropology is to examine their narratives of race and migration. In contrast to the overly optimistic view that interracial marriage could serve as a solution to racial conflict in Boas and Park, Gamio and Hurston focus on how the everyday experiences of gender, race, and class constituted obstacles to the enjoyment of full citizenship rights. In this sense, their ethnographies could be viewed as collaborative texts. However, both writers distanced themselves from those who suffered from race and empire in the United States and Latin America in certain ways. Moreover, I am not interested in suggesting that Gamio and Hurston were political radicals. I am well aware of Gamio's patronizing view that the indigenous cultures of Mexico were "backwards" and of Hurston's indifference and antipathy toward leftist movements. Instead of presuming these writers' full control over their texts, I engage in an against-the-grain reading in which the texts contain a multiplicity of meanings and political potential that these writers could not foresee. Their texts register deep tensions between egalitiarian tendencies and hierarchical social arrangements: Gamio's ethnographic work registers the potential for a decolonizing hemispheric citizenship that refuses racial hierarchies yet is irresponsible and aloof in its methodology, while Hurston is deeply sympathetic toward African American migrant workers even as she rejects discourses of hemispheric citizenship and a corresponding discourse of alliance with Afro-Haitians.

Finally, a coda argues that current practioners of what one journalist has termed hemispheric citizenship can draw on the considerable intellectual resources developed by the earlier generations of intellectuals and activists discussed in this book on the periodization and methodology of waves of decolonization. To posit waves of decolonization, then, means to search for the mechanisms connecting histories separated by periodization, national specialization, ethnic or social identity, and language. I hope my readers will take this book as an invitation to further explore waves of decolonization and discourses of hemispheric citizenship.

Some cultural critics, particularly Latin Americanists, have voiced skepticism about a comparative approach that focuses on activists on both sides of the border. After all, as Hortense Spillers has pointed out, "Martí's 'our' and 'America' usually do not embrace the U.S. at all."[77] I hope that the two primary aims of this book will reveal the benefits of thinking across such borders: to challenge the disciplinary assumptions of U.S. American literature by pushing it beyond its recognized national boundaries into a dialogue with Latin American culture; and to reveal the ample precedents for such a move in the discourses and practices of hemispheric citizenship of the writers in this study.[78] In 1891, Martí opened "Our America" with a description of a provincial Latin American villager, "unaware of the giants in seven-league boots who can crush him underfoot" (288). Just nine years later, Du Bois would insist that black intellectuals cultivate a "wide and thorough understanding" of global forces so as to gain a broader perspective on the "bitter sting of proscription" that African Americans faced. Moreover, both writers persuasively argue that in an age of U.S. empire, each one's America must understand the "other America[s]." More generally, both suggest that a cross-national, comparative analysis will deepen our understanding of both the record and possibilities of history. The implicit duty of the writer in these two essays is to demonstrate the transformative potential of thinking, of informed action rather than merely action: we need to adopt the "cold eye of the historian and social philosopher," argues Du Bois, while Martí claims, "Trenches of ideas are worth more than trenches of stone" (288). Today, in an age of unabated imperialist wars, we certainly need to dig deep.

One

"WHITE SLAVES" AND THE "ARROGANT *MESTIZA*": RECONFIGURING WHITENESS IN *THE SQUATTER AND THE DON AND RAMONA*

◖ Helen Hunt Jackson's *Ramona* (1884) and María Amparo Ruiz de Burton's *The Squatter and the Don* (1885) deploy the discourses of sentimental melodrama and romantic racialism in representing conflicts over land, class position, and racial status in California in the 1870s. These novels portray Anglos, Californios, and Indians as struggling for social position following the U.S. annexation of half of Mexico as a result of the Mexican-American War of 1846–48.[1]

I want to address three related sets of questions. First, what are the ideological limits and possibilities of the traditions of sentimental melodrama and romantic racialism that Jackson and Ruiz de Burton use in structuring their novels? Second, what happens to one's understanding of the limits and possibilities of the form when sentimentalism travels from England and the U.S. northeast to areas that are politically contested zones of empire?[2] Third, to what extent are the discourses of sentimental melodrama and romantic racialism adequate to the task of not only representing imperial conflicts, but also promoting decolonization? I pose these three related questions because some would question a focus on sentimental discourse in a book about decolonization because of the form's longstanding association with the formation and consolidation of the middle classes in opposition to the lower classes in England and the U.S. northeast, as Nancy Armstrong and Ann Douglas have shown.[3] Douglas has charged that Harriet Beecher Stowe equated domesticity with middle-class leisure in such a way that the moral high ground claimed by sentimental women served to rationalize their privileged position in a consumer society.[4]

The argument linking sentimental culture to class exploitation is quite persuasive. But sentimentalism's rationalization of class exploitation is a *possible* outcome of the form, not a *necessary* one. The argument about the class politics of sentimentalism is persuasive only if one (incorrectly) assumes that the use of the form was restricted to Anglo-Americans in England and the U.S. northeast and that the form cannot be unmoored from its roots in the white middle classes. Sentimental discourse was ideally suited to representations of populations victimized by empire, whether related to the British empire, as Julie Ellison has shown in her analysis of Joseph Addison's *Cato* (1713), or the U.S. empire, as I show here. Contrary to the assumption that sentimental melodrama was restricted to England and the U.S. northeast, the racially oppressed and colonized used the form to "write back" against the empire, as is the case with W. E. B. Du Bois and José Martí (see chapter 2). My analysis of *The Squatter and the Don* and *Ramona* supports the claim that sentimentalism has reinforced hierarchies of social class. But it would be a mistake to claim that it necessarily entails a specific ideology on class and race; in fact, the form is remarkably protean.

One measure of the pliant character of sentimentalism can be seen in Martí's assessment of Stowe and Jackson as sentimentalist writers. He offers hints as to how sentimentalism could appeal to writers such as himself, who grew up in poverty in a colonized country and sought to end Spanish colonialism by forging an alliance with tobacco workers and Afro-Cubans (see chapter 2 on the centrality of this alliance in Martí's anticolonial activism). In the prologue to his translation of *Ramona* (1888), Martí makes a strong case for the continued relevance of Stowe's brand of sentimental melodrama in addressing the differing political context of U.S. expansionism after the Civil War.[5] He favorably compares *Ramona* to *Uncle Tom's Cabin*, whose sentimental qualities he had earlier recognized, praising it as "a tear that has something to say."[6] As this metaphor suggests, nineteenth-century sentimentalism appeals to readers' emotions and morals in an effort to shape their politics, often through tropes of family separation.[7] Martí claims that he found in *Ramona* "*our* novel," a model full of "fire and knowledge" for what he would call "Our America," a racially egalitarian Latin America opposing both Spanish and U.S. imperialism. Martí celebrates Ramona as "la mestiza arrogante" (the arrogant *mestiza*), implying that she is the ideal subject of the revolutionary interracial movement that he calls "our *mestiza* America."[8] Martí represents this collectivity as embodied by the product of interracial love, a mestiza of mixed Indian and white heritage; he thus implicitly recognizes the utility of sentimentalism in representing the intertwined character of the plights of the victims of U.S. racial politics and empire.[9]

Even as Martí is reinventing the figure of Ramona for his own purposes of decolonization and downplaying the moments in the novel that appear to consign Native Americans to menial labor, he is teaching a useful lesson about the potential of sentimental discourses. If on the one hand sentimentalists could represent national, linguistic, and ethnic differences in a favorable if patronizing manner; on the other hand sentimentalism traveled across national boundaries into new cultural and historical contexts and occasionally crossed into the hands of the lower classes and colonized. Sentimentalism, Martí implies, can be a tool of decolonization—did it promote decolonization in the hands of Jackson and Ruiz de Burton?

Cultural production on the aftermath of the Mexican-American War in California presents an ideal opportunity for investigating what happens when sentimental discourse turns its attention away from antislavery reform and toward defining political agendas in response to U.S. imperial expansion. Before I turn in chapter 2 to the overt politics of decolonization in Du Bois and Martí that strategically deploy and transform sentimentalist discourse, I would like to examine in this chapter how Jackson and Ruiz de Burton play out the limits and possibilities of the form in a context in which they had not identified an explicit project of decolonization but rather aligned themselves with various reformist movements and political causes in the shadow of U.S. imperial expansion.

Ruiz de Burton and Jackson corroborate Martí's insights on the continued usefulness of Stowe's version of sentimentalism by describing their own texts as indebted to sentimental antislavery novels like *Uncle Tom's Cabin*.[10] Although commonly deployed by both male and female writers, sentimentalism proved especially useful to northern white women writers, affording them a way of morally transforming "the values and practices of domination" in patriarchy in such a way that their activities were not stigmatized as political and hence unladylike, as Lauren Berlant has argued.[11] Sentimentalism thus comprises a cluster of tactics by which writers effect reform by representing the public sphere in terms of domestic tropes —emotions, love, and family—and thereby claim moral authority through representations of areas of life that were commonly construed as irrelevant to political concerns.

The use of sentimentalism as moral critique in Jackson and Ruiz de

Burton is structured by the discourse of romantic racialism/feminism uti-
lized in reformist writings from Stowe to Du Bois and beyond. Romantic
racialism is most often intertwined with its double, romantic feminism, the
pair equating blacks and women as pious victims of—and hence morally
superior to—white men.[12] Romantic racialism is a more benign version of
racialist thought than scientific racial determinism because it holds that
various national and cultural groups are fundamentally different, with
distinct racial "gifts," but that blacks and women are inherently superior
rather than inherently inferior in that they allegedly possess a greater degree of Christian morality, reverence, and deeply felt emotions than white
men.[13] Depending on how the writer uses romantic racialism, the groups
defined as victimized by race, gender, or region can be white women and
Indians, as in *Ramona*, or, in a reversal of Stowe's portrayal of blacks as
victims, landed white southerners and elite Californios, as in *Squatter*.[14]
Romantic racialism provided women writers with a vocabulary to yoke
their protofeminism to more legitimized traditions of racial reform. Hence
sentimentalism in its romantic racialist mode intervenes in politics by
specifying morally superior victimized groups whose values should define
the priorities of a given polity.

The mechanisms by which these novels simultaneously affirm and re-
work dominant discourses can be explained in relation to the novels' allegorical structures. The key strategy of the mode of melodrama in these
novels is to imaginatively resolve social conflict through the allegorical
union of differing national constituencies in marriage. I use the term
melodrama because it is itself defined by its allegorical structure: characters
embody "primal ethical forces."[15] These allegorical unions at once expand
and contract the privileged sphere of whiteness to include and exclude
groups other than Anglo-Saxons. In 1870s California, recently conquered
by the predominantly Anglo United States, being identified as white con-
ferred a social and economic advantage quickly solidifying into law. In this
chapter I join a growing body of scholars who focus on the ways in which
white identity, understood as a socially constructed category, has been
assumed or rejected in the process of redefining a socioeconomic order.[16]

Minority characters in *Ramona* and *Squatter* exploit the protean character of whiteness, reconfiguring its bounds and meanings so as to realize
differing versions of hemispheric citizenship in relation to the U.S. empire.
Sentimentalism in these novels thus redefines the ethnic boundaries of
whiteness in order to undermine the cultural authority of male Anglo-
Saxons, condemning the alleged materialistic tendencies of white men,

particularly squatters, as immoral. These forces of "immorality" are ar-
rayed against the virtue of the marginalized, whether white women, Californios, or Indians.[17]

In the novels' redefinition of whiteness, the race/class politics are quite
complex, including positions that are at times egalitarian (expanding whiteness through incorporating groups marginalized by ethnicity and/or class)
and at times biased against the lower classes (in Jackson sympathy for
Indians coincides with a representation of their willingness to serve the
upper classes, and in Ruiz de Burton the Californios' scorn for the squatters
partly stems from their class position). If sentimental melodrama in Ruiz de
Burton and Jackson results in similarly contradictory class ideologies, the
two novels construct sharply contrasting discourses of hemispheric citizenship along the lines of region, ethnicity, and nationality: whereas *Squatter*
calls for the allegedly victimized regional populations of white southerners
and Californios to claim U.S. imperial citizenship, *Ramona* focuses attention on the ways in which Indians and Mexicans have been victimized by the
U.S. empire.

To briefly summarize, *Squatter* and *Ramona* both endorse the infusion
of the virtue of the victimized into the white male–identified dominant culture through sentimentalism, a form of *engagé* writing constituted through
the narrative strategies of the melodrama: defending morally superior victims; adopting conciliatory approaches to avoid direct, violent conflict; and
forging alliances among the elite of different cultures and regions through
marital and other unions that expand whiteness. In my analysis of *Squatter*
and *Ramona*, I will examine the tension between the exclusionary logic of
whiteness and the cross-cultural alliances in the melodrama that alternately
reinforce and undermine it. By exploring how these novels contract, expand, and sometimes even disrupt the ideology of whiteness, I explain their
strikingly distinct versions of hemispheric citizenship in the shadow of U.S.
empire.

MELODRAMA, ROMANTIC RACIALISM, AND THE KEYWORD OF *SENTIMENT*: CHILD, KINMONT, STOWE, AND BEYOND

An examination of the uses of the keyword *sentiment* from the 1830s to the
early twentieth century will serve to explain the protean political uses of
the term as it traveled among differing historical contexts, some beyond
Europe and the United States, and was employed by writers in oppressed

populations.[18] Sentimentalism's racial politics are particularly controversial. Euro-American racial discourses in the nineteenth century generally portray the darker races as naturally subservient, yet differ on the question of their specific attributes and capacities. Their assessment of nonwhites ranges from the assertion in ethnology and in evolutionary anthropology that the so-called lower races are inferior (Josiah C. Nott and George R. Gliddon, Edward Burnett Tylor) to the romantic racialist and sentimentalist view that Negroes and Indians are subservient yet morally superior (Alexander Kinmont, Stowe, Jackson).

Antislavery writers like Lydia Maria Child, Kinmont, and Stowe adopted an account of the Negro in which the keyword *sentiment* both defined the specific attributes of Negroes and delineated the proper emotional and ethical responses of whites to Negroes. Both Child and Stowe adopted and popularized many of Kinmont's ideas, and Stowe was the chief literary model for Jackson.[19]

Sentimentalist discourse was by no means limited to abolitionism. Scholars have uncovered a distinguished philosophical pedigree for the term. Nineteenth-century uses of *sentiment* are rooted in an Enlightenment debate between those who emphasized the role of reason in social improvement and those who emphasized the emotions. Responding to the perceived dangers of the empiricist views of John Locke (1632–1704), Anthony Ashley Cooper, the Third Earl of Shaftesbury, writing in 1711, "formulated his idea of the moral sense, an additional human faculty that could innately perceive right and wrong by allowing one person to experience another's pains and pleasures through the power of sympathy"—an idea that caught on with the Scottish common sense philosophers, ranging from Francis Hutcheson to Adam Smith, who were deeply indebted to his pioneering work.[20] Thus sentimentalism's early development in moral philosophy suggests that it was ideally suited to represent pressing ethical and political problems. Stowe, the best-known U.S. sentimental writer, reported that she read Archibald Alison's writings while she was a student and teacher along with those of two other Scottish philosophers, Hugh Blair and Lord Kames.[21] In addition, Stowe may have been exposed to these writers' ideas through Kinmont, who from 1833 to 1834 gave a series of public lectures employing the Scottish Enlightenment doctrine of moral sentiments in explaining the characteristics of Negroes in Stowe's home of Cincinnati.[22]

Stowe also drew on an allied narrative tradition that similarly linked the expression of emotions to morality: melodrama. Stowe's main exposure to

melodrama was by reading the novels of Charles Dickens.[23] As Linda
Williams has argued, melodrama represents the virtue of victims who are
caught in a clash among characters who embody primal ethical forces of
good and evil: "If emotional and moral registers are sounded, if a work
invites us to feel sympathy for the virtues of beset victims, if the narrative
trajectory is ultimately concerned with a retrieval and staging of virtue
through adversity and suffering, then the operative mode is melodrama."[24]
Although sentimentalism and melodrama are commonly associated with
somewhat different intellectual traditions (moral philosophy, the novel,
and poetry for sentimentalism; drama, the novel, and film for melodrama), Williams's definition alerts one to their considerable overlap. Although sentimentalism and melodrama are difficult to distinguish from
one another, they do differ in emphasis: while the discourse of sentiment
calls to mind efforts to stimulate social change through the eliciting of
sympathy in the minds of its readers, melodrama focuses attention on the
contest between primal ethical forces.

A generation of scholars of sentimental melodrama has uncovered what
June Howard has termed the "transatlantic and philosophical antecedents
of the form."[25] At least two more steps are required for the proper assessment of sentimentalism. First, there needs to be more attention to the ways
in which romantic racialism shaped sentimentalism.[26] A second step would
be to examine how the sentimental melodrama in its romantic racialist
mode traveled beyond the United States and endured into the twentieth
century and, having been transformed by new writers, promoted not only
the political causes of abolitionism and women's rights, but also those of
decolonization.[27]

To understand the political valence of the term *sentiment* in Kinmont
and Stowe, one has to understand how they constructed Negroes as ideal
Christians as a result of certain racial attributes. Kinmont, in his *Twelve
Lectures on the Natural History of Man* (1839), and Stowe articulate the
most fully developed discourses of romantic racialism. Both argue (here
in Kinmont's terms) that Negroes' racial "genius and temperament" are
rooted in the "milder and gentler virtues" that epitomize the moral values
of Christianity, while the "Caucasian" excels in political and intellectual
life.[28] Stowe articulates these "gentler virtues" as follows in *A Key to Uncle
Tom's Cabin*: "What God asks of the soul more than anything else is faith
and simplicity, the affection and reliance of the little child. . . . The negro
race is confessedly more simple, docile, child-like and affectionate than
other races."[29] For Kinmont, these character traits mean that Negroes are

morally superior to whites in certain ways: the "Negro race . . . may, as respects an innate love of goodness, and the majesty and strength of the moral discriminations, as far surpass our present civilization, as we now excel them, in all the distinctions of a daring and successful intellect" (195).[30] Kinmont suggests that the moral superiority of the Negro corresponds to the virtue of "primitive times" in which Christianity prevailed over science.[31]

Thus Kinmont's use of the term *primitive* serves two classifying functions: it characterizes an earlier chronological era and it describes the distinctly Christian sensibility of Negroes. *Sensibility* was a keyword that revolved in sentimentalism's conceptual orbit. In *Strictures on the Modern System of Female Education* (1799), Hannah More defined *sensibility* as "that exquisite sense of feeling which God implanted in the heart as a stimulus to quicken us in relieving the miseries of others."[32] So *sensibility* describes a particular person's level of attunement to the life of the emotions and to moral issues—a person of sensibility is expected to work to lessen the suffering of others. *Sensibility* therefore combined the etymological meaning of *sympathy*, which signifies feeling with someone else, with the moral imperative to act to remedy suffering.

In Kinmont the implicitly aligned terms *primitive* and *sensibility/sentiment* are crucial in reevaluating what counts as knowledge and therefore in reassessing the place of Negroes as members of what he terms the "divine brotherhood of the human race." This "brotherhood" is evident in the cross-cultural constant of "natural sentiments" and familial love in particular (77):

> Our minds are . . . an invisible mirror, which receive and constantly retain . . . a true image of nature. . . . And this is exhibited principally, in those natural sentiments, which are found to be universal among mankind: they are . . . always . . . the spontaneous expression of some universal law, the reflected image of nature's voice caught from the human soul. . . . And this copy . . . of the true laws of nature, is oftentimes more legible as a *transcript*, than the bright original, which is sometimes too bright for our *intellectual* reading. The *sentimental* knowledge is not only the best, but sometimes the only knowledge which can be had. (209)

For Kinmont, "natural sentiments" stand as proof—the divine "transcript" —of the human unity underlying the variety of the human races. This universal brotherhood acknowledges the coexistence of differing "species of intellectual and moral greatness" rather than equating greatness with European civilization alone (221). Further, because "sentimental knowledge" faithfully copies nature, it provides the "best" knowledge to be had—and this is the knowledge in which Negroes allegedly excel. For Kinmont, then, sentiment is a form of cognition enhanced by feeling, leading to a higher form of human reason and moral clarity in which Negroes show the way to a more advanced form of civilization. In other words, Negroes surpass whites in one of the key areas in which whites allegedly excel—intelligence.

This idea that Negro moral superiority would lead to a superior civilization did not end up being a dead letter in Kinmont, as remarkable and counterintuitive as it sounds in the climate of racial discourse of the mid–nineteenth century. Child takes up this line of reasoning when she argues in *The Anti-Slavery Standard* in 1843, "Among the races of men, I believe, too, that the type of the highest civilization is now the lowest; and it is so because the *affections*, the *sentiments*, have hitherto been made 'hewers of wood and drawers of water,' to *physical force* and *intellectual power*." In other words, a combination of physical and intellectual domination has enslaved sentiment, which she associates with Negroes and with women. Child claims that this state of affairs will soon change: "As the intellectual age passes into the moral age, women and the colored race are both rising out of their long degradation. The progress of both will be more and more perceptible, as men learn to respect *goodness* as much as *knowledge*."[33] This clever upending of conventional, racially charged hierarchies of intellect and emotion in Kinmont and Child is potentially promising because it plots a future in which blacks are "co-worker[s] in the kingdom of culture" in Du Bois's terms.[34]

As if to follow through on Kinmont's theory of "sentimental knowledge," Stowe in *Uncle Tom's Cabin* explores the possibility that a careful attention to feelings can improve or replace reason. After Senator Bird has agreed to help the fugitive slave Eliza elude her captors, Mrs. Bird says, "Your heart is better than your head."[35] As a metaphor for human sentiment, the word *heart* links affect to moral ideals through what Stowe terms "the magic of the real presence of distress"—an idea literalized through the presence of Eliza (156). Stowe implies that such "sentimental knowledge" (Kinmont's term) can indeed motivate racial reform: listening to the heart rather than the head ushers in what Child refers to as the new "moral age." It remains to be explored whether such sentimental knowledge can exert critical leverage on discourses that uphold racial hierarchies, resolving the tension between racial reform and racial status quo.

Whereas Stowe suggests that the heart can transform the head and lead even legislators to oppose unjust laws in order to alleviate human suffering, Kinmont, in an argument about melding the political ideals of the Enlightenment with the Christian ideals of "primitive times," explains in more abstract terms how sentimental knowledge can realize higher moral and political ideals. Kinmont's discussion is useful in assessing the conditions that must be met to transform sentimentalism into a tool for building racial egalitarianism, not just reform. There are three principal suggestions in Kinmont's argument about the long-term effects of "engrafting" Enlightenment political ideals of "truth" and "justice" to the religious achievements of "primitive times" (and allegedly primitive peoples such as Negroes) (178). First, he writes that this engrafting results in the transmission of ever-nobler attributes to the offspring of Negroes and whites. Thus rather than finally consigning Negroes to primitive times, Kinmont, like Child in the *National Anti-Slavery Standard* and Du Bois in *Souls*, implies that blacks will help to create a better future. Second, whites need to cultivate the "nobler passions" that implicitly meld religious "sentiments" and egalitarian social ideals so that they can transform the racial status quo. Third, Kinmont's text further implies that because the characteristics of blacks and whites will tend to approximate each other as they move toward what Child calls the "moral age," racial attributes will become increasingly less important. However, while Kinmont and Du Bois envision a future in which Negroes could potentially take the vanguard of social change and usher in what Child calls the "moral age," in *Uncle Tom's Cabin* Stowe, as a variety of scholars have pointed out, consigns Negroes to a racially separate future via George Harris's desire for "an African nationality."[36] Thus the tension between racial egalitarianism and racial essentialism in romantic racialist vocabularies of sentimentalism revolves around the question of the extent to which a text represents the potential for Negroes to transform white-dominated societies through exercising "sentimental knowledge" themselves, rather than retreating to separate enclaves that reinforce the notion of permanent racial differences.

To briefly summarize, the term *sentiment* in Kinmont and Stowe includes the following meanings:

1 as universal human affect, the term offers evidence of unity among the races; but since the term is yoked to romantic racialism, it creates a differential unity that relies on stereotypical notions that construct Negroes as childlike, ideal Christians;

2 the term implies that "sentimental knowledge" is a form of emotion-

ally enhanced, morally righteous cognition that is superior to mere reason (and it is in this "sentimental knowledge" that women and Negroes·
excel);

3 while Stowe ultimately assigns agency to mixed-race African Americans
such as George Harris and victim status to the full-blooded Uncle Tom,
Kinmont's notion of "engrafting" implicitly posits a cultural mixing that
will allow sentimental knowledge to shape U.S. society in accordance with
the morally superior sensibilities of white women and Negroes and therefore foregrounds the potentially transformative role of nonwhite agency
in social change even while insisting that whites will need to reform
themselves. However, the question remains as to the extent to which
whites will relinquish their self-flattering leadership roles and make room
for the agency of nonwhites achieved through their expression of such
sentimental knowledge.

There are contradictory political consequences of the use of *sentiment* in
Kinmont and Stowe. On the one hand, the universalizing thrust of sentimentalism in Kinmont and Stowe has the valuable effect of refuting the
claims of Negro emotional, moral, and intellectual inferiority present in
Thomas Jefferson's *Notes on the State of Virginia* (1787) and in *Types of
Mankind* (1854) by Nott and Gliddon. On the other hand, the sentimentalist attempt to equate differing affective responses to suffering as evidence of
human brotherhood runs the risk of encouraging an oversimplified view
that flattens out differences in the social and political circumstances of
whites and nonwhites, in a strategy that in a different context the critical
race theorists Kimberlé Crenshaw and Gary Peller have termed "disaggregation." Crenshaw and Peller define *disaggregation* as "a narrative technique that narrows the perception of the range of illegitimate racial power
by divorcing particular episodes from their larger social context." During
the Rodney King trial of 1992, defense lawyers showed a video of King's
infamous beating at the hands of police in frame-by-frame stills. They then
used these decontextualized fragments as the basis for their questions to
experts on prisoner restraint, which served the purpose of "the reframing
of King as a threat rather than a victim."[37] Sentimentalist versions of disaggregation similarly employ the strategy of decontextualization in order to
piece together disparate evidence from differing social conditions so as to
equate white and black affective responses to oppression and suffering.
They therefore risk downplaying both socioeconomic differences and the
inequalities that are built into discourses that assert Negroes' enhanced

sensitivity regarding emotions and religion. As Lauren Berlant has argued, "The turn to sentimental rhetoric at moments of social anxiety constitutes a generic wish for an unconflicted world, one where structural inequities, not emotions and intimacies, are epiphenomenal."[38]

Indeed, Stowe's aim is to demonstrate the common humanity of whites and slaves through an appeal to shared sorrow, as when Uncle Tom cries upon confronting the prospect of being sold and separated from his family: "Just such tears, sir, as you dropped into the coffin where lay your first-born son; such tears, woman, as you shed when you heard the cries of your dying babe. For sir, he was a man,—and you are but another man. And woman, though dressed in silk and jewels, you are but a woman, and, in life's great straits and mighty griefs, ye feel but one sorrow!" (91). This emphasis on commonality—"ye feel but one sorrow!"—is undermined by the fact that Stowe's pitch is to those among her readers who are separated from family members not because of slavery, but because of naturally occurring death. The abstract figure of "one sorrow" relies on tying together decontextualized moments of crying, in a strategy that one critic has viewed as a decisive flaw of discourses of sympathy: you can sympathize only with someone who resembles you.[39] But in a distinct move that is evident when one recognizes the centrality of romantic racialism to Stowe's version of sentimental discourse, Uncle Tom's tears mark a particular trait of Negroes—their alleged heightened emotions—a trait that paradoxically emphasizes racial difference as much as it does a shared humanity. So even if a white reader recognizes a certain shared humanity in the expression of sorrow at the loss of a loved one, the belief that Negroes (and women) are naturally more emotional could undermine that sympathy. Thus Stowe builds her universalism, such as it is, on the shaky foundations of racial distinctions. While Kinmont and the Du Bois of *Souls* suggest that the particular racial traits of Negroes suit them for participating in white society, Stowe betrays ambivalence—ambivalence built into the logic of romantic racialism—when she suggests at the conclusion of *Uncle Tom's Cabin* that Negroes belong outside of the United States.[40]

Sentimentalism's appeals to universality, then, are susceptible to contradictory impulses, the simultaneous invoking and dismissing of class and racial hierarchies, as if to loudly banish them while wishing them to remain. This is because the alleged racial traits that make blacks the embodiment of universal Christian values are paradoxically what mark them as a particular group, distinguishing them from white men. In practical terms, if "sentimental knowledge" in Stowe shows potential in that it construes blacks as morally superior to whites and compels readers to join movements of antislavery reform, it falls short in the crucial area of imagining blacks as intrinsically equal rather than as crucially different.

Indeed, sentimentalism's attempts to construct unity emphasize those specific traits of nonwhite groups that allegedly make them ideal servants or workers, confirming the link between sentimentalism and the exploitative tendencies of the middle classes in the arguments of Armstrong and Douglas. Stowe's disciple Jackson, writing in the 1880s, transfers the sentimentalism of Kinmont and Stowe into the new context of racial conflict in California with similar advantages and disadvantages. Jackson portrays Indians as appealing to white readers in a double-edged manner. On the one hand, Indians are morally upright, ideal Christians. On the other hand, these Christian virtues of their racial character, which predispose them to a "willingness to serve" in Kinmont's terms, consign them to occupying politically and intellectually subordinate positions (191). In the case of Jackson, sentimentalism insists on the personhood of Indians while upholding the status quo that constructs them as menial laborers. Du Bois drew on this deep and contradictory legacy of sentimental antislavery reformism in framing the ethical imperative of his anticolonialism, even as late as 1919 in his reports on the Pan-African Conference (see chapter 2 for an account of how his use of sentimental discourse differs from that of Jackson and Stowe). In divergent ways, both Jackson and Du Bois employ sentimentalism in attempting to articulate the consequences of U.S. imperialism.

Sentimentalism, then, is a highly protean form that aspires to persuade readers in various ways to adopt attitudes of sympathy toward those who suffer. One cannot fully determine the limits and possibilities of the form by examining solely its philosophical antecedents in the writings of, say, Adam Smith. Instead, the precise political significance of sentimentalism depends on the combination of which discourses (romantic racialism) and political ideals (antislavery, full equality, Pan-Africanism, imperial citizenship, or hemispheric citizenship) those attitudes of sympathy deploy in attempting to follow through on representations of deeply felt connections to other people. In the following analysis of two sentimental melodramas that sharply diverge in their assessment of who gets to count as victims in late nineteenth-century California, I want to assess the extent to which they shift sentimentalism's uneasy balance between the countervailing logics of

racial ontology and universal rights. In this analysis the question of agency
is crucial: to what extent do nonwhite groups exercise sentimental knowledge in attempting to secure their own rights?

THE "DOUBLE LOOP": UNITING "WHITE SLAVES" IN *THE SQUATTER AND THE DON*

Struggles over land dominated the maneuvering for racial caste position in
late nineteenth-century California. The California State Land Law of 1851
called for a thorough examination of Californio land titles on the fictitious
grounds that such titles were confused; the real motivation was the desire
to make *ranchero* land available to Anglos through squatting, or home-
steading. Costly legal fees forced the Californios to sell their land, and
squatters took advantage of such legal irresolution to stake their claim on
Californio ranchos. The Californios engaged "in relentless backyard guer-
rilla warfare with settlers bent on outright confiscation."[41] From 1851 to
1875, Anglos took control of "thousands of acres" of Californio land by a
variety of legal and illegal methods.[42] Such conflicts over land, class and
racial status, and male privilege take center stage in the *The Squatter and
the Don*, as the title suggests.

Ruiz de Burton's life was shaped by such disputes over land in the
U.S. Southwest and the Mexican North. U.S. imperial expansion led her
to move north from Mexico to the United States, and smaller-scale land
grabs in California itself threatened to displace her a second time. Born in
Loreto, Baja California, in 1832, María Amparo Ruiz lived through the U.S.
invasion of Baja California in the Mexican War. Her mother accepted the
offer the United States made to Baja Californians: transport to the United
States and citizenship. Ruiz and her mother moved to Monterey, California, where Ruiz later married U.S. Army Captain Henry S. Burton. When
the Burtons moved to San Diego, they encountered the same problems
over Mexican land grant titles that plagued landowning Californios. They
purchased the Jamul Ranch from the Pico family, but when Pico's claim to
the ranch came before the Land Commission, his claim was rejected. As a
result, the Burtons' purchase was contested as well. Squatters began to
settle on parts of the ranch. The Land Commission finally validated the
Mexican land grant title for the Jamul Ranch in 1875. Burton petitioned for
a homestead in 1887 and was granted 986.6 acres of the Jamul Ranch. The
grant was validated by the California Supreme Court in 1889.[43] This pro-

tracted, costly process was typical of the difficulties that beset the Californio elite class. This biographical sketch demonstrates the dizzyingly conflicting loyalties and identities that defined Ruiz de Burton as an early U.S. Latina: she was simultaneously Mexican, a U.S. (imperial) citizen, the wife of a U.S. army captain, and a non-Anglo landowner of a ranch formerly owned by a Californio.

Squatter intervenes in the conflicts over land and class position that shaped Ruiz de Burton's life by creating an array of moral oppositions within its sentimental melodrama. The novel contrasts two means of securing class position: a conciliatory style, characterized by the cross-cultural alliance politics of Mrs. Darrell, her son Clarence, and Don Mariano Alamar; and a violent, confrontational style, characteristic of William Darrell and other Anglo squatters. The narration emphasizes the important moral role that the wife and mother play in the politicized familial sphere by employing war metaphors in describing Mrs. Darrell's role in her debate with Mr. Darrell over the ethics of squatterism. Acknowledged by her husband to be a "comandante," Mrs. Darrell fights a holy war on behalf of virtue (*S* 57). However, when Mr. Darrell insists on staking a claim to Don Mariano's land, Mrs. Darrell responds by instructing her wealthy son Clarence to purchase the property against her husband's will, thereby employing the more subtle tactic of avoiding conflict and channeling male agency. When he learns of the transaction, Mr. Darrell accuses Don Mariano of "bribing" Clarence with the offer of Mercedes, the Don's daughter. "Livid with rage," Darrell attempts to strike the Don with his horsewhip, but before he can, Gabriel Alamar tosses a *reata* (lasso) around Darrell, containing his movement (*S* 248). To the horsewhip and *reata* of violent conflict, *Squatter* counterposes its morally upright, sentimental alternative, the "double loop" of marital union, which later unites Clarence and Mercedes in marriage, thus joining Anglo and Californio elites (*S* 123). The "double loop" refers to the ceremonial lasso tossed over the heads of bride and groom in Mexican Catholic wedding ceremonies. At this point in *Squatter* the families forging an alliance are the Californio Alamars and the Mechlins, Anglos associated with banking interests in New York. Gabriel Alamar marries Lizzie Mechlin, and Elvira Alamar marries George Mechlin.

Don Mariano takes a similarly conciliatory approach in his dealings with the squatters. Although they routinely destroy his property, Don Mariano proposes a compromise: he offers his cattle to the squatters so that they will stop killing them (as is their legal right), and he advises them to grow fruit rather than grains, suggesting a change that indeed made California agriculture more profitable in the 1880s.[44] If they cooperate, the Don promises to help pay for the irrigation of their fields and to drop his appeal against their land claims (S 91–96). The Don's plan for peaceful coexistence represents a shrewder, more rational capitalism than that enacted by the squatters, a capitalism that avoids conflict to ensure higher productivity. The Californios' conciliatory manner of interacting with Anglos is evidence of a sentimental culture that is represented as being rooted in the elite culture of northern Mexico rather than in Europe or the U.S. northeast.

Ruiz de Burton represents characters from differing cultures as embodying morally upright qualities in order to suggest political compatibilities, as in the parallel between the Californios and the white southerner Mary Moreneau Darrell, the mother of Clarence. The narration implicitly compares the restraint, manners, and Catholicism of Mary and the white South she represents to similar qualities in Don Mariano, contrasting these traits with the Protestant, violent temper of William and the northeast (S 60). Mary's refined manners signal a potential alliance between southern and Californio elites.

Moreover, the South and California are both represented as the sectional victims of the corrupt monopolies and of the lower classes: "Well, the poor South is in pretty much the same fix that we are," George Mechlin says to his wife, Elvira (S 297). Thus the melodrama's plot of villains and victims calls for these victimized regions and classes, white southerners and Californios, both of whom embody old money, honor, traditional values, and a stable social hierarchy, to morally redeem the nation by displacing the monopoly capitalists. The North-South alliance creates an entrepreneurial and finance capitalism offering paternalistic control of the lower classes as opposed to unfettered monopoly capitalism, a system symbolizing chaos at both ends of the class hierarchy.

This North–South alliance marks Ruiz de Burton's departure from the antislavery version of sentimental politics à la Stowe, as is clear in the use of the Texas Pacific Railroad scheme in the novel's plot. In the novel, the Texas Pacific Railroad proposed by the southerner Tom Scott embodies an economic alliance between elite Californios and white southerners. As a historical figure, Scott, the president of the Texas and Pacific, was also the president of the Pennsylvania Railroad, "the biggest freight carrier in the world and probably the most powerful corporation in America at the time."[45] Scott's railroad proposal challenged the monopoly of the Union Pacific and Central Pacific on transcontinental routes and to some symbolized an alliance between the South and the West. In 1877 Congressman Lucius Lamar of Mississippi praised the bill establishing Scott's transcontinental railroad for its promotion of a sectional reconciliation, but that year President Rutherford Hayes announced his opposition to the bill. Southern Democrats called for a western alliance in 1878, proclaiming their defiance "of Eastern capitalism, its banks, monetary system, railroads, and monopolies."[46] But by the end of 1878 the conservatives prevailed, and the South courted northeastern economic interests instead. *Squatter's* Gabriel Alamar and Clarence plan to start a bank in San Diego when the Texas Pacific Railroad is constructed (*S* 296). Their fight to bring the railroad to San Diego (the attempt is unsuccessful) reveals their hope of transforming southern California and the South into the leaders of an expanding capitalist economy, with white southerners, Californios, and sympathetic northeasterners like Clarence at its helm.[47] By establishing commerce between elites of different cultures and regions, the railroad thus epitomizes *Squatter's* political project of postbellum sectional reconciliation and interethnic alliance.

In the conclusion to the novel, in which the narrator directly addresses the readers, Ruiz de Burton again emphasizes that "the entire Southern States," among which she includes southern California, are suffering a common plight—the region "must wait and pray for a Redeemer who will emancipate the white slaves of California" from monopoly capitalists (*S* 372). With the phrase "white slaves," the narrator turns Stowe's antebellum brand of romantic racialism on its head, portraying the white elite rather than the black slaves as those who are oppressed. Indeed, while Mr. Darrell was courting Mary Moreneau in Washington, D.C., she kept a black servant named Letitia, who "was devotedly attached to her" (*S* 59). This brief reference to black–white race relations in the South marks southern institutions as benevolent, allowing Ruiz de Burton to elide race and class hierarchies.[48] Moreover, here again we have Negroes' alleged "willingness to serve," in Kinmont's terms, in which the egalitarian tendencies of romantic racialism are undercut by a hierarchy of occupation and race (191). Whereas Stowe attempts to reconcile the races through antislavery sentimentalism, Ruiz de Burton promotes a racially homogeneous reconciliation between white representatives of the South and California. In Ruiz de Burton's paradoxical logic, the expansion of whiteness via the Californio–

white South alliance paradoxically depends on an expansion and inversion of the meaning of slavery. The historical irony here is that the white slaves, if redeemed, would go on enslaving Indians and blacks.

Calling the white upper classes "white slaves" is possible in part because of what Immanuel Wallerstein has termed the dual appropriation of surplus in the capitalist world system: its appropriation by an owner from a laborer and its appropriation in peripheral zones by core zones.[49] Ruiz de Burton's inverted romantic racialism that portrays the South and California as victims represents the relationship of "unequal exchange" obtaining between European and U.S. capitalist core zones and their underdeveloped peripheries and regional semiperipheries. Indeed, California was a semiperipheral zone in the 1870s and 1880s.[50] Thus the story Ruiz de Burton tells is not a provincial example of literary regionalism, but rather a variation of a global pattern of capitalist core–periphery disparities. Ruiz de Burton strategically emphasizes regional exploitation in the capitalist world system so as to create a discourse of white unity that obscures exploitation by race and class.

The South provides an ideal model for such a strategy that downplays race and class inequality. Since the United States defeated both California and the South as a result of the Mexican-American and Civil wars, both can claim regional victim status.[51] The postbellum ideology of the "prostrate South" mistakenly held that physical damage to the South during the Civil War had devastated the southern economy, thereby articulating the reunion discourse on southern terms.[52] Northerners bought into this ideology in the 1870s, expressing a newfound sympathy for the white southern upper classes as allegedly victimized by Reconstruction. Governor Henry Haight of California subscribed to the prostrate South ideology in his victory speech in 1867, blaming nonwhites for the ills of California and the South: "I will simply say that in this result we protest . . . against populating this fair state with a race of Asiatics—against sharing with inferior races the Government of our country. . . . and this protest of ours will be re-echoed in thunder tones by the great central states until the Southern States are emancipated from negro domination, and restored to their proper place as equals and sisters in the great Federal family."[53] Haight uses the South as a model for white unity at the expense of nonwhites, just as Ruiz de Burton utilizes the prostrate South discourse in an attempt to secure a stable foothold for elite Californios in a racially hostile climate.

As the elite Californio–Southerner parallel makes clear, Ruiz de Burton's alliance between these regions would not lead to a more egalitarian social order. Rather, by portraying themselves as morally righteous victims the Californios are able to maintain their embattled white elite status. The class status of both the Californios and the Anglos depends on the exploitation of mestizos, Indians, and blacks. Clarence becomes a multimillionaire partly by speculating in western mines, mines that in California exploited primarily Mexican mestizo labor in supplying raw materials for the capitalist world system.[54] Their common exploitation of nonwhites links the squatters and dons, otherwise separated by culture and class. When Don Mariano proposes that the squatters raise cattle instead of growing grain, a squatter protests, "I don't want any cattle. I ain't no '*vacquero*' to go '*busquering*' around and *lassoing* cattle. I'll *lasso* myself; what do I know about whirling a *lariat?*" The squatter implies here that his white racial status precludes his working as a cowboy. Don Mariano, white in caste himself, attempts to reassure the squatter by responding, "I don't go '*busquering*' around *lassoing*, unless I wish to do so. You can hire an Indian boy to do that part" (*S* 94).

Don Mariano's reference to the "Indian boy" for hire has historical resonance. The Treaty of Guadalupe Hidalgo (1848) marked a dramatic shift in the rule of California from Mexico to the United States, but the condition of Indians as exploited and unfree labor remained the same or worsened. The California state constitutional convention in Monterey in 1849, drafted by both Anglos and Californios, adopted a white supremacist policy of depriving Indians of political rights and according them inferior legal rights and a subordinate status as laborers. Moreover, under U.S. rule most Indians worked under a condition of peonage, forced to remain with a single employer because of a creditor–debtor relationship. James Rawls likens such peonage in California to the Black Codes of the post-Reconstruction South. Indian peons composed most of the labor on Californio cattle farms like the Alamars' during their boom in the 1850s. Moreover, both Californios and Anglos participated in the kidnapping and slave trade of four thousand Indian women and children in 1852–67.[55] Thus the enslavement of Indians persisted in this ostensibly Union state even after the Civil War, revealing yet another commonality between the nineteenth-century elites of California and the South.[56]

Indeed, *Squatter* proposes a race and class hierarchy that differs only slightly from that proposed by the squatters and the monopoly capitalists. The squatters' hierarchy would racialize all Anglos as white and all Californios, regardless of class status, as nonwhite "greasers," in the squatter Matthew's words (S 73). By contrast, the novel proposes a hierarchy on the terms of the elite Californios, racializing the Anglo elite and Californio elite as white at the top of the social order, while grouping the Anglo "riff-raff," the squatters, paired with other alleged "thieves," the Indians, at the bottom, along with mestizos and African Americans (S 67, 315). According to Don Mariano, "Unfortunately . . . the discovery of gold brought to California the riff-raff of the world" (S 67). In both systems the subordinate position of those racialized as nonwhite remains constant.

The novel's cultural work of maintaining racial hierarchies signals the necessity of shoring up the Californios' shaky elite status. The Californios' class status is unstable because the squatters threaten to dispossess them not only of their land and wealth but also of their racialization as white. Similarly, Clarence worries that his father's attack on Don Mariano has made him "lose caste" (S 274). As in Ramona, the Californio mother's prohibition of the cross-cultural union results from her anxiety that it will diminish her family's social standing. Before sanctioning the union, Doña Josefa demands proof that Clarence can distinguish himself as superior to the squatters by distancing himself from his father's behavior. The union between Clarence and Mercedes offers a potential resolution of the two families' social instability. Clarence offers the Alamars wealth, business savvy, and financial connections; the Californios offer Clarence land, aristocratic traditions, and an elite status commensurate with his fortune.

But the alliance proposed through the marriage plot is destabilized by a sexual tension in the structure of the melodrama. The mother's prohibition shows that the erotic pull of the proposed marital union must be tempered and legitimated by the mother's moral authority. The allegorical expansion from the individual to the collective story involves a sublimation of disruptive sexual energies and interracial ties.[57] The nation as a sentimental imagined community needs the figure of the mother to secure its respectability, a respectability threatened by the culturally and racially diverse elements it must consolidate ideologically to maintain its authority.[58]

The representation of the Alamars as blue-eyed Spaniards similarly legitimates the proposed national alliance, in this case by strategically concealing the sexually charged issue of mestizaje (racial mixing). Historically speaking, money did tend to "whiten" Mexican families in formerly Mexican territory, but only figuratively in terms of class status. David Montejano has argued that Mexicans in the late nineteenth-century United States were racialized according to their class status: landowners were considered Spanish; laborers were considered "half-breeds."[59] Portraying the Alamars as physically resembling fair Europeans enables Ruiz de Burton to avoid figuring the union between Mercedes and Clarence as miscegenation, distasteful to the intended Anglo readership of C. Loyal, Ruiz de Burton's pseudonym.[60] This shadow plot of miscegenation results in ostensibly cross-cultural unions that blur the racial bounds of the national community imagined as white Anglo-Saxon—"the white slaves of California" to be redeemed comprise both Anglos and "half-savage" Californios. The elements marking *Squatter* as a sentimental melodrama are thus crucial to its political project: unmasking the Big Four monopoly capitalists as the true "invaders" of California (rather than Anglo U.S. imperialists) and promoting an alliance of Californios and sympathetic Anglos in an effort to reconfigure whiteness. This reconfiguration of whiteness to include the Californios works within existing frameworks of U.S. citizenship (and its accompanying racial hierarchies) rather than challenging such frameworks with a discourse of hemispheric citizenship à la Martí.

Squatter's romantic racialism integrates the Californios—ostensibly white yet racially ambiguous—into whiteness as caste through marital union, overtly expanding whiteness yet at the same time paradoxically blurring the racially homogeneous limits of the nation understood as an imagined community. By contrast, *Ramona*'s romantic racialism, through its overt plot of marital union, criticizes the ways in which the marginalized —Indians and Californios—are excluded from whiteness and rule and relegated to the exploited lower classes. Even more so than *Squatter*'s, *Ramona*'s overt plot of marital union is shadowed by a plot of racial ambiguity and homoerotics figuring a multiracial alliance that unsettles the nation's claims to racial and sexual propriety. If forgetting "is a crucial factor in the creation of a nation," then what is most forgotten is the twinned sexual underside of the sentimental plots focusing on maternal authority, marital union, and homoerotics (a countercultural form of national fraternity).[61] Such shadow plots constitute what Raymond Williams has termed an "emergent structure of feeling": new practices and experiences "at the very edge of semantic availability" because they serve as alternatives to dominant understandings.[62] Thus what I term the overt plot reinforces dominant discourses, while the shadow plot subverts them by revealing their undersides and contradictions. The overt plot and shadow plot correspond to romantic racialism's contradiction between a vocabulary of racial characteristics and aspirations of racial reform. The writer of the text does not exert full control over the shadow plot. Instead, it is a result of what could be called a textual surplus, in which the text "knows" something the writer does not. In Mikhail Bakhtin's terms, the "centripetal forces" of a novel—the elements the writer attempts to control—exist alongside "centrifugal" forces that elude the writer's control and reveal the heteroglossia of a novel, or competing visions of the world.[63] Moreover, in contrasting overt and shadow plots, I am distinguishing between the successful allegorical marital unions comprising the historical romance described by Doris Sommer—the overt plot in my terms—and other modes of allegorical union that fall out of her discussion owing to her privileging of the term *romance* over the more neutral term *melodrama*.[64]

THE "ARROGANT *MESTIZA*" AND
WHITENESS IN *RAMONA*

In *Squatter* Indians are represented as lowly thieves to be enslaved by southerners and Californios. By contrast, *Ramona* takes seriously Indians' struggles for rights in its portrayal of the consequences of Anglo expansion on the Indian Alessandro and his mestiza lover, Ramona, even if at a time when Indians no longer posed a threat to white expansion. The novel takes us on a California version of the Trail of Tears, as Euro-American squatters, reviled as "thieves and liars," stake claim to entire Indian villages, forcing Ramona, Alessandro, and his fellow villagers to undergo a series of displacements to less and less desirable land (*R* 177).

The dire condition of Indians in California resulted from the California Constitution of 1849 and the subsequent history of white aggression against Indians. Drafted by forty Anglos and eight Californios, the constitution deprived Indians of the right to vote and of other legal citizenship rights of whites, a category comprising both Anglos and elite Californios (as in *Squatter*). Between 1850 and 1870, Indians were considered obstacles to Anglo settlement. Indeed, in 1851 Governor Peter Burnet endorsed a policy of extermination against Indians. During the 1850s, Indian villages suffered repeated assaults by volunteer military companies and by U.S. army troops, often resulting in the destruction of entire villages.[65] In 1856, U.S. Army Captain Henry S. Burton, the husband of Ruiz de Burton, led his troops in a confrontation with the very Indians featured in Jackson's novel—the Luiseño Indians of Temecula, California, in San Diego County.[66] As a result of such policies, which exacerbated problems of poverty among Indians, the population of Native Americans in California plunged from 100,000 in 1850, to 20,000 in 1870, and finally to 17,500 in 1900. Only in the 1870s, when Indians no longer posed a direct threat to Anglo settlement, were they granted basic civil rights by California, gaining the right to testify in court in 1872 and the right to vote in 1879. Nevertheless, as if confirming the relevance of *Ramona*'s indictment of whites' mistreatment of Indians, as late as 1886 the California Supreme Court, in *Thompson v. Doaksum*, ruled that Indians had no legal claim to land they previously occupied, a decision upheld by the U.S. Supreme Court in 1889. Indians were not granted U.S. citizenship until 1924.[67]

Helen Hunt Jackson, born in Amherst, Massachusetts, in 1830, attended a lecture in Boston by Chief Standing Bear of the Poncas in 1879 and thereafter decided to devote her life to improving the conditions of U.S. Indians. The U.S. Army had forcibly removed the Ponca tribe from their Missouri River Reservation in what is now South Dakota to Indian Territory in 1877. Jackson's history and denunciation of U.S. Indian policy, *A Century of Dishonor*, was published in 1881. Jackson sent copies of the book to every member of Congress at her own expense. In the same year, she traveled to California on commission by *Century Magazine* to write a series of articles on the Franciscan missions. Jackson used these articles to publicize the largely unsuccessful efforts of the "Mission Indians"—the Luiseño, Cahuilla, Cupeño, Ipai, and Serrano—to retain rights to the lands they had settled. Appointed by the U.S. government as a special agent to the Mission Indians in 1883, Jackson ordered land surveys and visited scores of Indian villages. The official report she submitted in 1883 formed the basis for a Mission Indian Bill that aimed at securing Indian land rights. Although the bill failed to pass Congress in 1885, it was eventually approved in 1891.[68]

Despite the importance of the history of white–Indian conflict in *Ramona*, the figure of the Indian in the novel should not be read only in literal terms as the embodiment of the systemic racial oppression of diverse Indian populations in California; rather, one should also attempt to understand the character of the mestizo American future that Jackson's Ramona embodies. I thus shift from the political-economic analysis prominent in my reading of *Squatter* to a more speculative tack in my analysis of *Ramona*. In my reading of *Squatter* it was necessary to go into considerable historical detail to demonstrate the specific political resonances of the term *white slave*. By contrast, gauging the import of Ramona's contestation of

whiteness as an "arrogant mestiza" calls for a different approach: here I
spell out the narrative techniques by which the novel blurs racial boundaries, staking out novel conceptions of North American racial identity in the
domain of common sense. Common sense, of course, is no less a political
realm than the economic, as the theory of hegemony has shown. *Ramona*
responds to the political and economic conditions of capitalist expansion
—national consolidation and displacement of indigenous peoples—with
an anguished, tragic narrative, but also with a shrewd reconfiguration of
whiteness.

As an emergent structure of feeling, *Ramona*'s shadow plot calls into
question racial hierarchies—its own and those endorsed by *Squatter*. *Ramona* undermines whiteness by proposing cross-racial alliances through
the ambiguous figure of the blue-eyed Ramona, the daughter of an Anglo
and an Indian, who, as Martí suggests, chooses a politicized Indian identity,
and through Ramona's successive marriages to Alessandro, an Indian, and
Felipe, a Californio. *Ramona* also disrupts whiteness through the homoerotic relationship between Alessandro and Felipe. Both novels construct
national identity as fractured and haunted by racial oppression and interracial desire. The shadow of fraternity as the basis for national imagining is
interracial homoeroticism, and the shadow of maternity and sibling affection is incest. These national/narrative "shadows" cast a pall over national
respectability in terms of race, gender, and sexuality.

While *Squatter* portrays a marital union linking two cultures, in *Ramona* the ostensibly racially homogeneous marriage between Alessandro
and Ramona solicits the reader's sympathies.[69] Their union constitutes the
core of the novel's overt political strategy, which aims to turn its readers
into reformists by exposing them to sentimental discourse. Exemplifying
the aims of this strategy, the Iserian implied reader of the novel, Aunt Ri
Hyer, a white migrant from Tennessee, gains "heaps er new ideas inter
[her] head"—and a newly conciliatory reformist stance—as a result of her
acquaintance with the "Indian" couple (*R* 349).[70] The couple's devotion to
their baby gradually warms Aunt Ri's heart until "the last vestige of her
prejudice against Indians had melted and gone" (*R* 347). Aunt Ri's change
of heart suggests how the reader can similarly empathize with Indians.

This transformative potential of women's religious and moral influence
is brought home even more dramatically in the description of Sam Merrill,
an Anglo settler in Indian territory and a neighbor of the Hyers. After Aunt
Ri criticizes Merrill's callous assumption that murdering any Indian is

justified, invoking, in typical sentimental fashion, the higher "law o' God," the narrator describes Merrill as a typical frontiersman. In a passage reminiscent of Stowe's description of the southern plantation owner Augustine St. Clare in *Uncle Tom's Cabin*, Jackson portrays Merrill as a man whose violent experiences in the western "frontier" bury and conceal his virtuous New England heart:

> Young Merrill listened with unwonted gravity to Aunt Ri's earnest words. They reached a depth in his nature which had been long untouched; a stratum . . . which lay far beneath the surface. . . . Underneath the exterior crust of the most hardened and ruffianly nature often remains—its forms not yet quite fossilized—a realm full of the devout customs, doctrines, religious influences, which the boy knew, and the man remembers. . . . The wild frontier life had drawn him in and under, as in a whirlpool; but he was a New Englander yet at heart. (*R* 346)[71]

This "romantic feminist" passage opposes the purportedly female restraint and religious morality characteristic of women, New England, and the South to the male "wild frontier life."[72] In *Ramona*, as in other sentimental novels, the job of women is to restore morality to men: Aunt Ri and the wife of the Anglo usurper of Alessandro's house perform the same function as Mrs. Darrell in *Squatter* and Mrs. Bird and Aunt Ophelia in *Uncle Tom's Cabin*. Jackson charts a gendered geography of moral influence in which Merrill's westward and wayward path fails to fully leave behind the moral heart of the nation, New England. Thus Jackson's sentimental project, like Ruiz de Burton's, seeks to revive national morality, in the case of *Ramona* by according greater cultural authority and influence to the maternal sphere.

The novel attempts to achieve such sentimental reform by countering the racial ideologies used to portray Indians as inherently criminal. Unlike *Squatter*, *Ramona* combats several negative stereotypes of Indians. Alessandro argues that Indians are not born thieves, but rather they are sometimes compelled by hunger to steal (*R* 308). Aunt Ri attacks another pillar of white supremacy when she argues that killing an Indian—despite California law—is indeed murder (*R* 345–46). Jackson thus aims to reinstate the personhood of Indians in the minds of Euro-American readers.

But in *Ramona* Indians also appear as lower-class laborers such as Alessandro and "human ruins" to be pitied with "imperialist nostalgia" (*R* 324).[73] *Ramona* thereby replaces the "male" policy of displacing and exter-

minating Indians—as exemplified by the unreformed Merrill—with the
sentimental policy of viewing them as exploited lower-class victims and
members of the empire. Indeed, the last name of Pablo and Alessandro,
Assis, associating them with Saint Francis of Assisi, could be read as signifying that Indians must take a vow of poverty to be included in the
nation. The overt reformist plot invites Indians into the imagined national
community as long as they remain subordinate—here the romantic racialist notion of nonwhites' "willingness to serve" implicitly turns the victims
of U.S. empire into its second-class citizens.[74]

Since Alessandro is a "natural" man, "not a civilized man," and therefore experiences "only simple, primitive, uneducated instincts and impulses," he needs to prove himself worthy of citizenship (R 54). Alessandro
wins the favor of Señora Moreno through what she calls his "devotion" to
her son (R 96). When Felipe faints while packing sheep's wool, Alessandro
rushes to his rescue, proclaiming, "I am very strong" (R 58). Alessandro
plays a central role in bringing about Felipe's recovery, singing him to sleep
and then keeping vigil. Their relationship embodies an opposition between
the "primitive" and the "civilized," to use Jackson's terms that are simultaneously markers of a race and class hierarchy. Alessandro is associated with
the body and nature, exemplified by his physical strength, singing talent,
and motherly nurturing, while Felipe is associated with "training" (R 74).
Felipe alludes to the homoerotic character of their relationship with his
remark that when Alessandro sang, "I thought the Virgin had reached
down and put her hand on my head and cooled it" (R 74). One wonders
whether the homoeroticism is meant to seduce the reader into accepting
the desirability of a very limited "reform" of Indian relations that would
bring Indians into proximity with whites at the price of turning them into
servants.

Portrayals of homoeroticism and racial ambiguity provide a way for
Ramona both to maintain and bypass national, racial, and sexual respectability, as if national prohibitions of racial heterogeneity and extramari-
tal sexuality were coterminous. Racial ambiguity—exemplified both by
Ramona's blue eyes and by the Californios' anomalous status as members
of the upper class yet different from the Anglo norm in culture and color—
seduces the reader into contemplating illicit affective and political unions,
both homoerotic and cross-racial. However, such homoeroticism and
cross-racial unions do not earn the national sanction figured in the mother's approval—be it Doña Josefa in *Squatter* or Señora Moreno in *Ramona*.

Accordingly, the discourse of moral reform, in relying on the authority of the nation conceived as family, must overtly satisfy expectations of racial and sexual homogeneity: Ruiz de Burton represents the Californios as white, and Ramona's Indian husband, Alessandro, dies. Egalitarian longings, then, are for the most part relegated to the subterfuges of the shadow plot. Overtly Alessandro is a faithful member of the U.S. empire, but at the same time to the extent that this narrative endorses his full rights he embodies resistance to that empire.

Ramona simultaneously forbids and invites its shadow plot, which is more fully developed than *Squatter*'s. Through the shadow plot the reader swallows "a big dose of information on the Indian question, without knowing it," as Jackson once described her project.[75] Hence *Ramona* proposes a cross-racial alliance more implicitly than explicitly, operating on the hegemonic terrain of transforming common sense. To the extent that the homoerotic relationship functions as an allegorical union no less than the heterosexual union in the covert plot, the relationship between Felipe and Alessandro undermines the dominant racial hierarchy. Moreover, Felipe's ambiguous racialization as a "half barbaric, half civilized" Californio invites white readers to indulge in transgressions of race and gender norms without fully implicating themselves (*R* 11). After all, the Californios are only part white. Similarly, although Jackson marks the union between Ramona and Alessandro as a racially homogeneous marriage of "Indians," Ramona's blue eyes suggest that she is also the site of identification for whites.

By soliciting the identification of readers with racially ambiguous subjects, the shadow plot undermines romantic racialism's tendency to rely on racial difference to construct meaning. Ramona is physically whitened, inviting the readers' identification, but emotionally, intellectually, and spiritually Indianized. Señora Moreno gives Ramona the chance of "marrying worthily" with a non-Indian, but Ramona refuses, rejecting the lure of whiteness and casting her lot with Indians instead (*R* 132). Ramona's love for Alessandro makes her lose her "race feeling," and she ceases to think of him in a racially marked way (*R* 75). Here Ramona embodies a model for the white reader's disavowal of whiteness. Perhaps Ramona's rejection of whiteness explains why Martí celebrates her as an "arrogant *mestiza*."[76] For Martí, as for Ramona, Indianness is not merely a biological identity, a given, but also an identification, a choice. Señora Moreno's contradictory racialization of Ramona also undermines racialist discourses of blood:

she marks Ramona as predominantly white until her affair with Alessandro, after which she is viewed as predominantly Indian. As an alternative to such racialism, *Ramona* emphasizes upbringing; Alessandro's
manners prove him worthy of associating with whites.

As in *Squatter*, national respectability is secured via the prohibition of
the mother; but while in *Squatter* Mercedes obeys her mother, Ramona
defies Señora Moreno. Conflicts between the mother's desire for whiteness
and the daughter's desire for Indianness come to a head when Señora
Moreno strikes Ramona on the mouth upon encountering Ramona and
Alessandro in an embrace (*R* 113). "The story of Ramona the Señora never
told" (*R* 24) is so-phrased because to reveal Ramona's racially mixed ances-
try would threaten the social standing of Señora Moreno's family as white,
a fact that confirms my argument that national respectability is secured
through both racial homogeneity and sexual propriety. Ramona's racial
identity threatens Señora Moreno's sense of her family's propriety: when
she catches the "Indian" lovers kissing, she suspects a "disgraceful intrigue"
involving sexual intercourse (*R* 114). Moreover, Señora Moreno can't bring
herself to love Ramona because she is racially mixed: "I like not these
crosses. It is the worst, and not the best of each, that remains" (*R* 30).
Señora Moreno tolerates Ramona as a family member only because she can
physically pass for white with her blue eyes and fair skin. Thus when
Ramona falls in love with the Indian Alessandro it is as if the repressed has
returned—and speaks: "Terror for herself had stricken her dumb; terror for
Alessandro gave her a voice" (*R* 112). It is the Indian who allows the mestiza
to speak in her own voice, a voice marked as distinctively American, female, and part Indian. Thus while *Squatter* is concerned with carving out a
space for Californios in whiteness, *Ramona*'s protofeminism enacts a reformist project upsetting racial norms and establishing the personhood of
Indians while leaving intact racialized occupational hierarchies.

In stark contrast to Señora Moreno's sexist and anti-Indian politics,
Ramona adapts conventional creole nationalist ideologies to stake a claim
to a uniquely mestiza American and women-oriented culture.[77] Ramona
embodies the libidinal and collective possibilities of a racially "crossed"
America that is suppressed. Indeed, Ramona's simplicity signifies an American identity that contrasts with the Señora's European complexity: "She
was a simple, joyous, gentle, clinging, faithful nature . . . as unlike as
possible to the Señora's" (*R* 31). In contrast to the Señora's incestuous
feelings for her son, Ramona's union with Alessandro expresses a simple,
desexualized love:

[To Felipe] nothing could have been farther removed from anything like love-making. . . . This is a common mistake on the part of those who have never felt love's true bonds. . . . They are made as the great iron cables are made, on which bridges are swung across the widest water-channels,—not of single huge rods, or bars, which would be stronger, perhaps, to look at; but of myriads of the finest wires, each one by itself so fine, so frail, it would barely hold a child's kite in the wind. . . . Such cables do not break. (*R* 162)

While the Señora's love is selfish and mired in the past, Ramona's asexual yet productive love symbolizes the novel's sentimental, romantic racialist project of rule: the possibility of exploited groups—Indians, Californios, and women—making "common cause" with each other against tyrants (*R* 165).[78] The "myriads of the finest wires" of love elicit a cross-racial alliance between Anglo readers identifying with Ramona and Indians. However, the allegedly Indian qualities that compose the wires that hold the nation together—kindness, generosity, fidelity, obedience—themselves reaffirm racial subordination, contracting whiteness to exclude Indians. Even so, Jackson's project of white–Indian national reconciliation sharply contrasts with the intercultural yet racially homogeneous national reconciliation in Ruiz de Burton. More important, this representation of the aspirations of the oppressed to forge alliances with one another gestures beyond the ideological limits of the novel itself to unforeseen futures of grassroots organizing, in a Bakhtinian "centrifugal" textual moment.[79]

Toward the end of Jackson's novel, the overt and shadow Ramonas approach each other in the representation of her multiracial family in Mexico. The overt Ramona, as I've noted, is Indian by blood, while the shadow Ramona is ironically a blue-eyed, racially ambiguous model for Anglo readers. Whether Ramona is viewed primarily as Indian or as European, her marital union with Felipe creates an explicitly multiracial family. The decision of Felipe and Ramona to move to Mexico expresses their disgust with the United States as dominated by greed and a need to search for models of potentially racially egalitarian rule (*R* 359).[80] By the end of the novel, then, the mantle of Americanness passes from the United States to Mexico. Foreshadowing Martí's "Our America," Jackson even figures a would-be Indian and mestizo anti-imperialist uprising against the United States: Alessandro says that Indians would join Mexicans if they were to "rise against" the United States (*R* 238). This stunning moment in the text not only undermines faith in a rehabilitated whiteness (a faith that pervades *Squatter*), but also constructs a potentially potent discourse of hemispheric citizenship that rejects U.S. identity in favor of an Indianized Mexican identity. Here is romantic racialism at its most promising, a moment of Kinmontian "engrafting," in which "sentimental knowledge" combines Enlightenment egalitarianism with Christian discourses of sympathy to result in a representation of assertions of rights by nonwhites. Indeed, for Jackson, as for Martí, Señora Moreno represents the tyranny not only of Europe, but also of the United States: while North America "drowns its Indians in blood," "Our America" will be "saved by its Indians," as Martí writes.[81] Thus both Jackson and Martí find in Latin America a polemical alternative to U.S. race relations.

However, the representation of the anti-imperialist rebellion by North American Indians and Mexicans against the United States exists in tension with the text's portrayals of Native Americans as ideally suited to manual labor. In a more skeptical vein, one could argue that the sentimental melodrama's ethical aims of redressing victimization with an assertion of rights are undermined by its reliance on romantic racialist stereotypes for the building blocks of its ethical structure—Alessandro's "simple, primitive, uneducated instincts and impulses" (R 54). Indeed, the Native American–Mexican uprising never materializes, and readers are left with the less challenging but more reassuring representation of the willingness of Indians like Alessandro to serve those who stand above them in the racial hierarchy. Such representations thwart the momentum created by the rebellion scenario, which implicitly invokes a sort of "common cause with the oppressed."[82] By contrast, in Martí, "common cause with the oppressed" is the means through which it is possible to move from anticolonial imaginings to a more developed, broadly egalitarian project of decolonization (see chapter 2 for an extended analysis of Martí's writings).

THE ENDURING HEGEMONY OF WHITENESS

If *Ramona* and *Squatter* deserve to be read and reread because of their complex allegorical engagement with U.S. race relations and imperialism, their politics must be viewed as shaped by their use of the sentimental melodrama as an ethical discourse. Their engagement with social issues through sentimentalism thrusts one into a confusing thicket of contradictory political stances exemplified by the simultaneous expansion and contraction of whiteness. Stuart Hall has described such contradictory politics as exemplifying cultures of imperialism.[83] Conquerors and conquered, in other words, cannot always be easily distinguished. This was especially the case for elite Californios, conquered with the annexation of California, yet still conquerors in terms of race and class.

Even as *Squatter* and *Ramona* attempt to secure reform—an expansion of opportunities for certain non-Anglos—by expanding whiteness culturally in the overt plot and racially in the shadow plot, these novels simultaneously contract whiteness in a variety of ways. In *Squatter* the incorporation of the Californios into whiteness through allegorical union produces an elite class discourse subordinating nonwhites and the lower classes, thereby contracting whiteness, as the squatter's comment "I ain't no *vaquero*" indicates. In *Ramona* the contraction of whiteness—the Indians' obligatory low-class status—is countered with an expansion or undermining of whiteness; Ramona's blue eyes can be read as either pandering to the expectations of white readers or as signaling her racial ambiguity and the possibility of multiracial alliances. Such a tension between the expansion and contraction of whiteness can be understood as its dual assimilative and exclusionary operations.[84]

The expansion of whiteness in *Squatter* unleashes a shadow plot of miscegenation implicit in the cross-cultural union by representing Mercedes as physically Nordic rather than mestiza. By contrast, *Ramona* teases out the contradictions inherent in the dominant constructions of the nation as sexually respectable and racially homogeneous through its treatment of homoeroticism, racial ambiguity, and miscegenation and in its suggestion of the possibility of a multiracial uprising against the United States. Moreover, it is possible to read *Ramona* as further challenging the bounds of whiteness by allowing its readers to identify only as marginalized or displaced subjects: with the Hyers, a poor white migrant family from Tennessee; the racially ambiguous Morenos; and Ramona, an Indian made more palatable through mestizaje.[85] Jackson's representation of Hartsell's "Mongrel establishment," as at once a tavern, a den of vice and white supremacy, and a life-sustaining farm, readying itself for the harvest of a utopian interracial society, best captures the emergent structure of feeling embodied by Ramona, her Jamesonian "protopolitical impulses" attempting to create a more egalitarian social order despite cultural limitations. Such emergent structures of feeling constructing a politics of interracial alliance were waiting to be activated in a more explicit fashion by contemporary readers of the novel such as Martí. The abundance of Bakhtinian "centrifugal" moments in the text indicates that it was groping toward or attracted by possibilities of more egalitarian social relations that it couldn't (or wouldn't) explicitly endorse. Thus I would argue that *Ramona*'s enduring value to today's readers resides in an against-the-grain reading.

As a dual romantic racialist/romantic feminist strategy of vindicating groups exploited by region, race, culture, class, and gender, sentimentalism links gender politics to racial caste politics. While *Squatter*'s female characters confirm their husbands' attempts at maintaining white elite caste privilege, *Ramona*'s rejection of whiteness enhances the power of those women who choose to upset U.S. imperialism's racial hierarchies.[86] *Ramona*'s critique of whites' hostility toward Indians shapes its dismantling of whiteness as a strategy of white sectional reconciliation and dual racial and gender oppression.

I have focused on whiteness as the central point of contention in these texts for several reasons. First, whiteness has long shaped the subjective experience of class in the United States, as David Roediger has argued. Thus maintaining or upsetting class hierarchies necessitates a reinforcement or dismantling of whiteness, as in Ruiz de Burton's and Jackson's nineteenth-century California. Second, since the dismantling of whiteness is directly related to the degree of women's political agency in these texts, whiteness provides a way of linking gender and racial oppression. Third, the rehabilitation of whiteness in *Squatter* and the attempts to challenge it in *Ramona* are directly related to their differing versions of hemispheric citizenship: *Squatter* buys into U.S. imperialism by embracing the allegedly victimized groups of the post-Reconstruction era, white southerners and the Californios, while the Indian–Mexican rebellion in *Ramona* rejects the U.S. empire. The regional, interethnic alliance in *Squatter* solidifies racial hierarchies, while the transnational and interracial alliance in *Ramona* links the racial struggle to the anti-imperial struggle, gesturing toward the potential of sentimentalist discourse to promote decolonization.

Two

"THE COMING UNITIES" IN "OUR AMERICA": DECOLONIZATION AND ANTICOLONIAL MESSIANISM IN MARTÍ, DU BOIS, AND THE SANTA DE CABORA

> Universal history has no theoretical armature. Its method is additive; it musters a mass of data to fill the homogeneous, empty time. Materialistic historiography, on the other hand, is based on a constructive principle. Thinking involves not only the flow of thoughts, but their arrest as well. Where thinking suddenly stops in a configuration pregnant with tensions, it gives that configuration a shock, by which it crystallizes into a monad. A historical materialist approaches a historical subject only where he encounters it as a monad. In this structure he recognizes the sign of a Messianic cessation of happening, or put differently, a revolutionary chance in the fight for the oppressed past.
>
> —WALTER BENJAMIN, "Theses on the Philosophy of History"

◗ In 1889, José Martí took up his pen in exasperation to write a response to two newspapers in Philadelphia and New York, one which questioned Cubans' capacity for self-rule and the other which opposed annexing Cuba because of the "near a million blacks" in its population. Martí's letter to the editor of the *New York Evening Tribune* critically reflects on the popular conception that the United States is "the typical nation of liberty." Cubans, Martí writes, "admire this nation, the greatest ever built by liberty, but they dislike the evil conditions that like worms in the heart, have begun in this mighty republic their work of destruction. . . . We love the country of Lincoln as much as we fear the country of Cutting."[1] In elegantly condensed phrasing, Martí counterposes the "country of Lincoln," which he credits with having freed the slaves, to "the country of Cutting," referring to Francis Cutting, a leader of the Annexationist League, and more broadly to the history of U.S. imperial aggression in Latin America. These two "countries" lay claim to two opposed conceptions of liberty, one that allegedly attempts

to eradicate racial oppression, and the other that invokes the ideal of freedom only to "set aside" the rights of other countries, as Martí would write
in a subsequent essay.[2] A generation later, W. E. B. Du Bois similarly identifies a divided legacy of U.S. freedom. In *Darkwater* (1920), Du Bois argues
that the "Philosophy of Democracy" of the French and American revolutions was imperiled by "wave on wave . . . of whiteness" that divided the
globe along a "color line" constructed by race and empire.[3]

For Martí and Du Bois, to view the United States as the "typical nation
of liberty," in Martí's phrase, was not to uncritically celebrate its achievements. Instead, implicit in Martí's phrase is the need to respond to the
considerable impact of U.S. ideals and actions on the world. This impact
includes, on the one hand, the promise of freedom and, on the other, what
Martí terms its "work of destruction" and what Du Bois analyzes as the
global "color line." Martí and Du Bois implicitly construct decolonization
as a response to the United States as the "country of Cutting," a phrase that
implicitly conjoins domestic politics and imperial foreign relations. Decolonization, they suggest, is not external to the United States but rather
figures prominently in the battle to make the United States live up to its
egalitarian ideals. Martí calls for a "genuine and vigorous freedom" that
would contest U.S. imperialism ("WA" 139). Du Bois suggests that only the
"dispute of the white man's title by the darker world" will remedy the
shortcomings of the French and American revolutions and their "Philosophy of Democracy" (*DW* 499, 550). For both Martí and Du Bois, then, race
and empire constitute the main aporias of U.S. democracy, and for both,
1898 was a moment of truth in the history of the contest over the chief
legacy of the Enlightenment, the ideal of freedom.

THE "EVENT" (BADIOU) OF 1898 IN
MARTÍ AND DU BOIS

The careers of Martí and Du Bois respectively end and begin with 1898,
which historians have associated with the Cuban War for Independence, the
Spanish-American-Cuban War (1895–98), and the Philippine-American
War (1896–1902). Their careers end and begin with 1898 not merely in a
chronological sense, but in the sense that this date served as a touchstone for
their political aims as activist-intellectuals. It is true that Martí didn't live to
see 1898 and that Du Bois reflected on that historical moment only after the
fact. Moreover, for Du Bois, 1898 was one touchstone among many. It is

equally true that Martí and Du Bois worked under vastly different political circumstances. Martí helped to organize the war for Cuban independence, while Du Bois sought to achieve black civil rights and to oppose colonialism across the globe. Whereas Martí died on the battlefield in 1895, Du Bois's career spanned six decades into the twentieth century. Martí privileged national unity over racial grievances, while Du Bois most often prioritized racial grievances over national unity.[4] But because in the writings of Martí and Du Bois 1898 captures both the plight and promise of those oppressed by the U.S. empire, it serves as something more than a rough chronological dividing line between their careers: 1898 marks a previously unrecognized zone of convergence in their lives as writers. While it is well known that Martí was one of the primary architects of the Cuban War for Independence and literally devoted his life to the cause, the possibility that 1898 was a touchstone in Du Bois's ongoing assessment of the prospects for the darker peoples through the 1920s has gone unexplored.

Martí and Du Bois both viewed the Spanish-American-Cuban War of 1898 as an event of potentially messianic and world-historical importance, a war that had to be fought (in the case of Martí) or rethought (in the case of Du Bois) in order to achieve the "genuine and vigorous freedom" that would finally fulfill the promise of the Enlightenment ("WA" 139). Martí died before he could see the results of the Cuban War for Independence. However, he was such an attentive observer of U.S. imperial ambitions and had so much at stake in their results that he predicted the hijacking of the War for Cuban Independence—one of the bitter lessons of 1898. In a prescient letter to Gonzalo de Quesada in 1889, Martí angrily refers to "the darkest plan that we have known up to now, and that is the iniquitous one to rape the Island, to precipitate war, for the pretext of invading it and, under the guise of mediator and guarantor, to hold on to it. There is no more cowardly act nor colder evil in the annals of free countries."[5] Martí accurately predicts the setting aside of freedom that actually did occur about a decade later as the United States maneuvered to control the nascent Cuban republic and inaugurated a long, oppressive reign of neocolonialism that only the Cuban Revolution of 1959 would topple.

While Martí writes of the irony in the fact that the first independent republic in the hemisphere would turn out to be the "only enemy" of Latin American freedom in the last decade of the nineteenth century, Du Bois uses his metaphor of the color line to place U.S. imperial ambitions in Latin America within the broader context of European imperialism's rapidly increasing control of the globe: by 1878 Europe held 67 percent of the earth's surface, a figure that rose to 85 percent by 1914.[6] One of the early defining moments of Du Bois's career was a speech he gave to the American Negro Academy in 1900 in which he argued that the "most significant" event of his age was the Spanish-American War because "the colored population of our land is, through the new imperial policy, about to be doubled by our own ownership of Porto Rico, and Hawaii, our protectorate of Cuba, and conquest of the Philippines."[7] Twenty years later, looking back at the same period in *Darkwater*, Du Bois writes that the "zenith" of "the silent revolution" that introduced color as a mark of social distinction occurred during "Boxer times," around 1900: "White supremacy was all but world-wide, Africa was dead, India conquered, Japan isolated, and China prostrate, while white America whetted her sword for mongrel Mexico and mulatto South America, lynching her own Negroes the while" (*DW* 504). In this single, sweeping sentence, Du Bois links 1898 to the aftermath of the scramble for Africa (1884) and to colonialism in India and the rest of Asia through the figure of the "silent revolution" of race. He forcefully argues that African Americans' struggles for civil rights do not occur in isolation from those of other "darker peoples," but rather attack a single edifice of white imperial power. Moreover, by referring to "Boxer times," Du Bois shifts attention away from the defeat of Cuba and the expansion of the U.S. empire in the Spanish-American-Cuban War and suggests that the fate of democracy lies in the agency of the colonized peoples themselves.[8] During the next three decades Du Bois would continually return to 1898 as a defining moment in the shaping of the global color line and in the responses of "the darker world that watches" (*DW* 507).

In both Martí and Du Bois, then, the moment of 1898 must be understood through reference to a larger trajectory of events in imperial history, to waves of imperialism and anticolonialism. For Martí, the War for Cuban Independence was shaped by the point-counterpoint of, on the one hand, the democratic promise of the French and American revolutions and the reality of imperial control, and, on the other hand, the rebellion of those subjected to imperialism in such events as the Haitian Revolution (1791–1804), the Mexican War (1846–48), and Cuba's Ten Years' War (1868–78). Thus in his assessment of the legacy of the political Enlightenment, Martí emphasized the role of Afro-Caribbean peoples in remedying the shortcomings of the French and American revolutions. Du Bois similarly situated the events of 1898 as part of a larger cluster of imperial conflicts, including what he terms "the scramble for Africa" by the colonial powers beginning in 1884; the defeat of Italy at Adua, Ethiopia (1896); the Boxer Rebellion (1900); the Boer War (1899–1902), which pitted Great Britain against the South African Republic and the Orange Free State; and the ongoing British control of India.[9]

The work of Alain Badiou can serve to clarify how historical dates such as 1898 can create ethical imperatives that exert a shaping influence on a writer's subsequent work. In his theory of the event, Badiou argues that any period, such as France between 1789 and 1794 or situation, such as "a personal amorous passion," can lead to a rupture with the past that will reconstitute the subject and the political and social fields. The resulting event (the French Revolution or a relationship in the above examples) unleashes a "process of truth" that consists of the subject developing a "fidelity" to an event—"thinking . . . the situation 'according to' the event."[10] In other words, the subject perceives the possibilities of future situations from the perspective of the event. In Slavoj Žižek's account of Badiou's theory, "Fidelity to the Event designates the continuous effort of traversing the field of knowledge from the standpoint of Event, intervening in it, searching for the signs of Truth."[11] The event does not necessarily follow from a situation; the event is fully constituted when subjects achieve agency through what Badiou terms a "political thought-process" that shapes their sense of an event and the way in which it compels them to reevaluate their aims (*Ethics* 13). Badiou argues that this evaluation is "militant" in that it goes beyond mere thought, in "a feverish exploration of the effects of a new theorem."[12]

There are two key consequences of thinking from the event: (1) it requires subjects "to exceed [their] own being," and (2) it "deposes constituted knowledges" and "outmodes established meanings" (*Ethics* 50; *El ser* 440). As Žižek summarizes Badiou, the event and the process it unleashes reveal "how injustices are not marginal malfunctioning but pertain to the very structure of the system"—these injustices Badiou terms "symptomal torsions."[13] The main result of the perception of such social contradictions is "a prolonged disorganization of life" (*Ethics* 60). This disorganization entails "a sustained investigation of the situation, under the imperative of the event itself" (*Ethics* 69).[14] I shall show how Du Bois and Martí attempt to create what could be by working according to what they perceive as the imperative of the event of 1898 (and the other events clustered around 1898).

ROMANTIC RACIALISM AND SENTIMENTALIST
DISCOURSE IN STOWE, MARTÍ, AND DU BOIS

Badiou's concept of a "political thought-process" unleashed by an event serves to clarify the extent to which available discourses on race—especially sentimentalism and the allied discourse of romantic racialism—were, in the work of Martí, Du Bois, and their predecessors, especially Harriet Beecher Stowe, adequate to the task of developing a critique that could penetrate to the core of a given social structure and thereby contribute to the project of overturning it. The degree to which sentimentalism and romantic racialism could obtain critical purchase on the status quo lies in the differing political commitments of these writers, commitments that are tied to the major historical events that shaped them and that they shaped in turn. The key event for the Stowe of *Uncle Tom's Cabin* is the Fugitive Slave Act of 1850, while a "fidelity" to the War of 1898 shaped the aims of Martí and Du Bois.

Stowe's commitment to African American emancipation was spurred by her despair over the Fugitive Slave Act of 1850.[15] The act politicized Stowe and led her to engage in a "sustained investigation" of slavery in texts such as "The Freeman's Dream" (1850) and *Uncle Tom's Cabin* (1852). In "The Freeman's Dream: A Parable," a combination sketch and manifesto on the Fugitive Slave Act that appeared in the *National Era*, Stowe tells of a white farmer who refuses to hide a slave fugitive and his family from their pursuers. The consequences of his refusal to help are dramatized by the slaves' screams as they are recaptured—screams that unsettle the farmer. That night, as the white farmer sleeps, an "awful voice pierce[s] his soul," the voice of Jesus, and insists that when the farmer failed to help the fugitive slave he failed to help him. The farmer's dream implicitly invokes "higher law" doctrine; Stowe explicitly invokes this discourse when she concludes her article by asserting that the laws of Christ are higher than the laws of men. It is Christian duty to help "the hungry, the thirsty, the stranger, the naked, the prisoner, and every form of bleeding, suffering humanity."[16]

In "The Freeman's Dream," Stowe turns the slave fugitive into a figure of "suffering humanity," the quintessential object of sympathy in sentimental melodrama. Christian duty is to "*feel right*," that is, to adopt a sympathetic stance, and to relieve this suffering, but there the relationship ends.[17] In her construction of human unity through the universal capacity to feel sorrow,

Stowe presumes to already know (1) the inherently limited capacity of the sufferer—blacks are represented in the romantic racialist manner as "more simple, docile, child-like and affectionate than other races"—and (2) the remedy for this suffering—"freedom" as resettlement in Africa.[18] Thus the hidden figure behind the putatively universalist figure of "suffering humanity" is the *white* intellectual who, rather than engaging in an extended dialogue with blacks, witnesses and acts to remedy that suffering. Thus in *Uncle Tom's Cabin*, the Fugitive Slave Act creates an imperative to insist on the freedom of African Americans but not on their equality.[19] As Badiou has persuasively argued in a critique of human rights discourse, if we already recognize evil—and the recognition of evil defines melodrama in Stowe—"how are we to envisage any transformation of the way things are?" (*Ethics* 14). The a priori recognition of evil entails an unwillingness to explore what freedom consists of beyond simple emancipation or "freedom from" slavery.[20] Stowe's political imagination, bound up in the figure of "suffering humanity" epitomized by the slave, is therefore stymied by what Wendy Brown has termed the static "language of being" of romantic racialism as opposed to a more dynamic and democratic "language of wanting," in which the white intellectual could contribute to the processes by which blacks take control of their political destinies.[21]

In other words, "The Freeman's Dream" creates a tension between the higher law's potentially radical and messianic discourse of equality and the sharply circumscribed potential of the figure of "suffering humanity" central to sentimentalist romantic racialism. This tension between representations of radical social upheaval and a tendency to imaginatively manage and curtail social change is also evident in Helen Hunt Jackson's *Ramona*, in the glaring contradiction between the representation of the potential Indian–Mexican uprising against the U.S. empire and the characterization of Indians as ideally suited to manual labor. Here one sees the narrative conflict between what Bakhtin termed the "centripetal forces" that represent a writer's efforts to control the ideological content of a novel—in this case embodied by romantic racialist discourse—and the "centrifugal forces" that elude the writer's grasp and instead point to the conflicting worldviews that have penetrated the novel's linguistic fabric, as I noted in chapter 1.[22] As Bakhtin recognizes, even if centrifugal forces are always present in a given text, the writer can choose to provide them with more space to take on a central role in the unfolding of the narrative. Du Bois's theory of double-consciousness in *Souls* can be read as an implicit critique of the tendency of romantic racialist discourses of sympathy to use white norms and perspectives as the measure of all peoples. Du Bois writes of "this sense of always looking at one's self through the eyes of others, of measuring one's soul by the tape of a world that looks on in amused contempt and pity."[23] Du Bois's theory of double consciousness therefore sets the stage for a shift away from white sentimentalist discourses of *pity* toward his own emphasis on the *agency* of the darker peoples and a corresponding marginalization of the white sympathetic witness.

While for Stowe the Fugitive Slave Act of 1850 creates the ethical imperative of freedom, in Martí and Du Bois the event of 1898 problematizes freedom as the ultimate political goal. Indeed, it took Cuba, a nominally free country, until 1959 to rid itself of U.S. neocolonial rule. Narratives of decolonization in Martí and Du Bois move beyond a focus on emancipation and other negative definitions of freedom by exploring the preconditions for full democracy, or what Martí calls a "genuine and vigorous freedom" ("WA" 139). In Martí and Du Bois, the event of 1898 unleashes a "political thought-process" that characterizes the French and American revolutions as an unfinished and flawed project that only a protracted series of anticolonial struggles and decolonization can remedy. For Martí and Du Bois, the imperative of 1898 is decolonization; this is a "fidelity" that leads Martí to devote his life (and to lose it) to the cause of Cuban independence—as early as 1891 Martí refers to "the death sentence in life which is the Cuban's heritage" ("WA" 141)—and Du Bois to construct coalitions linking the darker peoples from different points along the global color line. For both writer-activists, decolonization in the shadow of 1898 requires a commitment to liberation that goes beyond one's own ethnicity and nation. As Martí writes Quesada in 1889, "Cuba . . . and our America [Latin America] . . . are one in my precautions and in my affections."[24] And as Du Bois writes on the expansion of U.S. territory through the Spanish-American War and the Philippine-American War in 1900, "What is to be our attitude toward these new lands and toward the masses of dark men and women who inhabit them? Manifestly it must be an attitude of deepest sympathy and strongest alliance."[25] While sympathy in Stowe resembles a monologue, because the evil and the remedy are presumed to be already known, sympathy in Martí and Du Bois unleashes an exploration that approximates a dialogue: in that the methods and outcomes are unknown because they are bound up in unfolding efforts to attain both freedom and full democracy.

If 1898 can be viewed as the animating "ethical imperative" in the work of Martí and the early Du Bois, expressed primarily through figures of sympathy and cross-national alliance, how does that imperative shape their evolving use of available literary discourses for figuring social reform? In other words, how do they utilize and transform the allied discourses of sentimentalism, melodrama, and romantic racialism in devising narratives of decolonization? Martí and Du Bois express their sympathy for those oppressed by race and imperialism both through the discourse of romantic racialism and through what I am terming anti-imperial messianism. Anti-imperial messianist discourses figure the redemption of the racially oppressed and the subjects of empire, often through their alliance with one another.[26] The question of the degree of emphasis on nonwhite agency in the work of Stowe and Jackson, on the one hand, and in that of Du Bois and Martí, on the other, reveals a shift away from romantic racialism (without abandoning it altogether) and toward anti-imperial messianism, a shift in part impelled by the imperative of 1898 in the thinking of Martí and Du Bois. This shift involves displacing the centrality of traditional sentimental discourse, which tends to hold open the possibility of a rehabilitation of white male morality and white rule, and instating a countervailing emphasis on anti-imperial messianism and hence on the agency of those oppressed by race and empire, deemphasizing, though not excluding, sentimental melodrama. In Du Bois and Martí an anti-imperial messianist sensibility shapes sweeping surveys of the history of the Americas as involved in a vast melodrama of empire and race in which nothing less than the fate of democracy and freedom is at stake.

For both Martí and Du Bois, Mexico constituted one of the central cases in the palimpsest of 1898, which includes its prehistory and aftermaths. In 1886, Martí writes of "the memory of the victory that strength and betrayal won in 1848 over justice and heroism."[27] Pitting the betrayal of the United States against the heroism of Mexico in a melodrama of history, Martí views the annexation of one-half of Mexico in 1848 as driving a wedge between the competing visions of the United States as a beacon of freedom and as imperialist aggressor. Similarly, in 1914 Du Bois argued that the Mexican Revolution's "million of brown peons" had caused the U.S. empire to lose the confidence it had gained in 1898 (and, I would add, in 1848), when it allegedly "liberated Cuba and benevolently assimilated the Philippines": "We have Cuba by the industrial throat and the philippines [sic] on its knees, albeit squirming. Why not Mexico with its million of brown peons? Because the fact is that we, with all our success, are not only uncomfortable, but we scent danger. . . . Can the white world always hold the black world by the throat and keep it to work?"[28]

In this chapter I place Martí and Du Bois in a triangular, comparative framework with Teresa Urrea, known as the Santa de Cabora, or "Mexican messiah," to a host of indigenous groups in the 1890s, in order to explore (1) the limits and possibilities of anti-imperial messianism as an avowedly antiracist and anti-imperialist melodrama of victimhood, sympathy, and vindication, and (2) to assess differing conceptions of the role of the intellectual in relation to anti-imperial movements. In Du Bois, Martí, and the Santa de Cabora, the processes of imperial aggression, expansion, and exploitation that discussions of U.S. citizenship typically ignore serve to redefine citizenship in two ways. First, if under U.S. neocolonialism there is an extension of economic and political control beyond national boundaries, there is an accompanying void in the citizenship of affected countries. That void is evident when Du Bois writes in 1900, "The colored population of our land is, through the new imperial policy, about to be doubled."[29] Du Bois prematurely (and wrongly) assumes that the United States will open its floodgates and incorporate the populations of its neocolonies as citizens (he mentions Cuba, Hawaii, the Philippines, and Puerto Rico). But on a deeper level, Du Bois is right to suggest that these populations should be treated *as if they were* U.S. citizens by those who oppose U.S. empire. In Du Bois's account, the limits of U.S. citizenship implicitly constitute its true meaning—and the "most significant" development of the age.

Second, U.S. imperial expansion is defined by the denial to the affected countries and groups of the full exercise of sovereignty: Cuba after 1898 was defined by U.S.-controlled puppet governments, sham democracy, and the inability to exercise rights in relation to the imperium. Therefore, the meaning of citizenship in Cuba must be transformed to address this imperial thwarting of sovereignty. But Du Bois, Martí, and Urrea do not simply propose an inclusion of those excluded from citizenship rights—they do not want to turn imperial subjects into U.S. citizens. Instead, their discourses of hemispheric citizenship deploy anti-imperial messianist figures in order to critique U.S. imperialism and its Latin American allies (such as the Porfirio Díaz dictatorship in Mexico) and to create a vision of alternative possibilities of alliance among the oppressed. Following Giorgio Agamben's analysis of Walter Benjamin's messianism, I want to view anti-imperial messianism as a way of addressing the constitutive paradox of imperial citizenship: the simultaneous engulfing and exclusion that defines neocolonialism's denial of sovereignty to affected countries or social groups or both. In Agamben's reading, messianism addresses the constitutive limits and contradictions of a legal regime: the law vanquishes the Messiah (as in the crucifixion of Jesus), but the Messiah returns to vanquish and reconstitute the law: in the Judeo-Christian tradition, the Messiah is "both redeemer and legislator."[30] As Agamben writes, "In Judaism as in Christianity and Shiite Islam, the messianic event above all signifies a crisis and radical transformation of the entire order of the law. . . . The Messiah is . . . the figure through which religion confronts the problem of the Law, decisively reckoning with it" ("Messiah" 162–63). In Agamben's view, the Messiah is both the victim of the existing legal order and the founder of an entirely new one. Therefore the Messiah is less a figure of "a life lived in deferral and delay," as some prominent scholars of messianism have alleged, than a figure for the radical critique of both the legal order and the state of exception that paradoxically both suspends and constitutes the legal order.[31]

More specifically, the Messiah insists on the illegitimacy of institutionalized power by creating a counterstate of exception. However, rather than extending the powers of the state by blurring the distinctions between an inside and outside of the law, and therefore suspending individual rights (as in the state of exception under the George W. Bush administration following 9/11), the Messiah suspends the law in order to erase all social distinctions, insisting on writing a radical equality into the law.[32] Anti-imperial messianism affords one a postcolonial reading of Agamben's theory of the state of exception, for the suspension of law takes place not only within a given state during wartime, as in Agamben's account, but also through an imperial state's denial of sovereignty to another state or a neocolonial state's denial of citizenship rights to minority groups within its folds.[33] In this imperial state of exception, the "threshold of indeterminacy between democracy and absolutism" appears both within and across states, deploying racial discourses as a principle of exclusion.[34]

A Messiah-like figure of suffering humanity is common to both romantic racialism and anti-imperial messianism. But whereas romantic racialism privileges white witnesses and agents of redemption, anti-imperial messianism upends white privilege and the imperial foundations of the world order. Indeed, Du Bois, Martí, and the Santa de Cabora organize history as a messianic vindication of 1848 and 1898. I will explore the shift in the discourse of sympathy and race from a romantic racialist emphasis on racial character—and a corresponding focus on the agency of whites as witnesses of suffering and agents of redemption—to an anti-imperial messianist emphasis on the potential for rebellion against empire in Martí, Du Bois, and the Santa de Cabora. How do Martí and Du Bois theorize decolonization and anti-imperial messianism in relation to questions of gender, race, and cross-national solidarity in their essays and novels? On the one hand, the figure of the intellectual in the work of Martí and Du Bois plans and prophesies anticolonial revolution and decolonization. But on the other hand, intellectuals oftentimes cannot fully participate in those processes because they have blind spots on issues of race (Martí) or have Pan-African allegiances that tend to downplay class exploitation (Du Bois), or because their vocation as intellectuals makes them unsuited to the tasks required of a soldier (as was evident when Martí died on the battlefield in Cuba). The figure of the Santa de Cabora helps expose these limitations of the intellectual because rather than planning or prophesying revolution, she serves as a conduit of an indigenous uprising already under way, thereby showing that one needs to think through Badiou's theory of the event by paying close attention to the limitations of the figure of the intellectual it implicitly privileges. I focus on decolonization in this chapter in order both to emphasize the earlier chronology of postcolonialism in the Americas and to account for the broad, transnational scope of the egalitarian thinking of Martí, Du Bois, and the Santa de Cabora. As Martí understood, colonialism's mode of rule is formed in part by the "practical consciousness" constituting the indirect rule of hegemony: "The task is not to get Spain out of Cuba, but to get it out of our habits," Martí wrote in 1893. "Independence is one thing, and revolution another."[35] In Martí's notion of revolution, national development happens not through a purportedly inevitable progress but rather through multiple political struggles. Similarly, Du Bois expands what counts as political by emphasizing struggles for gender equality as equal in importance to antiracist struggles: as early as the essay "Of the Meaning of Progress" in *The Souls of Black Folk* (1903), he focuses on the plight of Josie, a woman oppressed by both gender and race. Allegory's ability to figure the individual and the social simultaneously provides an apt vehicle in novelistic form for capturing the dialectic between national and social liberation in Martí and Du Bois. Thus my analysis of the allegorical novels *Dark Princess* (1928) by Du Bois and

Amistad funesta (Fatal friendship, 1885) by Martí—also known as *Lucía Jerez*—focuses on the ways in which this dialectic of decolonization constitutes what is most innovative in their nationalist thinking.

My periodization of the history of the United States, Mexico, and Cuba between the 1880s and the 1930s as shaped by waves of decolonization follows such reconfigurations of history as shaped by diverse social movements. The first wave culminates with the war for Cuban independence from Spain, in which Martí was a key player, and the second wave following World War I features nationalist challenges to imperialism that Du Bois sought to theorize.[36] But the portrayal of 1898 as a palimpsest of former and future imperial conflicts exposes an anti-imperial messianist conception of history that collapses the past, present, and future, challenging linear conceptions of history. In other words, the "political thought process" that 1898 unleashes in Du Bois and Martí transforms conventional notions of periodization; they cast historical events into constellations, thereby fashioning a radically perspectival vision of history with the purpose of critique. They therefore transform historical narratives in a manner prescribed by Michel Foucault, who writes, "Knowledge is not made for understanding; it is made for cutting."[37]

DECOLONIZING SENTIMENTALISM: THE QUESTION OF AGENCY IN MARTÍ AND DU BOIS

Recent scholarship on sentimentalism has deepened and extended our understanding of the discourse by exploring its roots in eighteenth- and nineteenth-century philosophy (Adam Smith et al.) and literature.[38] Departing from a careful exploration of the keywords of sentimentalism—*sensibility*, *sentiment* itself, and *sympathy*—these scholars have limned the ideological limits and possibilities of the discourse as used by white and black men and women in England and the United States. A logical next step in the analysis of sentimentalism would be to examine how this discourse travels outside the United States and beyond the nineteenth century and to what extent it could be deployed in antiracist projects of decolonization. Did anti-imperialist writers have to turn their backs on sentimentalist discourse? or could they sentimentalize decolonization and decolonize sentimentalism?

The discourse of romantic racialism in Kinmont, Child, Stowe, and Jackson—defining Negroes or Indians through their allegedly Christian

racial traits and viewing such traits as positive attributes—provided a foundation for the early understandings of race in Martí and Du Bois: both
employed the allied conception of racial gifts (see chapter 1 for a discussion
of romantic racialism in Kinmont, Child, Stowe, Jackson, and Ruiz de
Burton). Much like Stowe, Martí uses romantic racialism in a discourse
of universalism that paradoxically relies on a conception of equality-in-
difference. In his crónica "The Charleston Earthquake" (1886), Martí views
the catastrophe as a geophysical and social leveling: "The blacks and their
ex-masters have slept beneath the same canvas tents and have eaten the
same bread of sorrow."[39] This leveling effect lays bare the natural state of
the equality-in-difference of blacks and whites: "Every race brings to the
world its mandate, and one must leave the way open for every race, if one is
not to obstruct the harmony of the universe, so that it employs its power
and completes its duty, in all the decorum and fruit of its natural independence" (1748). This is the romantic racialist argument that nonwhite races
embody "variety without inferiority," in Child's terms.[40] Nevertheless, notions of inferiority tend to slip into romantic racialist discourse, as when
Martí praises blacks for their alleged ability to have an "intimate communion with Nature" and "loyalty" (1748). Martí's otherwise admirable antiracism butts up against the limitations of romantic racialism in these
passages. On the one hand, Martí insists that each race should be allowed
to develop to its full potential. On the other hand, that potential is characterized through the notion of a racial mandate or a set of racial gifts that
both characterize and set sharp limits to the alleged capacity of Negroes.

Nearly twenty years later, Du Bois pushes up against the same limits of
romantic racialism in "Of Our Spiritual Strivings," the opening chapter
of *Souls*:

> All striving toward that vaster ideal that swims before the Negro people, the
> ideal of human brotherhood, gained through the unifying ideal of Race; the
> ideal of fostering and developing the traits and talents of the Negro, not in
> opposition or contempt for other races but rather in large conformity to the
> greater ideals of the American Republic, in order that some day on Ameri-
> can soil two world-races may give each to each those characteristics both so
> sadly lack. . . . all in all, we black men seem the sole oasis of simple faith and
> reverence in a dusty desert of dollars and smartness.[41]

Du Bois's paradox of the "unifying ideal of race" proposes that race can be
a principle of cooperation rather than conflict if one accepts the view that

each race possesses a certain set of gifts that can make a distinct contribution to the United States and to the world. However, in order to make this argument, Du Bois is forced to make at least provisional concessions to the racial discourses that allege the superiority of whites in money making and intelligence, echoing Kinmont's notion that whites are defined by their "daring and successful intellect."[42] Kinmont, Child, Stowe, Martí, and the early Du Bois of *Souls* certainly do value Negroes for allegedly being superior to white men in the Christian virtues, yet to some extent those virtues fall within conventional racial hierarchies built on the oppositions between civilization and nature, body and mind, the emotions and intellect, and adults and children. Thus the romantic racialist notion of equality-in-difference ultimately undermines beliefs in racial equality.

If sentimentalism ultimately fell into the pitfalls of discourses of racial inequality when it deployed romantic racialism, it could also approach questions of race and colonialism in very different ways, ways that deemphasize the whole question of racial difference in favor of constructing alliances based on analogous political plights, as in Martí's short play *Abdala*, one of his earliest literary texts. Sentimental discourse shapes *Abdala*, which he published in 1869 in the shadow of Cuba's Ten Years' War against Spanish colonialism. However, rather than being set in Cuba, this play is set in the ancient African country of Nubia (in northeastern Africa). The title character and hero of the play is the leader of Nubia.

Abdala sentimentalizes decolonization and decolonizes sentimentalism. First of all, the "sympathetic transactions" among the characters in this play do not take place across ethnic or class differences, but rather among equals in Nubia, thereby displacing the putative centrality of the white intellectual as witness and agent found in Stowe and Jackson.[43] And rather than attempting to establish the personhood of Negroes through the contradictory logics of shared sentiment and distinct racial character, as in Stowe or in his own writings on Charleston, Martí views the personhood of the Nubians as axiomatic—it goes unmentioned in the play. The writer's stance of sympathy toward the Nubians works by establishing an analogy between colonial situations that links Cuba to Nubia, rather than attempting to turn posited racial differences into virtues. Indeed, Martí does not mark Abdala and the Nubians in terms of race at all: he neither describes his skin color, nor remarks on the putative racial character of Nubians in any way.

The play's disciplinary cultural work is to channel all expressions of sentiment into the service of nationalism. As if the nationalist bent of this play needed further emphasis, Martí writes under the title of the play, "Written expressly for *la patria* [the fatherland]." This play participates in the long tradition of expressing republican manhood in the language of sentiment, as in English Roman republic plays like Nathaniel Lee's *Lucius Junius Brutus* (1680), John Dryden's *Absalom and Achitophel* (1681), Joseph Addison's *Cato* (1713), and Robert Rogers's *Ponteach or the Savages of America* (1766). In these texts, the hero stoically suppresses emotions, and other men cry for him. In *Cato*, which is set in another ancient northern African region, that of Numidia (today's Algeria), the eponymous republican hero cries over the Roman state rather than over the death of his own son and comes to epitomize "the republican hero [who] earns his cultural keep by justifying other men's tears."[44] Tears can be shed over people as long as they embody the interests of the imperial state. Cato welcomes Juba, a Numidian prince, into his family as his son-in-law because Juba renounces his African identity and defends Rome's civilizing mission.

Although *Abdala* does not directly allude to this earlier tradition in British drama, it shares the tradition of the stoic republican hero. But in this case, the hero is himself African, and rather than epitomizing the imperial state, he heads a state that must fight an anti-imperial war. Once Abdala decides that Nubia must wage war against a "ferocious conqueror," he cries, "Oh! These tears/Are witnesses of my terrible anxiety,/And the hurricane that growls in my gut."[45] Abdala's tears speak of his all-too-human frailty and make him accessible as a heroic figure to Martí's readers. At the same time, they signify his fierce determination to conquer the colonizer and regain liberty for Nubia. This patriot's tears stand in stark contrast to those of Espirta, his mother, who cries in sympathy with his fears and because he is leaving to fight in the war. When the mother tries to place familial love over love for the patria ("So much love for this little piece of land?"), Abdala summarizes the conflict, then swiftly resolves it in favor of the patria: "My mother cries . . . Nubia claims me . . ./I am a son . . . I was born a Nubian . . . I no longer have doubts,/Goodbye! I am off to defend my country!" (*A* 30). Although Abdala's sister, Elmira, forcefully reproaches her mother for crying over the loss of her son ("Cowardly tears bathe your breast!"), Espirta's unsanctioned expression of sorrow commands the reader's respect and offers tangible evidence of the sacrifice necessary to defend one's country (*A* 32). Martí devotes an entire scene to

Espirta's tearful premonition that her son will return to her "without life, without color, motionless, ice cold!" She then considers the possibility that tearful mothers are traitors to the cause of Nubia: "The tyrants,/do they want to drown love of country/with the love of a mother? Oh no! They unleash/Their ardent tears and complain/Because their sons march off to die!/Because if they are Nubians, they are also mothers!" (*A* 31). So even if Elmira and Abdala reserve their tears for the fatherland, Espirta persuades readers of her right to cry for her son as well.

In other words, there is an unresolved tension in the play between the mother who cries for her son and the son who cries for his country. While Elmira suggests that these are incompatible figures, the mother's soliloquy forcefully argues that they are in fact compatible. The text thus considers the possibility that tears—the defining trope of sentimentalism—may not in fact be traitorous, but rather a tool of decolonization. Indeed, in the final scene of the text, the mother's worst fears are realized: Abdala returns wounded and dies in the arms of his fellow soldiers as Elmira and Espirta look on. Abdala's final words restore the figure of the stoic patriot to center stage: "Oh! How sweet it is to die, when one dies/Fighting bravely to defend the patria!" (*A* 33). This text invites the reader's sympathy for the figure of the mother and her son, the patriot, and his anticolonial cause (these figures are intertwined and build sympathy for one another), but also requires an interethnic and cross-national identification with an African hero. This cross-national identification paradoxically takes place both by provoking sympathy for Abdala and by suppressing one's feelings for individuals in favor of one's feelings for la patria. Further, it epitomizes the alliance between whites and Afro-Cubans that would have to take place if the Ten Years' War was to achieve its objectives.

If Martí's experiments with romantic racialist discourse in 1886 would temporarily distract him from this vision of racial equality and inter-ethnic, cross-national alliance, he would return to the antiracist approach of *Abdala* in his writings of the early 1890s, in which he defines his broad vision of decolonization undergirding the Cuban War for Independence. In the speech "With All, and for the Good of All" (1891), Martí writes, "Will we fear the Negro—the noble black man, our black brother—who for the sake of the Cubans who died for him has granted eternal pardon to the Cubans who are still mistreating him?. . . . From the Negro's love for a reasonable freedom, I know that only in a greater natural and useful intensity does his differ from the white Cuban's love of freedom. . . . Others may fear him; I love him. Anyone who speaks ill of him I disown, and I say to him openly: 'You lie!'" ("WA" 141). In this account, black and white Cubans differ only in the degree of "intensity" of their love of freedom; blacks' love of freedom is more intense because they constantly face mistreatment by their compatriots. Martí's "love" for blacks stems from his commitment to the patria; as in *Abdala*, interpersonal and national sympathies converge. Thus even if the romantic racialist version of sentimentalism could be said to run counter to the egalitarianism of decolonization in some of Martí's writings, in other writings discourses of sympathy form the very fabric of his ideology of decolonization.

Du Bois similarly drew on the deep, contradictory legacy of sentimental antislavery reformism in framing the ethical imperative of his anticolonialism, even as late as 1919 in his reports on the Pan-African Conference. Surveying the history of European imperialism in Africa, Du Bois concludes that the colonialism of his day presents a grave problem for all those concerned with the fate of democracy and self-rule:

> The number of souls thus under the rule of aliens is astounding, amounting in the case of England, France, Germany and Belgium to more than 110,000,000. . . . It is the question of the reapportionment of this vast number of human beings which has started the Pan-African movement. Colored America is indeed involved.

"If we do not feel the chain
When it works another's pain,
Are we not base slaves indeed,
Slaves unworthy to be freed?"[46]

Du Bois uses a kind of sentimentalist rhetoric in this passage similar to that employed by Stowe in asserting interracial sympathy—"ye feel but one sorrow!"—to counter what he calls "the rule of aliens" in colonized lands. As if to underscore the importance of sentimentalist discourse to his ethics, Du Bois quotes from an antislavery, sentimentalist poem in arguing the case that black Americans should indeed be concerned with colonialism abroad. Here again is an attempt to yoke the strikingly different living conditions of reader and slave in order to create a universalist appeal: the reader, comfortably reading in a chair, is asked to "feel the chain" of the slave (here a figure for the colonized).

Unlike Stowe, Du Bois combines this stock sentimentalist appeal with uncompromising assertions of full equality and a call for self-determination. Moroever, Du Bois defuses and decolonizes sentimentalism in two key ways: (1) in his writings of the 1920s, he no longer assigns a differing racial character to Negroes, thereby avoiding some of the pitfalls of decontextualization in the sentimentalist discourse of Kinmont and Stowe (see the discussion of Kinmont and Stowe in chapter 1); (2) while the discourse of romantic racialism implicitly uses the achievements of white civilization as the measure of blacks' racial "gifts," by the 1910s and 1920s Du Bois dramatizes the darker world's commitment to securing its own equality, by force when necessary, as in the Mexican Revolution. Thus Du Bois's version of sentimental universalism eschews representations of a vague common humanity in favor of insisting on universal political ideals of full democracy and self-rule for all. Sentimentalism in Du Bois is a tool of activism, not a substitute for it. As I argued in chapter 1, because sentimentalism is a protean form, in order to properly assess its political significance I need to trace the varying combinations of discourses (romantic racialism, sympathy, romantic racialism) and political ideals and movements (antislavery, full equality, Pan-Africanism, imperial or hemispheric citizenship) those attitudes of sympathy invoke in representing deeply felt connections to other people.

THE "NECESSITY OF GREATNESS": DECOLONIZATION IN MARTÍ'S *AMISTAD FUNESTA*

In constructing its narrative of decolonization, Martí's novel *Amistad funesta* (Fatal friendship, 1885), unlike *Abdala* and "With All, and For the Good of All," curiously does not directly draw on the legacy of antislavery sentimentalism. Instead, *Amistad funesta* opts for the moral certainties of melodrama rather than the ethical uncertainties that would have come with antislavery sentimentalism's project of reconciling the interests of different ethnic groups. By imaginatively projecting the dilemmas of Cuban anticolonialism onto an unnamed Latin American country with an indigenous rather than a black population, Martí sidesteps the vexed question of the future citizenship of blacks in the Cuban republic. He presumes the sympathy of his readers for his white creole characters rather than addressing the problem of cross-ethnic identification that black and white readers alike would have had to face in imagining a multiethnic nation. Martí's decision to avoid addressing the issue of postemancipation citizenship in *Amistad funesta* raises three related questions. First, how does one reconcile Martí's avoidance of the racial dilemmas of Cuba in *Amistad funesta* with his subsequent activism that brought together black and white Cubans across differences of class, ethnicity, and geography in a shared revolutionary project? Second, to what extent does Martí's unsettling tendency to downplay racial difference in *Amistad* continue in his later writings of the 1890s, in which he asserts his "love" for blacks? Keeping in mind the significant obstacles that stand in the way of that love's consummation, so to speak, what are its bounds and limits?

Martí's biography demonstrates why he has been celebrated both as a founding father of Cuba and as a Latin American icon of revolution, a nationalist, and an antiracist and also serves to explain the convergence of his *amor patriae* and "love" for blacks. Martí was born in Havana in 1853, a time when Cuba was a colony of Spain and slavery fueled the economy of the island. His father, Don Mariano Martí, came to Cuba as a sergeant in the Spanish army, and his mother, Leonor Pérez y Cabrera, grew up in the Canary Islands. The Martí family, including his sisters and mother, survived economically by making uniforms for the army at home. Thus despite the fact that Mariano was loyal to the Spanish crown, the Martís were a working-class family.[47] At the age of nine José accompanied his father to the sugar-producing zone of Matanzas—where the slave poet Juan Francisco Manzano had lived—and witnessed the suffering of slaves at firsthand. In *Versos sencillos* (1891), Martí recalls this first encounter with slavery, putting to verse his abolitionist fervor:

> Scarlet as in the desert,
> the sun rose in the horizon:
> it shone upon a dead slave
> hanging from a mountain *ceiba*
> A child saw him and shook
> with passion for those who suffer:
> and, beneath the dead man, swore
> to expiate with his life the crime![48]

Martí honed his poetic craft under Rafael María Mendive, an anticolonial poet. Martí attended numerous literary and political gatherings at Mendive's house. Following Spain's tax increase on Cubans in 1866, journals critical of Spanish control proliferated; there were no fewer than twenty-seven by 1869. Committed both to his craft and to politics, Martí published two of these journals. Reacting to such anticolonial activism, the Spanish military soon arrested and deported Mendive. Colonial officials then arrested and imprisoned Martí when in October 1869 they found him in possession of a letter critical of the Spanish military. Martí was sentenced to six years of hard labor in 1870, at the age of sixteen. His term in prison left him half blind and physically debilitated for life.[49]

In 1871 Martí's sentence was commuted, and he was deported to Spain, a journey that marked the beginning of his first exile (1871–78), leading him from Spain to France, Mexico, and Guatemala. In Spain, Martí studied at the Central University of Madrid for two years and then transferred to the University of Zaragoza, where he earned his bachelor's degree in philosophy and letters in 1874. After a brief return to Cuba, Martí embarked on his second exile (1880–95), this time settling in New York. During this second exile Martí proved to be a brilliant essayist and journalist and an accomplished poet: *Ismaelillo* (1882), *Versos sencillos* (1891), and *Versos libres* (1893) are classics in Latin American literature. His chronicles of U.S. culture and politics, collectively known as *Escenas norteamericanas* (North American scenes), also include some of the most famous essays in Latin American literature. Martí's *crónicas*, a highly imaginative, creative form of journalism, appeared in newspapers in Spain, Argentina, Colombia, Mexico, and Venezuela, among other countries. Martí grew so famous in Latin America that three countries, Argentina, Paraguay, and Uruguay, named him their national consul in New York.[50]

Martí's writings, particularly his essays and journalism, played an integral role in his revolutionary organizing, in which he emerged as a leader among Cuban exiles: in 1880 Martí became head of the New York Revolutionary Committee, and in 1892 he founded the Partido Revolucionario Cubano (Cuban Revolutionary Party). In the early 1890s Martí began organizing Cuban emigré cigar workers in Florida, especially in Tampa and Key West. In these varied efforts, Martí sought to unite diverse sectors of the Cuban emigré population divided by geography, race, and class in a single effort to bring a halt to Spanish colonial control of Cuba. He used the New York newspaper he founded in 1892, *La patria*, to reach the Cuban and Puerto Rican emigré communities with his simultaneously national and transnational anti-imperialism. Unlike other nationalist leaders, who were perceived to be insensitive to issues affecting union laborers and Afro-Antilleans, Martí was well regarded by these exile groups because he introduced a broad social agenda into the revolutionary movement, supporting, for instance, the rights of workers to organize and to strike. In addition,

Martí expressed outrage over racism in essays such as "Nuestra América" ("Our America," 1891) and "Mi raza" ("My Race," 1893). His commitment to antiracist projects was also apparent in his activist projects: he worked as a teacher for La Liga, an educational society in New York for black and mulatto Puerto Ricans and Cubans.[51]

As befits his selfless dedication to the patria, Martí was known by many names that demonstrated his popularity among the Cuban people. Cuban exiles and writers referred to him as *Maestro* or *Apóstol* (teacher and apostle), those who voted for him to serve as the delegate of the Cuban Revolutionary Party called him *el delegado* (the delegate), and the Cuban peasants who saw him accompany Generals Máximo Gómez and Antonio Maceo to battle simply and affectionately called him *Presidente*. Martí became the martyr of the Cuban independence movement—and therefore forever equated with the aspirations of Cuba—when he died in battle on May 19, 1895.[52]

Martí's *Amistad funesta*, written during his exile in the United States, avoids the issue of race and instead relies on allegorically figuring gender and sexuality in establishing the aims and bounds of a broad project of decolonization through the mode of melodrama. Such questions of gender and colonialism, despite being joined through this ethically charged allegory, have been viewed as separate by the novel's critics. Critics have used two distinct approaches to the novel: the study of modernity and the Latin American literary movement of Modernismo, an approach that often addresses issues of imperialism, generally the province of male critics, and an analysis of gender, almost entirely confined to female critics.[53] By bringing into alignment gender and imperialism, my analysis reveals the ways in which Martí utilizes gender so as to infuse an otherwise institutionally construed Cuban anticolonial movement with the social issues proper to a more broadly construed decolonization movement. Moreover, such an approach brings into focus an array of conflicting positions taken by Latin American writers on how to utilize gender in figuring national unity, from the male–female unions in the Latin American "national romances" studied by Doris Sommer to the male–male relationships in Martí.

Amistad funesta is set in an unnamed Latin American country populated by Indians rather than by African slaves, as in Cuba. The novel thus exemplifies Martí's *latinoamericanismo*, his concerns with the independence of Latin America as a whole. Chapter 1 introduces the male hero, Juan Jerez, a lawyer, poet, patriot, and *indigenista*, that is, a white creole advocate of Indian rights. Juan's "winged words" enchant his cousin and girlfriend Lucía Jerez, who imagines that his kiss magically fills the room with flowers.[54] Chapter 2 describes the history of the Del Valle family: Don Manuel, who has emigrated from Spain to America, his wife, Doña Andrea, their son, Manuelillo, and their daughter, Leonor, or Sol, a talented pianist renowned for her extraordinary beauty. Chapter 3 tells of Lucía's growing jealousy of Sol, who, Lucia mistakenly believes, loves Juan. Ultimately Lucía murders Sol with a gun and then commits suicide.

The novel's politics emerge through its allegorical structure, which defines the ethical oppositions of melodrama—its individual story of a love triangle tells a larger collective story of the threat of greed to the forging of the nation, to borrow Fredric Jameson's definition of allegory.[55] Juan's honesty, dedication, and defense of Indian culture and land rights embody the alliance that Martí would later call "Our America," a confederation of Latin American countries united against colonialism. By contrast, Lucía routinely mistreats her rival, Sol: "Ardent and despotic . . . she exercised . . . a powerful influence on Sol's timid and new spirit" (*LJ* 153). Sol is "the wholly American flower, ardent and rich" (*LJ* 144). Young and innocent, Sol "needed a boss, and Lucía was her boss." In allegorical terms, then, Lucía embodies the "despotic" Spanish colonial oppressor of Sol, who epitomizes the innocence and vitality of *América* (*LJ* 153). Thus the title *Amistad funesta*, fatal friendship, refers both to Lucía's creation of a lethal love triangle with Sol and Juan and to the oppressive colonial "friendship" between Spain, embodied by Lucía, and Cuba, embodied by Juan and Sol.[56]

The allegory of the fatal friendship between Spain and Cuba is constructed through the melodrama form. I use the term *melodrama* because it is defined by its allegorical structure, fusing ethics and aesthetics: characters embody "primal ethical forces," according to Peter Brooks.[57] The Latin American "national romances" studied by Sommer are melodramas in the romance mode, constructing heterosexual pairings that embody successful efforts at national consolidation in the wake of Latin American independence (1810–25).[58] By contrast, in his tragic melodrama Martí emphasizes the failure of national formation in Cuba, which, like Puerto Rico, did not gain its nominal independence from Spain until 1898.

In using the term *melodrama* I avoid the pitfalls of Sommer's definition of romance, which excludes Cuban and Puerto Rican novels that emphasized national conflict over cohesion in their tragic views of Spanish colonialism. For instance, Sommer excludes from her study Eugenio María de

Hostos's novel *La peregrinación de Bayoán* (The peregrinations of Bayoán, Puerto Rico, 1863) because it constructs a "rather un-American [here Sommer means un–*Latin* American] competition between erotics and duty."[59] Like Hostos, Martí was suspicious of sexual love as the basis for national consolidation, as is evident in his statement that friendship is superior to love: "Friendship is superior to love in that it does not create desire, neither the fatigue of having satisfied it, nor the sadness of abandoning the temple of sated desires for that of new desires."[60]

It is perhaps because of Martí's suspicion of sexual desire that two of the Latin American national romances studied by Sommer appear as corrupting forces in *Amistad funesta*. Pedro Real, a "frivolous" man markedly less honorable than Juan Jerez, attempts to woo Sol by reading to her José Marmol's *Amalia* (Argentina, 1851) and Jorge Isaacs's *María* (Colombia, 1867) (*LJ* 165). As Pedro's library of Latin American literature suggests, Martí's novel should be studied along with Sommer's canon of national romances because its "competition between erotics and duty" does link the personal and the political, in this case through its *rejection* of romantic love as a vehicle for politics.[61] In his prologue to the novel, Martí implicitly constructs the allegorical move from the individual to the social as a means of transcending the pitfalls of sexual desire. After humorously asking God's forgiveness for his sins as a novelist, he proceeds to place the onus upon his readers to transform an ostensibly frivolous novel—potentially similar to those read for selfish reasons by Pedro Real—into a politically engaged text: "I want to see the brave person who can create from the [unintelligible word] a good novel" (*LJ* 109). Martí seeks to benefit from the wide popularity of the national romance while disputing its harnessing of sexual desire.[62] By constructing *Amistad funesta* as a melodrama in the tragic mode, Martí polemicizes against the popular melodramas in the romance mode because they often call for a partnership between men and women that he could conceive of only in sexual terms and as therefore corrupted— as exemplified by Lucía's overly possessive love for Juan. Martí's use of the *tragic* melodrama signals his preference for homosocial politics over the heterosexual erotics present in popular melodramas in the *romance* mode.

In the episode on the Del Valle family, Martí genders decolonization by utilizing such homosocial bonds of male friendship to avoid heterosexual desire and signify the desired "revolutionary fraternity."[63] In this chapter, the antimonarchical *peninsular* Don Manuel proves his worth by founding a school, yet dies from the financial strain of paying for Manuelillo's education abroad, an exile necessitated by the young man's criticisms of the colonial regime in journalism and poetry.[64] "Aristócratas de la inteligencia," aristocrats only by dint of their intellects because the colonial regime denies them material well-being, Don Manuel and his son would belong to the upper classes of an uncolonized country, but in Cuba they lack the economic means to survive (*LJ* 132). In his portrayal of the Del Valle father–son relationship, Martí reveals the political repression and lack of opportunities for creoles under Spanish colonialism. Colonialism literally unmans Latin America by crippling its patriarchs and sending its sons abroad; colonialism postpones national development, thereby halting history. Thus the homosocial bond between father and son constitutes the would-be Cuban nation by compensating for the colonial "unmanning" of Cuba.

Such representations of a "national fraternity" responded in part to the pressures created by portrayals in the North American press of Cuba as an "effeminate" country.[65] In an essay written after his novel, Martí responds to such attacks on the manliness of Cubans with what he calls "la palabra viril" (the virile word).[66] "La palabra viril" encapsulates the decolonizing politics of "Nuestra América" in a three-pronged manner: it opposes the positivists, apologists for the contemporary politics of racial oppression, as "feeble thinkers" who "string together . . . bookshelf races";[67] it compensates for the alleged effeminacy of poets such as Martí himself;[68] and it asserts the masculinity of Cuba in the face of U.S. annexationist images of Cuba as a white woman to be rescued by Uncle Sam.

If homosocial bonds provide one gendered strategy of decolonizing resistance to colonialism's unmanning of Latin America, Fanonesque visions of violent rebellion provide another.[69] Martí fantasizes a violent anticolonial rebellion in Manuelillo's deathbed vision of a palm tree aflame (*LJ* 131).[70] Similarly, in the fanciful parable of the "portero soñoliento," or sleepy doorman, the portero is surrounded by a thousand little goblins who prevent him from rousing himself by pouring sleeping potion into his ears:

> There, in a corner of the chest, the necessity of greatness sleeps like a drowsy porter. . . . He sleeps as if he would never awake. . . . In things of greatness the human soul is deeply sleepy, above all in these times. Thousands of goblins, of repugnant figure, with hands like spiders', swollen stomachs, inflamed mouths, doubled rows of teeth, round and libidinous eyes, turn constantly around the sleeping porter, and pour sleeping potion into his

ears, and let him relax, and dampen his temples, and with delicate brush-
strokes moisten his palms, and grab onto his legs and sit on the back of the
armchair, looking towards all sides with hostility, so that no one approaches
to wake up the porter: so often greatness sleeps in the human soul! But
when he awakes, and stretches his arms, his first movement sends running
the whole band of goblins with swollen tummies. (*LJ* 139–40)

In this parable Martí portrays in the vivid, starkly drawn images of children's fairy tales the internalized, indirect rule of hegemony: the goblins
pour sleeping potion into the ears of the doorman in whom "the necessity
of greatness sleeps like a drowsy porter."[71]

Lucía embodies an internalization of the goblinlike oppressor, a woman
in whom "the necessity of greatness sleeps." Lucía's actions are dictated by
her jealousy and by her "encarnizado pensamiento"—her thinking pre-
occupied by desire and trapped by flesh.[72] Indeed, Martí describes Lucía as
if she is caught in her own corporeality, just as the goblins are marked by
their "swollen bellies" and "libidinous eyes": "Lucía, in whom desire tore as
hooks tear at fish, and who when she had to renounce some desire, was left
broken and bleeding, as when the hook is reeled in, leaving the bloody flesh
of the fish" (*LJ* 116). Lucía, then, is debilitated by her treacherous sexual
desire for Juan.

While Lucía lets herself be captured by her desire, Juan proves his worthiness by suppressing his desires for the nation's good. Juan is "one of
those unhappy souls who can only do good and love pure things," a poet
who also defends Indian land rights (*LJ* 115, 144).[73] Martí thus constructs an
opposition between a woman who embodies the treacherous character of
sexuality and an ascetic male nationalist, a figure prominent in *Abdala* as
well. However, contrary to some readings of the novel, Martí does not
construct a simple female–male opposition in portraying underdevelopment and decolonization.[74] "The necessity of greatness sleeps" in both
women and men: like Lucía Jerez, Pedro Real is portrayed as "frivolous" in
his sexual pursuit of Sol (*LJ* 124). And just as Lucía has her male counterpart in vice, Juan has his female counterparts in virtue. In addition to the
artistic Sol, there is Ana, a dying artist with a "pure spirit" like Juan's, who
sings so beautifully that she inspires the listener to do good deeds (*LJ* 117,
168). Thus even if Juan creates social change in the male realm of law and
political activism, by similarly realizing their "necessity of greatness" in the
artistic realm—a realm dear to Martí—women like Ana and Sol positively
transform the minds of those who consume their art. In Martí's view of

decolonization as a transformation of colonial "habits," then, virtuous men and women play equally important roles, even if restricted by conventional gender roles dividing the home and art from the public sphere. Martí's representation of Ana and Sol departs from the nationalist tradition of "Republican Motherhood" because rather than representing women as exclusively mothers, producers of citizens, Ana and Sol achieve greatness independently of men through their artistic skill.

In Martí such decolonizing virtue always requires a suppression of sexuality, a suppression that often relies on a crossing of gender roles. Juan, for instance, embodies a virtue described in terms of feminine decency: he regards "his virtue with as much reverence as the most modest woman" (*LJ* 167).[75] Ana similarly crosses gender divisions when she says that she feels like an altar boy paying tribute to the "sacred" beauty of Sol and Lucía (*LJ* 155). The conflicting political projects in this novel, then, do not result from differences between men and women, but rather from competing embodiments and constructions of femininity and masculinity which do not correspond directly to women and men. Such contrasting politics emerge in differing views of Sol, who embodies "Nuestra América," as we have seen. While Lucía views Sol as a sexual threat, Juan appreciates her for her sound ethics: "You are already famous for your beauty, but I will spread word of your goodness" (*LJ* 167). The value of women is not restricted to the reproductive realm or to their embodiment of beauty, but rather is bound up in their role as coproducers of ethical goodness and artistic beauty.

Thus in Martí, decolonization is articulated through a discourse of ethical and artistic "greatness" that suppresses sexuality in both men and women. Such a fusion of ethical and artistic attributes, of Goodness and Beauty, has been described as a key aspect of Modernismo, a movement within Latin American literature between 1875 to 1918 that exalted the figure of the poet, employed poeticized prose, as in *Amistad funesta*, and adopted new literary currents such as French symbolism.[76] If, then, Martí's *Amistad funesta* was "the first Modernista novel" in Latin America, I would add that it inaugurates this movement by infusing the aesthetics of Modernismo with the gendered ethics of the colonial opposition, an ethics that values women not only as objects of beauty but also as producers of beauty understood in its full artistic and political dimensions.[77]

The absence of any extensive thematization of racial issues in *Amistad funesta* reinforces Martí's tendency to privilege revolutionary unity over the redress of racial oppression. By emphasizing the importance of the ethics of sexuality and gender to creating a decolonizing movement, Martí strategically sidesteps the divisive issue of race relations in Cuba. Martí's subsequent essay, "Mi raza" ("My Race," 1893), demonstrates the strengths and weaknesses of a more explicit argument calling for a color-blind society. On the one hand, Martí rejects allegations of Negro inferiority and insists on the bravery of Afro-Cubans who fought in Cuba's wars for independence. As in *Abdala* and "With All, and For the Good of All," he also rejects the discourse of racial character that defines romantic racialism. Indeed, the very structure of Martí's writing in this essay—unique for its abundance of strikingly symmetrical pairings of sentences that set in parallel the feelings and aspirations of Afro-Cubans and creoles—dramatizes his belief in the meaninglessness of racial categories and the innate equality of blacks and whites: "What do blacks think of a white man who is proud of being white and believes he has special rights because he is? What must whites think of a black man who grows conceited about his color?"[78] In order to combat such pride in color, Martí constructs a race-blind nationalism: "'Cuban' means more than white, more than mulatto, more than Negro" ("MR" 319). For Martí, the consequence of racial equality and the independence struggle against Spain is that national unity must take priority over ethnic loyalties.

On the other hand, the grammatical symmetry of sentences illustrating the equality of Afro-Cubans and whites belies a structural asymmetry in social positions and life opportunities. Given such a social context, the "pride" of whites and of Afro-Cubans cannot be equated because white pride often produces social inequality, while Afro-Cuban pride often expresses a protest against such inequality. Martí's race-blind discourse dismisses claims of biologically based racial differences at the risk of minimizing differences in political perspective stemming from racial position.[79] His faith in the social progress that will take place following national independence leads him to assert, "There will never be a race war in Cuba. The republic cannot retreat." ("MR" 320).

Yet less than twenty years later, nearly three thousand Afro-Cuban members of the Partido Independiente de Color died in the Race War of 1912. This slaughter of Afro-Cubans was justified in part through an appeal to the very race-blind discourses that Martí and other *independentistas* used as the bedrock of their nationalism.[80] These race-blind discourses were subsequently written into the laws of the Cuban Republic. La Ley

Morúa, a law ironically penned by the Afro-Cuban novelist and politician Martin Morúa Delgado, outlawed the formation of political parties on the basis of color in 1910.[81] By contrast, at the onset of his career as a public intellectual, Du Bois called for race-based organizing, even as he cast doubt on rigidly deterministic scientific conceptions of race: "As a race we must strive by race organization, by race solidarity, by race unity to the realization of that broader humanity which freely recognizes differences in men, but sternly deprecates inequality in their opportunities of development."[82]

DISCOURSES OF RACIAL MYSTERY AND "THE COMING UNITIES" IN DU BOIS (FROM *THE SOULS OF BLACK FOLK* TO *THE NEGRO*)

While for Martí the ideal anticolonial revolutionaries combine male and female characteristics and profess a racially unmarked *Cubanidad* (Cubanness), Du Bois's female characters embody and help to push forward his broad Pan-Africanism as a cross-national discourse and movement that moves beyond racially bound modes of association. In *The Souls of Black Folk* (1903), Du Bois most famously formulates his Pan-Africanism as antiimperial alliance when he proclaims, "The problem of the twentieth century is the problem of the color line,—the relation of the darker to the lighter races of men in Asia and Africa, in America and the islands of the sea," describing the interrelations between domestic racism and global imperialism.[83] But in a little-known rewriting of those well-known lines, Du Bois reveals that underdevelopment also operates along gender lines: "The meaning of the twentieth century," he wrote in 1915, "is the freeing of the individual soul; the soul longest in slavery . . . is the soul of womanhood."[84] Thus even if struggles for women's rights do not occupy a central role in Du Bois's efforts to dismantle the color line, they do play a role in shaping his conception of decolonization as encompassing diverse yet interrelated political aspirations. Indeed, the logic of decolonization in Du Bois operates by expanding the range of his potential collaborators, whether by national affiliation or by gender.

Even as early as *Souls* Du Bois aligns gender oppression and racial oppression as equally important signals of the failure of what passes as progress. In the essay "Of the Meaning of Progress," recounting his two summers teaching in a rustic log schoolhouse in the Tennessee backwoods while an undergraduate at Fisk, the character Josie embodies underdevelopment as the price of "progress." In his student Josie, a "thin, homely girl

of twenty," Du Bois encounters "a certain fineness, the shadow of an unconscious moral heroism," just as Martí finds virtue in the female characters Sol and Ana (S 254). Josie exemplifies heroism by her hunger for
knowledge and by her work in Nashville to support her family. Yet Josie's
hard work does not lead her to realize her dream of higher education, but
instead results in her untimely death. Josie, then, represents the frustrated
aspirations of black southerners such as her neighbors the Burkes, who can
never extricate themselves from debt because of the highly exploitative
conditions of peonage—this is, the "second slavery" that Du Bois mentions
elsewhere (S 220). Du Bois views the temporality of underdevelopment,
then, as circular, as reenacting prior stages of history such as slavery. But
Josie embodies such underdevelopment not only as a black, but also as a
black woman: the fact that she sacrifices her education to meet her brothers' needs testifies to gender inequalities compounded by racial oppression.

Du Bois signals the need to transform such gender roles when describing his quest for a school in the backwoods: "There came a day when all the
teachers left the Institute and began the hunt for schools. I learn from
hearsay (for my mother was mortally afraid of firearms) that the hunting
of ducks and bears and men is wonderfully interesting, but I am sure that
the man who has never hunted a country school has something to learn of
the pleasures of the chase" (S 253). Du Bois registers a distinction in male
gender roles when he reports that hunting is said to be "wonderfully
interesting," a remark that is bitterly ironic given the allusion to lynching, implicit in the mention of the hunting of men. In contrast to such a
code of rough masculinity championed by Theodore Roosevelt in his imperialist exploits in a racialized Cuba, Du Bois embodies honorable and
refined notions of manliness in his alternative hunt to provide education
for the masses.[85]

Josie's exclusion from what Du Bois calls the "kingdom of culture"
accessed through education shows that the culture concept does not mark
Du Bois's elitism but rather is deployed as a method of revealing inequality.
For Du Bois, the color line creates unequal access to high culture because of
underdevelopment. Access to culture, he reveals, is determined both by
global inequality—Europe and the United States are portrayed as "culture-
lands" that meet their wants through "force and dominion"—and by class
differences between the black masses (Josie) and scholars such as himself
(S 271). Du Bois's movement from the racialized and gendered subject in
distress to the imperial powers' control of access to high culture and then

back again exemplifies his methodology of transnational analysis. Du Bois is conscious of his own privileged access to high culture: "I sit with Shakespeare and he winces not. . . . So, wed with Truth, I dwell above the Veil" (*S* 284). As a lower-class woman, Josie, by embodying class and gender differences that disrupt assumptions of black unity, provides Du Bois with the opportunity for self-scrutiny.

Du Bois's concept of folk attempts to bridge such class divisions between black intellectuals and the masses.[86] Indeed, Du Bois disrupts the high culture/low culture opposition by placing black folk musical expression—encoded by the bars of music serving as epigraphs to each chapter of this "singing book"—on a par with the quotations of European literary high culture accompanying them.[87] Moreover, Du Bois signals his solidarity with black folk when he remarks, "And, finally, need I add that I who speak here am bone of the bone and flesh of the flesh of them that live within the Veil?" (*S* 209). Thus Du Bois attempts to make himself into a Gramscian organic intellectual capable of forming a cross-class "intellectual-moral bloc."[88]

Du Bois's teaching experience in Tennessee exemplifies this commitment to the black masses. But Du Bois was not simply content to teach the black masses: he also sought to teach others about black folk, as the title to his book attests. Du Bois represents education as bridging the distance both from his white readers and from the black folk. In "Of the Wings of Atalanta," education is an alternative to the national obsession with money, exemplified by the story of Atalanta: "You know the tale,—how swarthy Atalanta, tall and wild, would marry only him who out-raced her; and how the wily Hippomenes laid three apples of gold in her way" and she succumbed to temptation (*S* 263). In explaining the educational solution to such greed, Du Bois employs a cautionary tale of the need to safeguard female virginity: "The Wings of Atalanta are the coming universities of the South. They alone can bear the maiden past the temptation of golden fruit . . . they will . . . leave her kneeling in the Sanctuary of Truth and Freedom and broad Humanity, virgin and undefiled. Sadly did the Old South err in human education, despising the education of the masses, and niggardly in the support of colleges" (*S* 268). This passage constructs a dual audience consisting of the black "masses" and of the white South. Black folk can rise to a higher socioeconomic level by attaining an education, here figured as female chastity and virginity. Ironically, in this passage Du Bois's insistence on educating black women such as Josie is undermined by his emphasis on the female virtue of chastity, as if women's duty is to safeguard their virginity and men's duty is to safeguard the knowledge leading to "Truth and Freedom." The second intended audience, white southerners and their northern supporters, can learn by reading *Souls* how to dismantle the barriers they have erected to black achievement.

Josie's life serves to critique gendered and racial oppression even as it embodies national potential. Josie's "sorrowful" life serves to exemplify for readers the "shadow" of the widespread faith in wealth and in national progress, their seldom-seen undersides: "How shall man measure Progress there where the dark-faced Josie lies? How many heartfuls of sorrow shall balance a bushel of wheat?" (*S* 261).[89] Josie embodies the immeasurable human potential of Negroes that goes to waste owing to the veil of racial oppression.[90] Du Bois describes such oppression as a problem compounded by faulty knowledge: "Measuring one's soul by the tape of the world that looks on with amused contempt and pity" (*S* 215). This "tape" or "veil" of racialization, then, is not a natural characteristic of Negroes, but rather a social construct. Du Bois employs the veil metaphor to describe his childhood discovery of his black identity when a schoolgirl refuses his visiting card: "I remember well when the shadow [of the veil] swept across me. . . . Then it dawned upon me with a certain suddenness that I was different from the others; or like, mayhap, in heart and life and longing, but shut out from their world by a vast veil." (*S* 214) Du Bois suggests that the racialist discourses of the veil, themselves implicated in the discourse of progress, construct an absolute difference between whites and blacks as a difference between "higher" and "lower" races (*S* 219).

Du Bois transforms the "grounds of meaning" of such discourses of absolute racial difference with a discourse of racial mystery that insists on the inexhaustible human potential of Negroes such as Josie, not to be measured on the same scale as bushels of wheat.[91] His discourse of racial mystery, then, intervenes in the production of knowledge by cautioning readers about the limits of contemporary discourses on Negroes. In "The Conservation of Races" (1897), Du Bois had already argued that the differences separating "men into groups" are "subtle, delicate and elusive," oftentimes having "swept across and ignored" the lines of blood and descent.[92] In *Souls* he extends this argument by considering the "longings" and "souls" of Negroes: "We seldom study the condition of the Negro today honestly and carefully. It is so much easier to assume that we know it all. . . . And yet how little we really know of these millions,—of their daily

lives and longings" (S 302). In the same chapter, Du Bois points out, "Each
unit in the mass is a throbbing human soul," reminding his readers that the
vocabulary for discussing social life—particularly the social life of African
Americans—is inevitably reductionist (S 307). The prominence of the notion of soul, itself a discourse of racial mystery, demonstrates that this
discourse constitutes the text's "master narrative," organizing its diverse
and rich representational repertoire into a coherent narrative strategy.[93]
Du Bois's emphasis on the limits of contemporary discourses on African
Americans contrasts with Stowe's sentimentalist and romantic racialist
notion that Negroes are transparent to sympathetic white observers.

The discourse of racial mystery establishes narrative coherence by revealing the inadequacy of contemporary racial discourses in describing the
Negro, suggesting that the true ability of Negroes is as yet unknown and
thus runs alongside and contrary to the discourse of racial gifts. The sorrow songs, for instance, "tell of death and suffering and unvoiced longing
toward a truer world of misty wanderings and hidden ways" (S 380). Just as
Josie's potential could not be described from a perspective that interprets
"the world in dollars," so the sorrow songs require attention to the quality
of the "souls" of those who sing them. Du Bois rejects the notion of
progress as a historical category and as a predictor of the future and instead
attempts to offer a glimpse of the untold capacity of Negro souls through
the sorrow songs. When he describes the spirituals as "the most original
and beautiful expression of human life and longing yet born on American
soil," he deploys the discourse of racial mystery to show that the spirituals
are both distinctly American and of universal significance (S 338). Thus the
problem of the color line is in part defined by the ways in which the veil
of racialization inhibits cross-cultural understanding: in "Of Alexander
Crummell," Du Bois remarks that the tragedy of the age is "that men know
so little of men" (S 362). This tragedy is encoded graphically in the text at
the beginning of each chapter in the musical bars understandable only to
those familiar with the African American gospel tradition, as we have seen.

Yet if racialization inhibits understanding across the color line, Du Bois,
displaying his intellectual indebtedness to Johann von Herder, paradoxically argues that race can be a "unifying ideal," partly because the Negro
contributes distinct "gifts" in the making of America (220). Josie embodies
the "simple faith and reverence" characteristic of Negroes, in contrast to
the "dusty desert of dollars and smartness" and the "triumphant commer-
cialism" typical of whites (220, 241). Such racial gifts, however, are them-

selves historically determined because progress, according to Du Bois, is historically variable rather than evolutionary:

> The silently growing assumption of this age is that the probation of races is past, and that the backward races of to-day are of proven inefficiency and not worth the saving. . . . Two thousand years ago such dogmatism, readily welcome, would have scouted the idea of blond races ever leading civilization. So woefully unorganized is sociological knowledge that the meaning of progress, the meaning of "swift" and "slow" in human doing, and the limits of human perfectability, are veiled unanswered sphinxes on the shores of science. (S 386)

Du Bois transforms the veil of race, ordinarily a "prisonhouse," into a "unifying ideal" (S 220) by paradoxically emphasizing the unlimited potential for "human perfectability" within the previously limiting bounds of racial identity. Du Bois's use of the term *sphinx* enacts this paradox by emphasizing the unknowable "limits of human perfectability," while at the same time invoking the Ethiopianist faith that the past greatness of ancient African civilizations demonstrates that African peoples will once again rise to power.[94]

The full meaning of the seemingly paradoxical phrase "human brotherhood, gained through the unifying ideal of Race" emerges only in the context of Du Bois's commitment to a politics of alliance. As is clear in his construction of the problem of the color line as oppressing all darker races, Du Bois avoids making his folk alliance into a narrowly racial unity, contrary to what Kwame Anthony Appiah has claimed.[95] Du Bois's discourse of racial gifts coexists in tension with his discourse of racial mystery in *Souls*, and this becomes a movement *away from* racial thinking in his subsequent work. Just as he rewrites his formulation of the "problem of the color line" to include civil rights for women, Du Bois later rewrites his "bone of the bone" remark in "The Forethought" to *Souls*, in which he stakes a claim to racial authenticity: "Need I add that I who speak here am bone of the bone and flesh of the flesh of them that live within the Veil?" (S 209). While in *Souls* "the bone of the bone" remark signifies a racial unity, Du Bois's rewriting of that phrase in the essay "The Souls of White Folk" from *Darkwater* (1920) undermines notions of racial purity, suggesting his inescapable indebtedness to Euro-American intellectual discourse (even as he so boldly contests its assumptions and provides access to otherwise ignored historical perspectives): "Not as a foreigner do I come, for I am native, not foreign, bone of their thought and flesh of their language."[96]

Indeed, in *Souls* and in later writings Du Bois strives to extend his commitment to civil rights for Negroes to all peoples by calling for broader "unities" that would resolve previous power inequalities by forging alliances on the basis of class, gender, national identity, and common humanity. In "The Negro Problem" in the historiographical text *The Negro* (1915), Du Bois rejects "narrow racial propaganda" in favor of "the coming unities": "The Pan-African movement when it comes will not . . . be merely a narrow racial propaganda. Already the more far-seeing Negroes sense the coming unities: a unity of the working classes everywhere, a unity of the colored races, a new unity of men."[97] Here Du Bois turns Pan-Africanism, which is at least prima facie confined to black diasporic populations, into a model for the principle of expanding circles of membership beyond ethnicity, race, and nationality.

WAVES OF DECOLONIZATION IN DU BOIS: RECONSTRUCTION, 1898, WORLD WAR I, AND THE MEXICAN REVOLUTION

We can locate the roots of Du Bois's discourses of racial mystery—an ethnically elastic model of Pan-Africanism—in his extended response to the event of 1898, especially in the antiracist coalitions in which he took part. As an event, 1898 epitomizes the antinomies of a putative universalism—freedom—which Du Bois exposes as alternately shaped by waves of whiteness and waves of radical democracy. In Du Bois's writings on the color line in the 1910s and 1920s, he continually returns to three historical events whose meanings, in his view, can't be understood apart from one another: Reconstruction, 1898, and World War I. For Du Bois these three events signal the world's distance from realizing the universalist goals of full citizenship for all. One measure of this distance for Du Bois lies in the erroneous conventional perception of these events. That is, Reconstruction and World War I are both viewed as nationally or regionally specific events; Du Bois hopes to explain their true meaning by tracing their neglected links to the global history of colonialism.

While Du Bois recognizes the distinct character of Reconstruction, 1898, and World War I, he also emphasizes the ways in which they all embody a recurring nightmare of history: the waves of whiteness and colonialism that must be met with waves of antiracism, democratization, and decolonization. An important thread in his writings is the insistence that the United States has joined the ranks of European imperial powers in establishing and maintaining colonial and neocolonial regimes. In *Darkwater* and other post–World War I writings, Du Bois follows through on the innovative perspective on Reconstruction as a key event in the history of the global color line (in chapter 2 of *Souls*). He uses Reconstruction as a yardstick for the ongoing historical contest between what he terms the Enlightenment "Philosophy of Democracy handed down from the 18th century" and "the disfranchisement of the blacks of the South and a world-wide attempt to restrict democratic development to white races and to distract them with race hatred against the darker races" (*DW* 551–52).[98] More specifically, white southern efforts to vilify Reconstruction down-played its expression of the ambitions of the white and black working class and instead portrayed it as an expression of white racial unity against blacks: "Reconstruction became in history a great movement for the self-assertion of the white race against the impudent ambition of degraded blacks, instead of, in truth, the rise of a mass of black and white laborers" (*DW* 552). As the heading "Reconstruction and Africa" in "Letters from Dr. Du Bois" (*The Crisis*, February 1919) suggests, Du Bois uses this under-standing of Reconstruction in order to craft it into a metaphor for the conjoined processes of democratization at home and abroad, which in his view build momentum for one another.[99] Thus in *Darkwater* and other writings Du Bois elaborates on his portrayal of Reconstruction as a global event in *Souls*: Reconstruction recurs in new guises as successive waves of democratization and decolonization. Du Bois expands the received under-standing of Reconstruction in terms of both space—by linking it to de-colonization struggles—and time—by using it as a metaphor for democra-tization in later periods.

Du Bois uses Reconstruction to show how U.S. struggles for civil rights are themselves part of a larger global story in which the processes of disfranchisement and democratization at home run parallel to those of imperialism and decolonization abroad. Similarly, in the discussion of imperialist aggression during "Boxer times" and the War of 1898 that I mentioned above he uses the events of 1898 to show how those two sets of processes are intertwined in the projection of U.S. imperial power in Latin America. I will note here only that Du Bois regards Reconstruction and 1898 not only as key events in the ongoing construction and maintenance of the global color line, but also as opportunities for interethnic, cross-class, and, in the case of 1898, transnational alliance.

The globe-spanning character of imperial conflicts at the close of the nineteenth century serves as a model for Du Bois's analysis of both Recon-struction and World War I. Reconstruction and World War I are conventionally conceived as U.S. and European conflicts, respectively; Du Bois explains their applicability (Reconstruction) or links (World War I) to global struggles over the color line. Indeed, his accounts of the war in *Darkwater*, *The Crisis*, and elsewhere can be viewed as putting the "world" into World War I. (This "worlding" of World War I exists in tension with Du Bois's wartime nationalism at the expense of pacifist principles—his decision to initially support the U.S. involvement in the war, which he viewed as an opportunity for African Americans to prove their loyalty and thereby compel recognition of civil rights.)[100] First, Du Bois disputes the Eurocentrism of conventional stories of the conflict, pointing toward the tendency of accounts of World War I to eclipse the indisputable importance of imperial conflicts outside of Europe: "Think of the wars through which we have lived in the last decade: in German Africa, in British Nigeria, in French and Spanish Morocco, in China, in Persia, in the Balkans, in Tripoli, in Mexico, and in a dozen lesser places—were not these horrible, too?" (*DW* 502). Here Du Bois is suggesting that in order to understand World War I we paradoxically need to look to other, allied conflicts that explain its true meaning: the aftermath of the scramble for Africa (hence the mention of German Africa and British Nigeria) as well as a plethora of contemporary wars outside of Europe, for example, the Mexican Revolution of 1910–17 (I follow through on Du Bois's lead in relation to the Mexican Revolution in chapters 3 and 4). As in his account of 1900, Du Bois's focus on U.S. imperialism in Latin America plays a central role in his efforts to shift attention away from Eurocentric histories, pointing the reader toward accounts of U.S. imperialism and conflicts in the colonized world as their necessary corrective.

In a second move to "world" World War I, Du Bois implies that the eclipse of non-European conflicts by accounts of World War I conceals its true significance. At stake in the jockeying for power among the world powers after World War I was nothing less than the fate of democracy in the darker world, domestically and abroad. On the domestic front, for Du Bois the antiblack riots in East St. Louis, evidence of white backlash against returning Negro soldiers and the Great Migration, threaten U.S. democracy. In a move that once again highlights the importance of Reconstruction as a model for future democratization in his thought, Du Bois argues that the return of black soldiers to the United States should inaugurate "the great new day of coming Reconstruction," which would secure for blacks the vote and universal education.[101] In addressing the global scene, Du Bois points to U.S. efforts to use its supposed support for democracy in Europe as a smoke screen for its subjection of Latin America to neocolonial rule: "If America can go into the World Court and League of Nations with her hands red in the blood of Haiti and her pockets filled with the loot of Nicaragua, she will be free for further imperialism in Central and South America."[102] Bringing together the domestic and foreign in a figure of decolonization and implicitly alluding to his writings on 1898, Du Bois proclaims that World War I was "the prelude to the armed and indignant protest of these despised and raped peoples" (DW 508). In other words, the "horrible" and "shameful" violence of World War I pales before the justifiable violence of "that fight for freedom, which black and brown and yellow men must and will make unless their oppression and humiliation and insult at the hands of the White World cease" (DW 507).

In several essays, Du Bois suggests that Latin America and the Caribbean will be one of the main arenas for the fight against U.S. imperialism. If World War I was a "prelude" to the "fight for freedom" by darker peoples, Du Bois recognizes that the Mexican Revolution was an important battle in that fight. Du Bois assesses the importance of the Mexican Revolution in relation to 1898 and World War I. In 1914 Du Bois writes that the Mexican Revolution has led the United States to lose the confidence it gained in the Spanish-American-Cuban War of 1898 when it "'liberated' Cuba and benevolently assimilated the Philippines. . . . We have Cuba by the industrial throat and the Philippines on its knees, albeit squirming. Why not Mexico with its million of brown peons? Because . . . we scent danger. . . . Can the white world always hold the black world by the throat and keep it to work?"[103] In this account, while the conquering of Cuba and the Phillipines by the United States in 1898 implicitly constitutes a wave of whiteness, Mexico embodies the disruptive promise of what I am terming waves of decolonization. Here Du Bois uses his knowledge of the aftermath of 1898 to portray himself as an anticolonial prophet. Whereas the United States was able to control the events of 1898, it found itself unable to control the outcome of the Mexican Revolution. Therefore Du Bois finds in the Mexican Revolution a harbinger of the future uprising of the "black world."[104] The Mexican Revolution offers an important corrective to conventional accounts of the World War I because it demonstrates the agency of the darker peoples in attempting to achieve self-governance and move to the forefront of struggles for democracy. In contrast, the U.S. government abrogates its stated commitment to democracy by engaging in imperialist wars in order to serve the interests of what Du Bois terms "Big Business."[105]

Du Bois's aggressively comparative approach to these events crosses over

the geographical and temporal dividing lines that typically organize historical narratives. Du Bois expands the boundaries of each event outward into
other world situations that must be considered in order to arrive at the true
meaning of the event. And each event emerges out of the earlier event(s)
and replays their conflicts in a new guise. Much of the power of Du Bois's
analysis, then, stems from his refusal to view these moments as being
discrete. Instead, he brings together U.S. history (Reconstruction), the
histories of European and U.S. imperialism (1884 and 1898), and European history (World War I) as a single history of waves of whiteness and
decolonization (or democratization) that places special emphasis on the
abuse of democracy by the United States in Latin America and the Caribbean. It is as if Du Bois is suggesting that there exists complicity between
conventional historical categories and antidemocratic rule, so that the first
step toward decolonization is to reconceive history. Indeed, the "darker
world that watches" demands decolonization. In sum, if Du Bois's writings
in the 1910s and 1920s cannot be termed an anti-imperial encyclopedia,
which would imply the production of objective and dispassionate knowledge, it is because Du Bois employs their encyclopedic scope in order to
create an anti-imperial agenda around three defining events of his age. Du
Bois portrays these events as part of a larger history of waves of whiteness
and decolonization in which he lays bare the contradictions of the white
capitalist powers in order to make them more vulnerable to the coming
"fights for freedom" by the darker peoples. Du Bois uses each event to
confirm the centrality of race and imperialism to the history of the modern
world, but also to clarify their changing features under new circumstances
and to galvanize himself and his readers in a renewed commitment to
remedying oppression along the global color line. It is this sense of periodization that defines histories of decolonization—each moment is saturated
in the past and presages the future.

DECOLONIZING MESSIANISM IN *DARK PRINCESS*: DU BOIS'S WORLD ROMANCE, WORLD MOVEMENT, WORLD DEMOCRACY, AND WORLD SALVATION

Following World War I, Du Bois continued to update discourses of sentimentalism in order to build on the historical legacy of the antislavery movement and redirect its momentum against the new imperialisms through
discourses of hemispheric and diasporic citizenship (see the analysis of Du
Bois's 1919 reports on the Pan-African Conference in chapter 1). *Dark*

Princess: A Romance (1928) is Du Bois's most extensive retooling of sentimental melodrama to serve the purpose of constructing a global anticolonial movement, and this retooling occurs in large part through his use
of the term *romance*. Reviewers of *Dark Princess* recognized that Du Bois
was writing in the mode of sentimental melodrama or romance, which they
coded in negative terms. Tess Slesinger wrote in the *New York Post* of May 12,
1928, "Occasionally the very real problems rouse our indignant sympathy.
But the truth is obscured by sentimental melodrama, in which Mr. Du Bois
himself seems to find a consoling ration of sour grapes." Slesinger apparently found fault with "sentimental melodrama" because Du Bois used the
form to express "sour grapes," or, more charitably, to formulate a social
critique. Robert O. Ballou, writing in the *Chicago News*, on May 9, 1928,
argued, on the contrary, that the novel was marred by "a too great romanticism."[106] Ballou is apparently referring to the "miraculous coincidences
and striking reversals" that comprise the texture of melodrama and depart
from realist conventions.[107] But when one brings together the two reviewers' opposed assessments—Slesinger's that the novel is too sour, and
Ballou's that it is too sweet—one realizes that the Du Boisian form of
romance, itself a version of sentimental melodrama, as Slesinger argues,
both utilizes and departs from realism. That dual movement between what
Du Bois termed the "Pain of the Bone" and the "Dream of the Spirit" is
precisely what one needs to understand in order to assess the powers and
limitations of his novel.[108]

Du Bois theorizes the novelistic form of *Dark Princess* through the term
romance, which didn't escape the stigma meted out to sentimental melodrama, if Ballou's review is any indication. But Du Bois's theorization of
romance—accorded prominence by the subtitle of the novel—helps one to
perceive how a deeper understanding of romance and sentimental melodrama is necessary to understand the novel's political aims. Du Bois begins
to theorize the form of romance prior to *Dark Princess* in his essay "Criteria
of Negro Art" (1926), which is perhaps best known for his famous but
widely misunderstood pronouncement, "All art is propaganda and ever
must be."[109] In this essay, the term *romance* lies at the very center of his
conception of "propaganda." Perceiving the romance-propaganda link allows one to understand the Du Boisian conception of propaganda as a
relatively open-ended exploration of the links between aesthetics and politics rather than as a dogmatic prescription for political art. Du Bois first
mentions romance in referring to the ability of black artists to look beyond

social stigma to transform their own group's history into art. Referring implicitly to the romance of Negro history, Du Bois writes of the moment "when as artists we face our own past as a people": "There has come to us . . . a realization of that past, of which for long years we have been ashamed, for which we have apologized. . . . Suddenly, this same past is taking on form, color and reality, and in a half shamefaced way we are beginning to be proud of it. We are remembering that the romance of the world did not die and lie forgotten in the Middle Age; that if you want romance to deal with you must have it here and now and in your own hands" ("CNA" 326). Here the "Middle Age" refers to a crucial period in the development of the form of the romance, long associated "with love, chivalry, adventure, the Arthurian 'golden age,' the exoticism and fancy of a distantly imagined past."[110] Consciously opposed to this model of the form, the Du Boisian romance insists on building on the promise of the Negro past in addressing the contemporary moment (the "here and now"), utilizing cultural materials that pertain to the black storyteller ("you must have it . . . in your own hands"). Contrary to Ballou, then, the Du Boisian romance does not turn away from history in a "too great romanticism," but rather engages with present political realities, with the "here and now."

Du Bois clarifies the stakes of the black-authored romance in the surprising beginning of this address. He frames his discussion of the form of the romance in this speech to the Chicago NAACP by first asking the members of his audience to imagine what they would want if they were "suddenly . . . full-fledged American citizens." Du Bois initially conjures up visions of wealth and power, only to argue that blacks "really want" something else: "Pushed aside as we have been in America, there has come to us . . . a vision of what the world could be if it were really a beautiful world" ("CNA" 325). The problem is that beauty, like democracy and freedom, is elusive, and the task at hand is to make it fully present for all people: "The world is full of it; and yet today the mass of human beings are choked away from it, and their lives distorted and made ugly. . . . Who shall right this well-nigh universal failing? Who shall let this world be beautiful?" ("CNA" 325–26). Du Bois suggests here that even if the NAACP were to achieve its goals of full citizenship for African Americans in the United States, its task would not be complete because "the mass of human beings" lack access to decent living conditions. Du Bois suggests that the romance as written by blacks must combine tales of the past with visions of a better, "splendid future," in which "all mankind" enjoys equal access to beauty, an access whose preconditions include full citizenship rights and socioeconomic stability ("CNA" 326). Here is an early conceptualization of the "world romance" of *Dark Princess* in which Du Bois links aesthetic pleasure and the political desire for full democracy across the global color line (*DP* 61).

Du Bois's conceptualization of romance as entailing an egalitarian politics grows out of a defining characteristic of the romance: its representation of a clash of ethical and political worldviews. For Jameson, the generic form of nineteenth-century romances such as Stendhal's *Le rouge et le noir* (*Red and Black*, 1830), Alessandro Manzoni's *I Promessi Sposi* (*The Betrothed*, 1825–27, 1840–42), and, I would add, *The Scarlet Letter* (1850) by Nathaniel Hawthorne, can be defined as combining three key "preconditions": "the category of worldness" (by which Jameson means the politically charged struggle between "higher and lower worlds"); "the ideologeme of good and evil felt as magical forces"; and "a salvational historicity." For Jameson, the "ultimate condition" of the romance is that it express an "antagonism" between two contradictory sociopolitical visions.[111] Indeed, in "Criteria of Negro Art," Du Bois theorizes the romance as contrasting a just and fully democratic world that has achieved beauty with the actually existing world, which is marred by a color line capitalism that exploits both the darker world and the white lower classes. Ballou's "miraculous coincidences and striking reversals," which he views as a defect, express the melodrama's ethical vision of "good and evil felt as magical forces," in Jameson's terms. In "Criteria of Negro Art," Du Bois theorizes the romance as recasting the black past as evidence of a "universal failing" by white civilization that can be remedied only by an ambitious, interracial coalition that will dismantle the global color line—the "coming unities" in *The Negro*. Because the Du Boisian romance is defined by its ethical commitment to full democracy, it deploys the mode of melodrama, which typically aims to expose "the underlying moral process of the world" through a "retrieval and staging of virtue through adversity and suffering."[112]

In its melodrama in the romance mode, *Dark Princess* attempts to create the conditions for the "coming unities" from an ethical perspective that synthesizes Marxism, Pan-Africanism, and radical democracy. In spearheading this synthesis, the eponymous princess takes on the leadership role that U.S. segregation denies to Josie in *Souls*: she heads a "great committee of darker peoples" that resembles the League Against Imperialism in its assembly of a broad range of colonized peoples (*DP* 16). Princess Kautilya also acts as the ethical and political mentor of Matthew Towns, who is em-

bittered over the racial discrimination that prevented him from complet-
ing medical school: the dean, a white southerner, refuses to allow Matthew
to register for obstetrics. As a result of such racial oppression, Matthew has
"no country" to call his own (*DP* 7). The princess enables Matthew to
acquire the cosmopolitan experience that shapes the novel's broad Pan-
Africanism: finding her loyalty to England challenged by radical Indian
exiles in London after the close of World War I, she returns to India and
throws herself into the independence movement. She then travels to Moscow in 1922, where she reads a "report . . . from America" on blacks. This
report is apparently a reference to Claude McKay's "Report on the Negro
Question," an address to the Fourth Congress of the Third Communist
International in the fall of 1922, in which he declared, "My race . . . belongs
to the most oppressed, exploited and suppressed section of the working
class of the world. The Third International stands for the emancipation of
all the workers of the world, regardless of race or color." McKay's report
condemned U.S. socialists and communists for failing "to face the Negro
question."[113] The "Report on the Negro Question," together with the Comintern's adoption of the "Theses on the Negro Question," constituted a
powerful black/Bolshevik argument that the particular struggles of blacks
and the colonized could best be viewed as universal struggles, but also that
any claim to universality should not be used to deny the specific character
of black struggles.

Following her trip to Moscow, the princess travels to Berlin, where she
founds an anti-imperialist committee linking "Pan-Africa" and "Pan-Asia"
and urges it to cooperate with African Americans (*DP* 20). After a chance
meeting with Matthew, she ushers him into the movement. She sends
Matthew back to the United States to investigate a "rumored uprising"
of African Americans and then repeatedly and miraculously appears to
rescue him and return him to his high ideals when he loses his bearings as a
Pullman porter based in New York and as a corrupt politician in Chicago
(*DP* 247).

Dark Princess's persistent metacommentary on romance, which builds
on Du Bois's theory of romance in "Criteria of Negro Art," demonstrates
how the form shapes the entire narrative, creating a momentum pushing
out from narrowly individual interests to sweepingly global, anticolonial
futures. Romance, conceived as Du Bois's vision, in 1926, of a fully egalitarian, "splendid future" to remedy the "universal failure" of the color line,
furnishes the architecture for the novel. The romance framework, like the

melodrama framework identified by Linda Williams that deploys several genres in a single text, organizes the realism of the first three parts of the novel and the epistolary form of the last part, deploying the Bildungs-roman (the novel of education) throughout to portray the spiritual and political education of both the African American Matthew Towns and Princess Kautilya of the fictional Bwodpur, India (Williams 27).[114] The princess and Matthew meet when Matthew punches a white American for forcing his company on the princess at a café in Berlin and is hustled into a cab with her. The princess later explains her reaction to this moment in a conversation with Matthew: "I had a curious sense of some great inner meaning to your act—some world movement. It seemed almost that the Powers of Heaven had bent to give me the knowledge which I was groping for" (*DP* 17). The princess's reading of Matthew's act serves to instruct readers in how to read *Dark Princess* as a "world romance" that por-trays the incipient "world movement" as a kind of "world salvation," one evident in the divine intervention that the princess senses.[115] In other words, Kautilya perceives Matthew's individual act as part of a broader story of the collective efforts of darker peoples to dismantle the global color line, in keeping with the Communist International's resolution on the "Black Question."

Matthew similarly views the punch—and his affection for the princess—in broader terms. While peeling potatoes in the kitchen of a ship traveling from Europe to the United States, Matthew realizes that "his sudden love for a woman far above his station was more than romance—it was a long-ing for action, breadth, helpfulness, great constructive deeds" (*DP* 42). Much like McKay's conceptualization of a particularized universal—the *black* working class—the Du Boisian romance makes two related moves in constructing the relationship between particular and universal conditions, moves that are implicit in Du Bois's 1926 formula of the "universal failing" of the color line: the princess's attempt to divine the "inner meaning" of Matthew's defiance of the color line and Matthew's conviction that his attraction to the princess is "more than romance." First, because the uni-versal is infused by the particular, it is possible to access the universal only through the particular. Therefore there are no pure or abstract universal human categories. Second, and as a logical consequence of the first move, it is only through historical processes that social actors can reach a rough approximation of universal equality. Du Bois refuses to regard the univer-sality of the ideals of the French and American revolutions as a fait accom-pli, seeing it instead as a promise for the future.

Indeed, the "world romance" of *Dark Princess* is portrayed as encompassing a series of radical movements following on the heals of widespread disillusionment on the part of the darker peoples after their largely unrewarded participation in World War I—the "world movement." Before exploring the full meanings of the novel's messianic expression of "world salvation" implicit in the princess's mention of "the Powers of Heaven," I want to discuss the various anticolonial world movements afoot in the 1920s that created the conditions for "world salvation." Both the "world movement" and the "world salvation" are crucial to the central purpose of Du Bois's "world romance," which is to hasten his readers toward that "splendid future" of an egalitarian world that will do away with the color line of race and empire as well as with class exploitation.

A number of world movements are woven into the fabric of Du Bois's romance of the darker world. First, the novel contains multiple references to anticolonial movements of "home rule" and independence, the most prominent among which is unfolding in India, as is evident in the biography of the Princess Kautilya. At the close of World War I, as a teenager, the princess identifies as English. But when she travels to England, having accepted a marriage offer from an Englishman, her political views rapidly change. As she tells Matthew, in England she encounters a radical movement among Indian exiles: "I had met a new India—fierce, young, insurgent souls irreverent toward royalty and white Europe, preaching independence and self-rule for India. They affronted and scared and yet attracted me.... I sensed in them revolution—the change long due in Asia" (*DP* 242).[116] At stake in her decision as to whether to go through with the marriage is nothing less than the political fate of India, she suggests: "Should India emerge with new freedom and self-determination as a country entirely separate in race, religion, and politics from Mother England? Or as one allied by interest and even intermarriage?" (*DP* 238). When her fiancé calls her a "darky" on the day of their engagement party, she takes up "the side of young India against England" and cuts off the engagement (*DP* 239, 244). She joins the *swaraj* (self-rule) and boycott campaigns of Mohandas Gandhi and travels across the Middle East, North Africa, and Asia, meeting the Chinese revolutionary Sun Yat-Sen in Peking (*DP* 246). Prior to writing *Dark Princess*, Du Bois had followed Gandhi's career and had even met him at the Universal Races Congress in London in 1911. In "Gandhi and India" (1922), Du Bois wrote in support of *swaraj* and the boycott led by Gandhi and supported by Du Bois's friend Lala Lajpat Rai.[117] Du Bois had met the Indian nationalist Rai during the years Rai lived in New York.

Rai was Du Bois's most personal connection to the Indian anticolonial cause. Shortly after the publication of *Dark Princess*, and after the death of Rai, Du Bois wrote about their friendship in a letter to one of the Indian nationalist newspapers Rai had founded: "It was my good fortune to know Lala Lajpat Rai while he was in exile in America during the great War. He was at my home and in my office and we were members of the same club. . . . I hope that . . . out of the blood of his martyrdom very soon a free colored nation will arise."[118] Born on January 28, 1865, Rai was raised in Punjab, trained as a lawyer, and actively participated in the Indian National Congress from 1888 to 1889 and from 1904 until his death in 1928.[119] He lived in exile in New York City from late November 1914 until the end of 1919.[120] During his exile he established the Indian Home Rule League of America in October 1917 and beginning in January 1918 edited the journal *Young India*. In 1919 he established the Indian Information Bureau. By 1919 he argued for "economic and social justice to all classes of the Indian people."[121] During the period that Du Bois knew him in New York, Rai was a prolific writer: he published a history of Indian nationalism, *Young India* (1916), *England's Debt to India* (1917), *The Political Future of India* (1919), and *The United States of America: A Hindu's Impressions and a Study* (1919).

Although some critics have adopted a skeptical view of Rai's evolving politics, rightly faulting him for his inattention to the plight of Indian and Asian migrant laborers in the United States and for his support of World War I, he remains an intriguing political figure, one who shares important concerns with Du Bois.[122] The question of Rai's support for World War I clarifies his growing disenchantment with British colonialism. The shared support of Du Bois and Rai for their respective countries' war efforts was premised on their hope that black and Indian participation in World War I would lead to black civil rights and Indian self-government.[123] However, they were both sorely disappointed in their hopes that World War I would enhance the struggles of blacks and Indians for civil rights and self-rule and used that disappointment to argue for a more radical rejection of British and U.S. imperialism.[124] Equally important, Rai was one of the models for the princess: as I will show, their political views are strikingly similar in certain respects even if their views did differ in other ways. Moreover, Rai read the manuscript of *Dark Princess*, instructing Du Bois on Indian culture and history.[125]

On the question of anticolonialism, Rai differed from Du Bois and the character of Princess Kautilya—who represented "the only hope of inde-

pendence in Bwodpur"—in that he argued for home rule, not independence (*DP* 243).[126] Following World War I, Rai still believed that Indians
would "gladly remain in the Empire, if permitted to do so on terms of self-
respect and honor."[127] But even as he held open the hope for a reform of
the empire, he insisted that the empire accommodate Indians' demands for
self-rule: "The world cannot be safe for democracy unless India is self-
governed."[128] So Rai's advocacy of home rule was a pragmatic political
move designed to secure Indian self-governance under the prevailing political conditions.

As much as scholars today may champion those who called for full
independence, there is no disputing the fact that Rai had earned the confidence of the Indian National Congress after he returned to India from exile
in 1919. Two events that occurred in 1919 shaped Indian nationalism as
much as the antiblack riots of the Red Summer of 1919 shaped New Negroes in the United States and the race riots in Britain the same year
influenced African exiles there: the passage of the Rowlatt Acts (or "Black
Bills") in February and the Amritsar Massacre of April 13, in which British
troops fired on a crowd of 10,000 demonstrators protesting the Rowlatt
Acts' suppression of activism as subversion, killing 379 and wounding
1,200.[129] The Rowlatt Acts made permanent the repressive Defense of India
Act of 1915, extending the state of (colonial) exception that further stripped
Indians of their rights. Similar to the state of exception that besieged the
United States following 9/11, the Rowlatt Acts permitted trials without
juries and the imprisonment of suspects without trial. The Amritsar Massacre dealt a serious blow to the politics of accommodation of the British
colonial regime. Rai was elected to preside over the special session of the
Indian National Congress in July 1920 that served as the springboard for
the noncooperation movement. He advocated the boycott of government-
sponsored councils and participated in Gandhi's noncooperation movement. Rai was imprisoned from 1921 through 1923 under the provisions of
the Seditious Meetings Act. Rai's commitment to Indian self-rule is the key
to his career: Rai led a campaign of noncooperation in protest against the
British colonial Simon Commission in November 1927, which sought to
establish an Indian constitution without Indian participation. During a
mass demonstration against the commission in late 1928, Rai died of heart
failure after he was assaulted by police.[130]

Rai's activist career and martyrdom on behalf of Indian nationalism
would have been sufficient to draw Du Bois's attention, but Rai also per-

sistently spoke in solidarity with other groups. As many have pointed out, the politics of alliance are fraught with perils: *Dark Princess*, for instance, constructs an alliance of the darker peoples at the expense of falling into orientalist representations of India.[131] But to claim an alliance with other racially oppressed and colonized groups has three advantages: first, it situates a given nationalism's claims within the broader perspective of the claims for rights by other groups; second, it constructs the particular demands for rights by various darker peoples as constituting in the aggregate a universal, world-historical opportunity to fulfill the Enlightenment revolutions' ideals (or to change the meaning of revolution, as in the case of communism); and third, it exposes anticolonialists to ideas and strategies from other political contexts that may help them in their own struggles.

Rai's *Unhappy India* (1928), an extended critique of Katherine Mayo's defense of British imperialism in *Mother India* (1927), demonstrates some of the benefits of expressions of solidarity with other anticolonial movements. In his introduction, Rai points out that Mayo was the author of *The Isles of Fear: The Truth about the Philippines* (1925), which rationalized the continuation of U.S. imperial rule in the Philippines. Lionel Curtis, a British imperialist hardliner, wrote a foreword to the English edition of *The Isles of Fear*, calling for a system of neocolonialism in India modeled after the Jones Law in the United States (1916), which established a Philippine governor responsible to the U.S. president. Curtis also sought to counter Indian nationalists, who reportedly made U.S. policy in the Philippines a staple of their "propaganda" against British imperialism in India.[132] By taking on Mayo and Curtis together, Rai exposes the ways in which an apology for imperialism in one country can serve to bolster imperialism in another, providing an implicit, yet powerful rationale for anticolonial coalitions.

In the two chapters entitled "Less than the Pariah," Rai again takes on the U.S. empire, but this time via its domestic racial politics. His aim is to underscore the hypocrisy of Mayo's declaration that Indians are unfit for self-rule in the face of the U.S. denial of democracy to racial minorities. Drawing on accounts published in Du Bois's *Crisis*, and quoting Du Bois directly, Rai denounces the practice of lynching and the antiblack riots of East St. Louis of 1917, arguing that they contradict claims of white "moral superiority" (*UI* 118–19, 122). In an argument that resembles that of Du Bois's *Darkwater*, Rai goes on to link the denial of rights to "Red Indians" and blacks in the United States to the outrages of imperialism in various countries in Africa. His critique of imperialism as a "world menace" implicitly calls for a transnational anticolonial alliance to bring it to a halt.[133] In sum, Rai's long activist career in support of Indian home rule, his interest in the "black question," and his astute denunciations of British and U.S. imperialism made him an important interlocutor for Du Bois and a fitting model for the princess.

Dark Princess portrayed and was energized by a second world movement: the Communist International's ongoing efforts to tap into the energies of African American and anticolonial radical organizing. For African Americans of the 1920s, "ethnic nationalism and internationalism were not mutually exclusive," as we have seen in the case of McKay, and indeed, black nationalisms and communist internationalisms transformed one another.[134] For his part, while writing *Dark Princess* Du Bois took his first tour of the Soviet Union.[135] He had recognized the Communist International's promise on questions of racial oppression and anticolonialism; indeed, by 1925 the Soviet Union had followed through on its various reports on imperialism and racism by establishing a university for the training of African and Asian revolutionaries.[136] In the United States the Marxist African Blood Brotherhood (ABB) was founded in 1919 by Cyril Briggs of Nevis Island, Richard B. Moore of Barbados, and W. A. Domingo of Jamaica. In the early 1920s, Otto Huiswood of Surinam and Harry Haywood also joined the group, as did McKay.[137] In 1925 the ABB merged into the Communist Party.[138]

Like African American radical groups, Indian nationalists gravitated toward the Soviet Union in the 1920s. The importance of Indian revolutionary exiles to the Indian nationalist movement goes far in explaining the Bolshevik sympathies of Matthew and Kautilya. M. N. Roy, the most prominent communist among Indian nationalists, an important and critical participant in the Comintern congresses of the 1920s and one of the founders of the Mexican Communist Party, traveled the routes among India, Europe, and the Americas that make *Dark Princess* so exhilarating. Roy worked with an Indian Revolutionary Committee in Berlin that was linked to the Gadar Party from 1914 to 1916. Founded in 1913 and operating out of San Francisco, California, where it published the Hindi language newsaper *Ghadr* from 1913 to 1917, the Gadar Party "attempted to coordinate efforts with Indian nationals in Berlin to use German support to send arms and ammunition to assist independence struggles at home."[139] Although Matthew and Kautilya do not join any communist party, they are linked to the communist cause on numerous occasions. As we have seen, the princess credits the Communist International of 1922 with sparking her interest in the struggles of African Americans. And while working as a Pullman porter, Matthew is accused by his supervisors of holding Bolshevik sympathies. Indeed, one official warns him to keep out of the union and to stay away from "those radicals and Bolsheviks" (*DP* 48). Similarly, in late 1921, Du Bois wrote that some attendees of the Belgian phase of the Pan-African Congress of that year called him a Bolshevist when he read the resolutions adopted by the congress in London.[140]

The council of darker peoples in *Dark Princess*, with all its flaws, can be viewed as taking part in a third world movement: the council is both a fictional embodiment of the various Pan-Africanist movements and a critique of them. Du Bois attended the very first Pan-African Congress in London in 1900, planned and convened by the Trinidadian Henry Sylvester Williams, and wrote its famous address, "To the Nations of the World," in which he proclaimed, "The problem of the twentieth century is the problem of the color line."[141] Du Bois also played a prominent role in the Universal Races Congress of 1911 (which Gandhi attended) and in the Pan-African congresses of 1919 (Paris), 1921 (London, Brussels, and Paris), 1923 (London and Lisbon), and 1927 (New York). These congresses were ideologically limited because of the conservative views of their elite black leadership and therefore could not serve as a vehicle for Du Bois's more radical, socialist ideas, as George Fredrickson has argued.[142] More specifically, the Pan-African congresses called for self-rule but not for complete independence partly because of the power of Francophone Africans like Blaise Diagne, who, as Du Bois pointed out, held positions of power in colonial governments.[143] Because the official pronouncements of the Pan-African congresses were the product of a collective process and not simply the views of Du Bois, they eschewed socialism, communism, and anticolonial revolution.

Du Bois's bitter experience with the elitism of some of the attendees of the Pan-African conferences shapes his representation of similar organizations in *Dark Princess*. At the dinner of "the great committee of darker peoples" to which Kautilya invites Matthew after their chance encounter, there is certainly little romanticization of the meeting between "Pan-Asia" and "Pan-Africa." The dinner meeting exposes how the Egyptian, Japanese, and Indian associates of the princess construct an antidemocratic aristocracy of the darker races that inverts, without overturning, European racism

and combines that racism with class-based exploitation. Matthew is sur-
prised to hear their elitist fervor for social hierarchy, but he recognizes it as
being all too familiar: "It started on lines so familiar to Matthew that he
had to shut his eyes and stare again at their swarthy faces: Superior races—
the right to rule—born to command—inferior breeds—the lower classes—
the rabble. How the Egyptian rolled off his tongue his contempt for the
'r-r-rabble'! How contemptuous was the young Indian of inferior races!"
(*DP* 24). Matthew's description of their elitism is apt: "Suddenly now there
loomed plain and clear the shadow of a color line within a color line, a
prejudice within a prejudice" (*DP* 22).[144] Even if "Pan-Africa belongs logi-
cally with Pan-Asia," as the princess asserts, this coalition and even its
constituent elements are extremely fragile and vulnerable to rifts, rivalries,
and hierarchies of all kinds.

On the other hand, the Pan-African congresses were tied in innumerable
ways to radical Pan-Asian and Pan-African anticolonial movements, some
of which were aligned with the Communist International. To take just one
example, Du Bois's Pan-Africanist movement had connections to the National Congress of British West Africa, the leading African nationalist organization in the 1920s, which called for free elections, land rights, and self-
determination.[145] Moreover, it was no mistake that Du Bois chose Paris for
the Pan-African congresses of 1919 and 1921. After World War I, many
Africans and Francophone West Indians settled in France—620,000 soldiers from the colonies had served France in World War I, and 370,000
African Americans fought in France.[146] These Africans and diasporic blacks
forged connections with the anticolonial movement of Indians in England
and with the Indo-Chinese in France.[147] Thus Pan-Asia and Pan-Africa did
come together among nationalist exile intellectuals in Paris, several of
whom penned strong critiques of Diagne and his ilk.

In Paris, Ho Chi Minh (then Nguyen Ai Quoc) joined the Communist
Party in 1920 and founded the Communist Union Intercoloniale, the first
association to unite intellectuals from the French colonies.[148] He published
its official organ, *Le Paria*, between 1922 and 1926. A string of African exiles
also published anticolonial periodicals in Paris during this period. Tovalou
Houénou, a Dahomeyan and French army veteran who joined the French
Communist Party and Marcus Garvey's United Negro Improvement Association (UNIA), founded the monthly journal *Les Continents*, the organ
of the Ligue universelle pour la defense de la race noire in 1924, "after he
had suffered humiliation and racial discrimination at the hands of white

Americans at a Montmartre café"—an incident strikingly similar to the one that thrusts Matthew and Kautilya together in Berlin.[149]

The Senegalese Lamine Senghor founded the Comité de la defense de la race nègre in 1927. Its organ was *La Voix des Nègres*, which changed in late 1927 to *La Race Nègre*.[150] *La Race Nègre* reported on the Indo-Chinese nationalists in Paris and on the West African Students' Union of London. Senghor represented the Comité at the conference of the League Against Imperialism in Brussels in 1927. The 1927 Brussels conference is germane to Du Bois's own "fidelity" (Badiou) to 1898 and its aftermaths because it links Pan-Africa and Pan-Asia to the Americas. This conference hosted a stunning array of delegates from several countries in Europe, as well as China, Indonesia, India, Japan, Korea, Palestine, Syria, Africa, and the West Indies. The delegates included Diagne; Sun Yat Sen of China; Julio Antonio Mella of Cuba and Angel Sotomayor of the Workers' Union of Cuba; Jawaharlal Nehru, the secretary of the Indian National Congress; Sen Katayama of Japan, who had attended the Fourth Congress of the Communist International in 1922 along with Claude McKay; F. Martínez of Mexico; Víctor Raúl Haya de la Torre of Perú; Manuel Ugarte of Puerto Rico; the novelist Upton Sinclair of the United States; and the black communist Richard Moore of Barbados, one of the founders of the ABB and a leader of the American Negro Labor Congress.[151] China and Mexico provided funding for the conference.[152] The Mexican government's support for the conference confirms Du Bois's sense that the Mexican Revolution was a watershed event in the history of global decolonization. For the purposes of historicizing Du Bois's choice of Berlin as a key site for representations of pan-colonial organizing in *Dark Princess*, I note that Willi Munzenberg, a publicist for the Comintern and the organizer of the conference of the League Against Imperialism, held an organizational meeting prior to the conference in February of 1926 in Berlin.[153]

Marcus Garvey was the figurehead for a fourth, allied world movement: a "populist Pan-Africanism" that at its peak boasted six million adherents among Africans and diasporic Africans in Europe and the Americas. In 1914 Garvey founded UNIA in Jamaica, then moved to New York City in 1916 and revived UNIA in 1917. UNIA's convention in 1920 attracted thousands from around the world. Garvey argued that an independent Africa would safeguard the human and civil rights of blacks in the diaspora.[154] While Du Bois's Garveylike character Perigua espoused violent resistance to white rule in the United States, in 1919 Garvey argued that it would be foolhardy for blacks to engage in violence in the United States.[155] Through Perigua's brief employment by the Ku Klux Klan, Du Bois does rightly point to Garvey's policy of a rapprochement with the KKK in order to fund an emigration scheme to Africa in 1922.[156] However, while in 1922 Garvey rejected domestic civil rights struggles as futile, by 1923 he changed his argument and called for a "complete emancipation of the race" both in the United States and in Africa.[157]

Finally, radical labor movements at times intersected with Pan-Africanist movements and at times appeared to be somewhat autonomous, like the Brotherhood of Sleeping Car Porters (BSCP), which was founded in 1925. Du Bois's choice to have Matthew begin his adventure in radical politics as a Pullman porter was a brave tribute to a labor movement that was still embattled on all sides in 1928.[158] By the 1920s, the Pullman Company was "the single largest employer of black labor in the United States, with roughly 12,000 black men (and a small number of black women) on its payroll by the end of World War I."[159] Since the largest white railroad brotherhoods excluded blacks until the 1950s and 1960s, black railway workers had to organize themselves separately. The Pullman Company was infamous for its aggressively antiunion stance: "In the 1920s, it instituted an elaborate system of surveillance, fired union activists, and maintained its own employee representation plan . . . which effectively undermined porters' independent unions."[160] Founded in 1925 and headed by A. Philip Randolph, the black socialist writer and coeditor of the *Messenger*, the BSCP called for increased wages and the abolition of tipping; the reduction of work hours; and the right of porters to have time to sleep during longer trips. The BSCP had to organize Pullman workers in the face of a larger black community that tended to look favorably on the Pullman Company for employing so many black workers and for its charitable contributions to black organizations. Indeed, when the Pullman Company "took out half-page advertisements in black newspapers denouncing the Brotherhood of Sleeping Car Porters, the editors of the Chicago *Defender*, the Chicago *Whip*, the St. Louis *Argus* and other black weeklies leapt to the corporation's defense."[161] By the late 1920s, the BSCP had earned the support of Du Bois and the NAACP, the Chicago Woman's Forum, and the Northern District Association of Colored Women but was still in the process of expanding the level of its support among blacks.[162] Following an alarming decline in support after 1929, the BSCP gained recognition in 1935 and a contract two years later.[163]

Dark Princess is "more than a romance," then, in that it is permeated by references to these myriad political movements and explores the consequences of their aims and shortcomings through Matthew's travails as an exile, a Pullman porter, a politician in Chicago, and a construction worker. Indeed, according to Bakhtin, the novel is the literary genre best suited to establishing "a living contact with unfinished, still evolving contemporary reality."[164] How do the anticolonial world movements relate to representations of a messianic "world salvation" in *Black Princess*? The education of Matthew and Kautilya in the Bildungsroman is simultaneously their *education within* these movements and their efforts to engage in an *education of* those movements—a critique of them—in a great "dream of the emancipation of the darker races" (*DP* 102). This dream emerges in its full outlines only in its relationship to expressions of messianism in the text.

The princess attributes to the intervention of a higher power her sensation that Matthew's attack on the rude white American has inaugurated a world movement: "The Powers of Heaven had bent to give me the knowledge which I was groping for. " (*DP* 17). This reference to the heavenly origins of her epiphany signals that this dream of the emancipation of the darker peoples contains religious dimensions. Indeed, as the princess and Matthew become acquainted while drinking tea in the *Tiergarten*, she tells Matthew that while viewing an exhibition of new paintings at the Palace of Berlin she was particularly interested in one painting, "a weird massing of black shepherds and a star": "All the time I was thinking absently of Black America"; the painting "intensified and stirred my thoughts" (*DP* 17). The princess doesn't describe the painting in enough detail to explain exactly how it inspired her to think about African Americans, but the bare-bones description offers some tantalizing clues. By portraying black shepherds who perceive the sign of the coming of the Messiah, the painting picks up Du Bois's central theme in *Souls* of the "second-sight" of black folk, their enhanced powers of perception brought about by their "double-consciousness" that stems from being both "American" and "Negro." *Darkwater* develops the theme of the enhanced perception of African Americans by extending it to the world's colonized peoples with the phrase, "the darker world that watches." In the painting's messianic image, the representation of the coming of the Messiah doesn't inspire the princess as much as the suggestion that *African Americans* will *perceive* the Messiah's arrival (the princess associates the black shepherds with the "Negro Question" that she had explored in Moscow).

Indeed, the painting can be read as a religious allegory of the Communist International's assertion that black Americans constituted a political vanguard. The "Theses on the Negro Question" adopted by the Fourth Congress of the Third Communist International (1922) argues that African Americans' "spirit of revolt," together with "the post-war industrialization of blacks in the North," places them "in the vanguard of the struggle for black liberation."[165] The "Theses on the Negro Question" followed through on McKay's characterization of blacks as the "most oppressed, exploited and suppressed section of the working class of the world" by arguing, "The black question has become an integral part of the world revolution."[166] The resolution sounds strikingly similar to Du Bois's *Darkwater* and provides a blueprint for *Dark Princess* in its conceptualization of the multiple struggles against imperialism as a sort of united front. Even as it points to the importance of black struggles, the "Theses on the Negro Question" insists that black oppression takes place in the context of an epic, global struggle between capitalists and imperialists on the one hand and workers and colonized peoples on the other:

> The Communist International must show the black people that they are not the only ones to suffer capitalist and imperialist oppression; that the workers and peasants of Europe, Asia and America are also victims of imperialism; that the black struggle against imperialism is not the struggle of any one single people, but of all the peoples of the world; that in India and China, in Persia and Turkey, in Egypt and Morocco, the oppressed non-white peoples of the colonies are heroically fighting their imperialist exploiters; that these peoples are rising against the same evils, i.e. against racial oppression, inequality and exploitation, and are fighting for the same ends—political, economic and social emancipation and equality.[167]

This passage strikes a somewhat patronizing note in its insistence that the Communist International must demonstrate to black people the commonality among various oppressions, and it insists on a universality that flattens out historical differences among many different groups. However, by accepting McKay's argument concerning the centrality of blacks to the Marxist struggle, it acknowledges the importance of a pan-colonial coalition. Moreover, it represents a secular blueprint for the princess's suggestion that blacks are the first to perceive the messianic sign of the world movement as world salvation. By implicitly linking black anticolonialism to world salvation, the princess's analysis of the painting is an illustration of what Wilson Moses has termed "racial messianism," or the belief in the "redemptive mission of the black race."[168] Moses's term, however, doesn't fully capture the meaning of the painting. When viewing the painting at the museum, the princess embodies the "darker world that watches," in this case a darker world that is able to perceive the "second sight" of African Americans/black shepherds. Thus one could more properly term the messianism of *Dark Princess* a *decolonizing messianism* because it constructs an alliance of darker peoples against the global color line while also criticizing the hierarchies of power within the darker nations.

Later, in an implicit reference to the painting she had viewed in Berlin, the princess says, "I have started to fight for the dark and oppressed peoples of the world; now suddenly I have seen a light. A light which illumines the mass of men and not simply its rulers, white and yellow and black" (*DP* 34). In an initial reading, one could argue that the princess' guiding star is democracy as opposed to aristocracy and self-rule by the masses instead of self-rule by a colonial elite. She hopes to travel to the United States to explore the possibility that African Americans could enact this democratic model of rule. These two allusions to the painting bring together the princess's commitment to exploring the Comintern's view that black Americans are the vanguard of racially oppressed and colonized peoples, her interest in Matthew as a representative of black Americans, and her new, life-transforming messianic worldview.

When we read the star as also signaling the onset of a messianic age, the image takes on an even more radical political meaning, intelligible once we consider the study by Agamben of Paul's *Letter to the Romans*, the best analysis of the politics of messianism. Here the reader might object that decolonization and messianism are antithetical because messianism has long been associated with nihilism, "a life lived in deferral and delay."[169] However, Agamben has persuasively argued that one should overturn this association of messianism with a retreat from political concerns. Agamben argues that messianism serves as a sort of crossroads of the concerns of theology, philosophy, and legal theory.[170] According to Agamben, Paul defines messianism by the claim, "In the days of the Messiah the weak and unimportant things . . . prevail over those that the world considers strong and important."[171] This revolutionary state of affairs comes about via the messianic condition's "transformation of all juridical conditions."[172]

Dark Princess develops its program for overturning the existing legal order by addressing the princess's question during the meeting of the "the great committee of darker peoples" as to whether "the mass of the workers of the world can rule as well as be ruled"—here she is attempting to respond to the challenge of Bolshevism by exploring the possibilities of a radically democratic socialism (*DP* 16, 26). Matthew responds to the princess—and to the Egyptian's quip that no "art ever came from the *canaille* [riffraff]"—by arguing, "America is teaching the world one thing and only one thing of real value, and that is, that ability and capacity for culture is not the hereditary monopoly of a few but the widespread possibility for the majority of mankind if they only have a decent chance in life" (*DP* 26). Here Matthew restates Du Bois's argument in "Criteria of Negro Art" that the equal capacity of all peoples to produce beauty will emerge in full clarity only when all peoples enjoy equal opportunity.

There is a great deal at stake in Matthew's argument that U.S. democracy should promote equal opportunity for the "majority of mankind." First, he is implicitly calling on Europe and the United States to make good on the democratic promise of the political Enlightenment by granting independence to the darker peoples of the world before the darker peoples liberate themselves by violent means. Indeed, later in the narrative, in a letter to Matthew, Kautilya writes, "In 1952 the Dark World goes free—whether in Peace and fostering Friendship with all men, or in Blood and Storm—it is for Them—the Pale Masters of today—to say" (*DP* 297). Second, Matthew is advocating the decolonization of third world nationalist movements, the dismantling of their "color line within a color line, a prejudice within a prejudice" (*DP* 22). Combining these two calls would putatively transform the sham universalisms of the French and American revolutions and anti-colonial independence movements into a true universalism. *Dark Princess* uses messianic discourse to convey fervor for such a fully egalitarian future. In other words, the "dream of the emancipation of the darker races" encompasses both the anticolonial aims of national independence and the decolonizing aims of full equality and self-rule for all (*DP* 102).

Yet despite its close association with the ideal of full democracy for all and its related proximity to the pronouncements of the Communist International on the "Negro Question," the messianism of *Dark Princess* is more aspiration than attainment, more of a springboard or "protopolitical act" (in Jameson's terms) than the realization of some fully egalitarian framework for identity.[173] As Agamben writes in his revisionary analysis of Paul's *Letter to the Romans*, "The universal is not for him [Paul] a transcendent principle from which to look at differences . . . but an operation that divides nominal divisions and renders them inoperative, only without ever reaching an ultimate ground."[174] In other words, Agamben calls for the messianic to be read as expressing a set of critiques of the status quo rather than as constructing some secure alternative. Messianism links the perspective of the "come non" (as if it were not), which entails a distancing from the status quo in order to reimagine it, to the "non ancora" (not yet) of a redemptive vision of the future.[175] The "come non" and the "non ancora" capture the Du Boisian romance's interest in "what the world could be if it were really a beautiful world," as Du Bois states in "Criteria of Negro Art" ("CNA" 325).

Agamben's analysis of the redemptive ideal of messianism together with Du Bois's explication of the utopian vision of the romance help to explain the significance of the three perspectival layers in the painting of the star witnessed by the black shepherds. First, within the frame of the painting itself, the shepherds (who initially embody black America to the princess) watch the star. Second, the princess observes the shepherds watching the star, as if she embodies the perspective of the "darker world that watches" oppression along the global color line. Finally, as the princess emphasizes, the star itself sheds light on the masses as well as on the rulers, suggesting that normally the masses are overlooked. This third messianic standpoint makes the suggestions that the star provides a measure of the world's distance from higher ideals of justice; that the masses will come to prevail over the rulers; and that the Messiah is more of an epistemology than a person or resting place. To follow Agamben, this epistemology works by exposing the ultimately spurious character of social divisions (such as that between rulers and masses). Therefore, messianism does not evade reality by constructing a fantasy world, but instead drenches reality in an otherworldly light, illuminating alternatives to the reigning order.[176] Indeed, as Agamben argues, messianism brings to crisis the legal/political order because it requires that "another world and another time must make themselves present in this world and time."[177]

"The African Roots of War" (1915) serves to clarify Du Bois's use of messianism as critique in *Dark Princess* because it shows how he repeatedly used messianic language to describe the full attainment of democracy by the world's darker peoples. Indeed, this essay is so compelling because it simultaneously draws on the narrative structure of melodrama and the logic of messianism. Du Bois argues that Europe's accelerated imperialism following the Berlin Conference of 1884 calls for a "theory of this new democratic despotism." Du Bois formulates a preliminary version of that theory as follows:

> Most philosophers see the ship of state launched on the broad, irresistible tide of democracy, with only delaying eddies here and there, others, looking closer, are more disturbed. Are we, they ask, reverting to aristocracy and despotism—the rule of might?. . . . It is this paradox which has confounded philanthropists, curiously betrayed the Socialists, and reconciled the Imperialists, and captains of industry to any amount of "Democracy." It is this paradox which allows in America the most rapid advance of democracy to go hand in hand in its very centers with increased aristocracy and hatred toward darker races, and which excuses and defends an inhumanity that does not shrink from the public burning of human beings. ("ARW" 644–45)

This essay—strikingly relevant to the post-9/11 political scene—enlists the mode of melodrama in that it equates the denial of democracy to the figure of a racially beset victim, in this case the African American victim of lynching, and thereby outlines an underlying ethical dilemma that must be resolved. For Du Bois this underlying ethical dilemma is that the color line is produced as a sort of colonial and racial state of exception, defined by the contradictions between the ideals of democracy and the practice of capitalism, imperialism, and "hatred toward darker races." Under this state of exception, the "rule of might" has displaced the rule of law, in fact, actually passes for the rule of law. Indeed, Agamben has defined the state of exception as "the original structure in which law encompasses living beings by means of its own suspension," creating "a threshold of indeterminacy between democracy and absolutism." Agamben demonstrates the corrosive force of the antidemocratic claim of "full powers" throughout the history of the ostensible democracies of Europe and the United States, ranging from the state of siege declared during the French Revolution, to the Weimar Republic's steady slide into Nazism, to the Bush administration's suspension of law following 9/11.[178]

Du Bois and Agamben concur that the state of exception results in the distortion and, ultimately, the destruction of democracy. But Du Bois's account differs from Agamben's in that it exposes the racial and imperial dimensions of the state of exception. Du Bois argues that white laborers provide the social cement for this colonial and racial state of exception: "The white workingman has been asked to share the spoils of exploiting 'chinks and niggers'" ("ARW" 645). In other words, a discourse of white racial superiority rationalizes the plundering of Pan-Asia and Pan-Africa. Du Bois's thesis is that World War I can be explained by the competition within the European empire for access to the labor and raw materials of Africa, Asia, and Latin America: "The present world war is, then, the result of jealousies engendered by the recent rise of armed national associations of labor and capital whose aim is the exploitation of the wealth of the world mainly outside the European circle of nations" ("ARW" 647). Du Bois argues that the only remedy for this global exploitation is an equally global democracy: "We shall not drive war from this world until we treat [black men] as free and equal citizens in a world-democracy of all races and nations" ("ARW" 648). Who will participate in this "great work" of establishing democracy across the globe? Du Bois mentions the "New China," the youths of India and Egypt, and finally, "the ten million black folk of the United States, now a problem, then a world salvation" ("ARW" 650). In arguing that black folk, now a "problem," will become a "world salvation," Du Bois makes an unmistakable allusion to messianism's defining formulation, Paul's pronouncement that the weak will prevail over the strong. Thus Du Bois turns the ethical clash characteristic of melodrama into a messianic discourse of the inevitability of emancipation for the darker peoples of the globe.

Du Bois further theorizes the post–World War I racial and imperial state of exception and its messianic critique and remedy in *Dark Princess*. When a black preacher visits him from the South, Matthew feels compelled to explain the downside of the luxury that abounds in New York City: "This squeezed middle white class is getting its luxuries and necessities by inflicting ignorance, slavery, poverty, and disease on the dark colonies of European and American imperialism. This is the New Poverty and the basis of armies, navies, and war in Nicaragua, the Balkans, Asia and Africa. Without this starvation and toil of our dark fellows, you and I could not enjoy this" (*DP* 64). This analysis would have been familiar to anyone who had read "The African Roots of War" or *Darkwater*. But here the critique of the consequences of what Du Bois called in the earlier essay "the rule of might" (or the state of exception in Agamben's terms of analysis) takes on added poignancy because Matthew speaks these words as he takes the minister on a cultural tour of New York City that includes visits to a museum, to Grand Central Station, and to a theater. All who are privileged enough to read *Dark Princess* are implicated in the unequal distribution of the world's wealth. As the minister remarks, "And what are we going to do about it? That's what gets me. We're in the mess. It's wrong—wrong. What can we do? I can't see the way at all" (*DP* 64). Here, as in "Criteria of Negro Art," Du Bois portrays artistic beauty and the pleasures of the modern city as distinctly bittersweet because they cannot be disentangled from a global political economy that produces beauty for some, but "starvation and toil" for many millions more.

The interest of Du Bois and Agamben in both the state of exception and messianism may puzzle readers because they initially seem to be opposed phenomena. After all, what similarities could there be between, on the one hand, the messianic vision of the weak prevailing over the strong and, on the other hand, the executive's suspension of the law in order to expand its control over the law—a scenario of the strong prevailing over the weak? Agamben suggests that both the messianic event and the state of exception suspend or even abolish existing law in order to reconstitute it, redefining both the legal order and sovereignty in the process. "The messianic," Agamben writes, "is not the destruction of the law, but . . . the inability to follow the law [*l'inseguibilità della legge*] and its deactivation."[179] The messianic replaces the existing legal order with the "law of faith," understood as a kind of "justice without law."[180] More specifically, Agamben argues that the term *pistis* in Paul, rendered as "faith" in translations, refers not only to "the unconditional abandonment to another power," but also to "a pact or a treaty of alliance among peoples" in ancient Greek and Roman civilizations, a model of law that creates greater freedom than the more restrictive model of law as norms and obligations.[181] In other words, messianic faith draws on the constitutive ambiguity and confusion between religion and law in order to create a new model of the social order. It is precisely such ambiguity that Du Bois invokes in the novel's "Envoy," in which he writes, "Which is really Truth—Fact or Fancy? the Dream of the Spirit or the Pain of the Bone?" (*DP* 312). Du Bois suggests that one need not choose between fantasies of a better future and the critique of what exists because the two are interwoven, and each gains force from the other.

The concept of faith plays a similarly central role in messianism's proposed reconstitution of the legal order in *Dark Princess*. In the "Chicago Politician" chapter—in which Matthew has lost his faith in the possibility of a future, better world—Matthew disappoints the Chinese man, a member of the princess's great council of darker peoples, when he shows that he has failed to share his friend's stated political aims of "Freedom, Emancipation, Uplift—union with all the dark and oppressed" (*DP* 135). When Matthew

explains that he believes in competition rather than egalitarianism—"Dog
eat dog is all I see"—the Chinese man responds, "The most hopeless of
deaths, is the death of Faith" (*DP* 136). Given the fact that as a politician
Matthew has the power to turn aspects of his world vision into reality, faith
can be viewed as a material force, one that is equally religious and social in
its consequences. The novel addresses the issue of faith again toward the
end of the same chapter, when Kautilya rescues Matthew for a second time,
remarking, "I have sought you, man of God, in the depths of hell, to bring
your dead faith back to the stars" (*DP* 210). Here again the princess refers to
the stars that orient the black shepherds of the painting in Berlin, announc-
ing the birth of the Messiah. Having suddenly realized the error of his ways
and regained his faith, Matthew immediately withdraws his cynical bid for
a seat in Congress.

Thus in *Dark Princess* messianism, entangled with the person of the
princess, affords Matthew an ethical and political reference point by which
to restore his path in life. The dual function of messianism is evident in the
structure of the narrative, which moves from social critique in the first
three chapters to the construction of a utopian future in the fourth. Finally,
the messianic future is figured in the conclusion of the novel, in which
Kautilya gives birth to the child Madhu, or Matthew, who by bringing
together Pan-Africa and Pan-Asia in his very body, is "Messenger and
Messiah to all the Darker Worlds!" (*DP* 311). But the child's birth and the
alliance and intermixture he embodies is less a conclusion than a springboard to future work. Here again, Agamben's writings on messianism are
instructive. According to Agamben, past events and messianic time exist in
a "field of tension in which the two times enter into the constellation that
the apostle calls *ho nyn kairós*, where the past (the completed) rediscovers
topicality and becomes incomplete and the present (the incomplete) acquires a sort of completion."[182] Therefore the messianic is "the present as a
demand of completion."[183] Similarly, the child of Kautilya and Matthew, as
"Messenger and Messiah," confronts readers with the implicit demand that
Dark Princess take on a life beyond the text itself, in the readers' implemen-
tation of its political vision.

Although many have taken the title character of *Dark Princess* as epitomizing Du Bois's alleged fascination with an aristocracy of color—and
there may be some truth in that view—there is another set of possible
reasons for the centrality of a princess in Du Bois's romance. The figure of
the princess simultaneously invokes (on a superficial level) and disallows

(on a deeper level) a reading of this novel as a fairy-tale fantasy, just as Du Bois invoked and transformed the romance of the "Middle Age" in "Criteria of Negro Art." This prohibition of a putatively escapist, fairy-tale version of romance takes place through an associative link between the princess and the nineteenth-century black Atlantic tradition of Ethiopianism, which took as its central text *Psalms* 68:31: "*Princes* shall come out of Egypt; Ethiopia shall soon stretch forth her hands unto God."[184] George Fredrickson has argued that there were two primary strands of Ethiopianism: one used by intellectuals and another consisting in the work of black folk theologians and of a series of ecclesiastical, social, and political movements.[185] The two strands both viewed blacks as "a chosen people with a special and distinctive destiny—a providential role similar to that of the Jews of the Old Testament," but the political results were sometimes very different: some used Ethiopianism to condemn slavery; some deployed it to advocate African American emigration to Africa, the Caribbean, or Central America; others sought to establish separate African churches; and still others sought to civilize Africans by converting them to Christianity.[186]

Du Bois updates and transforms this long, complicated tradition of Ethiopianism by playing on the biblical passage that it used as its conceptual foundation. By focusing on the Princess Kautilya from India rather than on "princes from Egypt," Du Bois implicitly criticizes the common African American argument that black Americans would occupy the vanguard of social change. Matthew states his belief in a version of the black vanguard argument in a letter to Kautilya in which he contemplates what St. Paul referred to as the *parousia*, or the "the full presence of the Messiah, which coincides with the Day of Wrath and the end of time":[187] "I can only hope that after America has raped this land of its abundant wealth, after Africa breaks its chains and Asia awakes from its long sleep, in the day when Europe is too weak to fight and scheme . . . that then the world may disintegrate and fall apart and thus from its manure, something new and fair may sprout and slowly begin to grow. . . . The center of this fight must be America, because in America is the center of the world's sin" (*DP* 284–285). Matthew argues that the U.S. empire, as "the center of the world's sin," must also be the center of decolonization, here figured as a sort of fertilizing and reseeding. Kautilya's response to this highly messianic vision of social change is to strip it of its provincialism by questioning Matthew's use of the term *center*: "America is not the center of the world's evil. That center today is Asia and Africa. In America is Power. . . . Only Asia and

Africa, in Asia and Africa, can break the power of America and Europe to throttle the world" (*DP* 285). Here Kautilya is simultaneously educating Matthew and criticizing various world movements that proclaimed the priority of African American political struggles, whether African American missionary Ethiopianists in the nineteenth century who sought to civilize Africa by Christianizing it or black communists in the twentieth century who viewed African Americans as the vanguard of the working classes. On a very practical level, the messianic discourse of Kautilya in this passage intervenes in these debates over the degree of centrality to be accorded to black movements within and outside the communist movement, implicitly disputing African American vanguard claims even while granting the importance of black America, in a deprovincialization of African American political discourse.

More broadly, *Dark Princess* works to qualify the assertions of the "Theses on the Negro Question" that anticolonial and African American struggles oppose the "same evils" and propose the "same ends." *Dark Princess* asserts differences of class that subdivide these various movements and historical differences that differentiate the Indian nationalism of the princess from Matthew's commitment to a radical movement led by African American workers. In "The Comintern Program and the Racial Problem" (1928), Andre Shiek, a white Hungarian communist exile who worked closely with black participants in the Communist International, implicitly endorses such historicizing moves in *Dark Princess* when he questions the tendency of the theses on "The Negro Question" to collapse the difference between what he calls the "colonial question" and the "Negro question":

> It is impermissible simply to identify racial oppression and exploitation with national-colonial oppression, . . . it is impermissible to deal with the racial under a clause on the national question. . . . For when we speak of the oppression of colonial or other subject nations, we have in mind . . . groups . . . striving towards an independent national existence. There is no question of these factors existing among the American Negroes, or say the Hungarian or Polish Jews. . . . Communists should not allow themselves to be caught in such snares. . . . they should demand not the right to national self-determination (self-determination has no practical meaning here!) but complete political and social equality.[188]

Much like Shiek, James Ford, one of the five African American delegates to the Sixth Congress, argued that class differences among African Americans meant that national self-determination could play into the hands of an exploitative black elite.[189] But my point is to show the ways in which *Dark Princess* both enthusiastically embraces the possibility of a Pan-African and Pan-Asian coalition and submits it to a thorough critique, a critique that was under way in the various world movements that give the novel much of its intrigue and political content.

In "The African Roots of War," *Darkwater*, and *Dark Princess*, Du Bois excelled at sketching a sweepingly global mapping of the color line as the main *aporia* of modern democracies. However, Du Bois's practical application of theories of decolonization in relation to independent African nations wasn't quite so successful. As Cedric Robinson has pointed out, Du Bois was exceptionally uncritical of Liberia in the 1920s, minimizing "the injustices perpetrated by the Liberian ruling class and its foreign collaborators."[190] Moreover, he defended the enslavement of indigenous Liberians by the Americo-Liberian elite in 1933 when the United States attempted to place Liberia in a political receivership through the League of Nations.[191] Robinson points out that Du Bois responded to the Liberian government's appeal to diasporic solidarity, lured by the possibility that it would subsidize a book he had proposed. This is the same self-promotion at the expense of principles that Du Bois engaged in when vying for a captaincy in military intelligence in June 1918. According to David Levering Lewis, Du Bois "struck a deal" with the War Department in which he would publicly support the war effort in return for being considered for the captaincy.[192] Du Bois later withdrew his application for the position. Such acts of blatant self-interest stand in stark contrast to Du Bois's association of the messianic ideal with selflessness. Is one left to conclude that because Du Bois's solidarity with the workers of the world fell by the wayside when lucrative benefits pertaining to the middle classes presented themselves, his messianic solidarity with workers in *Dark Princess* is self-delusion or, worse, armchair radicalism?

There are additional problems with the novel's discourses of solidarity. As Dora Ahmad has argued, at times *Dark Princess* presents an orientalist representation of "India as inscrutable, rife with contradiction, hyperspiritual, and bizarre."[193] This orientalism is woven into the fabric of the text's messianism in such a way as to be inseparable from it. There are at least two consequences of such orientalist messianism. First, Du Bois's messianism, a representation of the emancipation of the darker races, is both constituted and contradicted by an orientalist discourse that tends to

erase historical specificities. Second, while one should regard with suspicion orientalism's evacuation of historical content and penchant for the
exotic, it comes as part of the Ethiopianist/messianist historical narrative
of the return of African and Asian countries to greatness. Therefore, on the
one hand, messianism plays a central role in articulating the text's program
of decolonization, but, on the other hand, messianism is part of the problem that requires decolonization. I examine below how the figure of the
Santa de Cabora served as a vehicle for the decolonizing messianism of the
indigenous groups that lionized her, thereby transforming the intellectual's
role from catalyst of revolution to instrument of it. Perhaps the problem
with Du Bois's messianism is not so much messianism per se as the fact
that, being an intellectual with global visions and ambitions, he cannot
possibly bring the figure of the intellectual into close proximity with all of
the world movements he describes.

DECOLONIZING MESSIANISM AND
THE SANTA DE CABORA

As a transnational discourse deployed both in *latinoamericanismo* and
Pan-Africanism, anticolonial messianism figures decolonization through
tropes of Republican Motherhood. In conventional nationalist discourses,
Republican Motherhood relegates women to the role of producing national citizens, as Mary Louise Pratt has shown. But Martí and Du Bois
transform the trope of Republican Motherhood to figure transnational
revolutions. A focus on anticolonial messianism also serves to reveal the
ways in which Martí and Du Bois contest imperialist notions of progress by
developing circular rather than linear narratives of history.

In his speech "Madre América" ("Mother America," 1889), Martí pro-
phetically envisions the future of Latin America as a messianic "redemptive
march" of a pan-national, multiracial army uniting creoles, *mestizos*, *gau-
chos*, Indians, and blacks: "To your horses, all of America! And over plains
and mountains, with all the stars aflame, redemptive hoofbeats resound in
the night. The Mexican clergy are now talking to their Indians. With lances
held in their teeth, the Venezuelan Indians outdistance the naked run-
ner. The battered Chileans march together, arm in arm with the mestizos
from Peru. Wearing the Phrygian or liberty cap of the emancipated slave,
the Negroes go singing behind their blue banner."[194] Mother America embodies the common victimization of this geographically and racially di-

verse bunch. Martí figures Mother America as messiah-like, "born with thorns upon her brow and with words and the heart's blood flowing out through the badly torn gag like lava."[195] It is for this suffering mother, embodying a pan-national collectivity, that creoles, Indians, mestizos, and Negroes fight colonialism. Thus rather than deploying a Republican Mother who figures a racially homogeneous nation, Mother America embodies a racially heterogeneous and transnational anticolonial collectivity.

Similarly, in *Dark Princess* Du Bois names the child of Matthew Towns and Princess Kautilya Madhu, "Messiah and Messenger to all of the Darker Worlds!" (*DP* 311). Here, to be sure, Kautilya is the producer of citizens, but Madhu is a new kind of citizen, an Afro-Asian who embodies resistance to racial oppression and global colonialism.[196] Without ignoring the gender-based critique that Pratt and others have leveled against the discourse of Republican Motherhood, I want to call attention to the ways in which Martí and Du Bois transform it so as to reconfigure history as a struggle against oppression, discovering what Benjamin has termed "chips of Messianic time."[197] Such racial messianism in Martí and Du Bois registers in the realm of high culture the global proliferation of "prophetic rebellions" among groups threatened by European expansion, rebellions that constitute hitherto unexamined "coordinates of meaning" for the writers' decolonizing projects and mark a largely unwritten chapter in the history of anticolonialism.[198]

Several such messianic rebellions coalesced around the figure of Teresa Urrea, a mestiza who came to be known as the Santa de Cabora, after the name of the ranch were she lived in the early 1890s in Sonora and was subsequently celebrated as the "Mexican messiah," the "Chicana Mystic," and, perhaps more aptly, the "Queen of the Yaquis."[199] What I term the Santa de Cabora's "messianic text" can be considered part of that previously neglected body of Latin American women's writing that Pratt has called the "gender essay," a rich vein of women's texts obscured by the towering male author/heroes of the Latin American canon such as Martí.[200] My aim in shifting to a discussion of Urrea is to show how the "Santa de Cabora," when viewed as a messianic text collectively authored by both Urrea and her followers and collaborators, most of whom were impoverished Mayo and Yaqui Indians, constitutes an intercultural, cross-class alliance against Porfirian neocolonialism; in this sense her construction of broad-based political coalitions resembles the transnationalisms of Martí and Du Bois. However, unlike the anti-imperial messianist projects of Martí and Du Bois, the figure of the Santa de Cabora positions the intellectual as more tool than catalyst of revolution.[201]

The biography of Urrea is essential to reaching an understanding of how the figure of the Santa de Cabora can be read not so much as a multi-authored messianic text. Urrea, a mestiza of Mayo or Tehueco heritage born in 1873 in the village of Ocoroni in the state of Sinaloa, Mexico, studied under a *curandera*, or healer, for six years. Her recovery in 1889 from a thirteen-day epileptic coma was seen as a miraculous near-death experience by many, who believed her to be a saint, which Urrea herself denied. However, Urrea did claim that in addition to healing the sick, she could see divine apparitions, and she said her soul could travel. According to some witnesses, she had the power to predict future events.[202] In any event, the Santa de Cabora attracted between five thousand and fifteen thousand people to her healings—they were reported to be "miracle cures"—in Sonora and Arizona, and she was revered by a wide range of indigenous groups: the Yaquis and Mayos of Sonora, the Gusaves of Sin-aloa, and the Tarahumaras of Chihuahua.[203] Urrea denounced the govern-ment and the church, reportedly telling Indians, "God intended for you to have the lands."[204] According to Brianda Domecq, "[The ranch of] Cabora was transforming into a center of reunion not only for the ill, but perhaps also for political discontents who met one another there and exchanged opinions or made plans."[205] Urrea's followers, the Teresistas, engaged in two major armed rebellions against the government: that of the Tomochi Indians in late 1891 and that of the Mayos in 1892. As a result, the Díaz regime arrested Urrea and her father, sending them into exile in Nogales, Arizona, in 1892. There Urrea continued her cures, working in nearby Yaqui communities. Moving from Nogales first to El Paso, Texas, then to Solomonville, Arizona, and finally to Clifton, Arizona, Urrea collaborated with the Mexican journalist Lauro Aguirre in Arizona in urging the over-throw of Díaz in articles published in the newspaper *El Independiente*. Aguirre's so-called paper revolution called for a halt to political assassina-tions and Indian wars under Díaz and for agrarian reform, free speech, and the reestablishing of the communal possessions of indigenous commu-nities. In 1902 Urrea moved to Los Angeles, where she lived in Chicano neighborhoods and in 1903 joined a strike by electric trolley workers. This border-crossing political and labor activist died of tuberculosis on January 11, 1906, at the age of thirty-three.[206]

The major indigenous groups of Sonora and Sinaloa turned to this messianic figure of salvation in large part because their plight was dire indeed. In a double-barreled assault on indigenous groups in the 1880s and 1890s, the Díaz regime deployed what Michel Foucault has identified as the two basic forms of "biopower," or power over life: (1) biopolitical power, which shapes the life of the species by regulating whole populations—the body en masse; and (2) disciplinary power, which shapes the life of the individual body.[207] Biopolitical power targets the "species body," or the collective body, that serves as the basis for the processes of propagation and mortality as well as segregation and social ordering (*History* 139). Foucault argues that while biopolitical power portrays itself as benevolent in that it seeks to improve "the birth rate, the mortality rate, longevity and so on," racism provides a mechanism by which biopolitical power creates discrepancies in the life opportunities of differing groups (*"SMBD"* 243). Disciplinary power, by contrast, constructs the body as a machine, optimizing its capabilities to increase its usefulness and docility. Through the discipline of such critical social institutions as schools, the military, and factories, people tend to internalize social norms. I mention these two forms of biopower because they explain the strategies of the Mexican government's campaign against Sonoran Indians and serve to clarify the inventive responses to those strategies by Urrea herself and by the Indians who rallied around her, who worked symbiotically in attempting to make the Mexican government's deployment of biopower backfire.

The Díaz regime sought to pacify the Apaches, the Mayos, and the Yaquis in order to clear the way for the developing of infrastructure to support a revitalized economy in the north of Mexico. The plan was to establish rail lines, reinvigorate mines, and settle the river lands of the Yaqui and Mayo, who were opposed to white settlement.[208] The Mexican federal government and the Sonoran elite viewed indigenous groups as obstacles to settlement and economic development.[209] The federal and regional elites conspired to remove the indigenous obstacles through the biopolitical techniques of displacement, segregation, and extermination. An 1873 amendment to Sonora's state constitution deprived the Yaquis and Mayos of citizenship as long as they remained in their towns and *rancherías* rather than in *pueblos* approved by the state.[210] The Mexican government waged wars against the Yaqui and Mayo in the south, the Seri on the coast, and the Apaches in the north.[211] The so-called pacification of Indians during the Porfiriato coincided, as Domecq suggests, with the awarding of contracts to U.S. companies to establish infrastructure in the Mexican north.[212]

By taking away indigenous lands through legal and military means, the

Mexican government was deploying biopolitical power to force indigenous groups into joining the labor force and submitting to disciplinary power. Such job prospects were hardly enticing because debt peonage was the prevailing form of labor in Sonora.[213] Moreover, female Yaqui war prisoners were compelled to work as servants against their will, and in some particularly remote areas ranchers "hunted down escaping workers like runaway slaves."[214] The biopolitical power of "making live and letting die," in Foucault's succinct yet seemingly paradoxical phrase, emerges with greatest clarity in various deportation programs from the 1850s to the late 1880s (*"SMBD"* 247). In a genocidal strategy of separating men and women, the federal government deported Yaqui women and children to the deserts of northern border areas in the 1850s and 1860s. In Foucault's terms, the government was attempting to "let" an entire people die off by separating its men and women. In the late 1880s, a similar Mexican government program deported Yaquis to the sugarcane fields of Oaxaca and the henequen plantations of Yucatán and put them to work under the prevailing conditions of peonage.[215] The Mexican government here followed a policy of "making live" under the disciplinary conditions of a punishing labor regime that was just a step removed from slavery.

Why use Foucault's seemingly tortured phrasing of "making live and letting die" in seeking to understand the Mexican government's Indian policy? Some would question the ability of sociopolitical relationships to interfere in processes of living and dying, which are presumably natural and untouched by the workings of power. However, Foucault argues that power is not external to social relationships, but rather is wrapped up within them: "Relations of power are not in a position of exteriority with respect to other types of relationships (economic processes, knowledge relationships, sexual relations), but are immanent in the latter" (*History* 93). As a result of the immanent workings of power, power eludes the person who presumes to know.[216] More specifically, "power is tolerable only on condition that it mask a substantial part of itself. . . . Its success is proportional to its ability to hide its own mechanisms" (*History* 86). In the light of this analysis of power's tendency to camouflage itself, the phrase "making live and letting die" makes sense, and one can see how the workings of power are paradoxical for Foucault. The Mexican government can rationalize its Indian policy as enhancing life, claiming that the programs of deportation are necessary for the Yaquis' own protection (in the case of the Yaqui women and children, who would be especially vulnerable on the battlefields of the Indian wars), for the economic progress of the nation, and for the economic betterment of the Yaquis themselves. These arguments can serve to distract the public from the sinister workings of biopower, which "*make* live" (turn the very conditions of survival into a coercive extraction of labor power) and "let die" (create the conditions for genocide without having to engage in direct military action).

Urrea became the reluctant figurehead for an incipient pan-Indian movement in Mexico that attempted to assert indigenous land rights in the face of military and legal campaigns to strip Indians of rights: all the major Indian communities of northern Mexico invoked the Santa de Cabora to justify their messianic rebellions, the most prominent of which included the Mayo uprising in Jambiobampo in Sonora in August 1890; the Mayo attack on Navojoa in May 1892; the Tomóchic rebellion in September-October 1892; the protest of the slaughter at Tomóchic in Las Cruces, Chihuahua, in April 1893; and the Yaqui assault on the Nogales customshouse in August 1896.[217] Urrea's widespread appeal among diverse indigenous groups is especially significant in Mexican history because only recently have the linguistically and culturally diverse indigenous groups of Mexico developed a notion of pan-Indian identity or struggle.[218]

Moreover, Urrea is an anomalous version of nineteenth-century *indigenismo* in which the elite, literate figure does not so much stimulate reform from above as find herself swept up into it from below (and here she resembles Subcomandante Marcos of the Zapatistas of Chiapas). The Santa de Cabora should be viewed as a collectively authored messianic text because she was as much a creation of the Indians' beliefs as an instigator of their rebellions: although she actively supported Indian rebellions and worked to overturn the Díaz dictatorship, she always, as noted, refused to call herself a saint. The Santa de Cabora nevertheless served as the focal point of the indigenous rebels' passions and concerns, authorizing their cause with divine sanction. Through modes of expression that resemble yet move beyond the racial messianist tropes of Republican Motherhood in Martí and Du Bois, Urrea and her collaborators transform Republican Motherhood into a collective project of defending indigenous rights and attacking neocolonialism.

What I will call Urrea's collectively authored messianic text—consisting of her own speeches and writings, the Indian rebellions that invoked her as prophet, the paper revolution of her associate Aguirre, Heriberto Frías's novel *Tomóchic* (1892), and her own book entitled *Tomóchic*, written with

Aguirre—constitutes a counterculture to the neocolonial, racist regime of Díaz.[219] Yet even as the Santa de Cabora serves as a text composed by her followers, Urrea takes control of her gendered body as text. And although some might view Urrea's work as a curandera as exemplifying the ways in which women were confined to serving as caretakers of others, she used her fame as a healer to publicly criticize the Mexican government's Indian policies.

While the Santa de Cabora's biography reveals that she can be considered a figure that shares with Martí and Du Bois the discursive strategy of constructing intercultural alliances through racial messianism, her career shares a greater degree of commonality with the political project of Martí. Like the Indians of northern Mexico who made the Santa de Cabora their prophet, Martí recognized the injustices of the Díaz regime, which waged large-scale wars of Indian extermination and encouraged European immigration to whiten the national stock.[220] The fact that Martí published "Our America" (1891) both in New York and in Mexico in *El Partido Liberal*, the official newspaper of the Díaz government, shows that he aimed his polemic as much against tyrannies within Latin America as without. Indeed, in "Our America," Martí calls for Latin Americanist alliances among Latin American countries to counter the threat of "the giants with seven league boots" about to crush the majority underfoot, referring not only to Spanish and U.S. imperialism, but also to Latin American dictators such as Díaz who were backed by businessmen from the United States.[221] Even in the independent republics of Latin America such as Mexico, as Martí puts it, "the colony has continued to survive within the republic."[222] U.S. imperialism and Latin American tyranny, Martí's dual enemies in "Our America," converged in U.S. economic and military involvement in Mexican neocolonialism: the Texas Rangers collaborated with Díaz's troops to massacre a rebellious band of Urrea's followers in order to protect U.S. investments.[223] Thus, much like Martí and Du Bois, Urrea opposed racial oppression conditioned by transnational neocolonialism.[224] Like Martí, she worked as an activist in the "belly of the beast." Moreover, Urrea embodied "Our America" by promoting interracial alliances: like Helen Hunt Jackson's character Ramona, much admired by Martí, Urrea was an "arrogant mestiza" who chose to struggle on behalf of Indian rights.[225]

Domecq's novelized biography of Urrea, *La insólita historia de la Santa de Cabora* (*The Unusual Story of the Saint of Cabora*, 1990), exposes the

dual racial and gender oppression instituted by the Porfirian cult of scientific progress—a key rationalization of biopower—and sheds light on
the messianic discourses deployed by the indigenous groups that claimed
Urrea as their Santa.[226] Domecq illustrates the positivistic faith in scientific
progress in describing a historical document encountered by the narra-
tor/*investigadora* (researcher) of the novel, who sifts through historical
accounts of 1890s Mexico in researching a book on Urrea. The investigadora discovers a speech by Díaz in which he argues that his accomplishments of order and progress have done away with the need for miracles and
revolutionaries:

> The waitress came by and she asked for another coffee. . . . At the adjoining
> table, a man was reading the newspaper; the headline read: MEXICO IS NOT
> NOR WILL IT BE A BREEDING-GROUND FOR REVOLUTIONS. Díaz had
> said something similar . . . : "There are no revolutionaries in this country
> today for the simple reason that there are no reasons to have revolutions.
> The governmental project of peace and justice, order and law, of much
> administration and little politics, has produced abundant fruits of pros-
> perity. . . . I assure you that there would need to be a perverse miracle" (once
> again the miracle) "in order to perturb the peace that this country has
> enjoyed under my rule." (*IH* 29–30)

These fragments from the speeches of Díaz register positivism's link between progress, modernity, national formation, and a European-style rational and scientific mode of secular rule, a rule that is threatened by the
"miracles" of indigenous rebellion and the accompanying fervent, messianist belief that a more egalitarian social order is imminent. The narrator
calls attention to Diaz's anxious repetition that only a miracle would obstruct progress by interrupting his speech with the comment in parentheses. This interruption of the male dictator by the female narrator can be
read as even more irreverent given the contemporary political scene that
the passage invokes by citing the praise that is "still" meted out to Díaz by
historians (*IH* 29). Domecq's novel was published during the presidency of
Carlos Salinas de Gortari (1988–94), at a time when there was a concerted
effort by the distinctly antidemocratic government party the Partido Revolucionario Institucional (PRI), or the Institutional Revolutionary Party, to
refashion Díaz into a national hero despite his atrocious human rights
record.[227] The novel's critique of the present political scene is made possible by its very form, which alternates between the story of a present-day

historian's efforts to research the life of Urrea and a chronological recounting of Urrea's life. In light of the Díaz–Salinas continuity established by the
narrator, the novel's focus on miracles joins Mexico's search for political
alternatives in the 1990s era dominated by state neoliberalism and intran-
sigence in the face of neo-Zapatista demands for indigenous rights.

In the middle of a chapter in which the investigadora attempts to resolve
in her mind a series of disjointed and conflicting opinions and historical
documents on the Díaz regime and Teresa Urrea, the narrator arrives at an
epiphany in which the "miracles" and "magic" necessary to the Indians'
messianic rebellions obtain a revolutionary force: "Intuitively those pre-
cursors knew that in the hours of revolution it is not the sober, nor the
audacious, nor the brave, nor the wise who triumphs: it is the magician"
(IH 49). Here the use of magic to combat the cult of rationalism is viewed
as a way to thwart the seemingly inevitable march of Porfirian progress.
Indeed, Teresa's miracles are said to "mortally wound" the patriarchal
patrón Don Tomás Urrea, her illegitimate father, who despite "aligning
himself publicly with the antiporfiristas" subscribes to the Porfirian cult of
progress (IH 24, 188).[228]

Here the narrator critiques a cultural assumption that went unspoken in
the speeches by Díaz but was central to his ideological project: male dominance. A good deal of the investigadora's fascination with Urrea is the fact
that she is a woman with power in a male-centered society. At one point
Don Tomás remarks, "La niña tiene los pantalones" (the girl is the one
wearing the pants) (IH 197). At another point the narrator again remarks
on the threat that the Santa de Cabora presented to the hacendado Don
Tomás: "Marx had mistakenly argued that religion was the opium of the
people: it was in reality the oprobrium of husbands" (IH 188). Here the
narrator disputes the orthodox Marxist disdain for religion as a revolutionary force from the perspective of a critique of gender relations. Similarly, for Benjamin, religious belief is instrumental in devising a revolutionary consciousness, rather than an obstacle to it. For Benjamin, the task
of the historical materialist is to find the "chips of Messianic time" in the
past and present that reshape history into a struggle by the oppressed.[229]

Although the novel soundly criticizes Don Tomás for his womanizing
and initially patronizing treatment of his daughter Teresa, it also portrays
him as deftly negotiating a modus vivendi with the Mayos and Yaquis who
live on the rancho de Cabora. His attitude is in stark contrast to the prevailing tendency of mestizos to view Indians as obstacles to progress. Realizing
that he needs to make peace with his Indian employees, Don Tomás meets

with Aniseto Wichamea, a leader of the Yaquis on his ranch. Domecq has Wichamea speak frankly to his *patrón* about whites' campaigns of extermination against Indians during this period: "The boss is a *yori* [non-Indian]. The *yoris* take away our lands, kill our women, enslave our children. But the land belongs to us and our women and children are sacred; for that reason we also kill the '*torocoyoris*' and burn their ranches and kill their women and children. The Yaqui people don't want war; they want to live in peace; they want the whites to leave, to go away from their lands, to go away from its river, to go away from the sacred sierra of Bacatete" (*IH* 38). The fact that Don Tomás moved to Cabora in 1880 places their conversation squarely within the Cajeme era of Yaqui leadership: José María Leyva Cajeme, a famous Yaqui war leader, successfully sustained a "separate Yaqui state" during this period (1875–85).[230] He pushed into the forefront the ancient Yaqui custom of "the popular council, in which every Yaqui man and woman had equal participation"—he made it into "the major decision-making body and professed to abide by its consensus."[231] Cajeme also achieved success in forging an alliance with the Mayos: four Mayo municipalities swore their loyalty to him.[232] Indeed, Wichamea mentions that Cajeme is the leader of all the Yaquis but insists that he must answer to the Eight Pueblos, emphasizing the radical democracy that characterized Cajeme's leadership (*IH* 39). The next day Aniseto sets out with Don Tomás on a ten-day horse ride to the Eight Pueblos of the Valley of the Yaqui and engages in "three days of deliberations and spitting" (both allegedly rituals of the Yaqui) in a negotiation that on the third day involves Cajeme himself (*IH* 40). The exchange involves an agreement on the part of Don Tomás to protect the Indians on his ranch from persecution by the Mexican military and to trade food and goods with the Yaquis. In return, the Yaquis will not attack his ranch.

In addition to countering the positivist notion that indigenous groups constituted an obstacle to the progress of the Mexican nation—Don Tomás's efforts to establish a modus vivendi with Indians rather than trying to exterminate them—Domecq's novel demonstrates that Teresa Urrea and those who celebrated her as the Santa de Cabora countered biopower and the allied discourse of progress by exerting control over their collective bodies (in the case of the rebellious Indians), telling new stories about the meaning of the Santa de Cabora's body (Aguirre, the Yaquis, and the Mayos), and, in the case of Urrea, healing individual bodies and claiming unexpected powers for her own body and mind.

Urrea herself took control of her body in two ways, at least in Domecq's account of her life. First, at a time when Mexicans "of mixed heritage made it a point to deny their indigenous roots," she kept a close relationship to indigenous culture through her apprenticeship with Huila, the curandera.[233] More generally, Urrea occupied a liminal position that is truly betwixt and between class and racial positions in northern Mexico. Many mestizos in Sonora identified as white in order to claim a position on the highest tier of the race and class hierarchy. Teresa Urrea could pass for white, but she was constantly reminded of her humble origins. Although she embodied the Sonoran physical ideal in that she was quite tall at five feet, seven inches and had a "tez blanquíssima" (the whitest face), she also had "manos de vaquero" (cowboy hands) that were better suited to manual labor than to the domestic chores of a *señorita* in the *casa grande*.[234] Moreover, she was an illegitimate child, the daughter of Cayetana, a Tehueco Indian woman, who is of "carne morena" (brown skin) in Domecq's novel, and Don Tomás Urrea, from an important family of political and military leaders in northern Mexico.[235] She initially lived with her mother and with the predominantly Mayo and Yaqui laborers on her father's rancho, and only at age fifteen did she begin to live in her father's house.[236] Thus Teresa Urrea was culturally Indian even if visibly white. To say that Urrea was culturally Indian, however, does not mean that she claimed a Tehueco identity identical to that of her mother, but rather that she had immersed herself in the diverse indigenous languages and cultural practices at the rancho de Cabora: in Domecq's novel, she speaks Mayo as well as Spanish, and her mentor, the curandera Huila, speaks Yaqui (*IH* 94). Don Tomás best captures Teresa Urrea's mestiza identity when he says she is an "india blanca" (white Indian). In sum, like Martí's portrayal of Ramona (see chapter 1), Urrea chooses a mestiza identity that maintains active ties with indigenous culture (*IH* 117).

Second, Urrea transformed her body into what is believed by many to be an instrument of God's benevolence—a saint's body. Urrea, as noted, repeatedly denied being a saint, but her extended trances following her cataleptic coma, her claims to be able to predict the future, and her extraordinary healing abilities meant that her followers' conclusion that she was a saint was inevitable. The claim that she was a saint gave her name formidable cultural and political clout, which both Aguirre and indigenous groups used for political purposes, explaining Urrea's identity and aims in keeping with the narrative forms of melodrama and messianism.

In August 1890, Colonel Antonio Rincón witnessed a large gathering at

Jambiobampo, a settlement near Cabora. Some twelve hundred people had gathered to listen to a sixteen-year-old Mayo youth named Damián Quijano, who reported that he had been inspired by the Santa de Cabora. Mexican soldiers had joined the crowd, as General M. Carillo reported in a letter to his superiors, because they feared "that this [assembly] would hide some conspiracy that would disturb the public tranquility."[237] In his speech, Quijano, who would come to be known as "el santo niño de las visiones" (the boy-saint of visions), prophesied a flood that would "liberate all Indians of the oppressive yoke of the *yori*, of the traitorous and thieving white and of the servile mestizos. 'Then the *yori* will die, the white will swallow his own mud, and that which is not well with our gods will be lost in the waters and the Mayos of true faith will return to reign over the valleys and the mountains that have always belonged to them' " (*IH* 210).[238] Quijano attributed this prediction to several saints, including the Santa de Cabora, who, as he claimed in Domecq's retelling of the story, "in a dream had seen the future when the Mayos will return to be the owners of their lands" (*IH* 210). Quijano was a historical figure who had deep roots in indigenous resistance: his uncle, Cirilo Quijano, had fought with Cajeme.[239]

Colonel Rincón responded to Damián Quijano's speech by arresting him and nearly sixty other Mayos.[240] Aguirre recounted these events to Don Tomás and to Teresa Urrea. According to Aguirre, Colonel Rincón ostensibly sent two hundred Mayo prisoners to work in the mines of Baja California.[241] In Domecq's retelling of the story, Rincón ordered that they be drowned in the ocean en route (*IH* 213–14). When Urrea heard this story, she fainted and went into another trance—she literally feels and embodies history.[242] For the purposes of my argument, the significance of Quijano's messianic narrative about the Santa de Cabora is that it imagines an apocalypse that would overturn white rule over Indians. Similarly, according to Aguirre, Cruz Chávez, the leader of the rebels at Tomóchic in 1892, proclaimed, "It is our fate, so I have learned through revelations, to be the first victims of the new era that is coming to humanity and which will be prepared by the *niña de Cabora*."[243] While Quijano's vision constructs the Santa de Cabora as one among many prophets of the destruction of whites, Chávez reportedly prophesies a redemption of all of humanity spearheaded by the Santa de Cabora.

Aguirre respected the power of Teresa Urrea to move indigenous groups to engage in acts of revolt against the Díaz dictatorship so much that he not only shared his editorship of *El Independiente* with her, but placed her name above his and in larger print in the staff box on the second page of the newspaper. I will quote at length from Aguirre's remarkable narrative of Mexican history in *El Independiente* because it characterizes the postcolonial plight of Mexico as necessitating a messianic overturning of the juridicopolitical order. In the lead article, "5 de Mayo de 1862! ¡Glorias Perdidas!" (Cinco de Mayo of 1862! Lost Glories!), Aguirre writes,

> In modern times no people has struggled so much and with such heroism as the Mexican people. . . . [T]he Father of the Nation . . . sought at once to conquer the independence of the Nation, and to conquer human equality, and for that reason was the first to decree the liberty of the blacks and their entrance into the category of men. . . . Once independence was gained, the clergy and the military, . . . the eternal enemies of the equality and liberty of man, united in an inseparable consortium to spoil the struggles for independence and to take advantage of them, . . . as in the times of the Government of Spain.[244]

Commemorating Mexico's defeat of the French forces of Napoleon III, the Cinco de Mayo featured in the essay's title is Mexico's national holiday and the culmination of the legal and political transformations of *La Reforma*, which began in the mid-1850s to democratize and decolonize Mexico, deposing the dictator Antonio López de Santa Anna and stripping the military and the church of their power. The centerpiece of La Reforma was the Constitution of 1857, which abolished slavery and protected freedom of speech and of the press. "The father of the nation" Aguirre refers to is Benito Juárez, one of the masterminds of La Reforma and the president of Mexico from 1861 to 1872.

Aguirre moves from a narrative of La Reforma to the contemporary moment, arguing that Mexico under the Díaz dictatorship is in need of a second Reforma, but one that this time will be ushered in through divine intervention:

> Invoking peace, one can burn and kill, assassinate women and even children, as has been done during ten years to the unhappy children of the Yaquis and Mayos. . . . Will this last long? No. Because God watches over you, He who governs all the Universes—and without whose Will not even a leaf on a tree can move—will make your children awaken to duty, and upon awakening He will give them valor, abnegation and faith to sweep away even the embers of tyranny. . . . Have faith, beloved Patria, your days of sorrow will soon end, because the descendants of Hidalgo and Juárez have not died.

They only sleep. They will awaken, and when they awaken, *guay!* to the tyrants of cassock, saber, and mercantilism.[245]

Here Aguirre implicitly takes the resuscitation of Urrea and her channeling of divine power as a metaphor for the awakening of the Mexican people as a whole. In this account of Mexico's future, the melodrama of embattled virtue pitted against the dominion of evil is resolved through a messianic narrative of awakening. This awakening is both a future event and a repetition of the past events of the independence movement—Aguirre figures Mexicans as "the descendants of Hidalgo and Juárez," leaders who fought against Spanish colonialism and Mexican neocolonial dicatorship and foreign intervention. This passage portrays the messianic event that St. Paul termed *parousia*.[246] But in Aguirre, the fullness of time is achieved via a rerouting of history back to a period of the past that it will bring to completion (as in Du Bois and Martí), displacing despotic government with the rule of God, "who governs all the Universes." Here again is a representation of "the messianic event [as] above all . . . a crisis and radical transformation of the entire order of the law," but in this case there is an emphasis on a decolonizing transformation that overturns a juridicopolitical order that relies on racial distinctions.[247]

For Aguirre, the messianic event simultaneously brings to fruition the history of independence movements in Mexico and the "law" Jesus lived by and held up as a guide to behavior:

> The general law that must govern the relations of men . . . is the law of love, a law synthesized by the Savior and Teacher Jesus in these words: "Love your neighbor as you love yourself." That this law does not govern humanity . . . is a fact. . . . because there is no love nor is it possible that there can be love in the exploitation of man by man. . . . there is no love nor is it possible that there can be love in the distinctions and hatred among men as a result of distinctions of race, nationality, caste and religious or political ideas.[248]

It is this law of love—the sworn enemy of all social distinctions—that provides a key to understanding the continuity between Urrea's life as a healer and her reputation as the Santa de Cabora. As Urrea herself writes in an issue of *El Independiente*,

> I believe that by virtue of the law of love and justice, God listens to all of us and the speech by the most insignificant of his children that is elevated in the spirit towards Him He hears better than the mechanical speech by the

most powerful of beings; . . . I believe that Jesus is the Savior and Teacher in the sense that by following his teachings and above all his EXAMPLE we will walk according to the laws of the true and the good . . . and not in the sense that the merits of Jesus will save us, because that would not be correct.[249]

For someone who gained the fame of a "saint" through miraculous healings, this is a refreshingly modest and practical call to subordinate the professed *belief* in the Messiah to the need to follow his *example*. As in the case of *Dark Princess*, Urrea gives evidence of the radically interventionist character of messianism—its insistence on transforming the here and now rather than waiting for a distant future of redemption.

Decolonizing messianism in Martí, Du Bois, and the Santa de Cabora produces speculative thought that breaks with the tyranny of the "real," the tendency of thought to "asphyxiate" in a culture that is unable to "imagine anything other than what it is," to quote Jameson.[250] Indeed, decolonizing messianism breaks away from the contemporary discourses of social identity in the 1890s and 1920s, constructing potent, intercultural narratives of resistance. Decolonizing messianist narratives figure collaborative, egalitarian struggles by marginalized groups that cross divisions of ethnicity, language, and race. Decolonizing messianism therefore insists that intellectual work should not take place in a vacuum. Martí's revolutionary cross-class, cross-ethnic, and cross-national coalition building, Du Bois's Pan-Africanist conferences, and Urrea's collectively authored messianist text push the boundaries of conventional intellectual activity, turning the intellectual into an activist who dreams of bringing together disparate peoples but who also works assiduously to turn that dream into reality. Of all three "leaders," Urrea perhaps most unsettles notions of top-down leadership and "manda obedeciendo" (leads by obeying), in the words of Subcomandante Marcos: indigenous groups fashion her into a figure of a messianic overturning of the existing juridicopolitical order.[251] Messianism's imperative of overturning existing social relations therefore carries within it an overlooked corollary that requires all intellectuals to be activists and to subordinate their individual aspirations to the needs of a transnational coalition. Finally, decolonizing messianism builds on the tradition of sentimental, romantic racialism in its construction of a sympathetic response to the victims of race and empire. However, it moves beyond antislavery sentimentalism by foregrounding the agency of nonwhites in redressing wrongs to the subjects of empire and racially oppressed groups.

Three

TRANSNATIONALISMS AGAINST THE STATE: CONTESTING NEOCOLONIALISM IN THE HARLEM RENAISSANCE, CUBAN *NEGRISMO*, AND MEXICAN *INDIGENISMO*

In the mid-1920s, two special issues of the *Survey Graphic* appeared within one year of each other. The first and lesser known of the two was "Mexico: A Promise," which appeared in the May 1924 edition of the magazine. This issue announces an exuberant "New Mexico" emerging from the Mexican Revolution (1910–17). The contributors included pivotal figures in Latin American art, literature, politics, and social science, including the anthropologist Manuel Gamio, the Mexican secretary of education and essayist José Vasconcelos, the essayist Pedro Henríquez Ureña, the painter Diego Rivera, and the president of Mexico, Plutarco Calles. The U.S. intellectuals Carleton Beals, a leftist poet, novelist, historian, and journalist, and Katherine Anne Porter also contributed. This issue captures the postrevolutionary resurgence of pride in indigenous Mexican cultures, at a time of cultural foment that an editorial compares to the "Italian renaissance."[1] Did "Mexico: A Promise" serve as the model for Alain Locke's "Harlem: Mecca of the New Negro," which came out in the same journal just a year later?

In a move that implicitly acknowledged his familiarity with the 1924 *Survey Graphic* issue on Mexico, Locke includes, in his foreword to his own special issue, Mexico and the "Negro Renaissance" among an international array of "nascent movements of folk-expression and self-determination which are playing a creative part in the world to-day."[2] This chapter unravels the interrelations among three such movements in the Americas: the Harlem Renaissance, Cuban *negrismo*, or Afro-Cubanism, and Mexican *indigenismo*.

The Harlem Renaissance, Cuban negrismo, and Mexican indigenismo are rarely studied together because cultural critics have separated them according to distinct ethnic and national categories. But such limited frames fail to account for the transnational dimensions of these movements, evident in their shared institutional and discursive spaces, in their common use of primitivist discourses, which also cut across national lines, and in the broad alliances that artists and writers constructed among the poor and racially oppressed.[3] The hemispheric ties among 1920s nationalisms are occluded by the conventional accounts of these movements, which gather evidence of the linkages among them in a fragmented fashion.[4] Many scholars of U.S. American literature now know that an interest in African diasporic vernacular expression and music, particularly the blues and the *son*, was common to Nicolás Guillén, a founder of Cuban negrismo, and Langston Hughes, the leading poet of the New Negro movement. But few know that Cuba's *Revista de Avance* (1927–30) published the European and Cuban avant-gardes along with U.S. writers, including Hughes, H. L. Mencken, Eugene O'Neill, and Countee Cullen. Even fewer have heard that artists and intellectual currents also crossed freely between Mexico City and New York, particularly those associated with Boasian anthropology, and that the Harlem Renaissance shared its name with the contemporaneous Mexican Renaissance in the arts, which turned Indians into a national icon.[5] Such evidence of continuities among arts movements in Cuba, Mexico, and New York provides merely a slice of their converging interests (in shared publishing circles, for instance) and multiple collaborations.[6]

Once these multiple collaborations come into view, it is possible to construct a revisionary approach to 1920s culture that emphasizes the ways in which primitivisms and nationalisms meet on the contested terrains of neocolonialism. In part, this is the project of showing how the Harlem Renaissance "exceeded the bounds not only of Harlem, but also of the United States," to quote Eric Sundquist.[7] Their use of primitivist discourses reveals commonalities among these nationalisms. Chief among these commonalities are three kinds of cross-national cultural flows associated with the "primitive" groups that were in vogue in the 1920s. First, these 1920s nationalisms were movements organized around representations of putatively primitive marginalized groups that were vying for increased visibility and rights—self-determination, in the contemporary idiom—but lacked the ability to seize the state apparatus.[8] Second, the term *primitivism* is rooted in the history of colonialism: it is associated with the interest in supposedly primitive art objects acquired in colonial expeditions—an interest further stimulated by increased migrations of indigenous and African diasporic populations to urban centers in Europe and the Americas in the post–World War I era. Third, the use of primitivism as a frame for analysis has the additional advantage of suggesting that 1920s nationalisms adopt and adapt transnational discourses and stereotypes on nonwhite groups. Indeed, while Locke's term "folk-expression" suggests a static, locally rooted, and "traditional" cultural production, the equally vexed term *primitivism* has the virtue of suggesting a cosmopolitan engagement with culture.

To be sure, primitivism's defining project of rejecting aspects of European civilization in favor of the alleged characteristics of so-called primitive culture is fraught with perils, not the least of which is the tendency to define the primitive in an ahistorical manner, as many have argued. And there were important differences between ethnographic primitivisms (whites writing on nonwhites) and autoethnographic primitivisms (nonwhites writing about their own group). However, my emphasis on the transnational scope of primitivism allows me to engage in a different sort of analysis from that of scholars who have deployed primitivism to dismiss cultural texts as confined within stereotypical discourses, as when Henry Louis Gates Jr. asserts that the Harlem Renaissance is based on "the primitivistic defense of the racial self" and when another scholar condemns primitivism as a "fraud."[9] While developing critical perspectives on primitivism is undeniably important, at the same time one must explore what other scholars have called its "ideologically diverse" manifestations, and what Marianna Torgovnick has called its "rich history of alternative meanings."[10] In other words, my primary aim is to use primitivism as a broad frame for the analysis of cross-national cultural flows under the shadow of empire rather than as a term that solely denotes the limited horizons of stereotypes. Moreover, my approach traces the shifts in social scientific discourses of the primitive that set the conditions for uses of the term in cultural production.

By replacing the common disparaging notion of primitivism with a historically grounded analysis of primitivisms, one can arrive at a more nuanced account of the political projects of 1920s nationalist texts. Primitivist discourses in the post–World War I era fall into three broad categories: residual, dominant, and alternative.[11] Residual primitivist discourses conform to evolutionary notions that construct nonwhite peoples as racially inferior. Opposing the primitive to the civilized, residual primitivisms opt for the ways of the civilized, or Euro-American. In 1934, one of the foremost essayists on Mexican nationalism, Samuel Ramos, argued that Mexicans occupied a lower stage of civilization: "[Mexico], still being a very young country, wanted to jump to the heights of the older European civilizations in one bound, and then the conflict erupted between what one wants and what one can achieve."[12]

By contrast, dominant primitivist discourses oppose the primitive to the modern to point out the faults of the modern. These discourses often nostalgically long for the primitive as what European culture has left behind in the processes of modernization. Edward Sapir's "Culture, Genuine and Spurious" (1924) argues that "genuine culture" is more likely to be present at "a lower level of civilization" and is "inherently harmonious"— free from the class conflicts and geopolitical and social inequalities that for Roger Bartra are characteristic of a modernity more accurately termed "desmodernidad/desmadre" (roughly, a demodernized mess).[13]

While dominant primitivist discourses disavow sociopolitical relations by condensing them into broad historical stages (primitive versus modern in Sapir), alternative primitivist discourses construct more explicit articulations of racialist stereotypes that reveal the cultural production of social inequality and expose the workings of empire. Alternative primitivism contests the racial determinism of residual primitivism by simultaneously replaying and altering racial stereotypes through three key strategies. The use of parody calls our attention to the contested character of representations of race; the historicizing move describes the systemic production of racial and imperial inequalities; and the discourse of pride lays the foundations for alternative narratives of history.[14] In a 1924 report from Africa, W. E. B. Du Bois articulates the historicizing strategy by calling the reader's attention to the "other paths" followed by peoples termed primitive.[15] Thus if alternative primitivism shares dominant primitivism's idealization of "genuine culture," it differs by working through the social contradictions of capitalist modernity rather than by attempting to elude them through a reversion to the past. Moreover, as is implicit in Du Bois's reference to the "other [historical] paths" taken by Africans, alternative primitivism aspires to utilize its transnational perspective in order to realize antiracist and anticolonialist aims, as in Du Bois's texts *Darkwater* and *Dark Princess* (see chapter 2).

Indeed, the utility of alternative primitivist discourses must be assessed within the context of the "stretched out" character of social relations under neocolonial capitalism.[16] Following the devastation of European economies in World War I, the weakening foothold of European business interests in Latin America presented enhanced opportunities for U.S. business. As a result, by the 1920s U.S. investment in Latin America exceeded that of Europe for the first time.[17] But if the United States emerged as the dominant neocolonial power in Latin America in the 1920s, it did so unevenly, joining France, Germany, and Great Britain in attempting to repress labor and decrease wages so as to profit from the use of Latin American resources such as labor, land, and oil. At times these foreign neocolonial interests worked in concert with domestic forces of neocolonialism in Latin America.

The neocolonial regimes of Cuba and Mexico in the 1920s differed in their intensity, in the degree of control by the United States, and in their construction of racialized subjects. Neocolonialism in Cuba was to a great extent imposed from without: Cuba's sovereignty had been controlled by the United States from the ratification of the Platt Amendment in 1903. By contrast, the impetus for neocolonialism in Mexico developed from within the country itself, as the leaders of the politically triumphant Sonoran Dynasty (Presidents Alvaro Obregón and Plutarco Calles) sought to restimulate the economy following the devastation of the Revolution by favoring production for export, which sharply curtailed the land distribution and nationalization of resources that the Constitution of 1917 had set in motion.[18] These competing neocolonialisms in Latin America, in which domestic, European, and U.S. interests unevenly converge and diverge, demonstrate the shifting processes of exploitation and repression combated by decolonization movements.

Following World War I, the United States emerged as the leading neocolonial power in Cuba and Mexico as well as in other Caribbean countries. In an effort to reverse a postwar production surplus and recession and gain political influence abroad, U.S. State Department policymakers sought to promote foreign trade and investments.[19] In 1919, the National Bank of Commerce issued a programmatic statement: "For the first time in our history of a nation, the assurance of our continued prosperity rests with the future of our foreign trade. The period of our industrial isolation is as completely behind us as is the period of our political isolation. . . . We have surplus to sell" (*Platt* 182). This policy goal led to the greatest degree of collaboration between foreign policymakers and U.S. capital ever seen in U.S. history (*Platt* 185).

U.S. business interests actively promoted the repression of egalitarian movements in countries under U.S. neocolonial control. In Cuba, U.S. corporations bankrolled politicians who rigged elections and violently repressed organized labor, beginning with the presidency of Tomás Estrada Palma (1902–06) and culminating in the dictatorship of Gerardo Machado (1925–33).[20] Similarly, beginning in 1915, the United States occupied Haiti and repressed protests with military force.[21] And in Mexico, the threat of U.S. invasion postponed for over a decade the nationalization of oil as mandated by the Mexican Constitution.[22] In all of these cases, U.S. foreign policy served as a repressive tool of upper-class businessmen who benefited directly from underdevelopment: the lion's share of surplus value from the production of Cuban sugar and Mexican oil went to a U.S. business elite. In Cuba, for instance, U.S. businesses owned 22 percent of all land by 1926 (*Platt* 258).

In chronicling such exploitation and oppression abroad, writers like Hughes and Beals, both of whom wrote texts constructing black diasporic peoples as primitives, allowed U.S. citizens to perceive the processes by which neocolonialism deprived Latin Americans of their citizenship rights. In so doing, the two writers devised discourses of hemispheric citizenship in which leftist U.S. intellectuals traveling to Latin America took responsibility for the consequences of neocolonialism (for a more extended definition of discourses of hemispheric citizenship, see the introduction).[23] My argument, then, is that however one assesses the extent to which a particular primitivist representation is caught within stereotypes or exposes the conditions of their production, primitivism provides a useful frame for the analysis of 1920s nationalism: the contradictory politics of primitivism open a window onto conflicts over U.S. neocolonialism in Latin America.

In the light of such neocolonial conditions and (contradictory) transnational resistance efforts, the notion of self-contained national histories and literatures must be revised because they offer merely "a slice of a vaster reality," in Antonio Cornejo Polar's phrase.[24] A comparative, transnational approach to 1920s nationalisms in the United States, Mexico, and Cuba thus unsettles the sedimented, ethnically and nationally based histories of these movements, allowing for a more nuanced account of the politics of primitivist discourses in relation to their representation of processes of exploitation and oppression both nationally and in a broader frame of competing neocolonialisms. By comparing nationalist discourses, which in their official, elite, and popular versions do not align with the varieties of primitivist discourses in a predetermined way, one can perceive their range of uses, which varied from Mexico's narrowly focused official nationalism which invoked the egalitarian ideals of the Constitution of 1917 while concealing their betrayal—to broad, transnational discourses of hemispheric citizenship and Pan-Africanism.

As a result of this comparative approach, one gains a new perspective on the overdetermined character of canonical statements and literary texts in these movements. In *The New Negro* (1925), for instance, Locke writes that the New Negro "has linked up with the growing group consciousness of the dark-peoples and is gradually learning their common interests. . . . As with the Jew, persecution is making the Negro international."[25] When viewed in the light of transnational practices within 1920s cultural nationalisms in Cuba, Mexico, and the United States, what otherwise might be dismissed as an empty gesture of solidarity achieves an enhanced resonance of possibility.

PRIMITIVE: A KEYWORD IN SOCIAL SCIENCE AND CULTURE FROM THE 1830S TO THE 1920S

While sentimentalist discourse shapes the earlier wave of decolonization that is the topic of the first two chapters, primitivist discourse shapes that of the 1920s. However, discourses of the primitive have a long history, bridging the culture of sentiment of the mid–nineteenth century and ethnography in the early twentieth century. The shifts in the use of the keyword *primitive*, which defined the racial politics of the field of anthropology in the mid–nineteenth century to the early twentieth and point to successive waves of decolonization, can be seen in the differences among Alexander Kinmont's *Twelve Lectures on the Natural History of Man* (1839)—which he regards as contributing to "the science of human nature, which, to designate by a learned name, we might call Anthropology"—Edward B. Tylor's *Primitive Culture* (1871), and Franz Boas's *The Mind of Primitive Man* (1911).[26] These writers engage in a series of debates over the groups who were viewed as the first peoples, following the etymology of *primitive*, which comes from the Latin *primitivus*, the "first or earliest of its kind."[27] The term *primitive* is doubly misleading because it falsely homogenizes diverse social groups and because it "suggests that . . . living peoples are culturally similar to the men and women of early prehistory."[28] Nevertheless, given the long history of discourses of the primitive, it is reductive to argue that primitivism is only or even primarily "an intellectual tendency that rejects the benefits of civilization in favor of a simpler society."[29]

Tylor's *Primitive Culture* defines the term *primitive* in keeping with late nineteenth-century evolutionary theories of race and culture. Recognized as one of the founders of anthropology, in 1883 Tylor accepted a position at Oxford University as keeper of the university museum and reader in anthropology.[30] Tylor regards "primitive culture" as the first stage in the progressive development of civilization, which he defines as follows: "Culture or Civilization, taken in its wide ethnographic sense, is that complex whole which includes knowledge, belief, art, morals, law, custom and any other capabilities and habits acquired by man as a member of society. . . . Its various grades may be regarded as stages of development or evolution, each the outcome of previous history, and about to do its proper part in shaping the history of the future."[31] Tylor subscribes to a tripartite division of humans into savages, barbarians, and civilized, running from the lowest stage of development (that of the "lower races") to the highest (the "higher races" of Europe), from simple to complex cultural forms, and from primitive culture to modern, white Euro-American civilization—a similar evolutionary scale features prominently in the American anthropologist Lewis Henry Morgan's *Ancient Society* (1878) (*PC* 1:6, 1:500, 2:443). When these boundaries are breached, whether through intermarriage, cultural exchange, or cultural "survivals" (remnants of the primitive past of civilization), it is the duty of white civilization to protect itself by reestablishing the racial and cultural hierarchies and purity that facilitate "the advancement of civilization" (*PC* 1:16, 1:69, 2:453). Tylor had a chance to observe at first hand those he termed the "lower races" on a trip to Mexico in 1856. In *Anahuac, or Mexico and the Mexicans, Ancient and Modern* (1861), Tylor's account of that trip, he insists that Mexicans are incapable of self-government.[32]

Both Kinmont and Tylor use the term *primitive* to denote early human history and establish a rough correspondence with the culture of that age and that of various darker races. While for Kinmont elements of primitive culture can improve civilization—"the infantile simplicity of primitive times must be combined with the stern philosophy of the present age"—for Tylor the primitive stands in stark opposition to the civilized and should stay that way (*TL* 112). Whereas Tylor studies the primitive to understand the past of European civilization, a past that Europe should supercede, Kinmont studies the Negro to foresee the future both of the Negro race itself and of Euro-American culture, which should learn from the Negro how to match its scientific progress with moral and spiritual progress. Finally, whereas Tylor argues that one can currently understand the hierarchical ordering of human beings through the help of science, Kinmont says, "We see not yet the order" (*TL* 170). Kinmont's emphasis on the moral superiority of Negroes' "sentimental knowledge" and on incorporating the primitive in order to improve European civilization contrasts with Tylor's racial hierarchies and therefore lends itself to antiracist imaginings. But Kinmont relies on a notion of racial gifts that lends itself too readily to the very racial hierarchies it purports to contest. Moreover, Kinmont does not engage in a thorough analysis of racial oppression (as do Boas and Du Bois) or empire (as do Du Bois and José Martí).

In *The Mind of Primitive Man* Boas painstakingly refutes the logic of the evolutionary racial theories of Tylor and the notion of racial gifts that was a conceptual building block for the romantic racialism of Kinmont, Harriet Beecher Stowe, Helen Hunt Jackson, Martí, and the Du Bois of *The Souls of Black Folk*.[33] While Tylor asserts the inferiority of the "lower races" by positing a linear, evolutionary development from savagery to civilization, Boas argues in 1911 against any ascription of inferiority to the peoples deemed primitive, instead arguing for a plurality of civilizations, all to be valued on their own terms: "There may be other civilizations . . . which are of no less value than ours."[34] Boas later revises this characteristically cautious formulation with a bold summary in the preface to the 1938 edition of *The Mind of Primitive Man*: "There is no fundamental difference in the ways of thinking of primitive and civilized men. A close connection between race and personality has never been established."[35] Thus Boas attempts to drive nails into the coffin of evolutionary discourse and the potentially allied discourse of the primitive.

In addressing the question of national "genius"—a notion that is central to the racial imaginings of Stowe, Jackson, Martí, and the Du Bois of *Souls* and earlier—Boas argues that civilizations are not "the product of the genius of a single people," as in the *Volksgeist* theories of Johann Gottfried von Herder and Alexander von Humboldt, but are instead the result of multiple cross-fertilizations among people of different cultures (*MPM* 7).[36] The results of such cultural exchange are nowhere more evident than in the study of folklore. For Boas, folklore does not embody the soul of a people but rather demonstrates the interconnectedness of cultures (*MPM* 168). This twofold attack on evolutionary theories of race and the romantic racialist theory of national genius or gifts demonstrates why *The Mind of Primitive Man* has been read as a landmark text in the shift from race to culture that Boas did so much to promote. In Boas's own words, the shift from race to culture can take place when one realizes that "there is no close relation between race and culture" (*MPM* 196).

At the same time, there is a curiously contradictory use of the term *primitive* in *The Mind of Primitive Man*. On the one hand, Boas methodically dismantles previous racial definitions of the primitive through a variety of methods:

> Asserting that historical events rather than racial faculty led to the development of European civilization, Boas refutes the assumption of white racial perfection on which the opposition between primitive and civilized is based (*MPM* 2, 17).

Moreover, Boas argues that the category of race is itself invalid because "the differences between different types of man are, on the whole, small as compared to the range of variation in each type" (*MPM* 94). That these are the very same terms present-day biologists employ to refute the validity of race as a descriptor of human identity is a measure of the enormous impact of Boas's argument.

Boas argues that the category of primitive man was based on flawed evidence: travelers' accounts of the traits of primitive man were "too superficial," and the accounts of ethnologists such as Arthur Comte de Gobineau and Josiah Nott and George Gliddon and evolutionists such as Herbert Spencer and Tylor fail to adequately demonstrate "that they describe the psychological characters of races independent of their social surroundings" (*MPM* 99, 100). Boas's conclusion flies in the face of evolutionary orthodoxy by considering the possibility that people are indistinguishable in their mental attributes: "It may . . . be that the organization of mind is practically identical among all races of man" (*MPM* 102). Moreover, on the basis of his research findings among Native Americans along the northwest coast of the United States, Boas argues that the forms of social organization among primitive peoples are actually quite complex rather than simple, as evolutionary theory had alleged (*MPM* 111). Thus where evolutionists see racial causes, Boas sees historical and social causes, and where they view primitive culture as simple, Boas argues that every culture is complex when understood in its own terms.

This historically grounded, empiricist, skeptical approach to cultural analysis could lead one to believe that Boas would have no further use for the category of the primitive. Indeed, as he implies, the category of the primitive as used in racial science has no explanatory value: "We saw that the oft-reported claim that he [primitive man] has no power to inhibit impulses, no power of attention, no originality of thought, no power of clear reasoning, could not be maintained; and that all these faculties are common to primitive man and to civilized man, although they are excited on different occasions" (*MPM* 247). Boas suggests that the category of the primitive is a false construct that betrays the ambition of racial discourse to assert biologically based differences among diverse groups of people where none exist.

On the other hand (and here one sees Boas's contradictory use of the term *primitive*), Boas does not dispense with the category of the primitive, but rather uses it to root a new series of oppositions: "The change from primitive to civilized society includes a lessening of the number of the emotional associations, and an improvement of the traditional material that enters into our habitual mental operations" (*MPM* 250). Even if Boas no longer relies on the concept of race as a marker of difference to charac- terize primitive society, he now assumes that there exists an opposition and transition between traditional society and civilization, and that this tran- sition results in "improvement," or progress. Moreover, he tellingly asso- ciates primitive culture with emotional rather than rational behavior.[37] Charles Briggs and Richard Baumann persuasively argue that the reason Boas held onto the category of the primitive rather than dispensing with it altogether was that the category of the primitive was useful to him in rationalizing his activities as a professional scientist. In other words, in fashioning himself as epitomizing a highly rational and "improved" (Boas's term) culture, Boas found it useful to implicitly distinguish his own ac- tivities as a professional academic from those of primitive culture.

Why did the category of the primitive display such cultural staying power despite Boas's devastating critique of evolutionary racial science? Although a complete answer to this question would extend beyond the bounds of this chapter, the beginnings of an answer lie in the protean character of the term *primitive*. In the 1920s, primitivism could either be used as a foil for one's own identity as a self-styled modern, civilized person, or scientist, or it could be used to register ambivalence toward Euro-American modernity, pointing out what civilization loses as it sup- posedly progresses. The term *primitive* thus alternately registers approba- tion or critique of the status quo to varying degrees.

The pliant character of the term is on full display in *The Mind of Primitive Man*. There are two slippages in Boas's use of *primitive* that indicate the persistence of hierarchical terms of identity even within the new orthodoxy of cultural discourse that has displaced older racial discourses. First, there is a slippage between using the term *primitive* as a construct, a fictional creation of Euro-Americans, and referring to the primitive as if it were real, as if it could describe current social groups: Boas intersperses references to "primitive man" with references to "the negro," as if the two were interchangeable (*MPM* 115). Boas even concludes the book with a chapter entitled "Race Problems in the United States," which addresses the plight of African Americans. Although Boas disputes allegations of the racial inferiority of both "primitive man" and "the negro," by associating the two via the indeterminacy of the category of Negro itself (he uses it to refer both to "African tribes" and to African Americans), he risks reinforcing the connection between *primitive* and *Negro* in the minds of his readers. In this line of argument, *The Mind of Primitive Man* paradoxically foregrounds and reifies the very term it purports to expose as ahistorical.

Second, it is often difficult to distinguish among Boas's use of *primitive* as racial category, cultural category, and historical category. When Boas writes that the shift from primitive to civilized society entails "an improvement of the traditional material," how does this statement relate to those passages that describe African Americans as implicitly contemporary primitives, yet who no longer engage in traditional cultural practices (*MPM* 250)? Why is Boas still including them among primitive groups?

A different sort of indeterminacy is evident when Boas argues, "no large groups of primitive man are brought nowadays into conditions of real equality with whites" (*MPM* 105). Here Boas usefully employs the term *primitive* as a political category that brings together indigenous peoples and "the negro" as groups who have been denied equality. *Primitive* is a vexed and politically charged term, and to use it is to incur considerable risks that the hierarchies of racial thinking will slip in through the back door of cultural discourse. At the same time, Boas's political use of the term here strikes me as potentially useful because it insists on the necessity of creating the conditions for equality between the primitive and the modern. In this passage, the term does not quite break free from its troubling historical uses, but it does begin to chart new territory by clearing the semantic space for a recognition of the ways in which the putative primitives contest the inequalities that make the term possible to begin with.

The discourse of primitivism links Tylor's mental *evolution* to Gamio's "mental *revolution*" via Boas's attack on the racial claims of evolutionary science, the so-called "revolution in anthropology."[38] That is, the elite recognition of the agency of decolonizing groups was made possible by dislodging the racial claims of evolution and thereby questioning and transforming the meanings of the term *primitive*.[39] Kinmont and Stowe produce a contradictory early point in this process—the sentimental discourse of racial gifts—that comes to a head with Boas and writings by the "darker peoples" in the 1920s. At this point, "primitive" peoples were no longer the origin from which humans had evolved, the old that would gradually develop into the new, but at times were viewed as providing alternative forms of thinking and living that could transform Eurocentric models of culture—what I am calling alternative primitivisms.

Two strains within primitivist discourse obtain momentum in the 1920s. By adopting a skeptical attitude in texts such as *The Mind of Primitive Man* toward evolutionary theory and its sweeping claims about races (sentimentalism is guilty of such sweeping claims as well) and by discrediting common ahistorical uses of the term *primitive*, Boas lays the groundwork for the privileging of ethnographic fieldwork. The emergence of ethnography as the central practice of anthropology marks a new understanding that Euro-Americans cannot simply exhaust the meanings of a culture by deeming it primitive. In keeping with Du Bois's discourse of racial mystery in *The Souls of Black Folk*, Boas insists on a cultural opacity that undermines Stowe's assumption of a cultural transparency that allows whites to dictate the paths of racial reform. This new, more cautious approach to producing knowledge on nonwhites combines with the efforts of nonwhite writers themselves to reflect critically on unequal power relations.

Writers on race in the 1920s would portray members of the so-called primitive races as having developed ways of life that stood in protest against unjust, undemocratic, and racially oppressive neocolonial regimes. Such are the general outlines of primitivist discourse in Beals, Du Bois, Gamio, Hughes, Zora Neale Hurston, McKay, Masdeu, and Menéndez in the 1920s, although there were many variations and contradictions in their views (see chapter 4 on Gamio and Hurston). The celebration of the primitive in the twentieth century occurs not only or primarily in relation to fixed cultural traits or racial "gifts," as it did in nineteenth-century writers such as Kinmont, Stowe, and Jackson. Instead, primitivist discourse in Beals, Hughes, Hurston, McKay, Masdeu, and Menéndez now begins to claim self-determination for the dark races, dislodging whites from their foothold as the allegedly natural rulers of the world, the *zoon politikon par*

excellence. At times writers in the 1920s subscribe to earlier racial stereotypes that portray the darker races as lazy and sensual, but these residual
representations now contradict the concurrent insistence that the darker
races seize control of their own political destinies—an insistence made all
the more forceful by the participation of Afro-Cubans in the Spanish-
American-Cuban War and by the centrality of various indigenous groups
in the Mexican Revolution. And although not all writers engaging in the
discourse of primitivism were up to date with the shift from racial to
cultural discourses best exemplified by the work of Boas and his students,
including Gamio and Hurston, that epochal transformation similarly en-
abled and, at times, pushed forward the possibilities of the political agency
of the darker races. These political and social scientific preconditions for
the discourse of primitivism of the 1920s constituted a new wave of decolonization that was distinct from the earlier one between the Mexican-
American War and the Spanish-American War.

On the other hand, the ethnographic discourse that the Boasian shift
from race to culture ushered in could often be quite conservative—even
reactionary—in its political implications. Indeed, the production of ethnographic discourse was no assurance of the anthropologist's support of
decolonization. Two of Boas's star students, Margaret Mead, the author of
Coming of Age in Samoa (1928), and Ruth Benedict, the author of *Patterns
of Culture* (1934), ignored political economy and empire in their analyses of
what they termed primitive societies.[40] During the Vietnam War, Mead
attacked her fellow anthropologists Joseph Jorgensen and Eric Wolf for
having written a letter condemning those anthropologists who described
the structure of peasant huts for the U.S. Defense Department so that they
could be bombed.[41] Another scholar has identified in the work of Benedict
and other ethnographers a "complicity between the production of anthropological knowledge and the obfuscation of political forces."[42] Benedict's
ahistorical analysis of Japanese culture in *The Chrysanthemum and the
Sword* (1946) promoted the ethnocentric view that the Japanese, although
allegedly strikingly different from white Americans, could be assimilated
into Euro-American civilization.[43] In this case, ethnography constitutes a
shift from an evolutionary argument to one promoting an assimilation
paradigm, but the assumption of white cultural superiority persists. As I
argued in my analysis of discourses of sentiment, novel cultural forms may
emerge because of antiracist forces—Boas's opposition to evolutionism
and antiracist commitment paved the way for ethnography's new version

of primitivism—but those forms give rise to varied political meanings. The virtue of a focus on primitivism is not that it ensures that a particular text will adopt a particular political line, but rather that its embeddedness in cross-national cultural currents facilitates the development of a transnational frame of analysis that has the potential to be adequate to the task of deciphering the workings of U.S. imperialism in the Americas and beyond.

THE CAGE OF CIVILIZATION IN HUGHES AND BEALS

Langston Hughes and Carleton Beals both developed their dominant and alternative primitivist discourses through their firsthand experience of Latin American countries. At times Hughes and Beals romanticize non-white cultures in a way that evacuates historical specificities, as in Sapir's dominant primitivist discourse, but at other times they use primitivism to critique specific historical formations. It is precisely this oscillation between abstract stereotypes and specific critiques that the sternest critics of primitivism have missed. While primitivism precluded some forms of radical critique, it also made others possible, namely, the attempt to forge ties among divergent yet allegedly primitive nonwhite groups opposed to U.S. neocolonialism. The travel narratives of Hughes and Beals on Latin America illustrate the importance of such cross-fertilizations among nationalisms in Cuba, Mexico, and the United States

Hughes first came to know Latin America through his father, James Hughes, whom he visited in Mexico in 1919 and 1920. James Hughes had moved to Mexico City to make his fortune as a lawyer, a profession that typically excluded blacks in the United States. Unlike his son, James Hughes expressed contempt for the Mexican Revolution and disparaged Emiliano Zapata and Pancho Villa, known as defenders of the poor. This unfavorable view of the Mexican Revolution was shared by American diplomats and absentee landowners, the agents of U.S. neocolonialism, who opposed Mexican reforms such as land redistribution on the grounds that they threatened U.S. economic interests.[44] James Hughes despised both Negroes and Mexicans, whom he viewed as "ignorant and backward." In his autobiography, *The Big Sea*, Hughes writes that his father "spoke badly about the Mexicans. He said they were ignorant and backward and lazy. He said they were exactly like the Negroes in the United States. . . . My father hated Negroes. I think he hated himself, too, for being a Negro."[45] If James Hughes conflated Negroes and Mexicans in his self-hate, Langston Hughes's respect for Negroes and Mexican mestizos and Indians converged. Indeed, the son's perspective on Mexico differed considerably from his father's.[46] On his second trip to Mexico, Langston Hughes met Carlos Pellicer, a member of the avant-garde literary group Los Contemporáneos. Pellicer's poetry exalted ancient indigenous cultures as forming the bedrock of Mexican nationalism, much as Hughes's poetry romanticized ancient Africa.[47]

The importance of Mexican indigenismo to Hughes's work is evident in the fact that he wrote "The Negro Speaks of Rivers" (1921) while pondering his father's "strange dislike for his own people" on a train headed from St. Louis to Mexico.[48] Hughes's celebrated poem recounts the past greatness of African civilizations to lay claim to their future glory:

> I've known rivers:
> I've known rivers ancient as the world and older than the flow of
>   human blood in human veins.
> My soul has grown deep like the rivers.
> I bathed in the Euphrates when dawns were young.
> I built my hut near the Congo and it lulled me to sleep
> I looked upon the Nile and raised the pyramids above it.
> I heard the singing of the Mississippi when Abe Lincoln went down to
>   New Orleans, and I've seen its muddy bosom turn all golden in the
>   sunset.[49]

The rivers in the poem forge a diasporic link between African Americans along the Mississippi and Africans along the Euphrates, Congo, and Nile, whose Negro souls have "grown deep like the rivers." The rivers thereby establish a historical and geographical continuity between great ancient African civilizations and the know-how and dignity of current African Americans. Some may want to fault this primitivist discourse of pride for erasing differences between Africans and African Americans.[50] However, the advantages of asserting such a diasporic link are not only to provide the self-hating among African Americans with an alternative history that emphasizes black achievement rather than victimization, but also to renarrate dominant versions of U.S. history to emphasize the contribution of black labor—after all, the narrator of the poem is not only a poetic visionary, but also a worker. Hughes's commitment to workers in his early poetry constitutes a continuity between his early work that emphasized pride and his later work that emphasized the exploitation of workers, such as the bitterly and brilliantly ironic "Advertisement for the Waldorf Astoria" (1931).

The deep-rooted wisdom of those whom Locke termed "dark-peoples" similarly takes center stage in "Mexican Market Woman" (1922), but here the alliance constructed by the poem is not among Africa and its diaspora, but rather among workers and racially oppressed peoples more generally:

> This ancient hag
> Who sits upon the ground
> Selling her scanty wares
> Day in, day round,
> Has known high wind-swept mountains,
> And the sun has made
> Her skin so brown.[51]

In these two poems, "Negro" and "Mexican" "brown" identity, equally revered and nearly interchangeable, form the basis for a discourse of pride, which is central to the dominant mode of primitivism that collapses complex historical specificities, but which also forms the basis for alternative histories. On the one hand, such a conflation runs the risk of collapsing differences between African Americans and *indios* in an ahistorical, dominant primitivist attempt to make color an "emancipatory signifier," to quote Gayatri Spivak.[52] From this perspective, Hughes reverses the values of residual primitivist discourses but maintains their racialist terms. On the other hand, Hughes's romanticization of nonwhite cultures again produces transnational affinities between groups who would otherwise tend not to view each other as part of a shared political project. Thus Hughes's discourse of pride creates the conditions for an alternative primitivism that upsets the terms of racialist discourses by calling for the forging of alliances among workers and people of color from different nations.

If early in his career Hughes drew on his experiences in Mexico to construct a primitivist discourse of pride in the accomplishments of nonwhite peoples, his travels across the border forced him to confront the discrepancies between histories of racialization and inequality in the United States and Latin America. When he returned to the United States from Mexico, Hughes assumed a Latin American mestizo or mulatto identity at a San Antonio train station by ordering his ticket in Spanish to secure a sleeping-car berth.[53] Hughes's racial masquerade allows him to elude the indignities of southern U.S. segregation.[54] This cosmopolitan awareness of variations in racialization coexists in tension with Hughes's implicitly biologically based definitions of blackness as epitomizing the vitality of the African jungle—as he wrote in *The Weary Blues* (1926), "All the tom-toms of the jungle beat in my blood."[55] Moreover, Hughes complicates such assertions of continuity between the traditions of the African jungle and African Americans by invoking historical forces that his critics have chosen to ignore. In "Lament for Dark Peoples" (1924) Hughes establishes global imperialism as the historical referent in the first two lines of the poem:

I was a red man one time,
But the white men came.
I was a black man, too,
But the white men came.
They drove me out of the forest.
They took me away from the jungles. . . .
Now they've caged me
In the circus of civilization.[56]

The first stanza constructs an alliance between the "red man" who is a "black man, too," the composite figure a victim of imperialism and of "civilization." "Lament for Dark Peoples" proposes an alternative primitivism in that Hughes constructs the relationship between the contemporary African American and the inhabitants of the forests (Indians) and jungles (Africans) not as racially determined but rather as historically mediated through imperialism.

Early in his career Hughes drew on his experience of Mexico to construct a primitivist, anti-imperialist pride in the accomplishments of nonwhite peoples. His subsequent trips to Latin America and the Caribbean provided the basis for a fierce critique of U.S. neocolonial rule, one that displayed increasingly subtle understandings of differences and shared predicaments among nonwhites of the United States and Latin America. In "White Shadows in a Black Land" (1932), Hughes shows how neocolonialism impinges on the "darker world" of Haiti, where everything is run by blacks: "Imagine a country where the entire national population is colored, and you will have Haiti. . . . To a Negro coming directly from New York . . . it is like stepping into a new world, a darker world, a world where the white shadows are apparently missing, a world of his own people. . . . even the president of the Republic will have a touch of color in his blood. . . . the dark visitor from America will feel at home and unafraid."[57] Haitians in positions of political authority embody the hopes of the New Negroes to achieve self-determination and equality. Yet this darker world is haunted by what Hughes calls the "white shadows" of U.S. neocolonialism, with

U.S. marines subjecting the Haitian people to "a sort of military dictatorship backed by American guns" (91). Indeed, the U.S. marines massacred
three thousand peasants in the early years of the occupation. The U.S.
occupation also suspended the Haitian constitution and introduced segregation, forced labor, curfews, press censorship, and surveillance. In the
United States, the NAACP and Haitian exiles agitated against the U.S. occupation of Haiti (1915–34).[58] The "white shadows," then, figure a tentative alignment between domestic white racism and U.S. neocolonialism in
Haiti. With the term "white shadows," Hughes attempts to name structures
of oppression that cross from the United States to Latin America and the
Caribbean.[59]

Like Hughes, Beals, who was white, traveled to Mexico and Cuba in the
1920s. And like Hughes, Beals published in the journals that constituted the
fabric of the Harlem Renaissance: the *Survey Graphic*, the *New Masses*, the
New Republic, and the *Nation*. Beals soon grew famous through his leftist
travel writing and journalism in Mexico, where he lived from 1923 to 1928.
His historiographical study *Mexico: An Interpretation* (1923) won respect
from reviewers by demonstrating the political opposition of the conservative landed elite to postrevolutionary land reform. Beals's parents had
raised him to be supportive of egalitarian ideals: they participated in the
Populist Movement in Kansas in the 1890s, and his father helped to organize Mexican beet workers in southern California in the early 1900s.[60]

Beals moved in intellectual circles that were caught up in the binational
cultural foment moving between the United States and Mexico. In Mexico,
Beals was a friend of Diego Rivera, whose murals Beals defended against
critics who were offended by their sympathetic portrayals of the dark-
skinned poor. When the conservative, upper-class students at the National
Preparatory School in Mexico City tried to deface a Rivera mural at their
school in 1924, Beals circulated a petition in defense of the work.[61] He
associated with North American exiles in Mexico City, among them Porter,
Edward Weston, Tina Modotti, and Frances Toor, the founder of *Mexican
Folkways*, a binational and bilingual journal devoted to the study of Mexican folk and indigenous cultures. Moreover, Beals joined a bevy of famous
Mexican intellectuals, including Vasconcelos and Gamio, in contributing
an article to the *Survey Graphic* special issue on Mexico in 1924.[62] While
in Cuba, Beals interviewed Gustavo Urrutia, a principal activist in the
negrismo movement. He also met with Fernando Ortiz, an important
anthropologist who is recognized as the godfather of negrismo.[63] Beals not

only wrote about Mexico and Cuba, but also defended the most progressive political tendencies within the two countries. His respect for the common people of Mexico, including Indians, led him to defend the Mexican Revolution at a time when the U.S. State Department viewed Mexican reform as a menace to U.S. economic interests.[64] And living in Mexico turned Beals into an anti-imperialist—he vigorously opposed U.S. intervention in Mexico in 1927.[65]

Beals denounced U.S. neocolonialist abuses with equal vigor when he traveled to Cuba in the early 1930s. Horrified by the murder in Mexico City in 1929 of his Cuban friend Julio Antonio Mella, an exiled communist leader of student protests, Beals castigated the puppets of U.S. neocolonialism in Cuba in his exposé *The Crime of Cuba* (1933):[66] "The Machado despotism has overthrown the constitution, has overthrown the civil courts, has destroyed free press and the right of public assemblage and has ruled by force and murder. During this period that despotism was publicly praised by our highest officials. . . . What right have we to get exercised about Hitler when we helped to maintain a protectorate at our very doorstep, a government that has committed far greater crimes than those which have occurred in Germany?"[67] Beals's anger is informed by his knowledge of the history of U.S. neocolonialism in Cuba. An alliance between U.S. business and the U.S. and Cuban ruling elite had long maintained the protectorate status of Cuba established by the Platt Amendment (1903). This protectorate status consisted of a dual economic and political dominance by U.S. business interests. U.S. business dominated Cuban trade, raw materials, agriculture, infrastructure, and nearly all the major industries in the early twentieth century.[68] By 1927, U.S. business owned up to 82 percent of Cuban sugar production.[69] Owing to a depression in Cuba beginning in 1925, wages fell 50–75 percent, and poverty in Cuba, already widespread, deepened.[70]

U.S. corporations contributed to the dire straits of the majority of Cubans by making massive campaign contributions to corrupt presidential candidates, who were then able to rig elections. José Miguel Gómez became president with U.S. aid in 1909. In 1912 Gómez ordered a massacre of Afro-Cubans who supported the Partido Independiente Cubano. U.S. marines played a role in the killing, which resulted in the deaths of an estimated three thousand to five thousand Afro-Cubans.[71] Fraudulent elections continued in the next two decades: Mario Menocal became president by fraud in 1916, and Alfredo Zayas in 1920. Zayas responded to violent strikes by dockworkers, railroad workers, and sugar mill workers with severe repression, including assassination and deportation.[72] It was in this oppressive atmosphere that Machado, a former sugar mill owner committed to U.S. business interests, won the election of 1924 by exploiting nationalist sentiment.[73] When he illegally extended his mandate in 1927, students responded with anti-Machado demonstrations, which were severely repressed.

This same year Alejo Carpentier, a white Cuban novelist who had joined these protests, wrote ¡Ecue-Yamba-Ó! (May the Lord be praised! 1933) in a jail cell in Havana, a novel counterposing two crimes: that of an impoverished Afro-Cuban, Menegildo Cué, who kills a black migrant laborer from Haiti, and the greater crime of Cuban neocolonialism, in which the elite ruling class permits "the sale of the country to the highest bidder."[74] As Roberto González Echevarría has pointed out, the theme of crime in ¡Ecue-Yamba-Ó! must be viewed as invoking and rejecting the early work of Ortiz, who focused on Afro-Cubans from the perspective of criminology in Hampa afro-cubana: los negros brujos (Apuntes para un estudio de etnología criminal (Afro-Cuban underworld: black witch doctors [notes toward a criminal ethnology], 1906).[75] As if in response to the undervaluing of "trabajadores y campesinos cubanos" (Cuban workers and peasants) by Ortiz and Machado, Carpentier celebrates Menegildo, a "criminal," as being one of the Afro-Cuban "antidotes" to neocolonialism: "Orange Crush was becoming an instrument of imperialism, as in the memory of Roosevelt or of Lindbergh's flight . . . ! Only the blacks . . . jealously conserved an antillean character and tradition. The bongó, antidote to Wall Street! The Holy Spirit, venerated by the Cués, did not permit Yankee sausages within its votive bread-rolls! None of these hot-dogs with the saints of Mayeya!"[76]

The Crime of Cuba by Beals joins this dissident Afro-Cubanism, combining journalism, history, interviews, and a "photographic essay" by Walker Evans with photos of the poor, imprisoned students and murdered dissenters. In addition to imprisoning activists, Machado ordered the assassinations of many of his political opponents, including Mella. Moreover, Beals was shocked to discover that a Cuban citizen whom he had planned to interview in the early 1930s was assassinated the very day of the scheduled interview.[77] The text presents an unrelentingly grim picture of Cuba that contests, as did Guillén's poetry, the romanticized view of "Old Havana" then used to lure tourists.[78] Beals's Cuba is ruled by absentee landowners from the United States who make life "an elementary, savage struggle for survival" (22). A "thin Negro" whose poverty indicates that he knows that struggle well tells Beals that with the advent of U.S. neocolonialism, "we merely changed masters" (34). The absentee landowners formed the bulwark of U.S. neocolonialism in Cuba because they believed it was in their economic interest to maintain a dictator committed to repressing union organizing and democratic and socialist initiatives.

Beals's angry, impassioned, and exhaustively researched critique of U.S. neocolonialism in Cuba coexists with sexist and racially essentialist language in his passage on Fela, an "octaroon" dancer in a Havana cabaret.[79] The octoroon's body is this activist intellectual's sexual and ideological weak spot, a representation that threatens to undermine his critique of neocolonialism with stark oppositions between whites and nonwhites. As Fela dances, "her body became an instrument of racial purpose quite beyond itself," a potent racial signifier (42). Watching her, he finds "rhythms—so far from commercialized tunes—locked in her lovely tan and gold body," reiterating the dominant primitivist opposition between a commodified white culture and vibrant nonwhite cultures that Sapir had constructed (40). Fela's performance, then, coincides with another performance, that of the accomplished primitivist. That is, Beals attempts to grasp racial essences, revealing that the mannerisms of the "almost white" Fela, who is intently watching the black Toñico drumming, betray her African heritage: "Anyone more sensitized to Antillean racial vagaries would have noticed now in the way she sat the poise of loin and limb not Spanish but African; would have caught the significance of the haze gathering in her ebony eyes as she watched the black man in front of her, a smoldering stare that revealed her terrific duality—boiling in the cross-current of her unfused bloodstreams—of utter distaste and profound attraction" (40). Although elsewhere in the text Beals condemns those who have oppressed Afro-Cubans, the language of "unfused blood-streams" suggests that Africans and Europeans are biologically incompatible. The African allegedly predominates in the "smoldering" sexuality of the mulatto woman, as if she were divided between a primitive African body and an advanced Spanish mind.

Yet for Beals, witnessing Fela dance makes accessible a "primitive force" desirable to white and black alike: "Mind and will had been melted away in that quiver, slide and wheel of the flesh-covering; a constant flexing and unflexing that stripped off, even in us clumsy beholders, all civilized layers, and left some primitive force deeper, more important even, than symbolic orgy. It thrusts us, more than naked, into kinship with elemental attraction and repulsion of ions, that queer duality of matter that seeks unattainable unity in cohesion but can approximate it only by the upward spiral into form" (42). Here Beals casts in curious yet unforgettable terms the common 1920s notion that civilization is a cage (as in Hughes's "Lament for Dark Peoples") and that white regeneration is possible by approaching a primitive Other. Beals claims that the seduction of Fela's "flesh-covering" has created "quicksand underneath our smug cultural barriers," creating a cross-racial "kinship" (42, 44). Beals's hyperbolic reference to the "elemental attraction and repulsion of ions" registers what contemporary thinkers as diverse as Sigmund Freud, Bronislaw Malinowski, and the French Catholic theologian Romain Rolland called "the nirvana impulse," or "the oceanic," defined as "a dissolution of subject-object divisions so radical that one experiences the sensation of merging with the universe."[80]

However, Beals's desire for such a cross-racial "kinship" is undermined by his participation in the sexualized tourist economy of the cabaret. Moreover, Beals continually re-erects cultural barriers in the racial discourses he deploys while describing Fela. He emphasizes the distance between white and black cultures when he claims that Fela, exhausted by her dance, wants to return to the allegedly more civilized state of whiteness: "Unexpectedly Fela began singing white melodies, only a faint trace of negro-octaroon songs. There was a hint of defiance in her monodies, as if she wished to be reclaimed back to her whiteness. I was amazed at this obvious, though to her unconscious, inner antagonism of bloods and cultures" (44). Here Fela's alleged desire to be "reclaimed back to her whiteness" engages in a residual primitivist discourse of blood contested by the hegemony of Boasian anthropology attained by 1930. Beals constructs as an "inner antagonism of bloods" something that could just as well be read as Fela's outer defiance toward whites who racialize her as other.

Similarly, when describing the black-skinned drummer Toñico, Beals reverts to the outmoded discourse of phrenology, the nineteenth-century racial science of cranial measurements: "He was a big hunk of night, a mountain of darkness, beefy shoulders, sledge-hammer arms. In battering-ram posture, he shoved forward his bony close-cropped skull, composed of two half-spheres, frontal and paretic-occipital, looping up gourd-like to a form not white" (41). In his descriptions of Fela and Toñico, Beals constructs an opposition between whiteness, associated with the intellect, and blackness, associated with the body. By detailing the character of Fela's "flesh-covering" and Toñico's "sledge-hammer arms," Beals polices the constructed boundaries between a refined whiteness and an allegedly excessively corporeal and sexual blackness. So while Hughes and Beals transcend narrow racial ideologies by aligning themselves with the struggles of nonwhites from Latin America, they part ways in their differing valuations of blackness.

Despite primitivism's reputation for precluding rather than constructing resistance, both Hughes and Beals contest U.S. neocolonialism through primitivist representations of nonwhite Latin American women. However, each deploys primitivism with significantly different consequences for racial and gender politics. Hughes's alternative primitivist discourse figures Mexican "brown" and U.S. black identities as aligned against the "white shadows" of neocolonialism in Haiti and elsewhere. The "Mexican Market Woman" figures a transnational "brown" collectivity as much through economic exploitation—"selling her scanty wares"—as through her gendered position as a Republican Mother. Beals's career as a U.S. journalist has the advantage of bringing together the egalitarian impulses of the Mexican Renaissance and the opposition to neocolonialism that was central to Afro-Cubanism. But Beals's dominant primitivist discourse betrays his own participation within a sexualized tourist economy, as he figures Fela's female flesh as uniting men across national and racial divides. Moreover, Beals attempts to effect this cross-racial "kinship" through a simultaneous construction and effacement of biological racial difference. Fela's debilitating "inner antagonism of bloods" displaces the social antagonisms between neocolonialists and their opponents that Beals describes elsewhere in the same text.

The crucial difference between the primitivisms of Hughes and Beals, then, can be found in the degree to which they describe identities as produced within socioeconomic formations. In Hughes and Beals primitivist alliance politics oscillate between an evacuation of the historical determinations of race and a detailed specifying of the social production of racial difference. Primitivist discourses, then, must be evaluated according to their ability to signify racial pride while not erasing the historical conditions of racialization.

Through their travels in Mexico and the Caribbean, Hughes and Beals provide us with firsthand accounts of the social consequences of what Doreen Massey has termed "the spatial stretching-out of social relations," in this case in the context of U.S. neocolonialism in the 1920s.[81] Their recognition of the political, economic, and cultural interdependency of the "national" in the Americas—the paradoxical transnational production of the national under neocolonialism—carries far-reaching implications for current efforts to devise comparative approaches to U.S. and Latin American culture and history. By challenging U.S. foreign policy in Mexico and the Caribbean, U.S. citizens such as Beals and Hughes practice a kind of hemispheric citizenship, one that attempts to restore the rights of those exploited or repressed by the U.S. business elite in other nation-states. The "vaster reality" of neocolonialism in Haiti, Mexico, and Cuba sheds light onto lives seemingly remote from those of U.S. citizens yet bound to theirs by the forces of political economy and by transnational cultural threads.[82]

THE "CONTENTED ANIMAL" AND DECOLONIZATION IN MCKAY

As Hughes and Beals gained experience in their travels through Latin America, they grew more attuned to the ways in which neocolonialism, while often driven by motivations of profit and assumptions of nonwhite inferiority, nevertheless took on a particular shape according to nation and region—from the U.S. military occupation of Haiti to the U.S.-backed Machado dictatorship in Cuba to the U.S. opposition to the nationalization of oil by constitutional mandate in Mexico. Hughes and Beals traveled the routes of primitivism in the Americas, sustaining their circuits of transnational dialogue and exchange. Such a recognition of the transnational routes of primitivist discourses calls for a consideration of their impact on nationalist narratives that circulate within rather than across borders.

My readings of novels set in specific national sites—Claude McKay's *Home to Harlem* (the United States and Haiti), Jesús Masdeu's *La raza triste* (Cuba and the United States), and *Nayar* by Miguel Angel Menéndez (Mexico)—address the political consequences of the convergence or divergence between primitivist and nationalist discourses. The question of the degree of proximity between primitivisms and nationalisms can best be approached by considering how nationalisms construct the relationship between what Locke termed folk expression and self-determination. As Partha Chatterjee has shown, a common danger of nationalism is its tendency to assert an identity of interests between the governing and governed, thereby effacing political differences.[83] This occurred in Mexico, where official state discourses of nationalism constructed national unity as a process of ethnic homogenization via *mestizaje*, or intermarriage. Mestizaje discourse is like a parasite that destroys its host: it selectively appropriates the trappings of indigenous and peasant cultures for the national while "molding" Indians along the lines of the civilizationalist discourse of modernization as progress, thereby destroying indigenous social forms.[84] Mestizaje, then, splits off folk-expression from the right to self-determination. The producers of folk-expression—Indians and the lower classes of mestizos—are granted entrance into the national culture to the extent that they abdicate the rights of regional and ethnic-based self-determination.

While Menéndez's Nayar implicitly endorses mestizaje as a homogenizing project of national unity as opposed to exploring the possibilities of self-determination for indigenous groups in Mexico, McKay and Masdeu emphasize the violence committed by nationalism as a homogenizing project that suppresses self-determination by the marginalized. In identifying folk-expression with the "proletariat" (McKay) and with the "peon" (Masdeu), these writers specify the processes of racial oppression and class exploitation that undermine notions of an overarching national self-determination. Moreover, the meanings of proletariat and peon in McKay and Masdeu cull from these texts' attention to the workings of the U.S. empire. In the hands of McKay and Masdeu, proletariat and peon refer both to capitalist exploitation and to imperial oppression. The figure of the primitive in McKay and Masdeu thus brings together interests in folk-expression, self-determination, political-economic critique, and anti-imperialism, providing a model of analysis for transnational Americas studies. McKay and Masdeu thus construct alternative primitivisms in opposition to liberal ideologies of the national project that view folk-expression and self-determination as subservient to the interests of the state. By liberal ideologies, I mean the perceived necessary link among official or state-sponsored nationalism, modernization, democracy, and progress.[85]

In the context of the Harlem Renaissance, McKay differs from those like Locke and James Weldon Johnson, who argued that African Americans could gain civil rights by achieving excellence in the realm of art. In claiming that the recognition of the beauty of African American folk-expression would lead to their group's full inclusion within a widened sphere of democracy in the United States, Locke and Johnson express a gradualist faith in the process of assimilation in the United States that McKay did not share. Similarly, the Afro-Cubanismo of Masdeu contested the hegemonic race-blind discourses of the Cuban Republic that equated national independence with racial equality. These critical, minority nationalisms expose the contradiction between official nationalism's inclusion of folk-expression and rejection of minority self-determination. By insisting on self-determination for minority populations and the lower classes, McKay and Masdeu fashion themselves as Gramscian organic intellectuals in the sense that they provide their groups with "an awareness of (their) own function not only in the economic but also in the social and political fields."[86] In addition, they refuse the conservative ideologies that confer state privileges to token minorities: Johnson, the coauthor of "Lift Every Voice and Sing" (1900), the so-called Negro national anthem, ironically wrote a different sort of nationalist anthem, Theodore Roosevelt's 1904 campaign song, "You're All Right, Teddy," for which he was granted a consular position in Venezuela in 1906 and another in Nicaragua in 1908, where he supported the use of U.S. marines in suppressing a revolution.[87] That Johnson could support black civil rights while denying rights of self-determination to Latin Americans demonstrates the political stakes involved in the discourses of hemispheric citizenship of Beals, Du Bois, Hughes, and McKay.

Much like Hughes and Beals, Claude McKay, Jamaican by birth, contributed to discussions of 1920s race relations by historicizing neocolonialism in Latin America and the Caribbean as well as the plight of Negroes in Harlem, sites joined in *Home to Harlem* through the friendship of Ray, a Haitian immigrant, and Jake, a lower-class black from Harlem. His representations of travel, like those of Hughes and Beals, conceptually tie together the spatially "stretch[ed]-out" social relations that allowed U.S. business elites to make decisions that thwarted the rights of citizens in the Caribbean, especially in Haiti. Hughes, Beals, and McKay construct an alternative discourse of hemispheric citizenship in which narratives of class and racial subordination unseat narratives of national loyalty and racial belonging, creating the conditions for a politics of alliance among the oppressed of different nations. McKay constructs alternative primitivist discourses that focus on racial and class hierarchies as well as on the "sensibilities of geopolitical location" in his contrast between the lower-class African American Jake and the educated Haitian Ray.[88]

When McKay traveled from Jamaica to New York (via sojourns in Alabama and Kansas), he encountered what he regarded as a black proletariat —he called *Home to Harlem* a "proletarian novel."[89] Indeed, the rise of the Harlem Renaissance coincided with the transformation of Harlem into a slum. The political economic factors involved in this process have received scant attention from scholars of the Harlem Renaissance, yet could contribute to an enhanced understanding of nationalisms ostensibly based on the redress of the oppression of racialized groups.[90] Indeed, the conditions for the emergence of primitivist nationalisms of the 1920s in Cuba, Mexico, and the United States included frustrated economic expectations: the thwarting of land redistribution in postrevolutionary Mexico and the early advent of the Great Depression in Cuba and Harlem as economically peripheral sites.[91] The Great Migration of African Americans from the South to the North contributed to the ghettoization of Harlem, as the population of the area grew by more than one hundred thousand between 1920 and 1930.[92] An equally important factor in the transformation of Harlem into a slum was the systemic oppression of African Americans in a racially split labor market, which accorded them only menial positions. The majority of black men worked in the service industry—Hughes worked for a time as a busboy—and 70 percent of black women in Manhattan worked as domestics in the 1920s, as did Hurston.[93] Harlem families earned an average of $1,300 a year, well below the New York City average of $1,750.[94] To compound problems, because of racial discrimination in housing, Harlem tenants paid twice as much as white tenants for comparable apartments.[95]

Thus most African Americans were prevented from gaining a stable economic foothold in the urban North. New Negro representations of the black poor did not constitute merely an urban counterpart to the primitivist fascination with the "folk" left behind by modernization, but also grew out of the plight of African American artists and writers whose education and talent did not afford them consonant economic rewards. Any discussion of the discrepancies between standards of living in the United States and Latin America, then, must be joined by attention to the very low ceilings placed on the advancement of African Americans in the domestic racialized political economy. McKay portrays the contraction in the economic hierarchy among blacks in his comparison and contrast of the characters Ray, an uneducated Haitian migrant, and the working-class African American Jake. McKay's pairing of Ray and Jake reveals an intellectual disparity and an economic parity, highlighting the anomalous class position of black intellectuals. As he writes in *The Negroes in America*, a book of sociohistorical and political-economic analysis published in Moscow in 1923, "The ruling class of America wants to keep the Negro intelligentsia, as well as the masses, at the bottom."[96] McKay knew this from personal experience as well: while living in New York, after a failed attempt to own and operate a restaurant, McKay worked as a boiler room operator, bartender, and railroad porter and waiter.[97]

Despite their similarly dim economic prospects, tensions exist between Ray and Jake over differences in their gender ideologies. An opposition between sexuality and respectability similar to that in Beals's representation of Fela drives the plot in *Home to Harlem*: Jake's search for the faithful black woman Felice, who, he believes, made love to him not for money but for love. Hazel Carby has shown how "sexist" representations of black women in Carl Van Vechten and McKay grew out of the widespread "moral panic" over the allegedly immoral sexual behavior of black women migrants to northern cities.[98] In her argument, black female migrants had extremely limited employment opportunity, so either turned to occupations deemed immoral by the black middle class or relied on a husband for economic security. It is indeed true that Jake, a longshoreman who fought in World War I, expresses sexist views. As Carby points out, he chooses Felice as a partner over the arguably more independent blues singer Congo Rose, who threatens black male sexuality by offering to take on the bread-winning role and make Jake her "sweetman."[99]

However, contrary to Carby, other characters criticize Jake's condemnations of women in this multivoiced narrative.[100] While working on the Pennsylvania Railroad, Jake meets Ray who is reading a modern French novel entitled *Sapho*. He explains to Jake that the historical Sappho was a Lesbian. When Jake remarks that Lesbians are in his opinion "ugly women" and called "bulldykers" in Harlem, Ray asks Jake not to disparage them (129). Ray subsequently attempts to persuade Jake to question his sexist, homophobic ideologies. Rather than viewing McKay's text as sexist, as Carby does, one could view his representation of gender roles as forwarding the text's project of educating lower-class black men out of their provincial and homophobic attitudes, a project spearheaded by Ray.

It is precisely Ray's relationship with Jake that defines the novel's alternative decolonizing primitivism. In McKay, decolonizing primitivism pairs an anticolonial politics with a broadly radical vision that refuses to hierarchize differing oppressions: racial, gender, and class oppression all matter.[101] Indeed, McKay's speech to the Fourth Congress of the Third Communist International in Moscow in 1922 places racial subordination on a par with class hierarchies by castigating white American communists for their racial prejudice, while at the same time seriously engaging with communism as offering an alternative to the racialized political economy of the United States[102] Indeed, McKay participated in socialist student groups as early as 1912 and had declared himself a communist by 1920.[103] In the early 1920s, he joined the ABB, which proposed racial equality, higher wages, and lower rents (the ABB later merged with the Communist Party U.S.A.)[104] McKay's claim to fame was his poem "If We Must Die," published in *The Liberator* in July 1919. With the publication of "If We Must Die," McKay became the black voice of the Red Summer, in which whites attacked African Americans in twenty-five urban race riots. Black newspapers across the country reprinted McKay's poem.[105]

Moreover, the character of Ray introduces the problem of imperialism into McKay's "proletarian novel," creating an unusual combination for the day. Ray tells Jake that his father was imprisoned and his brother died while fighting the brutal U.S. military occupation of Haiti that began in 1915. The United States supported an extremely repressive regime during its occupation of Haiti between 1915 and 1934. In 1916 the Haitian government passed a law allowing the forced conscription of labor, leading to a peasant-based rebellion called the Cacos Insurrection in 1916–19. The U.S. military allegedly suppressed the rebellion with a "massacre" of fifteen thousand people. Finally, in 1929, U.S. marines responded to a student-led strike galvanized by the slogan, "Down with Poverty!" with a low-altitude bombing of Port-Au-Prince.[106]

Despite this sordid history of U.S. neocolonialism in Haiti, the country's promise as the hemisphere's only independent black republic stirs Jake's imagination: "It was incredible to Jake that a little island of freed slaves had withstood the three leading European powers" (132). Just as Ray's lesson about Sappho is intended to steer Jake away from sexist ideologies, Ray's history lesson about Haiti and U.S. imperialism helps Jake to grow out of the ethnocentrism he exhibits when he expresses hatred toward his Arab shipmates during his voyage home from the battlefields of Europe (2–3). Moreover, the story of Haiti inspires Jake to modify his prejudiced, residual primitivist attitude towards "foreign niggers," whom he considers "bush niggers, cannibals and . . . monkey chasers," and instead adopt an attitude of solidarity toward African diasporic peoples (134).

In Ray's analysis of oppression, anti-imperialism, antiracism, and a Marxist analysis of economic exploitation converge. Ray bitterly contends that the white agents of European and U.S. capitalism "invest" in imperialism:

> There must be something mighty inspiriting in being the citizen of a great strong nation. To be the white citizen of a nation that can say bold, challenging things like a strong man. Something very different from the keen ecstatic joy a man feels in the romance of being black. . . . Ray felt that as he

was conscious of being black and impotent, so correspondingly, each ma-
rine down in Haiti must be conscious of being white and powerful. What
a unique feeling of confidence the typical white youth of his age must
have! Knowing that his skin-color was a passport to glory making him one
with ten thousands like himself. All perfect Occidentals and investors in
that grand business called civilization. That grand business in whose pits
sweated and snored . . . all the black and brown hybrids and mongrels,
simple earth-loving animals, without aspirations toward national unity and
racial arrogance. (154–5)[107]

By ironically calling "Occidental" civilization a "grand business," Ray lays
bare the profit motives of the military occupation of Haiti and directs the
reader's attention to those who suffer from that business in the "pits"—
those who are "black and brown." By the time he wrote *Home to Harlem*,
McKay had witnessed the "grand business" of Western civilization and its
exploited workers of color in New York and London (as well as in Berlin,
Paris, and Marseilles) and had strengthened his Jamaican outsider perspective by living in Harlem and Russia and writing for socialist publications
in the United States (*The Liberator*) and England (*The Workers' Dread-
nought*). Ray's similar leftist black cosmopolitanism expresses itself in his
contrast between differing models of citizenship and manhood. He sar-
castically suggests that the sensation of power of white U.S. citizens, and
especially the marines in Haiti, is a prosthetic model of manhood in that it
derives from the unjust U.S. military intervention in Haiti. The alternative
to this violent white male imperial citizenship can be found in what Ray
terms "the keen escatic joy a man feels in the romance of being black," in an
implicit reference to Jake. Jake embodies a rejection of participation in the
white man's wars (World War I and the occupation of Haiti) with an
alternative, self-affirming model of citizenship and manhood that celebrates black culture and black physical beauty.

In an attempt to escape from his feelings of degradation and impotence,
Ray overdoses on two packets of heroin Jake kept in his coat pockets. The
epistemology of imperialist civilization condemns Ray, as it does Helga in
Nella Larsen's *Quicksand* (1928), to illness, but civilization itself is condemned to illness. Indeed, when Jake falls ill from drinking too much
alcohol, to Ray "life appeared like one big disease and the world a vast
hospital" (229). To Ray, European civilization's chief products are sickness
and suffering.

Although Ray attempts to educate Jake about imperialism in Haiti and the importance of a feminist perspective, Ray stands to learn much from Jake, as is apparent in their differing strategies of resistance against imperialism and racial capitalism. Ray's abhorrence of European civilization leads to self-deprecation and self-hate. He wishes to purge himself of European civilization, yet he cannot become what he calls "the contented animal that was a Harlem nigger strutting his stuff" (246). While Jake states his admiration for Ray's education at his farewell party, Ray devalues it, likening it to the vacated houses of Harlem, leftovers from whites: "When the whites move out, we move in and take possession of the old dead stuff" (243). Ray thereby implicitly subscribes to the view that there is "nothing outside" the discourses of colonialism and domination, to quote Henry Louis Gates Jr. from a different context.[108] Unable to tolerate the contradictory position he inhabits as a black intellectual, Ray leaves Harlem to work on an ocean freighter, taking the escapist path of wrapping himself "darkly in self love" (246).

Rather than rejecting white culture wholesale, as Ray does, Jake displays the advantages of strategically adopting elements from the dominant culture. While Ray contributes to decolonization by attacking oppression on an intellectual level, Jake shows how the "common people," as Jake's lover Rose is described, thrive despite oppression (114). McKay's description of the "block beautiful," the sole remaining white enclave in Harlem, reveals how he constructs black *joie de vivre* as constituting a protest and a strategy of survival against racial oppression and imperial citizenship: "With its charming green lawns and quaint white-fronted houses, it preserved the most Arcadian atmosphere in all New York. . . . But groups of loud-laughing-and-acting black swains and their sweethearts had started in using the block for their afternoon promenade. That was the limit: the desecrating of that atmosphere by black love in the very shadow of the gray gaunt Protestant church! The Ancient Respectability was getting ready to flee" (301–02). "Desecrated" by black newcomers, the "block beautiful," once a bastion of white wealth, is quickly losing its fragile hold on power: the "afternoon promenade" presages white flight and the subsequent claiming of the area by blacks. Using the terms of the dominant primitivist mode, McKay opposes the "Ancient Respectability" of white Protestants to the implicitly sexually liberated character of lower-class New Negroes, invoking the typical contrast between the modern and the primitive. The "block beautiful" passage suggests that by engaging in a radical critique of processes of imperialism, Ray has gained a critical sensibility at the expense of feeling pride in his identity as an African American—even though he recognizes that black pride in Jake constitutes an alternative to white imperial citizenship.

By contrast, in joining the afternoon promenade of black Harlemites on the "Block Beautiful," Felice and Jake enact a discourse of pride that marks blacks' claim on a significant piece of real estate in New York despite their exploitation and widespread exclusion from ownership—whites owned 80 percent of Harlem's wealth.[109] Lower-class blacks such as Felice and Jake reinhabit what Ray spurns as the "old dead stuff" in order to make the most of what they have been able to get from a hostile society. As Felice says when her favorite club is shut down by the police, "White folks can't padlock niggers outa joy forever" (336). Indeed, for Ann Douglas, the black reclaiming of Harlem as a "homeland" marks its Renaissance as "the 'post-colonial' phase of African-American culture."[110] If the Harlem Renaissance can be viewed as constructing a postcolonial sensibility, McKay searches for the methods of decolonization among the black proletariat, endowed with "simple, raw emotions and real" (338).

Although Jake shares Ray's critical take on civilization as governed by "hate and violence," unlike Ray he manages to "delight in love" (328). Ray's self-doubt and impotence contrasts with Jake's confidence, pride, and happiness through trying times—he is Ray's "contented animal" who exceeds the bounds of such stereotypes of the primitive with his critical consciousness. In McKay the figure of the primitive is the result of the political economies of race and empire and responds creatively to those conditions. Indeed, in *The Negroes in America*, in an extended discussion about the vogue for "Primitive Negro art," McKay roots the term *primitive* in colonial expeditions by the British, Germans, and French. McKay writes that the objects of African art these explorers brought back to London museums "lie like a silent reproach to British imperialism."[111] Both Ray and Jake respond differently to those imperial foundations of the primitive.

In opposing the characters Ray and Jake, McKay points to an enduring contradiction in the New Negro movement: its bifurcation by class. *Home to Harlem* suggests that if the New Negro is to foster social change, intellectuals of the middle class must construct alliances with the black "proletariat," to adopt McKay's term. The friendship between Ray and Jake signals the text's effort to construct a progressive class, gender, anticolonial, and antiracist politics rejecting black middle-class notions of uplift with a Marxist, black Atlantic vision.[112] McKay's attempt to encompass multiple political constituencies epitomizes what Cary Nelson has identified as "an emergent alliance politics of resistance" within a constellation of black, feminist, and white leftist publications in the 1920s, a scene in which Mc-Kay participated prominently as a contributor to Max Eastman's *Liberator* beginning in 1919 and as an associate editor beginning in 1921.[113]

"THE LIGHT OF THE SPANIARD DEFEATED THE SHADOW OF THE INDIAN": THE MEXICAN INDIGENISMO OF MENÉNDEZ

As in Haiti and Cuba, in Mexico the European and U.S. aspects of neocolonialism were sustained by a homegrown neocolonialism, one epitomized by the dictatorship of Porfirio Díaz (1877–1910), known as the Porfiriato. Díaz gave foreign companies unprecedented access to national resources and waged wars of extermination against indigenous groups.[114] The Mexican Revolution (1910–17) overturned the Porfiriato, making possible a wave of Mexican nationalism in the 1920s that consisted in various reformist measures such as land redistribution and the assimilation of Indians. As director of the National University in 1920 and secretary of public education in 1921–24, José Vasconcelos spearheaded the national reform effort: he launched a campaign against illiteracy (which was as high as 80 percent as late as 1910); he increased by 50 percent the numbers of schools and teachers and students in schools; and he initiated an ambitious public mural project.[115]

Indigenismo describes the variety of such reformist practices and discourses adopted by *ladinos* (non-Indians) on behalf of Indians and practiced by political officials, artists, and writers alike.[116] Indigenismo presented white and mestizo intellectuals in Latin America with a way of exploring their ideas on race, the exploitation of labor, modernization, mestizaje, social reform, citizenship, and empire. Indigenismo was common to Mexico, Guatemala, and the Andean region (Bolivia, Ecuador, and Peru). Although the most famous *indigenista* cultural texts were films and novels, the genre also included music, paintings, and poetry.[117]

Mexican indigenismo was prolific in literature and the visual arts. Among the most important Mexican *indigenista* novels were *La tierra del faisán y del venado* (The land of pheasant and deer, 1922) by Mediz Bolio, *Los hombres que dispersó la danza* (The men that the dance scattered, 1929) by Andrés Henestrosa, *El Indio* (The Indian, 1935) by Gregorio López y

Fuentes, *El resplandor* (Sunburst, 1937) by Mauricio Magdaleno, *Canek* (1940) by Ermilio Abreu Gómez, *Lola Casanova* (1943) by Francisco Rojas González, and *El luto humano* (Human mourning, 1943) by José Revueltas. The so-called "cycle of Chiapas" includes the novels *Juan Pérez Jolote* (1948) by Ricardo Pozas, *El callado dolor de los tzotziles* (The silent suffering of the Tzotziles, 1957) by Ramón Rubín, *Balún Canán* (The nine guardians, 1957) and *Oficio de tinieblas* (The book of lamentations, 1962) by Rosario Castellanos, and *La culebra tapó el río* (The snake stopped up the river, 1962) by María Lombardo de Caso. Important books in the genre of the essay included *Forjando Patria* (Forging the nation, 1916) by Manuel Gamio, *La raza cósmica* (The cosmic race, 1925) by José Vasconcelos, and *El perfil del hombre y la cultura en México* (Profile of man and culture in Mexico, 1934) by Samuel Ramos.

As secretary of public education, Vasconcelos commissioned a series of public murals, calling for an art "saturated with primitive vigor"; in doing so he launched the careers of "los tres grandes," the three most important Mexican muralists: José Clemente Orozco, Diego Rivera, and David Alfaro Siqueiros.[118] The work of Orozco and Rivera was particularly germane to indigenismo. In a series of frescoes at the National Preparatory School (1923–26), Orozco portrayed the costs and achievements of the Mexican Revolution and featured the heroism of mestizos and Indians, situating the revolution as part of an ongoing history of colonialism and its aftermaths (Rochfort 40–48). Rivera's famous murals in the Ministry of Education in Mexico City (1923–28) celebrated the diverse cultures of Mexico, the social achievements of the Mexican Revolution, and indigenous workers' and "proletarian" activism (as in "The Agitator," 1926) (Rochfort 50–77). Early Mexican cinema was similarly obsessed with Indians. Films dealing with Indian themes included *Tepeyac* (1918), *Tabaré* (1918), *Cuauhtémoc* (1919), *El rey poeta* (1920), *En la hacienda* (In the hacienda, 1921), *La raza de bronce* (The race of bronze, 1931), *Janitzio* (1934), *El Indio* (1938), *La india bonita* (The pretty Indian, 1938), *Rosa de Xochimilco* (1938), *La noche de los Mayas* (The night of the Mayas, 1939), *María Candelaria* (1943), and *Flor Silvestre* (Wildflower, 1943).

Mexican indigenismo was highly influential in other Latin American countries, but particularly in Guatemala.[119] One of the early indigenista novels in Guatemala was Carlos Wyld Ospina's *La tierra de Nahuayacas* (The land of the Nahuayacas, 1933), a "fictionalized ethnography" (Lienhard 50). The most important Guatemalan indigenista novelist was Miguel

Angel Asturias, the first Latin American prose writer to win the Nobel Prize; among his works were *Leyendas de Guatemala* (Legends of Guatemala, 1930) and *Hombres de maíz* (Men of maize, 1949). In Bolivia and Ecuador the figure of the Indian was similarly central to debates over how to construct a modern nation. In Bolivia, Alcides Arguedas wrote two influential novels, *Wuata Wuara* (1904) and *Raza de bronce* (Race of bronze, 1919). An early novel on Indian themes in Ecuador was *Cumandá* (1879) by Juan León Mera. The founder of institutionalized indigenismo in Ecuador was Pío Jaramillo Alvarado, the author of *El indio ecuatoriano: Contribución al estudio de la Sociología Indo-Americana* (The Ecuadorian Indian: Contribution to the study of Indo-American sociology, 1922). Jaramillo would go on to found the Ecuadorian branch of the Instituto Indigenista Interamericano, which he directed from 1941 to 1960. In 1927, Fernando Chaves wrote the indigenista novel *Plata y bronce*. The Mexican Moisés Saénz published *Sobre el indio ecuatoriano* (On the Ecuadorian Indian) in 1933. The most important indigenist novel in Ecuador was Jorge Icaza's *Huasipungo* (1934).[120]

Peru was the site of a similarly distinguished tradition of indigenista writing.[121] Nineteenth-century Peruvian writers on Indian issues included the socialist essayist and vitriolic defender of Indian rights Manuel González Prada and the novelist Clorinda Matto de Turner, author of *Aves sin nido* (Birds without a nest, 1889). Matto's first novel was preceded by other novels on Indian themes elsewhere in Latin America and the Caribbean, including the previously mentioned *Cumandá* (Ecuador, 1879), José de Alencar's *Iracema* (Brazil, 1866), and Manuel de Jesús Galván's *Enriquillo* (Santo Domingo, 1882). Moreover, two remarkable, lesser-known novels from Peru set precedents for Matto's writing: Nelson Aréstegui's *El Padre Horán* (1848), which portrays the social and political dilemmas surrounding the figure of the Indian, and Ladislao Graña's *Sé bueno y serás feliz* (1860), which denounces the forced labor of Indians.

Enrique López Albújar is said to have inaugurated the twentieth-century indigenismo literary movement in Peru with his *Cuentos andinos* (Andean stories, 1920), followed by the novel *Matalaché* (1928). The journal *Amauta* (1926–30), founded by José Carlos Mariátegui, Luis Alberto Sánchez, and Jorge Basadre, served as an important generator of indigenista thought across national boundaries, and the *Boletín Titikaka* (1926–30) was the main forum of indigenous writers. Other prominent Peruvian indigenista texts include Hildebrando Castro Pozo's *Celajes de Sierra* (Cloudy skies of the Sierra, 1916) and *Nuestra comunidad indígena* (Our indigenous community, 1918), the Marxist Mariátegui's *Siete ensayos de interpretación de la realidad peruana* (Seven interpretive essays on Peruvian reality, 1928), Uriel Garcia's *El nuevo indio* (1930), Ciro Alegría's *El mundo es ancho y ajeno* (Broad and alien is the world, 1941), Jesús Lara's *Surumi, novela quechua* (1943), and José María Arguedas's *Yawar Fiesta* (1941), *Los ríos profundos* (Deep rivers, 1958), and *Todas las sangres* (All bloods, 1964).

Although there were many national varieties of indigenismo, each primarily sought to intervene in a national sociopolitical scene rather than across national borders. Therefore, Mexican indigenismo can be regarded as a subset of Mexican nationalism along with *hispanismo*, an interest in the Spanish roots of Latin America, and *latinoamericanismo*, which emphasizes commonalities between Mexico and other Latin American countries.[122] Although indigenismo carved out important spheres of influence in the Mexican political scene of the 1920s and 1930s, newspapers routinely denounced the "savage customs" of Indians, pointing to the majority's belief in the inferiority of Indians in the postrevolutionary era.[123] Indigenismo's considerable influence within political circles despite its lack of popularity among the majority of acculturated Mexicans can be attributed in part to the postrevolutionary cultural consensus that Mexico needed to search for what Antonio Caso called in 1930 "nuestro destino" (our destiny) in its own traditions.[124] Another key factor in the influential role of indigenism was the high level of rural migration to Mexico City during and after the Revolution; this movement placed lettered elites in close proximity to representatives of the varied regions, cultures, and indigenous populations of Mexico. The most important reason for the influence of official indigenismo was its populist rhetoric, which sought to appeal to Mexicans of all classes via the unifying figure of Indian heritage.

Unlike New Negro reformist schemes, official indigenismo was initiated by whites and mestizos rather than by those who most suffered from racial oppression in Mexico.[125] Official indigenismo's goals of assimilation have been faulted for reenacting evolutionary schemes of progress that construct Indians as inferior.[126] The residual primitivist notion that Indians were stuck on a lower evolutionary level underwrote the attempts of President Plutarco Calles (1924–28) to exterminate the Yaquis of Sonora, who demanded the return of their tribal lands. Government troops massacred a great number of Yaquis and then proceeded to bomb their territory in 1926.[127] State-sponsored indigenismo was thus a bifurcated nationalism consisting of a rhetoric that stressed national unity based on indigenous heritage and a practice that enacted ambitious social reforms benefiting some Indian groups while at the same time making Indians the targets of neglect, exploitation, and, in some cases, extermination.

Gamio and Vasconcelos, the two leading proponents of Mexican indigenismo as Indian reform in the 1920s and the heads of the government's Department of Anthropology and the Department of Public Education, respectively, opposed what Vasconcelos called the "ejército de destructores" (army of destroyers) approach to Indians practiced by Calles and by Díaz before him, but similarly constructed Indians as being behind in an evolutionary scale of progress.[128] In *The Indian Basis of Mexican Civilization* (1926), a lecture delivered at the University of Chicago, Gamio calls for "redeeming the Mexican masses" by constituting them as subjects who think of themselves as Mexican rather than as members of their respective indigenous groups.[129] To that end, Gamio calls rural schools "Centers of Cultural Incorporation" (*IB* 150). Gamio views both Indians and mestizos as deficient in evolutionary terms: Indians have "stagnated miserably," and mestizos have a "defective hybrid culture" (*IB* 154, 169). So at least in its general outlines the "mental revolution" that for Gamio followed the Mexican Revolution resolves the Indians' condition of "utter wretchedness" by prioritizing the transformation of indigenous peoples into Mexican citizens—civilizing the "masses"—over uprooting the exploitative structures of the surrounding society (for a more extended discussion of the contradictory mixture of reformism and evolutionism in Gamio's indigenist politics, see chapter 4) (*IB* 169, 171).

Vasconcelos similarly operates under the assumption of what Gamio, despite his Boasian training, calls as late as 1923 "la ley inevitable de la evolución" (the inevitable law of evolution).[130] Because of what Vasconcelos calls an incomplete "blending process" that has maintained the existence of a "hundred different stocks," Mexico has failed to attain its evolutionary destiny as a nation: "Instead of an evolutionary series of events, as you may find for instance in the history of Europe, the history of Mexico will show you a number of glorious but lonely, disconnected efforts like sparks in the darkness."[131] In addition to the great heterogeneity of racial stocks, what Vasconcelos calls "the tropical problem"—the allegedly slower development of civilization in the tropics—similarly hinders evolutionary progress in Mexico (*LAB* 13). Vasconcelos takes the greater obstacles to civilization in the Latin American tropics as proof that "the race that shall conquer the tropics will be the master of the future" (*LAB* 24). Vasconcelos praises Indians as possessors "of as many good qualities as any other living race," ostensibly placing them on a plane equal to that of European civilization, yet criticizes Indian forms of social organization as an "oriental indigenous type of despotism" (*LAB* 52). Indians are not so much "primitive" as they are "provincial" in their inability to forge national unity among themselves (*LAB* 77, 90). Since the nation imagined as racially homogeneous is essential to Vasconcelos as a measure of evolutionary progress, Indians as such can only be obstacles to national unity. However, they can serve as passive ingredients in the process of mestizaje.

So while Harlem Renaissance intellectuals such as McKay rejected civilizationist discourse as contributing to oppression by race and class, Mexican nationalists had reached a consensus that a mestizo civilization built along European lines with indigenous trimmings could resolve social problems and place Mexico on an equal footing with other nations. In viewing racial homogeneity as a precondition of national unity and progress, Gamio and Vasconcelos subscribe to "Darwinian collectivism of the nationalist or racist variety," a residual primitivist discourse that relies on evolutionary notions of history as the unilinear progress of nations toward higher degrees of sophistication in civilization.[132] Gamio's imagined collectivity extends to the borders of the nation, while that of Vasconcelos includes all of Latin America. Vasconcelos's Latinoamericanismo, relying on a future racially homogeneous, international collectivity of mestizo Latin American nation-states, contrasts with McKay's Marxist, Pan-Africanist ideology, which presents a more skeptical view of civilization and nation-states as vehicles of oppression by race and class.

The evolutionary underside to indigenismo, evident in Gamio and Vasconcelos, shows that indigenismo did not resolve national problems of racial conflict, but to a great extent constituted such problems. Postrevolutionary Mexican nationalism was a contradictory discourse in that it set in tension the question of minority self-determination—official assertions of indigenous disfranchisement—with a homogenizing logic of national unity via mestizaje understood in Guillermo Bonfil Batalla's sense of "desindianización," or de-Indianization of Indians.[133] On the one hand, President Calles portrayed Indians as an oppressed population: "No government in Mexico can last unless it recognizes the age-long cry of the Indian for land."[134] In this statement, official nationalism calls for radical social reform that would disrupt prevailing social hierarchies, in this case through land redistribution. On the other hand, official nationalism sought to reconcile and even erase political, regional, cultural, and class differences. As Ricardo Pérez Montfort writes, the notion of "lo mexicano" relied on an increasingly geographically restricted stereotype of "el charro y la china poblana bailando el jarabe tapatío" (cowboy and a *china poblana* dancing a traditional tap dance), the most popular embodiment of Mexicanness by the mid-1920s.[135] Not only did this widely reproduced and widely performed spectacle of Mexicanness narrow Mexico's vast regional diversity down to three regions, the Bahío, Jalisco, and Puebla, it also emptied Mexicanness of any indigenous signs or traces of class conflict, since the *charros* and *chinas poblanas* signified a pastoral image of the hacienda. This pastoral version of Mexican nationalism was used by conservative landowners to portray themselves as intrinsically Mexican and therefore to oppose agrarian land reform on the grounds that it threatened a treasured national way of life.[136] By contrast, a cluster of indigenist discourses— ranging from those depicting "el indito," an icon of beauty and of an indigenous past viewed as the glorious prehistory of Mexico, to Gamio's indigenous subject requiring land reform—relied on a notion of "la raza doliente" (the suffering race) that at least implicitly invoked social injustice (but that failed to fully collaborate with indigenous social movements).[137]

These contrasting images of Indians within Mexican nationalism suggest the need for a discussion of the many Mexican nationalisms and indigenisms circulating in the 1920s, just as New Negro nationalisms spanned the political spectrum. Indeed, another contradictory vector slicing through Mexican nationalist discourses is the contrast between the homogenizing logic of official Mexican nationalism—"nosotros los mexicanos" (we, the Mexicans)—and the multiple and oftentimes contestatory nationalist discourses that proliferated beyond strict state control. In recognizing the diversity of Mexican nationalism, one must strike a balance between recognition of the state's increasingly proponderant role as a cultural patron and the fact that the state's hegemony over national culture was continuously contested by unequal partners and antagonists in Mexican nationalism.[138] These diverse nationalisms include the Marxist/indigenist class-based analysis of Rivera and Siqueiros;[139] the conservative landowners' discourse of the "rural eden";[140] and Yucatán governor Felipe Carrillo Puerto's socialist and feminist Mayan nationalism.[141] Although Carrillo Puerto came to power through a strategic use of violence and through pragmatic cooperation with *caciques* (local political bosses) and suppressed the autonomy of urban unions, his government (1922–24) aggressively attacked conditions of peonage on sugar plantations, achieving in Yucatán, after the state of Morelos, the most success in land redistribution and embarked on an extensive plan of instruction in the Mayan languages.[142] Moreover, Carrillo Puerto organized *ligas de resistencia* (leagues of resistance) of peasants and *ligas de feministas* (feminist leagues) of women, both of which served as hybrid political, social, and educational institutions linking "ethnic pride to class consciusness."[143] Such contradictions in Mexican nationalism emerge from the tensions between competing social groups in the new political order: in the Mexican Revolution the liberal opposition (the urban middle class) in alliance with the popular revolutionary movement (rural mestizos and Indian peasants) had ousted the old regime (Porfirian landowners, the military, and the clergy).[144]

A corollary to these contradictions of Mexican nationalism was the tension between the nation as the horizontal mestizo brotherhood of revolutionary reform and the vertical axis of the continued subordination of women. A key literary debate of 1925 associated "el afeminamiento en la literatura mexicana" (effeminacy in Mexican literature) with the betrayal of Mexican nationalism in favor of European cultural influences.[145] This association of the feminine with the betrayal of the nation demonstrates that the battle over the authenticity of national identities was fought along starkly drawn gender oppositions that denigrated the feminine.

The Mexican Constitution granted political rights to all Mexican citizens, including Indians, but excluded women from the category of citizen.[146] Mexican feminists engaged in an organized struggle to put women's rights on the reform agenda. Elena Torres, a Mexican teacher, Trotskyite socialist, and collaborator of Carrillo Puerto, participated in the First Pan-American Conference of Women in Baltimore in 1922, in which the delegates launched a movement to promote women's suffrage throughout the hemisphere. Torres was named the vice president of the newly formed Pan-American Association for the Advancement of Women.[147] In 1923, the Mexican branch of the association held a conference that drew one hundred women.[148] In 1934, Lázaro Cárdenas pledged to make good on the promises of the revolution by granting equal rights to workers, indigenous peoples, and women. In response to an effective mass campaign supporting women's right to vote, Cárdenas favored a constitutional amendment giving women the vote in 1938. The measure passed both the Senate and the House but was not ratified by the states until 1953, when it was finally made into law.[149]

Miguel Angel Menéndez's novel *Nayar* (1940) intervenes in debates over

Mexican nationalism by joining the gender question to the Indian question in its portrayal of the sexual betrayal of the mestizo protagonist's wife, which leads him to kill a judge and join a band of Cora Indians in the Sierra.[150] *Nayar*'s late publication date—it came out over a decade after the novels by McKay and Masdeu—demonstrates the protracted character of the sociopolitical conflicts of the Mexican Revolution. Indeed, although article 27 of the Mexican Constitution of 1917 held that oil fields were the property of the nation, it was not until March 18, 1938, that President Cárdenas nationalized Mexican oil, shocking the world. Cárdenas also sped up land redistribution, another central ideal of the Mexican Revolution, beginning in 1935, and maintained his political clout through an alliance with peasants and workers.[151] *Nayar* is set during the Cristero War (1926–29), a civil war that pitted peasant followers of the Catholic Church against the anticlerical state.[152] *Nayar* implicitly endorses this conservative backlash against the radical social reforms instituted by the state in the early 1920s by figuring women and Indians as equally unreliable, as a synopsis will demonstrate. In *Nayar*, the mestizo Ramón Cordoba goes into hiding after having murdered an unpopular judge whom he caught sleeping with his wife. In retaliation, friends of the judge kill an innocent man who resembles Ramón. Furious over Ramón's ostensible death, the townspeople set fire to the judge's house and to the workplace of Enrique Salinas, a disillusioned white federal tax agent in San Blás, Nayarit, who joins his mestizo friend.[153]

Enrique and Ramón flee into the Sierra del Nayar, commencing the narrative's journey, one that is picaresque in that as they travel they reveal a broad cross section of Mexican society, including a small provincial town of whites and mestizos, a series of Indian villages, and the Sierra Nayar mountains, home to Cara, Huichol, and Tepehuana Indians. The two move through a range of indigenous communities, finally witnessing the rebellion of Indian laborers against the *gringo* owner of a gold mine.[154] A leader of the Indian labor rebellion, Pedro Gervasio, a Cora Indian elder, or *tatouan*, allows Enrique and Ramón to travel with his people. The fragile bond Enrique and Ramón construct with Gervasio's band of Coras shatters when Gervasio accepts his people's ruling that the *hechicero*, or sorcerer, Uchuntu deserves to die for using his powers against the community. Believing that Uchuntu is innocent, Ramón betrays his trust with the Coras by alerting federal troops, who mistakenly kill him, Ramón, when they arrive.

Two alliances opposed to the putatively corrupt, institutionalized revolution form in the novel, alliances that comprise the text's alternative nationalism. The first is a male mestizo–white alliance embodied in the rebellion of Ramón and Enrique against government corruption. Enrique, the "jefe" (boss) of a federal tax agency, rebels against a "vicious cycle" of corruption apparent at his workplace: "Those who tell the truth go bankrupt" (37). State corruption is figured as a lapse of morals, much as the feminist movement was portrayed by the popular press in Mexico. Thus women's rights and state corruption comprise a composite figure of postrevolutionary "immorality," as evidenced by the fact that the judge was sleeping with Ramón's wife.

The second alliance is the fragile bond Enrique and Ramón develop with Gervasio's band of Cora Indians. The outlaw status of both Ramón and Enrique allows them to explore Indianness as signifying rebellion against the factors comprising neocolonialism in Mexico, including labor exploitation and socioeconomic inequality. Their rejection of the mainstream and their initial sympathy for the Indians mark a convergence between desires for governmental reform and for decolonization. This connection is most visible when Enrique and Ramón sympathize with the Indian rebellion against the gringo gold-mine owner. The gringo owner embodies the long-standing exploitation of Mexican citizens by U.S. and European companies—in 1925 foreign interests controlled one-half of national wealth in Mexico[155]—while Cometa, the military chief of the Sierra, embodies what Vasconcelos in 1920 called the "ejército de los destructores," referring to the Indian policies of Díaz and Calles, opposed to the postrevolutionary ideal of "el ejército de los educadores" (army of the educators).[156] Cometa proclaims, "There is no better Indian than a dead Indian" (155). Thus the shared antipathy of white, mestizo, and Indian characters toward these elements of neocolonialism allows them to forge an alliance among themselves. However, by portraying the culprits of neocolonialism as either foreigners or remnants of the Porfirian past, *Nayar* fails to explore the domestic contradictions of racial conflicts in the postrevolutionary present.

This cross-racial alliance is achieved through the subordination of women by all groups. When Ramón slashes his wife's face with a machete after she sleeps with the judge, he remarks, "The men of yesteryear would have forgiven me" (17). Here the "men of yesteryear" is ambiguous: it could refer to a past era of more heroic Mexicans, but it could also refer to the

Indians, other "men of yesteryear." "Indian cultures only can exist as a dead thing in the past, but never in the present or future," as Bonfil Batalla has written.[157] The masculinist dimensions of the cross-racial alliance fully emerge when the Coras humiliate a woman who breaks gender conventions. Skirt of Flowers, a Huichol woman whom a Cora man claimed as his wife by raping her, is caught sleeping with the man she loves. In a "cleansing ceremony," she is led naked by Gervasio through the plaza to her husband before the entire town (183). Neither Ramón nor Enrique objects to this public humiliation because they agree that an unfaithful woman deserves punishment.

If the alliance between Mexicans and Coras is forged through the subordination of women, it also forms through cross-racial homosocial bonds constituting a desired "national fraternity." The hopes for cross-cultural harmony are represented in the budding friendship between Enrique and Leandro, a Cora Indian. Enrique finally gains Leandro's trust by seeking his recommended cure for fever. As they speak, a swallow falls from the sky at their feet:

> Both of us saw the small tragedy and we sought each other's eyes, without speaking. We said everything with that look. He saw my soul, I saw his. In both souls there were dead swallows.
> —Tatoani Leandro: in this way dreams take flight and then die.
> —In this way they die, little white man (*blanquito*), in this way they die. (145)

The cross-racial male friendship created by this primitivist-humanist discourse of kindred souls relies on the male exclusion of women, as is evident in the fates of Ramón's wife and Skirt of Flowers. Vera Kutzinski's argument that in 1920s Cuban negrismo "the mestizo nation is a male homosocial construct premised precisely upon the disappearance of the feminine" holds equally true for this version of Mexican indigenismo.[158]

However, this bonding moment between Enrique and Leandro is followed by their dispute over the legacy of Manuel Lozada, the Tiger of Alica, who led a mass insurrection of Indians in 1853 and who later signed the Plan Libertador for the Pueblos Unidos del Nayarit in 1873, proclaiming the national independence of Cora and Huichol Indians.[159] The two friends differ on the cause of Lozada's defeat. Enrique maintains that the Mexican army defeated him, subscribing to a tragic narrative of indigenous rebellion in Mexico. By contrast, Leandro claims that Lozada failed because the Gods realized he had not liberated his brothers, as he had promised:

"But to liberate the Indians is to make the whites go away, that they leave us alone, as we were before they came. Or to kill them if they don't want to leave."[160] Rather than perpetuate a discourse of the tragic primitive, Leandro emphasizes Indians' continued liberation struggles. Liberty for the Indians, argues Leandro, would result in the expulsion of all whites from Mexico.[161] The fact that Leandro cannot imagine the independence of Indians as long as whites populate Mexico reveals the difficulties of decolonization in an independent yet neocolonial nation. Leandro's construction of Mexico as riven by an unresolvable conflict between Mexicans and Indians challenges the narrative's tentative resolution of racial conflict through the discourse of homosocial humanism in the swallow incident.

If the violent suppression of women and the disputed character of Indian–white conflicts reveal two aspects of the underside of the novel's project of indigenismo, the novel's ambivalent stance with regard to its project of assimilating Indians into Mexicanness reveals another.[162] *Nayar*'s pessimistic view of Indian assimilation becomes apparent when Gervasio orders the death of Uchuntu, the *hechicero*, and a storm looms as if to punctuate the crisis. Ramón is represented as being deeply troubled by the death sentence owing to his mixed racial heritage. Bandied about by his two heritages, Ramón embodies the storm, a metaphor for cultural conflict in Mexico. The mestizo, "his spirit dislocated by the clash between two heritages," is tragically divided and disoriented: "It may have been that the storm had placed itself in the body of Ramón. It may have been that the two immensities that the mestizo carries within him emerged in his blood" (260). When Ramón decides to alert federal troops of the impending lynching of Uchuntu, who is suspected by Gervasio's tribe of practicing black magic, his Spanish blood is said to have triumphed over his Indian blood: "His mestizo leaven finally defeated the color of his skin, the color of the dawn at the point of daybreak. The light of the Spaniard defeated the shadow of the Indian." Here the imagery of dawn versus shadow equates the Spanish inheritance with civilization and the faculties of reason, while consigning the Indian to the allegedly superstitious past, thereby perpetuating colonialist discourses. *Nayar*'s indigenismo, then, seeks to integrate Indians into Mexican culture, but only through Bonfil Batalla's process of "desindianización."[163] In this closing scene, *Nayar* turns its back on the possibilities of the implicit yet promising alliance between Enrique and Ramón and Indians. Ramón's rejection of his Indian heritage leaves no room for transculturation, for a negotiation between dominant and minority cultural traits, as in McKay, but rather calls for acculturation to white norms.

Although *Nayar* deploys indigenist discourses, it despairs of a true dialogue between whites and Indians, as the final image of Gervasio refusing to speak to a journalist while imprisoned for the murder of Uchuntu reveals: "Perhaps he understands when all is done that his tradition exists in conflict with the culture of his *conquistadores*, that it is useless to explain his sorrows because no one will understand them. In his very flesh he feels the defeat of his race once again" (266). Here, in contrast to the buoyant figure of Jake in McKay's *Home to Harlem*, it is Enrique's tragic narrative of Indian rebellion that prevails, rather than the competing version offered by the Indian Leandro, which calls for uncompromised freedom for Indians. In betraying his Cora friends, Ramón becomes part of neocolonialism, what the group of Indians he encountered in Mexcaltitán refer to as the "camichín," a vine that strangles jungle trees by entwining itself around them. When the villagers of Mexcaltitán expelled Enrique and Ramón from their town, they shouted, "camichín" (94).

"TO BE AN INTELLIGENT BLACK IS A CRIME": MASDEU AND CUBAN NEGRISMO

While Menéndez's character Ramón embodies state-sponsored Mexican indigenismo as a discourse of modernization via mestizaje, Cuban negrismo reveals the racial violence inherent in modernization. The negrismo movement is said to have been inaugurated by the Puerto Rican Luis Palés Matos in his poem "Danzarina africana" (African dancer) (1917–18), later included in his collection *Tun tun de pasa y grifería* (The drumbeat of the kinky-haired and mulattos, 1925–37). In Cuba, negrismo took root in letters with Fernando Ortiz's *Glosario de afronegrismos* (Glossary of Afro-Cuban terms, 1924) and Gustavo Urrutia's "Ideales de una Raza" (The ideals of a race) series in Havana's daily *El Diario de la Marina* (1926–31); these were followed by Nicolás Guillén's *Motivos del Son* (1930), *Sóngoro Cosongo* (1931), and *West Indies, Ltd.* (1934) and by the poetry of the Chinese-Afro-Cuban Regino Pedroso; and in painting with Eduardo Abela's *El triunfo de la rumba* (The triumph of the rumba, 1928) and *El gallo místico* (The mystic rooster, 1928) and Carlos Enríquez's *Tocadores* (Musicians, 1935). In popular music Afro-Cubanism dominated with various Afro-Cuban *conjuntos de son*, including the Septeto Habanero, the Septeto Nacional, and the

Quarteto Machín, the salon music of the white composer Ernesto Lecuona, the work of the Afro-Cuban singer and pianist Rita Montaner (who appeared with Josephine Baker in Paris in 1927 and with Al Jolson in New York in the early 1930s), and the mulatto singer and composer Ignacio Villa in the 1930s, said to be the Cuban Louis Armstrong.[164]

Negrismo unfolded during a tumultuous decade of activist organizing that witnessed the founding of the Radical Socialist Party in 1920, the Cuban Federation of Women's Associations in 1921, and the Communist Party of Cuba in 1925 along with numerous student activist groups. At a time when the race-blind public discourses of the Cuban Republic dominated, writers like Carpentier in ¡Ecue-Yamba-Ó! and the Afro-Cuban poets Guillén and Pedroso courageously foregrounded the problems and longings of Afro-Caribbeans as epitomizing the problems of Cuba as a nation.[165] Chief among these national problems were the great economic and social disparities caused to a great extent by the U.S. domination of the Cuban economy—as noted above, the United States owned 82 percent of sugar plantations and up to 22 percent of national territory.[166] In addition, by the provisions of the Platt Amendment (1903), the United States had the right to intervene to protect those economic interests, as in 1921 when General Enoch Crowder arrived in Havana in a battleship to intimidate those who were striking and demonstrating in protest of widespread unemployment and food shortages brought on by the collapse of sugar prices in 1920.[167] These two factors combined to constitute U.S. neocolonialism in Cuba.

The U.S. domination of the sugar industry and its willingness to use military force against Cuba are main ingredients in representations of the political scene in negrismo. But negrismo also insisted that the problem of neocolonialism was matched by the particular oppressions endured by Afro-Cubans. In his essay "El Camino de Harlem" (1929), Guillén argued that race relations in Cuba increasingly resembled racial oppression in the United States, setting Cuba on the "road to Harlem." He describes the plight of Afro-Cubans as the quintessentially postcolonial problem of the failure of the nation to live up to the promises of independence: "Is it possible that after the two great revolutions against Spain and after the installation of the *patria libre* [independent republic] . . . there could be one population of Cubans . . . who feel differentiated from the other?. . . . *Sí, señores*, the *raza de color* still has problems in Cuba. . . . [I]t is necessary to continue combatting innumerable prejudices."[168] Thus negrismo must be read both as participating to some extent in the activism that swept across Cuba in the 1920s in response to the dire economic plight of the majority, and, at its best, as also insisting on the specificity of the oppression of Afro-Cubans, whether of the lower or middle classes. In negrismo, as in the Harlem Renaissance and in indigenismo, discourses of race, anti-imperialism, and nationalism converge with global primitivism.

The publication of Jesús Masdeu's little-known *La raza triste* (The sad race, 1924) was delayed for over ten years, perhaps as a result of the chilling effect of the massacre of thousands of Afro-Cubans with the collusion of the U.S. marines in the Race War of 1912, a war that created the conditions for the travails of the mulatto protagonist of the novel.[169] In his preface, written in 1920, Masdeu claims that for years he delayed submitting his manuscript for publication because he feared exposing "the inconsolable cry of those who still suffer from slavery."[170] Masdeu does not reveal his own racial identity in the preface, but he does claim that he conceived the book while working in cane fields alongside blacks: "I wrote *La raza triste*, like other essays of mine, obeying impulses inseparable from my feelings: to vent my sadnesses as a slave, a vagabond pariah, a rebel against the justice that condemned me to an inferior position among human refuse" (7). Although it is uncertain whether Masdeu is Afro-Cuban, like that population he personally suffered the condition of exploited peon or "slave." Masdeu's *La raza triste* and Beals's *The Crime of Cuba* can be thought of as bookends to the social upheavals of the early years of the republic, which began with the massacre of thousands of Afro-Cubans and temporarily culminated in the overthrow of the Machado dictatorship.

This as yet untranslated novel focuses on the tragic love between Miguel Valdés, a talented mulatto doctor, and Gabriela Estrada y Céspedes, his white childhood friend. With the financial aid of two white men, Don Antonio, Gabriela's father, and Don Epicuro, Miguel is able to study in the United States. Upon his return, however, he discovers the limits of their generosity: both turn against him under the influence of the ex-slaveowner Don Enrique Reyes and his son Armando. The wealth and social status of Don Enrique and Armando allow them to persuade the newspaper *El Demócrata* to smear Miguel's reputation as a responsible citizen and doctor, even going so far as to allege that Miguel and Gabriela attempted to poison Don Antonio in order to claim his estate. With his clientele gone and all but a few friends avoiding him, Miguel loses hope, becoming an alcoholic. By the end of the novel, he has become the naturalist archetypal "brute" (304): he has murdered his friend, the mulatto Edmundo, mistaking him for the editor of the newspaper that has so maligned him. In a bitterly ironic ending, it is only after Miguel's prison stay has deprived him of all hope that he is set free, to live miserably as a homeless alcoholic for a short time until he dies.

The title of the novel, *La raza triste*, points to its use of the naturalist narrative strategy of social determinism, a strategy that is more egalitarian than *Nayar*'s biological determinism. The novel sets up a series of conspicuous contrasts that reveal the social mechanisms determining the fate of Afro-Cubans. Miguel's scholastic career begins auspiciously when he shows great talent as an orator but then ends in frustration when twenty-two medical schools in the United States expel him when his nemesis, a white Cuban youth, exposes him as a mulatto and when he can't find employment in Cuba.[171] Miguel's experience was representative of the plight of the Afro-Cuban middle classes aspiring to professional positions: in 1907, for instance, only 4 out of 1,345 lawyers in the census were Afro-Cuban.[172]

Such hopes and frustrations of Afro-Cubans are captured by the two contradictory poles in Cuban history shaping the conflicts in the novel. On the one hand, the interracial War for Independence (1895–98), in which Afro-Cubans comprised 85 percent of the troops and 40 percent of the officer corps, exemplifies suppressed national ideals of racial egalitarianism.[173] As Miguel says, "The war . . . was our culminating moment" (171). Or as Don Antonio says to his friend Anacleto Valdés, Miguel's father, "Nos hermanó la guerra" (the war made us brothers) (31). When Anacleto questions whether Miguel will be allowed to study abroad, Don Antonio reassures him: "All that black and white stuff was in the times of slavery, and pertains to what we should forget. Today we are brothers" (31).

On the other hand, the Aponte slave rebellion of 1811 and the Race War of 1912 loom as evidence of enduring conflict between whites and ex-slaves. Don Enrique invokes the Aponte controversy in arguing that the black is the "natural enemy" of whites: "What you want is to give wings to blacks," he tells Don Antonio, insisting that the scholarships be given only to whites. "And blacks are going to cause us quite a few headaches. Remember Aponte" (32). The Race War of 1912 erupted when the Partido Independiente de Color (PIC, Independent Party of Color) began pressing the government via demonstrations and strikes throughout Cuba to rescind the Morua Act outlawing the organization of race-based political parties.

The PIC stood for a democratized Cuba: it called for compulsory free education, the abolition of the death penalty, reform of the judicial and penitentiary systems, an end to the ban on nonwhite immigration, and expanded employment opportunities.[174] The spectre of the PIC is raised when the newspaper wrongly attributes Don Antonio's death to Miguel's "atavisms" as a mulatto in the same issue that it describes the uprising of ten thousand Afro-Cubans led by Pedro Ivonet and Evaristo Estenoz (287).[175]

The novel reveals that the public discourses constructing those two poles of Cuban history severely limit the scope of the debate on discourses of race in Cuba. On the one hand, what Aline Helg calls the "myth of Cuban racial equality" asserts equality between blacks and whites at the cost of downplaying racial oppression: "All that has ended," as Don Antonio claims.[176] On the other hand, the Reyes family scapegoats blacks for all social conflicts —indeed, they blame Miguel for everything from Don Antonio's heart attack to the alleged poisoning of the city's water supply. These two seemingly opposed political positions actually develop out of a shared discursive field. The scapegoating of blacks is made possible by the myth of Cuban racial equality, which holds that any assertion of racialized particularity by blacks is racist. El Demócrata makes just this claim about a meeting Miguel calls among "the race of 'color'" in order to discuss widespread poverty among Afro-Cubans (81). By blaming Afro-Cubans for airing racial grievances, the dominant public discourse avoids confronting social problems. La raza triste relentlessly exposes such racial oppression.

The myth of racial equality is also figured in the friendships between blacks and whites. Yet such friendships, apparent in the relationship between the Afro-Cuban Valdés family and the white Estrada y Céspedes family, dissolve under the pressure of racial antagonism. Don Antonio and his wife, Doña Carmen, fall prey to the Reyes's smear campaign and displace their former warm affection for Miguel with barely concealed hostility. Even Miguel and Gabriela, who have formed a strong bond, have to pursue their relationship on the sly.

Setting this novel apart from most novels dealing with race relations in Cuba is the fact that its anti-imperialism, evident in Miguel's rejection by the U.S. universities, is matched by its fierce critique of internal Cuban racism. Indeed, it is Armando Reyes, who attends college in the United States along with Miguel, who exposes Miguel's mulatto identity at every single university, forcing him to study at a Negro college in Atlanta. Kutzinski's argument that negrismo targeted U.S. imperialism to the exclusion of domestic conflicts points out the rarity and importance of La raza triste's critique in Cuban letters, which predates Guillén's "El Camino de Harlem" by five years.[177] At first Miguel serves as a spokesperson for the myth of racial equality when he tells Gabriela upon returning to Cuba from his studies in the United States, "In Cuba the black is a companion of the white, in the United States, the black is a dog" (69). However, Miguel soon changes his mind on the matter, even before Don Enrique Reyes refers to him as "that Negro dog" and espouses southern U.S.-style segregation (101). After Armando's libelous article in El Demócrata accuses Miguel of fomenting rebellion in a "racist" meeting of Negroes, Miguel fumes, "Hace falta una revolución, un cataclismo" (We need a revolution, a cataclysm) (84). Numerous incidents follow in which El Demócrata libels Miguel with absurd charges and successfully turns public opinion against him, depriving him of his livelihood. Cuba, Miguel finds, is a country in which "to be an intelligent black is a crime" (208). His critique of Cuba deflates claims that the country was a racially egalitarian nation.

After Miguel has become a hopeless alcoholic, he confronts Don Antonio, responding to the charge that he is a criminal. Miguel blames Don Antonio for having filled him with false illusions that Cuba was a color-blind society: "You are more of a thief, for having robbed me of my ignorance. . . . You were aware of the fact that it was impossible to convince your people that the brain of the black is equal to that of whites; that we have the same heart, the same feelings, the same concept of beauty . . . that blacks are more sentimental because the sadness of slavery has spoken more to the heart than to the intellect" (279). Miguel insists that supposedly politically neutral notions such as justice are themselves corrupted by the system of racial inequality in Cuba: " 'Justice' is a privilege of whites." Don Antonio dies at the conclusion of Miguel's tirade, as if he can't bear to hear that Cuba hasn't lived up to the ideals of its war for independence.[178] Miguel's speech provides an example of a dominant primitivist theme—the romantic racialist opposition between "sentimental" blacks and unfeeling whites—that simultaneously promotes an alternative primitivist critique of race relations.

Focusing on the mulatto's tragedy serves to expose the inability of a corrupt and racist republican Cuba to live up to the egalitarian ideals announced by Martí during the independence movement. In stark contrast to Nayar's Ramón, as a mixed-race character Miguel does not suffer from a tragic conflict between opposed racialized "bloods," but rather from the white culture that constructs him as entirely alien to them. What is important, then, is not so much the primitivist racial stereotypes that Masdeu inevitably falls into, but rather their use on behalf of the novel's firm commitment to a truly democratic Cuba, freed from the dual ills of racial oppression and neocolonialism. Indeed, as Alejandro de la Fuente has argued, Afro-Cubans were able to appropriate the "myth of racial equality" to their advantage by insisting that Cuba should live up to its egalitarian ideals, thereby claiming agency within a discourse that otherwise downplayed racism in Cuba.[179]

CONCLUSIONS: PRIMITIVISM AND NEOCOLONIALISM IN THE AMERICAS

These comparative studies of texts from the Harlem Renaissance, indigenismo, and negrismo show that the dominant and alternative modes of primitivism focus attention on local political conditions and neocolonialism to create a literature *engagé*, an anomaly in the age of high modernism. These cultural movements contest and reaffirm nationalist discourses of modernization and progress via the racialized figure of the primitive, whether indigenous or diasporic African. In Beals and Hughes, primitivism, antiracism, and anti-imperialism coexist with one another, if sometimes at cross purposes, as Beals's representatation of the cabaret dancer Fela demonstrates. In McKay, Jake is a lower-class, provincial "primitive" who receives an education in egalitarian politics from the educated Ray, but this primitive also has something to teach intellectuals: Jake embodies a model of everyday resistance that the despondent Ray cannot match. In Menéndez, the fragile alliance between acculturated Mexicans and Cora Indians shatters from irreconcilable differences on the questions of Indian resistance and the norms of social regulation. And in Masdeu, the supposed primitive is revealed to be a social construct rather than an inferior being. Thus while residual primitivism does indeed turn one's attention away from social conditions toward ahistorical conceptions of race as determining life chances, it would be unwarranted to regard this as the only mode of primitivism, which must be conceived as plural in its political strategies. All the texts discussed in this chapter deploy dominant and alternative primitivist discourses that reveal racial and class inequalities and efforts to resolve them, either by dominant or subordinated groups.

The wide range of primitivist narrative resolutions to racial conflicts demonstrates that the mere fact of employing primitivism is no guarantee of a particular brand of politics. Instead, the politics of a text are determined to a great extent by the version of primitivism deployed. The residual primitivisms in Beals and Menéndez, based on biological notions of "blood" and nonwhite racial inferiority, undermine their commitments to anti-imperialism and racial reform. By contrast, casting the primitive as a creation of socioeconomic problems allows Hughes, McKay, and Masdeu to issue stinging indictments of neocolonial politics in the United States, Haiti, and Cuba.

While no coherent strategy linked these nationalisms—even within a single country nationalism is always a matter of political contestation—all construct alternative primitivisms that focus on the resistance of racialized subaltern subjects to a neocolonialism viewed as both internal and external.[180] The differing neocolonialisms in Cuba, Mexico, and Haiti were based on an international alliance of U.S. and European business elites, the military and political arms of the U.S. state, and politicians and landed elites in Latin American countries. Hughes, Beals, and McKay contend with U.S. neocolonialism from their position as U.S. citizens, constructing "cognitive maps" (Jameson) of the "stretch[ed]-out" social relations (Massey) obtaining between the United States and Latin America.[181] They construct their "cognitive maps" of neocolonialism through transnational ties based on political affinity (Hughes, McKay, and the Cuban Mella were communists, and Beals was socialist), on diasporic African popular cultural forms such as the blues and the *son* (Hughes and Guillén), and on the artistic and political milieus that swept them into their folds.

While Hughes, Beals, and McKay construct transnational alliances that cross the divide of uneven development in the Americas, Menéndez and Masdeu emphasize the internally fractured character of nationalism in Mexico and Cuba. In Menéndez, Ramón and Enrique's disgust for political corruption within postrevolutionary state nationalism motivates their tentative—and temporary—alignment with Indians. In Masdeu the tragedy of the Afro-Cuban doctor Miguel Valdés, emblematic of the plight of Afro-Cubans, embodies a national tragedy: the failed ideals of racial egalitarianism (à la Martí) in the face of U.S. neocolonialism.

Dominant primitivisms oppose the primitive to the modern, sometimes producing a nostalgia that evades a full recognition of the political processes of oppression (Sapir). Dominant primitivism can also promote the creation of a nationalist amalgam of European modernization and indigenous or African spiritual and artistic "gifts." In this scenario, dominant primitivism accepts folk expression but rejects self-determination by the marginalized (Gamio, Menéndez, Vasconcelos). By contrast, alternative primitivisms align themselves with efforts at self-determination by specifying the dangers of modernization for the lower classes and racialized groups (Hughes, McKay, Masdeu).

I have focused on texts by male writers in order to examine the ways in which they construct the primitive through gendered categories. Following Mary Louise Pratt, I have emphasized the ways in which women are produced in "permanent instability" to the nation.[182] By "permanent instability" I mean to signify something in addition to Pratt's focus on the representation of women as partaking in processes of subordination, by also pointing out the ways in which these writers represent women as figures in opposition to dominant nationalist narratives. In Beals, Fela the octoroon provides an epiphanic moment of intimate communion across barriers of nation, race, and class. In Hughes, the "Mexican Market Woman," a woman who is oppressed by class, race, and gender, becomes a figure of "brown" rebellion implicitly aligning Mexicans and African Americans. In McKay, images of sexually liberated women abound: the Lesbian Sappho and Felice. In Menéndez the most prominent female characters defy male authority: Ramón's wife sleeps with the judge and Skirt of Flowers defies Cora traditions that prioritize duty over romantic love. In Masdeu the female protagonist is a race traitor, a white woman who defies the will of her father to remain loyal to her mulatto childhood friend and lover. The persistence of such constructions of women as rebellious can be explained by the uncertain status of women in the 1920s era in the United States, postrevolutionary Mexico, and the neocolonial Cuban republic. In all three cases, women pressed for social and legal freedoms and oftentimes resisted the liberal-nationalist link between modernization, nationalism, and progress. Where bourgeois men saw progress, feminist activists saw exclusion and exploitation.

What is truly remarkable about these 1920s nationalisms in Cuba, Mexico, and the United States is that within each one there was a significant transnational discourse/movement. All of the writers discussed here participated in transnational cultural currents, but these transnationalisms carried very different political meanings: while the indigenismo of Gamio and the latinoamericanismo of Vasconcelos were decidedly elitist and colluded with the state, the negrismo of Masdeu, the socialism of Beals, and the Marxist Pan-Africanism of Hughes and McKay adopted critical stances toward nation-states in general and the U.S. empire in particular. I propose that the transnational travels and imaginings of U.S. writers such as Beals, Hughes, and McKay be read as the practice of hemispheric citizenship—a critique of the repressive social consequences of the collusion between U.S. and European foreign policy and capital in Latin America in the 1920s. Adopting such a revisionary approach to 1920s U.S. culture as a whole would open an important transnational and intercultural perspective on the Harlem Renaissance. Rather than analyzing racial conflict in the terms of the more familiar black–white axis, such an approach would force one to understand the simultaneous construction of the domestic and foreign in discourses of race, whether in Hughes's alignment between black and brown or in a 1924 National Foreign Trade Council special report: "Foreign trade is an absolute necessity if the development of American life is to continue along the lines of which it has proceeded ever since the first white man landed on these shores."[183] The Foreign Trade Council tells a story of triumphant U.S. modernization for whites only. If U.S. capitalists and policymakers viewed neocolonialism in Latin America as the engine of white prosperity and progress in the United States, Beals, Hughes, and McKay took the politically radical approach of looking beneath the veneer of those countries to understand neocolonialism's devastating social consequences on the majority of citizens. A transnational, multilingual approach to the Harlem Renaissance could follow their cue by focusing comparatively on cultural production in Spanish-speaking Latin America, the Francophone Caribbean, and Portuguese Brazil, following the circuits of capitalism, social repression, and resistance.

Four

"RISING TIDES OF COLOR": ETHNOGRAPHY AND THEORIES OF RACE AND MIGRATION IN BOAS, PARK, GAMIO, AND HURSTON

> What the map cuts up, the story cuts across.
> —MICHEL DE CERTEAU, "Spatial Stories," *The Practice of Everyday Life*

During the 1920s, social scientists, their students, and theories of race traveled circuits linking New York, the U.S. South, Chicago, and Mexico City, producing a vibrant exchange among the Harlem Renaissance, Boasian anthropology, and the Chicago School of Sociology. These two leading centers of U.S. social science also evolved in dialogue with Mexican *indigenismo*, a literary and institutional reform movement fueled by a postrevolutionary efflorescence of national pride in indigenous cultures.[1] Manuel Gamio, a prominent Mexican nationalist and *indigenista* anthropologist, and Zora Neale Hurston both studied under Franz Boas and therefore may be seen as exemplars of my revisionary, comparative approach to 1920s cultural production, which joins the New Negro and the "New Mexico."[2] Although Gamio and Hurston have been canonized in Latin American and U.S. American literatures, respectively, their common debt to Boas illustrates the previously unacknowledged institutional and intellectual spheres shared by Mexican indigenismo and the Harlem Renaissance.

More specifically, when one stresses their overlooked contributions to U.S. social science, Gamio and Hurston can be viewed in a new light as differently marginalized intellectuals who adopted and modified Boasian anthropology and Chicago sociology. Working within and confronting the shift from race to culture under way in U.S. social science, Gamio and Hurston oppose the construction of a racially homogeneous U.S. culture forged through intermarriage in the theories of Boas and the Chicago School sociologist Robert E. Park. Park's accompanying notion of the "world melting pot" relies on the construction of quiescent, feminized, nonwhite subjects, evident in his romantic racialist formulation of the Negro as the artistic "lady among the races."[3] By constructing the Negro as the "lady among the races," Park emphasizes an allegedly distinctive contribution to the nation made by African Americans and thus criticizes nativism. Yet this famous formulation posits "racial temperament" as the inherited complex of an ethnicity's defining characteristics, with the consequence that Park accepts the racialist discourses that served as the building blocks for 1920s nativism.[4] As an alternative to the *racial* hybridity of these intermarriage schemes in Boas and Park, Gamio in his work on Mexican immigrants and Hurston in her representations of black migrants in ethnography and fiction emphasize *cultural* hybridity—alternative discourses, methodologies, and practices that form a more malleable cluster of strategies for political dissent because they emerge out of an interplay among differing cultural contexts.[5]

In conceptualizing migration, Gamio and Hurston follow Park's theorization of race in terms of geopolitical space inhabited by migrants in essays such as "Human Migration and the Marginal Man" (1928). But they place a greater emphasis on migration as an embodied space of recalcitrant subjects who refuse Park's assimilationist master narrative of "diminishing [racial] distances" with disruptive micronarratives of gender and class: Gamio's informant Isidro Osorio says that he works so hard that he "almost coughs up his lungs," and Hurston's migrant laborers are the "farthest down" on the race and class ladder.[6] These micronarratives produce notions of identity that emphasize alienation from the dominant culture. The popular term "La Raza" (the people or the race) in Gamio responds to the derogatory connotations of *Mexican* in the United States by constructing a transnational and cross-class solidarity of Latin American immigrants and Latinos that transforms "race" into an implosively heterogeneous category.[7] Similarly, Hurston figures migration not as a tale of absorption by the dominant, but rather as demonstrating the resilience of black folk culture in contesting the discourses that consign African Americans to a subordinate role. Gamio and Hurston thus exemplify Edward Said's notion of "critical consciousness" as "a sort of measuring faculty for locating or situating theory" by resituating Boasian and Parkian thought within the contexts of these micronarratives.[8]

Despite their own migrations and participation in 1920s counterculture,

Gamio and Hurston have been "transfixed," to adopt Said's term, within critical paradigms restricted by nation, ethnicity, geographical site, and discipline.[9] Gamio is seldom even mentioned as having been a student of Boas and, beyond his brief collaboration with Robert Redfield, has been ignored by students of the Chicago School, even though he taught as a visiting professor at the University of Chicago in the late 1920s.[10] Similarly, literary critics have mistakenly viewed Hurston as a pastoral regionalist.[11] Questioning the literary historian's claim that Hurston was "more of a novelist than a social scientist," I start from the hypothesis that Hurston was as much a social scientist as a novelist.[12] My revisionary account of Gamio and Hurston as migrant intellectuals who engaged with 1920s social scientific discourses that theorized race in terms of geopolitical space serves to extricate them from immobilizing critical "traps" and reveal their cultural production as disputing theories of migration that aimed at assimilation. These theories posited either a unidirectional mimicry of the dominant (E. Franklin Frazier) or racial hybridity via intermarriage (Boas and Park).

In crossing over into the territory of the dominant, theoretically and geographically, Gamio and Hurston define an alternative politics shaped by an attention to the theories and sensibilities of their subaltern subjects. This alternative politics consists of a hybrid cultural stance that adopts aspects of U.S. social scientific theory while refusing to accept either of the choices offered by the popular debate on migration: absorption by the dominant or racial subordination. Thus where Park and his followers represent race relations uncritically in terms of "communication and contact" leading to acculturation, Gamio and Hurston find conflict.[13] It is only through this immanent analysis of the ways in which Gamio and Hurston addressed issues of nation, race, and class that one can approach the broader, more elusive question of the relations among their ethnographies, discourses of hemispheric citizenship, and the wave of decolonization of the 1920s.

To gain a full understanding of how Gamio and Hurston transformed U.S. social scientific theory, it's first necessary to examine how Boas and Park countered nativist discourses of the undesirability of intermarriage between (im)migrants of color and Euro-Americans. Boas and Park differed from the nativists in casting intermarriage in a positive light, but this tactic of attacking nativism by imagining a racially homogeneous nation left them at odds with their broader strategy of proposing a shift from race to culture in social scientific theory, thereby creating space for the interventions of Gamio and Hurston.

THEORIES OF RACE, HYBRIDITY, AND MIGRATION IN BOAS AND PARK, 1894–1935

Debates over assimilation in the 1920s ranged from those who opposed intermarriage because of the alleged inferiority of nonwhites to those like Boas and Park who presumed equality among all ethnicities and therefore favored intermarriage. These differing positions sought to dispel the threat of migrants' mimicry of dominant forms but not their content either by excluding migrants from the imagined community of the nation or by incorporating them through intermarriage.

Corporate proponents and opponents of black and Mexican migration both asserted the undesirability of racial mixing. In arguing for Mexican immigration in 1930, Henry Chandler, an agricultural magnate and publisher of the *Los Angeles Times,* claimed that Mexicans "do not intermarry like the Negro with white people." In opposing Mexican immigration, a *New York Times* editorial from 1930 similarly argued that Mexicans were unassimilable: "It is folly to pretend that the more recently arrived Mexicans, who are largely of Indian blood, can be absorbed and incorporated into the American race."[14] Taken together, these two opposed positions on Mexican immigration express a consensus that Mexicans were an inferior race who should remain separate from whites. Partly owing to such widespread public hostility toward Mexicans, they were reclassified from white to "colored" in the 1930 U.S. census.[15]

Boas and Park differ from these dominant discourses on immigration by casting intermarriage in a positive rather than negative light. But by focusing on intermarriage, they accept the terms of this debate. In 1921 Boas argued that racial mixture could reduce racial prejudice: "The negro problem will not disappear in America until the negro blood has been so diluted that it will no longer be recognized."[16] Similarly, in "Our Racial Frontier on the Pacific" (1926) and in "Human Migration and the Marginal Man" (1928), Park posited a causal chain leading from migration through cultural hybridity to assimilation via intermarriage.[17] Moreover, by constructing intermarriage as a means to end racial conflict, Boas and Park locked themselves within an opposition to the corporate discourses that reject intermarriage. Both sides of this opposition posited a causal chain

linking migration to differing scenarios of racial hybridity—conceived either as the perils of mongrelization or as the progress of assimilation. By
constructing the nation as homogeneous, Boas and Park contradicted their
claims in other writings that a heterogeneous yet egalitarian nation is
possible through political and economic transformations.

By relying on racialist terms, these programs of racial harmony via
intermarriage ironically fall out of step with the shift from race to culture
that Boas and Park engineered. Boas and Park conceive this shift in very
different terms. Boas opposes the universalizing theories of racial evolution
with the study of culture, defined as a focus on the "unique history" of each
ethnic group, itself a product of multiple borrowings.[18] Like Boas, Park
defines cultures as produced through "contact and communication" as
opposed to the "interbreeding and isolation" that create races.[19] However,
Park's definition alludes to differing stages of a universal "race relations
cycle," an "irreversible" movement through "contacts, competition, accommodation" to "eventual assimilation" via amalgamation, a teleological
and ahistorical narrative to which Boas would object.[20] Thus the chief
negative consequence of the conceptual shift from race to culture in Park is
that his narration of the shift as the rejection of antagonistic isolation in
favor of "diminishing distances" strips him of the vocabulary that would
help him to explain difference, heterogeneity, and conflict, a vocabulary
that the "Marginal Man" essay begins to assemble, only to succumb to the
teleology of assimilation.

Whether couched in terms of culture or race, these academic and popular debates over hybridity in the 1920s focus on the alleged damaging effect
of migration on migrants themselves (the extent of the loss or retention of
cultural identity) or on the extent of the racial health of the dominant or
national culture, avoiding the threatening question of the extent to which
these "marginal" populations adopt politically dissenting positions. Gamio
and Hurston change the grounds of these debates by breaking the chain of
causality linking migration, hybridity, and assimilation, focusing instead
on hybridity and mimicry as modes of resistance to assimilation.[21] That is,
while Park worries about the extent to which "racial groups" adopt dominant cultural forms but not their content, Gamio and Hurston show how
such groups explicitly reject the content of dominant cultural norms, thus
shedding light on the strategic uses of cultural hybridity.[22] By refusing
Park's narrative of quiescent nonwhite and feminized subjects who consent
to assimilation on the terms of the U.S. dominant culture, Gamio and

Hurston reject the accompanying narrative of intermarriage as a means of creating social harmony in Boas and Park, thereby creating the space for dissent. Boas and Park help create this space by developing the shift from race to culture in their writings.

The appeal of Boas to both Gamio and Hurston and that of the Chicago School to Gamio can be partially explained by the ascendant international prestige of U.S. social science in the 1920s.[23] But Gamio and Hurston also found theories of cultural hybridity in Boas and Park amenable to their defense of Mexican and black migrants. These theories in Boas and Park decisively parted from their schemes of national homogeneity via inter-marriage and also from nineteenth-century biological determinism. When Boas secured a lectureship in physical anthropology at Columbia University in 1895, he had achieved enough institutional security to directly attack the biological racial thinking of his discipline. At the time, physical anthropology focused on the independent invention of traits in an effort to emphasize the absolute difference between racial "types" in a hierarchical scheme of evolutionary development. Sir Francis Galton, known as the founder of the eugenics movement, was so convinced that evolution proceeded along distinct racial lines that he argued that racial mixing led to the intermediate racial type of the "mule," which was infertile.[24] Among evolutionists, as George Stocking has argued, diffusion "served to explain departures from the normal evolutionary sequence [but] independent invention was much more central to their nomothetic purpose."[25]

By contrast, throughout his career Boas focused on the diffusion of cultural traits among peoples—the migration of people and ideas (what Park termed "contact and communication")—refuting allegations of the inferiority and infertility of hybrid races and even calling into question the notion of race itself.[26] Examining Indian folktales in North America in the late 1890s, Boas argues that "similarities of culture on our continent are always more likely to be due to diffusion than to independent invention."[27] The diffusion of culture via migration was part of the same process of intermarriage that undermined the notion of separate races prized by the evolutionists, and intermarriage would later play a key role in Boas's schemes for racial harmony. In "Race and Progress" (1931), Boas argues that even putatively pure races consist of a great variety of family lineages: "Every racial group consists of a great many family lines which are distinct in bodily form."[28] Rather than viewing such racial mixture as a hindrance to civilization, as Galton and the anti-(im)migrationists did, Boas, like

Park, argues that the "intermingling of racial types" instead leads to the "greatness" of a civilization.[29] However, as in Park's dissonant body of writings on "race consciousness," Boas emphasizes that such greatness would not come automatically, but rather only with a radical structural transformation bringing about racial equality: "As long as we insist on a stratification in racial layers, we shall pay the penalty in the form of interracial struggle," he warns.[30] Gamio and Hurston focus precisely on such struggle in their narratives, whether in the anger and defiance Mexican immigrants express toward Anglos or in the brilliant banter and fanciful tales told "behind the boss' back" in the lumber mills of *Mules and Men* (1935).

Park joined Boas in the assault on biological explanations of race relations, stating his opposition to immigration restriction measures such as the Exclusion Law of 1924 in the *Survey Graphic*, the journal that published *The New Negro* the following year.[31] In addition, Park provides a definition of *assimilation* that complicates colloquial uses of the term. For Park, assimilation consists of two processes. In the first, a process of mutual exchange, "individuals spontaneously acquire one another's language, characteristic attitudes, habits, and modes of behavior."[32] In the second, "individuals and groups . . . are taken over and incorporated into larger groups."

However, Park adds a pair of qualifications to this second sense of assimilation as absorption, which would otherwise accord with the colloquial use of the term. First, Park argues that assimilating groups stamp their "individuality" on the dominant cultural traits they appropriate: "Nations and races borrow. . . . Materials taken over in this way, however, are inevitably stamped with the individuality of the nationalities that appropriate them."[33] Second, he argues that assimilation requires the forging of a common "sentiment of loyalty" to the nation. However, such loyalty comes only when the state is structurally transformed to incorporate the needs of the minority group in what he calls a "reconditioning."[34]

Park's later theory of the "race relations cycle" avoids such a call for a structural transformation by producing an inevitable "diminishing [of] distances": "The race relations cycle, . . . contacts, competition, accommodation and eventual assimilation, is apparently progressive and irreversible."[35] How is it possible to explain the discrepancy between the Park of inevitable assimilation and the dissonant Park of "race consciousness"? I would argue that Park views Negro "race consciousness" as inconsistent with its racial temperament as the "lady among the races."[36] Indeed, in

"Negro Race Consciousness as Reflected in Race Literature" (1923), Park takes a patronizing approach to what he refers to as "the Negro renaissance" and Pan-Africanism, suggesting that Negroes are passive by nature: "The unrest which is fermenting in every part of the world has gotten finally under the skin of the Negro."[37] Since "race consciousness is the natural and inevitable reaction to race prejudice," Park suggests in his theories of assimilation that a color-blind society will eliminate race consciousness.[38] The "race relations cycle" provides a way of viewing conflict as a transitory stage, to be overcome in the long run by the forces of harmony.

Moreover, in "Our Racial Frontier on the Pacific" (1926), the logic of the global melting pot compels Park to dismiss Pan-Africanism and "national self-determination" movements as "rising tides of color [that] are merely incidental evidences of these diminishing distances" among peoples.[39] The "migrant man" figures in these "rising tides of color" in differing racial trajectories. While the Jewish variant of the "migrant man" is constructed as both geographically and economically mobile, Park constructs blacks and women as tied to the local, domestic sphere—as implied by the "lady among the races" remark. This formulation constructs blacks and women as passive rather than as activist New Negroes and New Women. Thus Park's "world melting pot" theory proves inadequate in theorizing both domestic and transnational activism by blacks and women and the forces of oppression and exploitation such activism confronts. Moreover, in his uncritical construction of the "diminishing distances" tending toward greater harmony, Park ignores the heightened postwar collusion between the U.S. State Department and corporations in promoting state repression in the Caribbean, Latin America, and Asia to increase profits for the elite business classes (see chapter 3).

Nevertheless, the dissonant vein in Park's "race consciousness" writings contains egalitarian possibilities. In his benchmark essay "Human Migration and the Marginal Man" (1928), which focuses on Jewish immigrants and African American migrants to northeastern U.S. cities, Park posits a causal chain leading from migration through hybridity to what he views as beneficial assimilation. Park viewed assimilation as occurring on a global scale, spurred by the export of U.S. cinema: "It is in the obscure, dream-haunted recesses of our inner lives that the future of the world is taking form and shape. . . . The melting pot is the world."[40] However, a contradictory strain in his work focuses on how discourses of racially homogeneous "national solidarity" have distinguished Negroes from immigrants on the path to assimilation: "The Negro has had his separateness and consequent race consciousness thrust upon him, because of his exclusion and forcible isolation from white society."[41] As a result, Negroes have formed a nation-within-a-nation and will not assimilate until the United States creates the conditions for the formation of a "sentiment of loyalty" among them by structurally transforming the state to incorporate the interests and needs of African Americans.[42] In a later essay, in a phrase suggestive of Antonio Gramsci's notion of the war of position within hegemony, Park argues that dominant society needs to undergo a "reconditioning" before Negroes will gain full civil rights.[43] Park later eludes the arduous work that such reconditioning would entail by crafting an overly optimistic, teleological narrative of assimilation.

In focusing on the two contradictory strands in Park's thought, one emphasizing increasing harmony and assimilation and the other focusing on exclusion and black nationalism, I depart from the received negative view of Park's theory of assimilation as maintaining the status quo by also focusing on the ways in which it produces a "dream-haunted," disavowed narrative of the potential for novel forms of affiliation and social critique to emerge from the process of migration. In observing that the migrant, as a "cultural hybrid," is "not bound as others are by the local proprieties and customs," Park suggests that African American and Jewish migrants and immigrants inhabit the productive social space of alienation, thereby capturing an important aspect of the cultural hybridity practiced by Gamio and Hurston.[44] However, by doggedly insisting on individualist terms of analysis—he locates social conflict in the "moral turmoil" present in the "mind of the marginal man"—Park eludes the radical implications of such a theory for collective action.[45] As if to follow through on Park's suggestion of migrant alienation, Gamio and Hurston emphasize migrants' feelings that they find themselves *in but not of* the dominant culture—an irreconcilable affiliation with the source culture that emphasizes the enduring character of inequality produced by such ties. This is evident in the coalitional ideology of La Raza in Gamio and in Hurston's focus on migrant laborers "broken from being poor" who mine the rich veins of the black vernacular.[46]

However, if Park has been scorned by contemporary critics because he often evades the question of conflict by adopting uncritical terms,[47] Boas and Park can be used to show that theories of hybridity do not necessarily bear the politically fatal taint of biological determinism, as a prominent postcolonial theorist has charged.[48] Instead, one finds a range of uses of hybridity in the 1920s: debates on migration invoked the specter of inter-marriage, a form of racial hybridity, to either dispute or confirm the bene-fits of immigration, while Boas and Park emphasized the benefits of both intermarriage and cultural hybridity (Park's "contact and communication" and Boas's "intermingling" between peoples).

Gamio and Hurston transform the social scientific theories of Boas and Park in three critical ways. First, by breaking the shackles of objectivity, they create a fundamentally ethical social science that utilizes novel methodolo-gies and promotes social programs with the aim of benefiting their infor-mants.[49] Second, a central motivating factor for such activism is their focus on the obstacles to social harmony that appear in various cultural problem-atics; they do not argue that a peaceful society would be guaranteed by intermarriage. Both writers engage in an analysis of race grounded in the specific social hierarchies of class and gender encountered by migrants and varying according to the geopolitical spaces they inhabit. Hurston addi-tionally focuses on a diverse range of African American folk discourses and practices that are hybrid in form yet alter and reject dominant ideological content. Third, without collapsing the social spaces that divide people, Gamio and Hurston call attention to efforts to create affinities across those divides, especially those based in race and class. In these ideologies of coalition, Gamio and Hurston remind one that by definition, hybridity can consist either of a fusion of different elements or a collection of distinct parts. Gamio and Hurston reject the easy hybridity of racial fusion in favor of the intellectually and politically more demanding version of hybridity as an assemblage of heterogeneous cultural elements. Such notions of cultural hybridity play a central role in the transformation of social science theories by marginalized populations: Gamio and Hurston move toward an analysis of racial oppression grounded in an "embodied" migratory space specified in geopolitical terms and in relation to social hierarchies of class and gender.

NATIONALISM, IMMIGRATION, AND "LA RAZA" IN GAMIO

Manuel Gamio, recognized today as the first professional Mexican anthro-pologist, has been honored posthumously with a postage stamp bearing his image. A student of Boas at Columbia University between 1909 and

1910, Gamio conducted excavations under Boas's direction in Mexico in 1912, and in 1913 succeeded Boas as director of the International School of Archaeology and Ethnology in Mexico City. Gamio later served as the founder and director of the Mexican national Department of Anthropology, 1917–24.[50] As founder and editor of the journal *Ethnos: Revista dedicada al estudio y mejoría de la población indígena de México* (Ethnos: a journal dedicated to the study and improvement of the indigenous population of Mexico) from 1920 to 1925, Gamio provided a forum for the new field of indigenista anthropology.

Gamio maintained a dialogue with U.S. social science throughout his professional career. In 1921 he earned a doctorate from Columbia University, and in 1926 he worked as a visiting professor at Park's school, the University of Chicago, where he delivered a series of lectures that, together with essays by José Vasconcelos, were published in English as *Aspects of Mexican Civilization*. Gamio's chief archaeological accomplishments were the restoration of Chichén Itzá and Teotihuacán. "The reconstruction of Teotihuacán at once converted the site into the greatest public monument in Mexico and effectively reinstated Indian civilization as the foundation of Mexican history," as David Brading has written.[51] Gamio's two-volume study *The Population of the Valley of Teotihuacán* (1922) was widely praised and proposed as a model of archaeological work in Europe and the United States.[52]

Gamio's indigenismo motivated little-known forays into screenplay writing and short-story writing. In 1919 he wrote the screenplay *Tlahuicole*, focusing on the tragic love affair between Tlahuicole, a warrior of the Tlaxcala people, and Copo de Algodón, the daughter of the Aztec king Moctezuma II—it was later adapted as a play and produced in the ruins of Teotihuacán in 1925.[53] A collection of his short stories, some of which dealt with indigenous themes, was published as *De vidas dolientes* (On suffering lives) in 1937. However, Gamio is best known in Latin American literature for his book-length nationalist essay *Forjando patria: Pronacionalismo* (Forging the nation: pronationalism, 1916). Gamio was lionized in the postrevolutionary era by government officials who viewed *Forjando patria* as central to their nationalist programs. President Alvaro Obregón (1920–24) stated in a letter to Gamio that the book deserved to be read by every literate man in the country.[54] President Plutarco Calles similarly honored Gamio by hiring him as an undersecretary of public education in 1925. Gamio soon resigned from this post upon discovering fraud in the agency. The course of Gamio's career through his work on Mexican immigrants replays the broader shift from racial to cultural analysis under way in social theory in a process defined by his own turn away from examining national formation in Mexico to the alienation of immigrant laborers in the United States. While Gamio's *Forjando patria* devises a theory of *mestizaje* in which national identity is formed through racial fusion, his *Mexican Immigration to the United States* (1930) moves away from a focus on racial fusion to the construction of cultural hybridity as an antiracist mode of association.

Forjando patria builds on the momentum of the Mexican Revolution by defending the worthiness of indigenous peoples as national subjects against those who denigrated the lower classes and nonwhites. The book begins with a historical allegory of Latin American independence. The independence leaders of the early 1800s sought to erect a statue symbolizing all of America, writes Gamio, but "the task was not well understood; they attempted to sculpt the statue of those countries with racial elements of Latino origin and consigned the indigenous race to dangerous oblivion."[55] In using the allegory of the statue to represent the social composition of Latin America, Gamio implicitly critiques the highly influential *Ariel* (1900) by José Enrique Rodó, an Uruguayan professor, journalist, and congressman. In *Ariel,* a book-length essay, Próspero, a teacher and the master of the slave Calibán, calls for his students to emulate the bronze statue of Ariel, embodying the spirituality characteristic of ancient Greece. Based on Shakespeare's "Airy Spirit" of *The Tempest,* Ariel represents "el imperio de la razón y el sentimiento sobre los bajos estímulos de la irracionalidad" (the reign of reason and sentiment over the lowly stimuli of irrationality).[56] Ariel thus embodies a *criollo* high culture contrasting with both European imperialism and with Calibán, a bodily "símbolo de sensualidad y torpeza" (symbol of sensuality and stupidity) (1). Calibán embodies a dual slavery: the "material slavery" of U.S. culture, dedicated to utilitarianism and commerce, and that of the degenerate indigenous and African masses of Latin America, allegedly incapable of self-government and hence dependent on the "voz magistral" (the masterly voice) of Próspero (2, 12).

In sharp contrast to the "shrinking of the human brain due to commerce" in the United States, Latin America aspires to "an interior freedom" through the cultivation of aesthetic, spiritual, and intellectual gifts (11, 12). Highly ambivalent toward democracy, Rodó seeks to create a synthesis of the modernity embodied by the democratic United States and the antiquity embodied by classical Greece, which he associates with hierarchical social orders. The concept of meritocracy, "el dominio de la inteligencia y la virtud" (the dominion of intelligence and virtue), allows Rodó to mediate between the two opposed social orders and to rationalize the subordination of "la masa anónima" (the anonymous masses) (25, 32).

By contrast, just as José Martí argues that the "trunk" of Latin American national identity is indigenous and African and has therefore been celebrated by Roberto Fernández Retamar as a defender of "the culture and history of Calibán," so Gamio opposes policies of Indian subordination, instead advocating the national incorporation of indigenous groups.[57] In Gamio, ancient indigenous cultures occupy the role that classical Greek antiquity plays in Rodó: a model for national formation. For Gamio, the statue embodying Latin America must be sculpted from a mixture of "el bronce y el hierro," "bronze" (dark-skinned peoples) and "iron" (white-skinned peoples). Thus while Rodó calls for a selective intellectual and spiritual melding of European cultural elements by Latin America, Gamio's "great forge of America" (5) melds indigenous and European races in a project of mestizaje (racial mixing): "Ahí está el hierro. . . . Ahí está el bronce. . . . ¡Batid hermanos!" ("There is the iron, there is the bronze. . . . Stir it, brothers!") (6).

In his early writings, then, Gamio's nationalism is inextricably bound up in his racial thinking. Since he understands the nation to be a "great family" (7–8) composed of "the same blood" (11), he worries that Mexico cannot be considered a nation because of the diverse pockets of indigenous groups that he calls "pequeñas patrias mexicanas" (little Mexican nations) (167). According to Gamio, most rural indigenous peoples identified with their "pequeñas patrias" rather than with Mexico, presenting an obstacle to the nationalist project. The solution, then, is to promote "the ethnic fusion of the population" (39). Gamio is thus vulnerable to Guillermo Bonfil Batalla's critique of postrevolutionary mestizaje as a violent project of "desindianización" (de-Indianization) that homogenizes the national population, perpetuating colonial structures of domination.[58]

Gamio anticipated the objection that mestizaje would lead to homogenization. In "The Utilitarian Aspect of Folklore" (1925), he constructs a racial nationalism that sets in tension its required reformism, which expands the size and power of the state by making Mexicans out of Indians, with his fears that the unfortunate consequence of such a political and racial "fusion" will be cultural uniformity. Returning to the metaphor of "molding" that begins *Forjando patria*, Gamio reveals the top-down character of his reformist aims: "To make progress easy through the gradual forming of the Indian mentality until it is molded into the ways of modern thought. This, of course, does not mean that we shall attempt to strip the Indian of his typical characteristics, for we are enemies of standardization, above all with respect to that which refers to artistic expression."[59] Here Gamio's insistence that his program of molding "the Indian mentality" will not result in stripping indigenous groups of their cultures is a mere token gesture that denies to *indios* a proper role in the shaping of their own future. In rejecting an artistic standardization, Gamio grants Indians the role of artists in a restricted, aesthetic sense while espousing a sociopolitical standardization that refuses political agency to Indians—they do not join the mestizo elite that decides what counts as progress and who carries out the "forming of the Indian mentality." As Bonfil Batalla has written in a critique of Gamio, the only people with a role in indigenista decision making are non-Indians.[60] The discourse of hybridity as fusion in Gamio is premised on two contradictory nationalist desires: on the one hand, the desire for national homogeneity and, on the other hand, the desire for national distinctiveness based on folk cultural particularities. Thus when the discourse of hybridity as fusion produces the contradictory phrase "we are enemies of standardization," it flies in the face of the foremost tenet of the ideology of mestizaje—the view that standardization in culture and race will create the homogeneity necessary for national politics. Gamio may never have been able to fully resolve this paradox between the conservation of folk culture and the homogenization of the national population. However, historians have argued that although Gamio defined the Mexican nation in biological terms, his Lamarckian view that acquired characteristics could be inherited lent itself to the reformist perspective that indigenous groups could contribute to national progress.[61]

The contradictory nature of hybridity as fusion plays itself out in *Forjando patria*'s emphasis on creating certain forms of social equality for indigenous peoples. On the one hand, Gamio asserts that Indians would embrace Mexican culture and jettison their own cultures if offered equal treatment, ironically undermining the possibility for true political equality among differing social elements. If Gamio argues that nations must be racially homogeneous and governed by the mestizo elite, on the other hand, he deplores the subordination of Indians in Mexico, comparing its system of race relations to that of colonialism in South Africa (9). More-over, he argues that Indians are just as intelligent as other races (21). And in theorizing the incorporation of the indigenous "pequeñas patrias" into the Mexican nation, Gamio employs a notion of incorporation resembling what Park would later describe as a mutual exchange between groups. While indigenous peoples are to become Mexicans, white and mestizo Mexicans are told, "we must forge ourselves an indigenous soul—even if temporarily. Only then will we be able to work for the progress of the indigenous class" (25). Thus Gamio deploys a metaphor of transparency in describing the social scientist's relation to the "indigenous soul," assuming that indigenous culture and worldview can be fully understood and even assumed by the white or mestizo Mexican intellectual. Even if such assimi-lation should not eradicate Indian traditions but rather lodge them within an "Indianized" national identity, the phrase " 'indianicemonos' nosotros un tanto" (let us 'Indianize' ourselves a bit) smacks of tokenism (24). Forging "an indigenous soul" is fully compatible with the subordination of actual Indians.

Gamio's conflation of race and class, evident in his call for Mexican revolutionaries "to work for the progress of the indigenous class," indicates that he does not content himself with indigenismo's token adoption of minority cultures by the dominant but instead advocates an alternative activist social science. Gamio has been described as a pioneer of "applied anthropology" because throughout his career in various governmental posts he advocated and achieved such radical reforms as land redistribu-tion to peasants.[62] His version of "Panamericanismo," or Pan-Americanist ideology, calls for Latin American republics to revise their constitutions to respond to the needs of their indigenous populations (73). In Mexico, he called for the distribution of reading materials to combat illiteracy, increased funding for education, land redistribution, and an "economic equilibrium" between racialized groups (183).[63] Later, in the mid-1920s, Gamio criticized the refusal of Presidents Obregón and Calles to return the communal lands of the Yaquis and the Mayas and called for their political autonomy.[64] Thus even early in his career Gamio equates the institutional practices of social science with increased justice and social change. However, much like the nineteenth-century sentimental reformists of the United States such as Harriet Beecher Stowe, Gamio fails to fully explore the possibility that the racially oppressed could take control of their own destinies and challenge his notions of what might count as progress.

It is precisely Gamio's commitment to an applied anthropology that marks his dissent from official projects of indigenismo and allows one to revise the otherwise devastating critique of Mexican indigenismo by scholars who have concurred in the view that "the ultimate and paradoxical aim of official indigenismo in Mexico was . . . finally to destroy the native culture which had emerged during the colonial period" and was indistinguishable from "ethnocide."[65] Although Gamio held government posts and is therefore indicted in this critique, he also dissented from official indigenismo in crucial respects. Official indigenismo rested on a gradualist politics that sought the future assimilation of Indians via education and mestizaje, yet instantiated the present suppression of indigenous demands in a range of political visions: from Vasconcelos's neglect of the plight of contemporary Indians to the efforts of President Calles to exterminate the Yaqui in the late 1920s.[66] By contrast, while Gamio's gradualism was confined to his endorsement of mestizaje, his applied anthropology enacted a politics of indigenous political autonomy that prefigured the 1970s Mexican state policy of treating indigenous groups as a "federation of nationalities."[67] By insisting that the Mexican government immediately honor indigenous demands for land and political autonomy, Gamio refuses a Parkian political gradualism.

In embarking on such a career of applied anthropology, Gamio also differs with Park's emphasis on the importance of maintaining a stance of objectivity.[68] Gamio's *Mexican Immigration to the United States* (1930), the version of Gamio's applied anthropology most familiar to U.S. readers, adopts the Chicago School's emphasis on the study of displaced peoples but differs from the work of Park and his student Redfield in its explicit advocacy on behalf of immigrants. While Redfield's introduction to Gamio's companion volume *The Life Story of the Mexican Immigrant* (1931) maintains a neutral stance toward immigrants, *Mexican Immigration* is avowedly pro-immigrant: Gamio argues that Mexican immigrants should be paid the same wages as U.S. citizens.[69] *Mexican Immigration* differs from *Forjando patria* by rejecting conventional racialist thinking and incorporating the perspectives of the immigrants themselves in its analysis of the ideology of La Raza. However, what could appear to be a principled act of advocacy on behalf of Mexican immigrants loses some luster when one considers the problems with Gamio's hands-off methodology. Indeed, Gamio conducted only a few of the 131 interviews from which the selections that comprised *The Life Story of the Mexican Immigrant* were made. The vast majority of the interviews were conducted by Elena Landázuri, a

Mexican citizen and a graduate of the University of Chicago in sociology who had worked under Park, and Luis Felipe Recinos, a Salvadoran journalist who worked for *La Prensa* in San Antonio. Landázuri and Recinos used questions drafted by Gamio. According to Devra Weber, the fact that Gamio hired Recinos a few days after having met him in a hotel indicates that the interviews of *The Mexican Immigrant* were much less important to Gamio than the sociopolitical analysis of *Mexican Immigration to the United States*. Moreover, Recinos turned out to be a poor choice for an interviewer. He interviewed a disproportionate number of the middle class and workers who were established in the United States rather than seasonal migrant workers. He also expressed disparaging views of the poor and unlettered. Finally, Recinos engaged in sexual relations with at least one of his interviewees.[70]

Sponsored by the U.S. Social Science Research Council, which granted him thirteen thousand dollars in 1926 to work on the project, Gamio's study was supposed to make policy recommendations. But his advocacy on behalf of immigrants can also be explained by his position as an autoethnographer of sorts in relation to his immigrant subjects. Even if Gamio's identification with immigrants would, from a Mexican perspective, be disrupted by the class differences between them, as he observes, U.S. "racial prejudice" does not distinguish between differences of color and class among Mexicans: "Individuals of Mexican origin but of white skin are also socially discriminated against. The stigma of indigenous blood is so deep that the word 'Mexican,' which implies a little or great deal of Indian blood and the corresponding pigmentation, has acquired in the South a derogatory character" (54). U.S. whites racialize Mexican identity in such a way that it overrides differences in class position and even skin color. Gamio's Mexican immigrant informants, "deeply offended at discovering a racial prejudice against [them] in the United States" respond with the self-denomination La Raza, which cuts across differences of color, class, and acculturation, uniting Mexican immigrants and Mexican Americans, laborers, and professors. "La Raza," then, is a racialist term that paradoxically combats biological determinism by extending racial identification beyond the conventional boundaries of skin color, like the discourse of mestizaje. But unlike mestizaje ideology, rather than claiming a biological essence, it convenes a multiplicity of identities shaped by differing nationalities, skin tones, and class locations in an act of defiance against U.S. racist discourses. Gamio himself adopts an implicit La Raza ideology by advocating on behalf of Mexican immigrants.

Two sets of questions that Gamio prepared for the interviews of *The Mexican Immigrant* construct the term "La Raza" as a creative response to U.S. racism. Under the heading "Racial Prejudice," Gamio asks, "What does the racial prejudice to which they are submitted by the white man consist of? Compare with the attitude of whites in relation to blacks and vice versa. How do Mexicans and Americans of Mexican origin react to . . . racial prejudice?" Gamio then links this sequence of questions to the self-denomination of La Raza. Under the heading "Patriotismo" (patriotism), Gamio asks, "Whom do you include within the general term *La Raza*? Do you include only the descendants of Mexicans or also South Americans or so-called latinos, such as the French and Italians, etcetera? Do you believe that those who constitute *La Raza* are destined for a happier future or will they be absorbed by the Anglo-Saxon race in this continent?"[71] Here Gamio characterizes "La Raza" as a term of identity that could provide a way for Mexican immigrants and others to resist absorption by "the Anglo-Saxon race." Moreover, La Raza, at least in Gamio's queries, is an open-ended collectivity that could potentially include even French and Italian immigrants. The point for Gamio is not a biologically or culturally defined essence but rather a political grouping that would contest the construction of the nation as a homogeneous collectivity both in the United States and in Latin America.

The culturally hybrid collectivity constructed by ideologies of La Raza thus presents an alternative to the racial hybridity of contemporary mestizaje discourse present in *Forjando patria* and in Vasconcelos's *La raza cósmica: Misión de la raza iberoamericana* (*The Cosmic Race: The Mission of the Iberoamerican Race*) (1925). In Gamio La Raza derails the harmonizing project of national homogeneity via mestizaje in favor of a more politically antagonistic version of cultural hybridity. Such an antagonism toward U.S. imperialism and race relations is also present in Vasconcelos, who rejects "an exclusively national patriotism" in favor of a Latin Americanism of "nuestra raza en conjunto" (our race en masse).[72]

But whereas Vasconcelos constructs a La Raza ideology of "Iberoamerican" alliance from his position as a resident of Mexico, Gamio constructs his version of La Raza as a political exile in the United States. In Vasconcelos, the antagonist of the hybrid collectivity of Latin American nations is the United States, viewed as an imperialist, "Anglo-Saxon" nation. By contrast, in locating La Raza within the United States, Gamio cannot avoid a discussion of nationally based exploitation and oppression, in contrast to Vasconcelos, who speaks only of imperialism. Gamio's movement away

from an "exclusively nationalist" ideology stems in part from his exile in
the United States after his resignation as undersecretary of public education and his denunciation of corruption in the Mexican Department of
Education in 1925. It was during this period of exile that Gamio began his
study of Mexican immigrants. Gamio's migration to the United States was
thus accompanied by a Saidian theoretical traveling of the term "La Raza":
the meaning of the term shifts from signaling the racial superiority of
mestizos to whites and Indians in the postrevolutionary nationalism of
Vasconcelos to denoting a culturally distinctive, diverse community of
Latinos and Latin Americans in Gamio.

While the racism that immigrants and Latinos encounter creates a transnational and interracial ideology of alliance in the term "La Raza," it also
promotes a new Mexican nationalism in many of the immigrants. Those
who become immigrants initially "have little notion of their nationality or
their country," instead identifying with what Gamio called "pequeñas patrias." But when they immigrate to the United States, they "learn immediately what their mother-country means" (128). Gonzalo Galván, an immigrant from the state of Chihuahua who worked as a railroad laborer and
lumberman in California, Oregon, and Washington, views his life in the
United States as a jail sentence: "I like it here in the United States because I
live here, but this is only a jail in disguise. One's life is a real struggle, for
what can one do but endure these *bolillos* ("white breads") who do whatever they want to with one especially when one doesn't know English. One
lives here to leave one's strength and then go back to Mexico when one is
old like I am. That is why I am taking my son while he is young so that he
won't forget his country" (25). Galván implicitly criticizes the U.S. capitalist
underdevelopment of Mexico when he argues that the United States exploits his labor, which he describes here as a sapping of his strength and
youth. By conceptually fusing his experience of U.S. class exploitation,
racial antagonism, and national chauvinism, Galván paves the way for a
nationalism strengthened by its ability to associate class exploitation with
the United States rather than with Mexico.[73] Ironically, Gamio had searched
for the keys to Mexican nationalism in regional indigenous cultures and in
the rubble of Teotihuacán, only to find that many rural residents of Mexico
identify as Mexican only when they immigrate to the United States. To
return to the metaphor of fusion that begins *Forjando patria*, the United
States, with its racial antagonisms and exploitative labor conditions, becomes the unlikely foundry of Mexican nationalism.

Mexican immigrants' resistance to assimilation in the United States via the embrace of Mexican national identity is characterized by Redfield (as the editor of *The Life Story*) as an "intense, even bitter, racial feeling" in his section remarks to the book, whose selections he arranged for publication.[74] This is an antagonism indistinguishable from expressions of fierce national loyalty. Carlos Ibáñez, who worked in beet fields and on railroads in California, remarks, "I would rather cut my throat before changing my Mexican nationality. I prefer to lose with Mexico than to win with the United States" (45–46). Thus while in *Forjando patria* Gamio speaks for Indians, in his work on immigrants he allows his subjects to voice their own concerns and protests.

By contrast, Redfield structures *The Life Story* according to a Parkian notion of the inevitability of assimilation: the penultimate section is entitled "Assimilation," while the last focuses on "The Mexican-American." This arrangement of the text runs counter to the "bitter racial feeling" he detects among the immigrants—and thus mutes the protest implicit in the self-denomination "La Raza." Redfield even discounts data that would challenge the teleology of assimilation. He claims that the documents in "The United States as a Base for Revolutionary Activity" "are not, properly speaking, immigrant documents at all, as they have little to say as to the experiences of Mexicans in the United States" (29). Ironically, to qualify as "Mexican immigrants," Redfield argues that the subjects of the study cannot move too much—they should not return to Mexico or participate in Mexican politics.

By adhering to the prior assumption of an assimilation that will gradually eliminate conflict, and by narrowing the definition of *immigrant* to conform to that assumption, Redfield closes off the potential for devising radically alternative political ideologies. In both his landmark ethnography *Tepoztlán, a Mexican Village* (1930) and his introduction to *The Life Story*, Redfield polices geographic boundaries in order to cleanse his texts of political conflicts, which are evidently antithetical to an "objective" social science. In *Tepoztlán*, Redfield refuses to analyze in any depth political forces that cross beyond the village boundaries, such as peonage and the state–church conflicts that were raging in that section of rural Mexico. For instance, Redfield remains silent on the fact that the beginning of his research in 1926 coincides with the outbreak of the Cristero War (1926–29).[75] Redfield's strict adherence to the theory of assimilation in his editing of *The Life Story* finally ignores at its peril what Said has called the "essential untidiness" of social phenomena that must be addressed by every theory.[76]

By contrast, Gamio is able to account for untidy "current changes" to a somewhat greater extent because his commitment to the well-being of his subjects sharpens his ability to account for the complexity of their position within social relations. Redfield's narrow definition of *immigrant* as including only those who remain in the United States differs from that of Gamio, who argues that it is precisely the immigrants' desire to return to Mexico that distinguishes them from other immigrants.[77] Gamio's recognition of Mexican immigrants' defiant wish to return to Mexico does not make his thought radical—after all, when Henry Chandler argues in the *Los Angeles Times* that Mexicans do not intermarry like the Negro, he makes a similar point from the position of corporate interests.[78] However, Gamio's emphasis on immigrants' defiant attitudes does show that his social science methodology was more attuned to the specificities of immigrants' narratives than that of Park and Redfield. Moreover, especially in the discussion of La Raza, Gamio creates the space for a more thorough refusal of U.S. nationalist discourses of assimilation than was possible in their versions of Chicago School sociology.

Yet while Gamio creates the space for a critique of U.S. nationalist discourses even as he reaffirms Mexican nationalism, his ideologies of gender prove incapable of accounting for his informants' revisions of Mexican gender norms. In *Forjando patria* Gamio explicitly theorizes gender, concurring with Park's construction of the political realm as exclusively masculine. Women enter into Gamio's discussion only in relation to reproduction, as a necessary ingredient in forging a racially homogeneous nation from what Gamio viewed as a lamentable collection of "pequeñas patrias." Gamio distinguishes between "la mujer sierva" (the woman as slave), valued only for her motherhood; "la mujer feminista," a "masculine" feminist "for whom pleasure is more sport than passion"; and "la mujer femenina" (the feminine woman), who occupies a middle ground (119). Much as Gamio constructs the ideal Mexican subject as a biological and cultural fusion of indigenous and white elements, here he views the ideal woman as a combination of the preindustrial servant and the modern feminist. But in the double-edged character of mestizaje, Gamio's commitment to the well-being of Indians and women—exemplified by his indigenista projects of applied anthropology—is contradicted by mestizaje's need to create Mexican citizens. That is, the mestizaje project of intermarriage requires Indians and women who are compliant in the face of the state's refusal of their citizenship rights—Indians who are willing to choose Mexicanness over Indianness, and women who are willing to choose femininity over feminism. Indians were legally granted citizenship rights in the 1917 Constitution, but women were not granted basic rights of citizenship —the right to vote and hold political office—until the Mexican senate ratified President Lázaro Cárdenas's amendment to the 1917 constitution in 1937.[79]

Gamio further confronts the threat of allegedly masculine Mexican women in his essay "El celibato y el naturismo indígena," ("The celibate and indigenous naturalism," 1923), in which he discusses the reasons the female celibacy rate was higher in Mexico's cities than in *pueblos* and *rancherías*. Gamio explains this discrepancy by utilizing a variant of romantic racialist theory, which typically constructs an opposition between the artificiality of whites and the alleged emotional and sexual spontaneity of nonwhites: "In our opinion, these differences stem from the fact that the indigenous race is eminently naturalistic, faithfully following . . . the dicates of nature, while the white race grows farther away from natural systems; its habits rapidly grow artificial. . . . For the Indian there do not exist the thousand economic and social barriers that in the white race create obstacles to marriage, because puberty is the only index that accurately signals the age in which sexual relations are to begin."[80] Gamio argues that Indians, especially Indian women, provide a model of liberated sexual relations for the allegedly more repressed whites and mestizos.[81] So when in *Forjando patria* he writes, "Let us 'Indianize' ourselves a bit," he is partly alluding to the necessity of increasing the rate of reproduction among whites and mestizos, thereby hastening the homogenizing process of mestizaje.

The repressive gender ideology integral to Gamio's mestizaje coexists in tension with his interviews of women in *The Life Story*, which confound his tripartite scheme of female identity with narratives of work and activism. Elisa Silva, a divorced immigrant from Mazatlán, earns a living by dancing in a ballroom five nights a week from 7:30 p.m. to as late as 1:00 a.m. for around five dollars a night, or ten cents a dance. Silva is conscious of breaking Mexican norms of respectability through her job but reports that she hasn't suffered any adverse social consequences: "In Mexico this work might perhaps not be considered respectable, but I don't lose anything here by doing it" (161). If, on the one hand, she doesn't fit into Gamio's earlier conception of womanhood, on the other hand, she doesn't exemplify Park's notion of the immigrant subject who assimilates to U.S. social norms: "If I do marry some day it would be with a Mexican. The Americans are very dull and very stupid. They let the women boss them" (162). Silva subscribes to traditional gender ideologies in criticizing U.S. gender relations but undermines them in her own line of work.

The interview of Señora Flores de Ándrade, a woman born in Chihuahua in 1877, shows that while immigration to the United States often initiated a revision of gender norms, at other times this process began in Mexico. When Flores de Andrade inherits a fifth of her grandparents' estate at age thirteen, she frees her peons and allows them to live and work on her portion of the land for free. Widowed at the age of twenty-five, she joins an anti-Porfirian women's club called Daughters of Cuahtémoc and suffers from "extreme poverty," partly owing to her decision not to remarry (31). In 1906 she moves to El Paso with her children, where she continues her campaign of liberal propaganda against the notorious dictator Porfirio Díaz. Soon thereafter she becomes president of a liberal women's club in El Paso and aids revolutionary forces in the armed struggle against Díaz, hiding Pancho Villa in her house for three months in 1911. As a mother taking a leadership role in revolutionary activism, Flores de Andrade combines Gamio's categories of female identity, thereby exceeding their limited bounds.

Gamio's interview-based text sets loose multiple voices, some of which conflict with his ideologies of nation and gender and others of which concur with them.[82] Thus in criticizing U.S. nationalism and reaffirming Mexican nationalism via his immigrants' narratives, Gamio produces a bifurcated nationalism that carries a critical weight in the United States while upholding the status quo in Mexico. While nationalism assumes importance in Gamio's analysis of the interviews in *Mexican Immigration to the United States*, the revision of gender ideologies by his female informants does not attain the status of a category of analysis. Nevertheless, in *The Life Story* the rigid gender division between masculine men and feminine women that underwrites Gamio's nationalist mestizaje ideology is eroded in the narratives of Elisa Silva and Señora Flores de Andrade, two divorced immigrant women who attain an unusual level of economic and ideological independence from men.

What, then, can one conclude about Gamio's relationship to the Mexican Revolution in particular and decolonization in general? On the one hand, Gamio hoped to reform Latin American governments so that they would develop more enlightened Indian policies. This desire reflected to some extent the uprising of Indians that propelled the Mexican Revolution. Moreover, he actively promoted and effected the most radical measures proposed in the aftermath of the Mexican Revolution, including the redistribution of land. On the other hand, Gamio's relatively privileged status, first as a government official and then as a social scientist who felt more comfortable writing at his desk than interviewing in the streets, distanced him from the socialist and indigenous movements that challenged the postrevolutionary status quo and worked to democratize Mexico. Nevertheless, his texts on Mexican immigrants are fascinating narratives that have taken on meanings that Gamio did not foresee and instead point to critiques of U.S. social and cultural norms, narratives of revolutionary activism, and potentially nonhierarchical conceptions of mestizo identity.

"BEHIND THE BOSS' BACK": COLLABORATIVE ETHNOGRAPHIC DISCOURSE IN HURSTON

Much like Gamio, Hurston focused on migrants' rejection of narratives of inevitable assimilation to the dominant. But any comparison between the two Boasian anthropologists must be qualified by accounting for their differing access to institutional power. Beginning in the 1920s, it was possible for Mexican anthropologists to obtain power in governmental posts and to exercise that power through "applied anthropology" to a degree unheard of in the United States. The prominence of Mexican anthropologists grew out of the government's need to gather information on Indian populations that did not identify as Mexican, which in some estimates constituted the majority of the country's population.[83] By contrast, Hurston never obtained a doctoral degree in anthropology, much less a prominent governmental post, as she lacked the will and the money (and, in part, the racial identity) to do so. While Gamio enjoyed a privileged position as a member of the white criollo dominant culture in Mexico, Hurston was a member of an oppressed racialized minority in the United States. Consequently, her dreams of promoting her version of applied anthropology took place on a much smaller scale than Gamio's.

Nevertheless, Hurston devised her own version of applied anthropology in attempting to utilize black folk culture as an economic resource. Her use of such a resource is evident in her attempts to capitalize on the vogue of Negro subjects in theater by writing and producing her own plays based on black folklore—such as the *Mule Bone* project and the relatively successful *The Great Day*—and by teaching drama in schools.[84] These time-consuming projects indicate Hurston's dedication to finding ways of turning her folklore collecting into a source of income for blacks. Hurston implicitly theorizes such a practice in her essay "High John De Conqueror," which describes the belief in the spiritual powers contained within the root of that name. In African American folk-medicine practices, High John is a root that protects against evil and helps the user navigate trying circumstances. Here Hurston suggests that the performance of identity can be used to profit blacks: "His people [African Americans] had their freedom, their laugh and their song. They have traded it to the other Americans for things they could use like education and property, and acceptance. High John knew that that was the way it would be. . . . John will never forsake the weak and the helpless, nor fail to bring hope to the hopeless. . . . They go on and laugh and sing. Things are bound to come out right tomorrow. That is the secret of black song and laughter."[85] Folk culture is Hurston's "High John De Conqueror" root: a vast reservoir of power that can be tapped by those who are knowledgeable enough to do so.

One of the ways to secure this advantage is Hurston's project of applied anthropology, which differs from prominent Harlem Renaissance intellectuals' gradualist faith in the erosion of white prejudice through African American excellence in the arts (James Weldon Johnson and Alain Locke). Hurston envisions equality as an immediate rather than a future goal. And alongside the issue of "acceptance" stressed by Johnson and Locke, Hurston emphasizes bread-and-butter issues such as "education and property." Thus, for Hurston, the "secret" of black folk practices such as song and laughter is that they can serve as strategic means by which black people secure power from the powerful, as in her projects of applied anthropology.

The similarly strategic function of her texts has long remained a secret as well. Writing in 1937, Richard Wright accused Hurston of perpetuating minstrel stereotypes of Negroes. To Wright, Hurston's characters stay in their place, "that safe and narrow orbit in which America likes to see the Negro live," thereby pandering to the prejudices of whites.[86] By condemning her for the minstrel performance of "making the 'white folks' laugh," Wright misses Hurston's strategic use of laughter as cultural critique in her essay "High John De Conqueror," which metonymically captures her emphasis on the use of black folk culture to gain strategic advantage. Hazel Carby has adopted Wright's position wholesale: "Has *Their Eyes Were Watching God* become the most frequently taught black novel because it acts as a mode of assurance that, really, the black folk are happy and healthy?" (89–90). Carby contrasts Wright's critique of minstrel stereotypes with Hurston's alleged maintenance of them: "Whereas Wright attempted to explode the discursive category of the Negro as being formed, historically, in the culture of minstrelsy, . . . Hurston wanted to preserve the concept of Negroness, to negotiate and rewrite its cultural meanings, and finally, to reclaim an aesthetically purified version of blackness. The antagonism between them reveals Wright to be a modernist and leaves Hurston embedded in the politics of Negro identity."[87] Although Carby is right to argue that Hurston is confined within the politics of Negro identity, I think she overstates her case. It is true that Hurston artificially extracts black communities from some of the conflicts they waged with whites, and, unlike Wright, she was certainly not a radical leftist. Indeed, as her biographer points out, none of the characters in *Mules and Men* tells stories of the Ocoee riot of November 1920, in which whites attacked blacks for protesting the denial of their voting rights.[88] Nevertheless, Hurston alludes to racial conflicts in more indirect ways. Ironically, Carby and Wright maintain that Hurston mimics the dominant white culture's representations of Negroes despite the fact that Hurston herself argued, "Mimicry is an art in itself," reminding us that mimicry can be employed on behalf of resistance by "reclaiming . . . borrowed characteristics."[89] Postcolonial theories of mimicry have created the space for the recognition that imitation, commonly viewed as a sign of inferiority in colonial and racist discourses, constitutes the subject as a heterogeneous collection of identifications and masks rather than as a coherent identity.[90] In contrast, by leveling the charge of minstrelsy against Hurston, Wright and Carby prematurely foreclose the possibility of a strategic reworking of dominant cultural tropes through performances of black identity.

The story " 'Member You'se a Nigger' " from *Mules and Men* reveals some of the ways in which Hurston turns mimicry into an art of reworking racial stereotypes. In this story John saves his master's children from drowning in a lake. Ole Massa sets John free with the reminder, "Member you'se a nigger" (89–90). Ole Massa's repetition of that phrase gives the story its bitter humor and its pointed critique of the efforts of slaveholders to deny the humanity of slaves even in the face of overwhelming evidence to the contrary. Slavery, like colonial rule, requires those constructed as inferior to "imitate" their oppressors in manners and morals. They must become like the rulers, but not identical to them. John has usurped the role of the white father by saving the children and therefore blatantly exceeds the role assigned to him. When John gains the master's respect, he threatens the black/white division, so he must be sent away, with the anxious reminder that he is still a "nigger."

This story perfectly illustrates the "'hybridization' of discourse and power," the threatening cultural sharing across race and class boundaries that for Homi Bhabha pervades orders of colonial and racial oppression. In Bhabha's view, "colonial ambivalence" consists in the contradictory character of stereotypes such as "nigger": "The stereotype . . . is a form of knowledge and identification that vacillates between what is always 'in place,' already known, and something that must be anxiously repeated."[91] As a calcified form of knowledge, the stereotype leaves the members of the dominant culture vulnerable to the ruses of the subordinated. In the U.S. context, the ambivalence in question here is what John Blassingame has termed the paradox of the fugitive "Sambo," who in the account of white slaveholder ideology views his master as a benevolent father yet runs away.[92] Indeed, elsewhere John is described as Ole Massa's "pet nigger," capturing the paradox of favoritism and degradation (113). At times Hurston's folktales contest such stereotypes outright, while at other times stereotypes are repeated without comment.[93] But taken as a whole, her folktales reveal the constructed character of the stereotype, its use in demeaning blacks but also its appropriation by them within strategies of resistance to the oppressive orders of slavery and segregation.

By having earned the right to leave slavery in "'Member You'se a Nigger,'" John mocks authority because he has demonstrated the inadequacy of the stereotype of "nigger."[94] John has earned the right to migrate North by becoming what the slaveholder regards as a faithful slave. Here migration becomes a particularly rich metaphor, figuring a certain mobility in class and geography, but also a racial indeterminacy in which the slave exceeds the bounds ascribed by the slaveholders' discourses of race. Why is this tale retold in the 1920s and 1930s? What "cultural work" does it perform—how does it redefine the social order—in the decades after slavery?[95] The allegory of the "good slave" who runs away alludes to the contemporary Great Migration of African Americans. This contemporary level of the allegory literally brings the South into the North: upon migrating the black southern folk become a northern urban population. With the Great Mi gration, then, it is no longer possible to view the "Negro Problem" as an exclusively southern problem. Migration threatens the white South with the loss of cheap labor and the white North with transformed neighborhoods. If one reads *Mules and Men* and *Their Eyes* as simply stories about the South or tales caught in "a discourse of nostalgia about the rural community," one runs the risk of joining with Ole Massa in attempting to keep John in his place in the rural South. Instead, these stories signify across geographic divisions.[96]

Hurston's stories of migration between rural and urban areas figure as part of a larger meditation on the choices available to African Americans in the North and the South: acculturation as opposed to a politically dissenting cultural autonomy. Hurston posits a third possibility when she positions herself within a hybrid cultural space as she "enters and eludes" modernity (as Néstor García Canclini would say) in her use of Boasian ethnography. On the one hand, by migrating North to gain an education, Hurston has undergone a process of "deterritorialization" in that she has lost "the natural relation of culture with geographic and social territories." However, Hurston enacts a "reterritorialization" in her imaginative reclaiming of that territory's culture as a resource for migrants in the North.[97] Hurston's reclaiming of black southern folklore through Boasian ethnography enacts "cultural reconversion," the practice of transferring "symbolic patrimony from one site to another in order to conserve it, increase its yield, and better the position of those who practice it."[98]

How does Hurston attempt to "increase [the] yield" of black folk culture? By representing black folk culture as a resource for cultural resistance in stories such as " 'Member You'se a Nigger,' " she bucks the persistent tendency of educated African Americans to denigrate black folk culture. In "Racial Self-Expression," an essay included in Charles S. Johnson's collection *Ebony and Topaz* (1927), E. Franklin Frazier, then, like Johnson, a doctoral student in sociology at the University of Chicago, argues that the American Negro was "practically stripped of his culture" when enslaved in the United States.[99] Further, Frazier argues that African Americans would only "impoverish" themselves by seeking strength in a "barren racial tradition," allegedly isolated from white America.[100] Frazier's notion of the barrenness of black culture confirms his teacher Park's notion of the inevitability of assimilation. By contrast, Hurston, like Frazier's antagonist, the anthropologist Melville Herskovits, amply demonstrates the resilience of African "survivals" and slave culture into the 1930s. Indeed, Herskovits cites Hurston in support of his argument.[101] This reading of Hurston in the context of the Frazier-Herskovits debate allows one to move away from viewing her as being trapped within a "narrow orbit" (Wright) or as "embedded" (Carby) within an overly provincial romanticization of southern Negro identity. Instead, Hurston moved between the urban life Wright knew so well and the black South. I am arguing, then, for a more dialectical view of Hurston's self-positioning as a black intellectual returning from a northern exile to the South, a view that emphasizes the ways in which her profound ties to the South are reconfigured by studying under Boas in New York City.

Hurston's immersion within the culture of the black South has led critics to exaggerate her proximity to it, as suggested in the metaphors of spatial confinement deployed by Carby and Wright. Yet Hurston constantly reveals her distance in class from the subjects of her anthropological investigations, even as she attempts to bridge that distance.[102] Hurston herself suggests that the black South is so close to her that it crowds out her ability to write effectively about it until she obtains the "spy-glass of anthropology." The South fits Hurston like a "tight chemise" until she migrates North and is able to view it differently, through metropolitan lenses (1).[103]

Hurston's description of the production of ethnographic knowledge is both more modest and more nuanced than similar descriptions offered by Boas and Park. Boas writes that Hurston "has been able to penetrate through that affected demeanor by which the Negro excludes the white observer effectively from participating in his true inner life" (xiii). Boas claims, somewhat patronizingly, that Hurston the autoethnographer can reveal to white readers the "inner life" of her subjects. Similarly, Park argues that sociology should focus on the "mind of the marginal man"—in this case a description extending to the marginal woman, Hurston herself —so as to allow sociologists to understand the process of assimilation. Thus like Gamio, Boas and Park use metaphors of transparency in discussing social scientists' objects of knowledge.

Hurston, by contrast, shows the ways in which what she calls "the spy-glass of anthropology" is rendered opaque. Hurston emphasizes the "evasive" responses of lower-class Negroes both to whites *and* to middle-class Negroes. In what Hurston calls a deceptive "feather-bed resistance," the Negro outwardly "satisfies the white person" with a response that conceals inward thoughts: "He can read my writing but he sho' can't read my mind" (3). Here "writing" refers both to the texts produced by Hurston's informants and to her own text, as if she learns how to write in a resistant manner from them. The second time the "feather bed tactics" are invoked is when Hurston attempts to collect folklore at the Everglades Cypress Lumber Company in Polk County, Florida: "The men would crowd in and buy soft drinks and woof at me, the stranger, but I knew I wasn't getting on. The ole feather bed tactics" (60). Hurston soon learns that the markings of her class difference have distinguished her from the others: "The car made me look too prosperous. So they set me aside as different" (60–61).

Hurston thus reveals the limits of her own autoethnography: her subjects withhold information not only from whites, but also from Hurston herself, who is viewed as being different in class despite her skin color. Her exile to the North has made strange her experience of the familiar, a desired feature of ethnography, but in the process she has also become strange to her familiars. Other limits of Hurston's role as an ethnographer stand out in the jook section, in which her proximity to men during the process of collecting makes Lucy jealous, leading Big Sweet to defend Hurston (149–54, 175–79). It is in these passages one learns that the sexual persona Hurston devises to aid her collection of folktales—she avoids being seen as Cliffert Ulmer's "property"—ironically creates rivalries with other women that threaten the ethnographer's life (143).

Hurston attempts to bridge this distance between ethnographer and subjects by assuming a lower-class identity: she gains acceptance only when she claims to be a bootlegger eluding the law, exemplifying the novel strategy that Fatimah Tobing Rony has aptly termed "observing participation."[104] Hurston also compensates for the limits of autoethnography by actively adopting the perspectives of her informants. Indeed, when Hurston declares that her task is to rescue black folk culture, George Thomas contests her theory of salvage ethnography—anthropologists' conviction that they had to record "primitive" cultures before they expired under the onslaught of modernization:

> "We want to set them [folktales] down before it's too late."
> "Too late for what?"
> "Before everybody forgets all of 'em"
> "No danger of that. That's all some people is good for—set 'round and lie and murder groceries." (8)

Thomas's response to Hurston constructs the folk culture as active, transforming, and in no danger of dying out, as the anthropologists fear. Thomas "teaches" Hurston one of the key aspects of her methodology—the placement of anthropological "data" within the daily life of the subjects. By allowing her informants to comment on the practice of ethnography, Hurston both blurs the divisions between ethnographer and informant, daily life and anthropological investigation, and calls attention to the stubborn persistance of those divisions. By refusing ethnography's conventional objective stance, Hurston disrupts the proprietary assumptions of social scientists such as Redfield, who claims, "The southern negro is our one principal folk."[105] Rather than a discourse of mastery, as signaled by the possessive used by Redfield, Hurston emphasizes the limits of social science. Thus Hurston practices an alternative, collaborative social science, one in which she incorporates the insights of her subjects on the practices of knowledge production.[106]

Such a collaborative social science is made possible by a decisive transformation in the culture concept. The modern period in anthropology marks the transition from a hierarchical, Arnoldian view of culture as the "best which is thought and known" to the pluralist notion of culture as consisting in a wide array of informal beliefs and practices in the age of ethnography.[107] This more inclusive array of cultural practices achieves a privileged position in Hurston's text, which lovingly describes sermons, card playing, a dance on payday, songs, children's games such as "Chick, mah Chick, mah Craney crow," and how to get warm by a fire, among many other cultural practices.[108]

Gamio and Redfield join Hurston by describing such informal cultural practices in their social scientific texts as well. But Hurston, honing her skills as a storyteller, takes this transition to informal culture a step further, describing culture as embedded within everyday practices. With this new move in ethnographic methodology, Hurston outpaces even her renowned teacher. In his own work Boas had not moved beyond a strict definition of culture emphasizing formal public affairs and myths over informal behavior, according to Stocking.[109] However, in his theoretical statements on ethnology, Boas called for a shift toward the description of informal behaviors. In "The Methods of Ethnology" (1920), Boas calls for a new ethnographic practice eschewing the "systematic enumeration of standardized beliefs and customs of a tribe" in favor of a more holistic approach that describes the ways in which "the individual reacts to his whole social environment."[110]

Hurston establishes a narrative line in *Mules and Men* by suggesting the "whole social environment" in representations of the banter and activities accompanying the storytelling. For instance, as the members of the swamp gang go fishing, they tell mostly animal tales, such as "How the Woodpecker Nearly Drowned the Whole World," about a woodpecker that pecks away at Noah's Ark until "Ole Nora . . . hauled off and give dat peckerwood a cold head-whipping wid a sledge hammer, and dat's why a peckerwood got a red head today" (102–03). Here "peckerwood" refers to the woodpecker and and also serves as a disparaging term for whites, a fact that explains the bitterness of the tale's conclusion: "Dat's how come Ah feel like shootin' every one of 'em Ah see. Tryin' to drown me before Ah was born" (103). This story is told after a foreman forces the swamp team to work in the sawmills rather than allowing them to take a day off. The swamp gang disobeys the foreman's wishes by waiting outside rather than going into the mill (84). The menacing presence of southern whites is also evident in the description of the "quarters boss" who "had a way of standing around in the dark and listening" (144). Whites exert not only economic but also social control of blacks: the quarters boss doesn't allow liquor in the jook (usually a combination bar and dance hall) on the property of the lumber company.

By revealing the varied uses of folk practices within everyday life, Hurston's discourse of collaboration creates what de Certeau has called a "science of the everyday."[111] That is, metropolitan social science allows Hurston to disseminate information on black folk cultural practices in order to legitimize those practices to black middle-class readers. Ironically, through her engagement with Boasian anthropology, a mode of social inquiry that construed itself as an objective science, Hurston sheds light on other, popular sciences generally dismissed as fraudulent, but which she dignifies by showing their utility within everyday practices. These technologies of knowing range in *Mules and Men* from the humorous explanations of the origins of things, as in "Why Negroes are Black" and "How the Gator Got His Mouth," to the more elaborate technology of voodoo, which places an emphasis on interpretive powers, as when a pair of eyes are painted on Hurston's cheeks in Luke Turner's initiation ceremony and when Father Watson prides himself on the ability to " 'read' anybody at sight" (200, 213). Hurston participates in these practices with a great deal of respect for both the practitioners and their clients. Thus dignified by Hurston, these practices can be best described via the etymological meaning of science: a technology of knowing.

In the section on New Orleans, "the hoodoo capital of America," conjure is used not only in "man-and-woman cases," but also as a way for powerless blacks to gain some power over whites (202). In one account of the uses of hoodoo, told in the section on "conjure stories," an "unreconstructed planter" in Georgia who has murdered his black servant finds his family gradually destroyed by hoodoo vexes (234–36). This cautionary tale to white southerners reveals conjure, in its dual sense of exerting magical powers and seizing "narrative authority," to serve as an alternative everyday science of resistance.[112] If racial sciences manipulated craniometric data, taken as the outward signs of intelligence, so as to create narratives of Negro inferiority, hoodoo practices can manipulate the occult workings of the mind to terrorize oppressors.

By refusing to dismiss hoodoo as mere superstition, Hurston uses the social scientific practice of ethnography to mend the rift between professional and everyday scientific discourses.[113] At a time when Negroes were systematically excluded from the realms of institutional power, Hurston reminds her middle-class Negro readers that black southern folk culture, a culture often disparaged as "barren" by observers such as Frazier, contains rich resources and tactics of resistance for use by the powerless. Thus by refusing to separate professional and everyday scientific discourses, Hurston makes a complex political intervention not confined to any one institutional or cultural sphere. In the realm of social science, Hurston deftly deploys its "objective" methodology even as she undermines such objectivity by showing how popular scientific discourses, themselves not even usually counted as science, often endow the powerless with power. Intervening in the politics of Negro identity, Hurston puts her own spin on "New Negro" ideologies by calling for the urban middle classes of the North to respect the resistant cultural tactics devised by the lower classes of the South, tactics which undoubtedly traveled north along with the wave of black migrants. By respecting the technologies of the folk, Hurston challenges the widespread faith in professionalization and modernization as a cure-all for problems of race and class, undermining the Parkian notion of the desirability of assimilation.

In *Their Eyes Were Watching God* (1937), Hurston again opposes the metaphors of merging, fusion, and melting typical of theories of assimilation and instead specifies multiple routes of migration and movement, some moving toward the centers of dominant culture, but others straying away from them. While Park's "marginal man" has migrated to the city, Hurston's characters typically live among the Negroes "farthest down," as she points out, using a phrase developed by Booker T. Washington and Park.[114] Janie and Tea Cake, for instance, do not migrate to the city, where they can aspire to upward mobility, but instead travel to the Everglades, joining migrant laborers who pick beans for a living, people "broken from being poor."[115] One of Hurston's most lyrical passages describes Janie's respect for these people: "Work all day for money, fight all night for love. The rich black earth clinging to bodies and biting the skin like ants."[116] While Park's "marginal man" is a migrant figure unmarked in terms of class, Hurston's migrants would find themselves at home in a proletarian novel.

Thus an attentiveness to class location and class division among African Americans, together with an emphasis on the "routes" of culture and the migrations of subjects, constitute Hurston's major contribution to social scientific racial theory in the 1920s and 1930s.[117] Hurston's careful description of class conflict among African Americans is evident not only in her self-critical representation of ethnography in *Mules and Men*, but also in the exchange between Mrs. Turner and Janie in *Their Eyes*. Mrs. Turner snubs Tea Cake because he is dark-skinned, identifying with Janie because she is light-skinned like her. "Us oughta class off," she proposes to Janie (135). As Hortense Spillers has written, " 'Race,' as a poisonous idea, insinuates itself not only across and between ethnicities, but within."[118] Here color functions as a marker of race/class within a racially oppressed group.[119] But Janie, eager to defend her dark husband, responds, "Us can't do it. We'se uh mingled people and all of us got black kinfolks as well as yaller kinfolks" (135). In other words, Janie argues that even a family living under the same roof often includes both dark-skinned and light-skinned members. Here Janie's tactic of using the coexistence of colors in the same family resembles that of Boas in arguing against racial difference by pointing out racial mixture. Mrs. Turner responds, "Always cuttin' de monkey for white folks. If it wuzn't for so many black folks it wouldn't be no race problem. De white folks would take us in wid dem. De black ones is holdin' us back" (135).

Through Mrs. Turner's words, a familiar black middle-class disparagement of the lower classes, Hurston anticipates Wright's criticism of her novel's alleged "minstrel" tactics. Hurston shrewdly places a Wrightian critique of the minstrel practice of "cuttin' de monkey for white folks" in the mouth of Mrs. Turner, whose class and color snobbery make her an unsympathetic character. Hurston's move here is to suggest that the charge of minstrelsy by middle-class blacks can conceal an elitist class politics. As we have seen, a collaborative discourse that adopts lower-class cultural forms accompanies this critique of class ambition. This incorporation of lower-class forms occurs at the narrative level of the text in Hurston's use of free indirect discourse, which evokes the voice, presence, and style of a character in third-person narration.[120] Thus the politics of color and class in Hurston refute the charge that she has created a pastoral "discourse of nostalgia for a rural community."[121] Instead, the playfulness and romance of *Mules and Men* and *Their Eyes Were Watching God* are literally carried on "behind the boss' back" (*Mules* 127).

In stark contrast to Gamio's interest in Mexican immigrants, Hurston's sympathies for the black working classes did not cross the border, as is evident in Hurston's patronizing and ethnocentric attitudes toward her Haitian informants in *Tell My Horse* (1938). In this mixed-genre text that combines ethnography, a travelogue of her journeys among Jamaican and Haitian peasants, and political analysis, Hurston departs from her first ethnographic text by dropping her collaborative discourse, which takes a sympathetic approach to her informants, in favor of a hermeneutics of suspicion. Without registering the slightest trace of irony, Hurston leaves behind her nuanced narrative of the multiple strategic uses of "big old lies" by African Americans in the U.S. South and instead castigates Haitians for their "habit of lying":[122] "It is safe to say that this art, pastime, expedient or whatever one wishes to call it, is more than any other factor responsible for Haiti's tragic history. . . . This lying habit goes from the thatched hut to the mansion."[123] Hurston posits a singular Haitian national trait of deception in order to homogenize a diverse assortment of class-based "lies," ranging from the denial of widespread cruelty to animals by peasants to the denial of voodoo and the upper classes' blaming of national problems on the marines' occupation of the country.

By blaming these multiple lies for Haiti's predicament, Hurston positions herself as an apologist for U.S. imperialism: she claims that the U.S. invasion and military occupation of Haiti from 1915 to 1934 "was the end of the revolution and the beginning of peace."[124] This assertion matches the claims of U.S. officials who argued that Haitians' inability to rule necessitated the military occupation.[125] Moreover, Hurston ignores the brutal use of U.S. military force in suppressing Haitian rebellions in 1915 and again in 1918–19 that resulted in the deaths of thousands of Haitians.[126] In claiming that Haitians overwhelmingly welcomed the U.S. occupation, Hurston ignores the protests within Haiti against press censorship, forced labor, and segregation as well as the transnational organizing by the NAACP and Haitian exiles in New York City who worked toward Haitian independence.[127]

Thus Hurston's relationship to the egalitarian tendencies of the wave of decolonization of the 1920s and beyond was as complex and vexed as that of Gamio. Both wrote ethnographic texts that exposed readers to the voices and perspectives of working-class people of color. Hurston's experimental ethnography championed black cultural forms at a time when some black social scientists viewed black culture as a liability rather than a strength. However, both Gamio and Hurston distanced themselves from their subjects in certain ways: Gamio left the interviewing to others, while Hurston's interest in black cultural resilience prevented her from fully portraying the predicaments of African Americans and Afro-Haitians in the context of imperialism and racial oppression.

CONCLUSIONS: THE "RECIPROCAL CONTAGION" OF THE HARLEM RENAISSANCE IN HEMISPHERIC PERSPECTIVE

The differences between Gamio and Hurston in terms of their institutional enfranchisement and class trajectories are also registered in the range of genres in which they write: Gamio's mainstream social scientific text *Mexican Immigration*, Hurston's experimental and iconoclastic text of ethnography and folklore, *Mules and Men*, and her novel *Their Eyes Were Watching God*. Having little access to institutional power, Hurston simultaneously conducts three lines of investigation identified by Spillers as crucial to politically transformative intellectual inquiry: "the contemplative," "the everyday," and "the practical," evident in the program of economic empowerment in the essay "High John De Conqueror." Hurston produces a "reciprocal contagion" among these three realms often maintained as distinct by social science.[128] By contrast, partially owing to his institutional enfranchisement, Gamio emphasizes the practical and the contemplative, avoiding a representation of the everyday in favor of cataloguing formally held beliefs. And while Gamio leads a cadre of social scientific investigators, thereby distancing himself from the people whom he studies, Hurston lives among her subjects, eating their food, cavorting at their dances, speaking in their idiom. Unlike Hurston, Gamio is limited by the ethnographic paradigms developed by British functional anthropology (Bronislaw Malinowski and Alfred Radcliffe-Brown) after World War I. According to Talal Asad,

functionalist anthropology structured its inquiries along the lines suggested by the question of what holds society together.[129] For Gamio, the
requirements of Mexican nationalism are the binding element for the social order. However, Gamio's goal of maintaining social order in Mexico conflicts with his own and Hurston's aims of enfranchising the lower
classes, partly through projects of applied anthropology. Ironically, it may
be Gamio's faith in the unifying force of nationalism that distanced him
from the forces of decolonization in Mexico. Similarly, Hurston's stubborn
insistence on the resilience of black cultural forms led her to downplay the
significance of white racism and set her at odds with more radical intellectuals in the black community who were more savvy in negotiating cultural
differences within the black diaspora and were thus better equipped to lend
their support to decolonization movements.

However, despite such drawbacks in their politics, Gamio and Hurston
excel at adapting metropolitan social science for use by writers from the
racialized periphery. In Gamio and Hurston's collaborative discourses, to
differing degrees the subaltern's concerns transform the methodologies
and narrative strategies of the metropolitan writer. The subalterns criticize
methodological practices, and their narratives assume a prominent position within the collaborative texts. The subalterns are not just represented;
they also represent. A collaborative discourse is produced, then, when
autoethnographers intervene within primitivist stereotypes and discourses
so as to turn the subalterns into coauthors of transformed metropolitan
discourses, even when the ethnographic subjects' views differ from those of
the ethnographer. Thus the autoethnography of Gamio and Hurston does
not fulfill François Lionnet's definition of autoethnography as the self-
description of the ethnic subject.[130] Their ethnographic coauthorship rejects such neutral and individualist terms of engagement, refusing the
guarantees of ethnic identity in favor of the possibilities of a politics positing an unstable, dialectical relationship between "self" and socius.

As migrants themselves, traveling the routes between metropolitan intellectual centers and putatively primitive peripheries, Gamio and Hurston
devise unconventional roles as intellectuals, identifying with the subjects of
their studies. Rejecting standards of objectivity, Gamio proposes policy
changes so as to better the condition of Mexican immigrants. Similarly,
Hurston invites black migrants and more established middle-class black
northerners to jettison their class pretensions so as to draw upon the
intellectual and economic resources within southern black folk culture.

Thus by partially rejecting the top-down discourse of mastery that structures social scientific texts by Boas, Park, and Redfield, Gamio and Hurston practice an early twentieth-century example of a politically engaged cultural critique that eschews the rigidity of objectivity. Indeed, as Renato Rosaldo has argued, "Dismantling objectivism creates a space for ethical concerns in a territory once regarded as value-free."[131] Nevertheless, there are sharp limits to their collaborative discourses: they spill over into certain reformist acitivities (Gamio) and into efforts to turn black folklore into an economic resource for the black community (Hurston), but both avoid joining leftist or working-class movements.

Gamio and Hurston contribute to social scientific discourses on race by refusing prefabricated theoretical templates. Instead, Gamio reveals the firm resistance of Mexican immigrants to assimilation, and Hurston situates folk practices within everyday life rather than simply cataloguing them. Moreover, the emphasis on migration in Gamio and Hurston provides them with the historical particulars they use to contest theories of mimesis as an unthinking mimicry or assimilation. These migrant subjects may travel the routes laid by capitalism in the Americas, moving into the exploited positions offered to them, but they also refuse to be trapped by those positions. As what Bhabha has referred to as "mimics," Gamio and Hurston adopt a "hybrid" cultural stance in which they accept aspects of the dominant culture while refusing to carry out its hegemonic dictates.[132] It is precisely through this concatenation of theories of hybridity, migration, and mimesis that the texts of Gamio and Hurston challenge narratives of progressive assimilation and modernization with a notion of politically recalcitrant "marginal" subjects.

Finally, a comparison of Gamio and Hurston reveals that the political debates identified with the Harlem Renaissance, focused on hybridity, migration, mimesis, and assimilation, among other subjects, outstrip its narrowly defined and ethnically restricted boundaries. By engaging with theories developed by the Chicago School of Sociology and Boasian anthropology, Gamio and Hurston negotiate cultural circuits linking metropolitan and peripheral sites in another sort of "reciprocal contagion." Moreover, the fact that Gamio and Hurston both attempted to refute popular press antagonism toward black and Mexican migrants to northern U.S. urban centers shows that the Harlem Renaissance can be profitably situated within a larger intercultural and transnational frame of debates on migration.[133] Indeed, while scholars such as Ann Douglas and George Hutchinson have emphasized intercultural ties in the study of the Harlem Renaissance, and Hazel Carby and others have done important work on class and gender, more work remains to be done in demonstrating the ways in which the Harlem Renaissance was produced within transnational circuits of culture.[134] As Eric Sundquist has written, scholars need to explore "the ways in which the Harlem Renaissance exceeded the bounds not only of Harlem but also of the United States."[135] In contesting the Harlem Renaissance paradigm, a paradigm that perpetuates a vision of what Richard Wright called "that safe and narrow orbit in which America likes to see the Negro live," culture critics should develop frames for an intercultural and transnational Harlem Renaissance that transgresses the ethnically and geographically restricted coordinates suggested in its name. As Hurston wrote, "I do not wish to close the frontiers of life upon my own self. I do not wish to deny myself the expansion of seeking into individual capabilities and depths by living in a space whose boundaries are race and nation."[136]

Coda

> Most philosophers see the ship of state launched on the broad, irresistible tide
> of democracy, with only delaying eddies here and there, others, looking closer, are
> more disturbed. Are we, they ask, reverting to aristocracy and despotism—the
> rule of might?
> —W. E. B. DU BOIS, "The African Roots of War" (1915)

○ Immigrant groups from both Latin America and the United States met at the Sixth World Social Forum in Caracas, Venezuela, from January 24 to February 2, 2006, to share experiences and strategize potential solutions to social and political problems in the Americas. Forum participants such as Oscar Chacón, leader of the U.S. Latino contingent and director of the Chicago-based immigrant rights group Enlaces America, sought to place what are commonly viewed as exclusively national problems, such as immigration, in a broader, hemispheric context. Indeed, Chacon has insisted on linking U.S. immigration policies to U.S. foreign policy in Latin America.[1] According to Roberto Lovato, the "radical vision [of immigrant rights groups] was perhaps best embodied by proposals for a hemispheric citizenship along the lines of the European model."[2] Other practices of hemispheric citizenship at the forum focused on more immediate solutions to problems facing immigrants and workers in the Americas. Indeed, Via Campesina, a Latin American organization of small farmers, used the forum to gain support and to develop strategies that would address the needs of the several countries it serves.[3] The Sixth World Social Forum demonstrates how contemporary activists are engaging in practices of hemispheric citizenship that resemble those of the earlier writer-activists featured in this book, particularly those who participated in the alternative Pan-American social movements that condemned U.S. intervention in

Latin America in the 1920s (see the introduction to this book). This brief account of the Sixth World Social Forum also shows how today's discourses of hemispheric citizenship can contest the U.S. government's version of inter-American relations and uncritical vision of its own history as an "irresistible tide of democracy," in Du Bois's terms.

The term "wave" as used by Du Bois in his phrase the "wave upon wave of whiteness" in *Darkwater* disrupts assumptions of an "irresistible tide of democracy" and a correspondingly linear historical periodization, pointing out the disruptive force of both race and empire. It also implies that contemporary activists would do well to investigate earlier discourses of hemispheric citizenship as a rich vein of conceptual resources. Over a century ago, the antiracist and anti-imperialist aims of Martí and Du Bois compelled them to develop novel conceptions of history and citizenship to create a sense of urgency for their readers and audiences. Both Martí and Du Bois contest dominant narratives of European and U.S. history as uninterrupted progress or as the consummation of democracy and freedom, and instead expose how the U.S. government "set aside" freedom for other regions (Martí) or participated in waves of whiteness that must be met by waves of democratization and decolonization (Du Bois). The notion of waves of decolonization challenges conventional historical periodizations by exploring how a historical event or a series of historical events shapes a given writer's outlook on the present and the future. Indeed, Martí and Du Bois braid narratives of past events into their understandings of the current political scene in order to frame an ethical response. More specifically, the narrative form of melodrama and the discourse of messianism provide ways of configuring the present and future as a response to the political dilemmas of the past: for Martí, U.S. imperialism in 1848 victimizes Mexico and creates the imperative for the Cuban War for Independence of 1895–98; for Du Bois, U.S. imperialism in 1898 victimizes a host of "colored populations" and creates the imperative for black alliances with the "darker races" all along the global color line. Thus as a methodology waves of decolonization plots historical events not along a continuum of unfolding time, nor along an upward slope of historical progress, but rather as a political and ethical drama (or melodrama) shedding light on efforts to make freedom and democracy live up to their names. The transnational, comparative aspect of the methodology of waves of decolonization is necessary to expose the unsatisfied character of freedom and democracy. Thus the methodology of waves of decolonization links domestic struggles for equality to broader, global struggles against empire.

To be sure, discourses of hemispheric citizenship—and transnational discourses more generally—are not necessarily politically progressive, as is evident in U.S. Secretary of State James G. Blaine's efforts to secure the "annexation by trade" of Latin America in the late 1880s, and in Hurston's xenophobic writings on Haiti—imperialism and ethnocentrism are among the potential pitfalls of a hemispheric approach. Decolonizing discourses of hemispheric citizenship require giving a full hearing to those who contest the U.S. State Department's characterization of hemispheric affairs and a sensitive navigation of class and cultural divides as well as linguistic and ideological differences. The cross-national frame of analysis inherent to discourses of hemispheric citizenship is necessary to keep pace with the transformations of U.S. imperialism—and the creative responses of oppressed groups throughout the Americas.

This cross-national frame also offers insight into an important, occluded field of political power. The transnational paradigm of rightlessness associated with the work of Hannah Arendt, that of the stateless refugee, remains pertinent today—think of the tortured prisoners held in Abu Ghraib, Guantánamo, and the secret CIA prisons in Europe in the post-9/11 age. However, Arendt's account fails to capture another sort of transnational rightlessness: the plight of those imperial subjects who retain the ostensible rights of their own nation-states, in a situation in which those rights are undermined and to some extent made irrelevant by the political economy—and biopolitics—of imperialism. The gap between the rights of the citizen and human rights that is so irrefutably present in the person of the refugee or tortured "enemy combatant" is equally present, if less visible, in the imperial or neocolonial subject. While Arendt views the gap between the rights of the citizen and human rights as a central flaw of democracy, Jacques Ranciere views it as one of the secrets of its biopolitical power, the power exerted over bodies in the aggregate, setting the conditions for fertility and mortality as well as segregation and social hierarchies.[4] The contention of this book is that a full account of that biopolitical power requires moving beyond the nation-state, but also beyond the traditional international human rights framework toward a transnational analysis of the denial of rights to imperial subjects. With the aid of the concept of the biopolitical as a less-recognized form of power, one can perceive discourses of hemispheric citizenship as redressing not only the contradictions of democracy, but also its limitations, joining efforts to expand our notion of what constitutes the political itself.

INTRODUCTION

1 W. E. B. Du Bois, *The Souls of Black Folk, Three Negro Classics*, 221. All further references to *Souls* are cited parenthetically in the text as *S.*

2 Du Bois, "The Present Outlook for the Dark Races of Mankind," 47. All further references to this speech are cited parenthetically in the text as "PO." I am indebted to Nahum Chandler for having suggested the relevance of this text in a brief seminar on Du Bois ("Reading Seminar: 'The Problem of the Twentieth Century Is the Problem of the Color Line'").

3 Mikhail Bakhtin, *The Dialogic Imagination*, 84.

4 According to M. E. Chamberlain, the term *decolonization* "came into general use in the 1950s and 1960s although it seems to have been coined in 1932 by the German scholar Moritz Julius Bonn" (*Decolonization*, 1). For other studies of decolonization, see R. F. Holland, *European Decolonization*, and Presenjit Duara, *Decolonization: Perspectives from Now and Then*. Mary Louise Pratt has described the Latin American independence movements of the 1820s as the "first wave of decolonization" (*Imperial Eyes*, 175). My use of "waves of decolonization" is deeply indebted to Pratt's entire project.

5 The term *transnational* has increasingly been associated with the current "globalized" regime of capital accumulation (see, for instance, Roger Rouse, "Thinking Through Transnationalism," 368). In relation to earlier historical periods, I use the term *transnational* in a different way to distinguish certain activities from those termed international, which identifies a consortium of nationally based entities. In my use, the term *transnational* instead denotes modes of affiliation that elude the national and activities beyond the purview of the state, such as those implied by the term "darker races" invoked in the NAACP journal *Crisis: A Record of the Darker Races*, edited by Du Bois beginning in 1910. See also Paul Gilroy's analysis of "outer-national" cultural flows in *The Black Atlantic*, 16; the distinction between "international" and

transnational in Leslie Sklair (*Sociology of the Global System*, 2–4); Francesca Miller's work ("Feminisms and Transnationalism," 1); and the exhaustively detailed transnational history by Benedict Anderson, *Under Three Flags: Anarchism and the Anti-Colonial Imagination.*

6 Pratt, "Edward Said's *Culture and Imperialism*," 4.

7 José Martí quoted in Peter Turton, *José Martí*, 52; Manuel Gamio, *The Indian Basis of Mexican Civilization*, 171. Prasenjit Duara has similarly argued that decolonization is a prolonged process that includes but is by no means limited to the anticolonial attainment of independence: "Decolonization represented not only the transference of legal sovereignty, but a movement for moral justice and political solidarity against imperialism. It thus refers both to the anti-imperialist political movement and to an emancipatory ideology which sought or claimed to liberate the nation and humanity itself" (2). *Colonialism* refers to direct territorial rule, while *neocolonialism* refers to a combination of indirect political and economic rule. The term *imperialism,* first used around 1880, refers more generally to a range of efforts to impose rule (*imperium*) on others (Winfried Baumgart, *Imperialism*, v).

8 Gramsci, *Selections from the Prison Notebooks*, 165. In this summary of Gramsci I am indebted to Raymond Williams's *Marxism and Literature* and to Roger Rouse ("Thinking Through Transnationalism," 361–62).

9 David Forgacs, "National-Popular: Genealogy of a Concept," 88.

10 Williams, *Marxism and Literature*, 125.

11 Gramsci, *Selections from the Prison Notebooks*, 22.

12 This cultural war consisted in many fronts in which Mexican revolutionaries sought to foster social change through campaigns of rural pedagogy, by establishing secular fiestas, by broadcasting anticlerical radio shows and by establishing civil marriage and divorce. On these cultural struggles of Mexican nationalists against the Catholic Church, which opposed agrarian reform, see Alan Knight, "Popular Culture and the Revolutionary State in Mexico, 1910–1940," 393–444. These struggles against the Catholic Church went well beyond the scope of the Cristero War (1926–29), extending into the 1930s.

13 On the "war of position," see Gramsci, *Selections from the Prison Notebooks*, 238–39. Calles' phrase the "psychological revolution" is cited in Knight, "Popular Culture and the Revolutionary State," 402.

14 Frederick Cooper has argued that George Fredrickson's comparative historical studies, *White Supremacy: A Comparative Study in American and South African History* (1981) and *Black Liberation: A Comparative History of Black Ideologies in the United States and South Africa* (1995) isolate the history of ideology from social history to their detriment and therefore obscure "the agency of black people" ("Race, Ideology and the Perils of Comparative History," 1129–31).

15 Pan-Africanism probably emerged in response to what Franz Ansprenger has termed "supra-regional colonial movements" (*The Dissolution of the Colo-*

nial Empires, 125–44). Such movements used nationalism as a rationale for imperialism. Charles Dilke, the author of *Greater Britain* (1868), argued that the strength of the British empire was based on the superiority of the "British race" and argued for the extermination of inferior races. The Pan-German League, founded in 1891, similarly argued for more aggressive imperialism. Pan-Africanism transculturates such imperialist pan-nationalisms to create movements of solidarity between African and colonized peoples that are oftentimes, but not necessarily, anti-imperialist in politics. Pan-Africanism is a transnational and intercultural ideology and practice both because it often merged into a pan-colonial alliance (as in Du Bois's *Dark Princess*) and because "Africans" themselves are quite diverse, as observers such as Malcolm X and Franz Fanon have noted. On pan-nationalist movements, see Ansprenger, *Dissolution of the Colonial Empires,* and Baumgaurt, *Imperialism,* 52–89. On Pan-Africanism, see St. Clair Drake, *The Redemption of Africa and Black Religion,* and "Diaspora Studies and Pan-Africanism"; Immanuel Geiss, *The Pan-African Movement;* and Sidney J. Lemelle and Robin D. G. Kelley, eds., *Imagining Home.*

16 *Latinoamericanismo* (Latin Americanism) refers to the enduring efforts by the lettered elite to construct a unified Latin American identity attempting to resolve conflicts stemming from imperial underdevelopment. Since the traditional Latin Americanist canon refers to a large trajectory of (nearly exclusively male) Latin American writers, especially essayists, from Domingo Faustino Sarmiento, Martí, and José Enrique Rodó to José Vasconcelos and José Carlos Mariátegui, among many others, Latin Americanism is marked by a variety of conflicting political stands. While both Martí and Rodó criticize United States imperialism, Martí calls for a multiracial revolution of the oppressed, while in *Ariel* (1900), Rodó calls for hegemony by the lettered elite to control the masses. Latin Americanism asks the question of national/pannational identity: *¿Quiénes somos?* (Who are we?). For discussions of Latin Americanism, see Roberto González Echevarría, "The Case of the Speaking Statue," in his *The Voice of the Masters,* and Julio Ramos, *Desencuentros de la modernidad en América Latina.* For a critique of the male-centered construction of the Latin Americanist canon, see Pratt, " 'Don't Interrupt Me.' " The most important difference between Latin Americanism and Pan-Africanism, as Brenda Plummer has argued, is that Pan-Africanism could not redress African Americans' political grievances through a confederacy of nations because African Americans constituted a "nation" within a nation ("Firmin and Martí at the Intersection of Pan Americanism and Pan Africanism"). I would like to thank Julio Ramos and his students in the "Crítica de Latinoamericanismo" graduate seminar at the University of California at Berkeley, fall 1995, for providing me with the opportunity to develop my views on *latinoamericanismo.*

17 Angel Rama has similarly referred to "successive waves of democratization" (*La ciudad letrada,* 137).

18   William A. Williams argues that as the 1930s wore on, United States govern-
     ment officials and corporate leaders such as Nelson Rockefeller sought to
     make United States foreign policy less intrusive in political affairs and more
     "equitable" in its pursuit of economic expansion. However, he notes that the
     State Department in the early 1930s aggressively thwarted radical reform in
     Cuba. Secretary of State Cordell Hull pointed to the enduring character of
     United States imperialism when he called the United States pledge of non-
     intervention in Latin America that he signed in 1933 "more or less wild and
     unreasonable" (*The Contours of American History*, 458–60).

19   Under the Platt Amendment (1903), an appendix to the Cuban Constitution
     of 1901 following on the heels of the United States intervention in 1898 and
     subsequent occupation, Cuba "ceded territory for the establishment of a
     foreign naval station, acquiesced to limitations of national sovereignty, and
     authorized future United States intervention." Thus Cuba "inaugurated the
     republic with the task of decolonization incomplete and unfinished" (Louis
     A. Pérez, Jr., *Cuba Under the Platt Amendment*, xvi–xvii).

20   In 1823, Thomas Jefferson wrote to James Monroe that Cuba's "addition to
     our confederacy, is exactly what is wanting to round out our power as a
     nation to the point of its utmost interest" (Pérez, "Between Meanings and
     Memories of 1898," 501). For a historical survey of European and United
     States imperial designs in the Gulf–Caribbean area, see Lester D. Langley,
     Struggle for the American Mediterranean.

21   Du Bois, *Darkwater*, 500. All further references to *Darkwater* are cited paren-
     thetically in the text as *DW.*

22   Du Bois's writings during this period abound in long lists of the myriad parts
     of the world subjected to colonial rule: "[Colonies] belt the earth, . . . but they
     cluster in the tropics, with its darkened peoples: in Hong Kong and Anam, in
     Borneo and Rhodesia, in Sierra Leone and Nigeria, in Panama and Havana—
     these are the El Dorados toward which the world powers stretch itching
     palms" (*DW*, 505–06).

23   Here is an example of the "perspectival knowledge" that Michel Foucault
     would later endorse as opposed to objective knowledge ("Nietzsche, Geneal-
     ogy, History," 382).

24   Moreover, because Du Bois uses the categories of "Negro" and "the darker
     peoples" interchangeably in *Darkwater*, both terms take on the charge of a
     transnational politics of alliance.

25   *Provincializing Europe*, 5. In his use of the story of Prometheus in closing
     "The Souls of White Folk" and in his repeated references to the Enlighten-
     ment and democracy, Du Bois uses the master's tools to dismantle the mas-
     ter's house. In the closing paragraph of "The Souls of White Folk," Du Bois
     refers to the figure of the white as a "modern Prometheus,—hang bound by
     his own binding, tethered by a fable of the past" (*DW* 509). In Hesiod's
     Theogony, after Prometheus tricks Zeus, Zeus punishes him by hiding fire
     from man. Prometheus steals it and restores it to humans. In response, Zeus

ordered a number of gods and goddesses to create a "beautiful curse" to accompany "the blessing of fire"—"the damnable race of women" (*The Theogony*, 69). Du Bois ignores the misogyny of this tale and instead focuses on the figure of Prometheus. In Hesiod's telling of this myth, Prometheus is both the source of human civilization and the source of the woes of humankind, which is precisely what Du Bois wants to argue about whites. What does Du Bois mean when he claims that Prometheus is "hang bound by his own binding"? This phrase echoes Hesiod's conclusion of the tale of Prometheus: "In spite of all his cleverness he lies helplessly bound by a great chain" (*The Theogony*, 70). Prometheus's self-defeating behavior captures Du Bois's sense that the "horrors" committed by whites in events such as World War I are not some kind of aberration; instead they define white civilization.

26 "Fiestas de la Estatua de la Libertad," 1:1764. Subsequent references to this essay will be paginated in the text as "Fiestas." Since the existing English-language translation of this text made the unfortunate move of translating "tu" as "thee," which fails to register the familiar manner with which Martí addresses the statue, I include here my own translation; see his "Dedication of the Statue of Liberty," 133–57.

27 Martí, "Nuestra América," in *Sus mejores páginas*, 90.

28 "With All and For the Good of All," 139. Subsequent references will be cited in the text in parentheses as "WA."

29 Bakhtin, *The Dialogic Imagination*, 250.

30 In addition to the better-known category of the postwar literary "renaissance" in the Americas, Roger Bartra has pointed to "the legend of the new man" in Vasconcelos's notion of "la raza cósmica" and in the muralists' Marxist notion of the working vanguard (*La jaula de la melancolía*, 128).

31 For a recent articulation of this split, see René Prieto, "The Literature of *Indigenismo*," 138–39. For others who have characterized textual politics based on an *indianista/indigenista* split, see Concha Meléndez, *La novela indianista en Hispanoamérica*; Antonio Cornejo Polar, "La novela indigenista: un género contradictorio." As Analisa Taylor has suggested, the discourses of progress common to twentieth-century Mexican *mestizaje* and *indigenismo* rest on a foundation of exoticism: while *indigenista* writers "may condemn Mexican society as a whole for its indifference to the marginalization of 'its' indigenous populations, they ultimately condemn indigenous peoples themselves for being unable to 'rise above' these supposed cultural limitations to which they stubbornly cling" ("Between," 114).

32 See Immanuel Geiss, passim. In the same vein, St. Clair Drake defines nineteenth-century Ethiopianism as a web of movements that were "pre-political" because they often didn't assume institutional form (*The Redemption of Africa and Black Religion*, 11). Emerging among ecclesiastical intellectuals and church-based social movements, Ethiopianism consisted of varied efforts to bring about the differently construed "liberation" of Africa, ranging from literary texts to missionary projects to Africa with the aim of

"civilizing" Africans, to separatist African-run church movements in West Africa and South Africa in the 1890s, to the Zulu uprising of 1906 in South Africa. At times Ethiopianist discourses converged with imperialism, as when Edward Blyden, a West Indian minister who worked in Liberia, argued that European imperialism was a necessary step for preparing Africans for self-government. However, at other times Ethiopianism coincided with anti-imperialism, as in texts by Du Bois and Pauline Hopkins, editor of *The Colored American* magazine and author of the Ethiopianist novel *Of One Blood* (1902–03). The founding text of Ethiopianism can be found in Psalms 68:31: "Princes shall come out of Egypt; Ethiopia shall soon stretch forth her hands unto God." Important proponents of Ethiopianist ideologies include Martin Delany, Alexander Crummel, Edward Blyden, and Du Bois. For a discussion of Ethiopianism, see George Fredrickson, *Black Liberation*, chapter 2. In addition to the texts already mentioned by Geiss and Drake, see also Wilson Jeremiah Moses, "The Concept of Messianism, Sacred and Secular"; Moses, "The Poetics of Ethiopianism: W. E. B. Du Bois and Literary Black Nationalism," in *The Golden Age of Black Nationalism*; Eric Sundquist, *To Wake the Nations*, chapter 6.

33 Park, "Education in its Relation to the Conflict and Fusion of Cultures" (1918), in *Race and Culture*, 280; on romantic racialism, see George Fredrickson, "Uncle Tom and the Anglo-Saxons: Romantic Racialism in the North," in *The Black Image in the White Mind*, 97–129.

34 Juan Comas, "La Vida y la Obra de Manuel Gamio," 10. As evidence of the Carnegie Insitute's participation in the United States government-sponsored version of Pan-Americanism, see *Conferencias Internacionales Americanas, 1889–1936*.

35 Gamio, "The New Conquest," 192.

36 Ibid., 194.

37 See Nancy Stepan, *The Hour of Eugenics: Race, Gender and Nation in Latin America*, passim.

38 Bonfil Batalla can be taken as a theorist of decolonization as related to the history of *indigenismo* in Mexico and therefore deserves to be widely read by those interested in postcolonial studies; see his *México profundo*, which has been translated.

39 "Nuestra América," in *Sus mejores páginas*, 90.

40 Moreover, discourses of hemispheric citizenship provide a transnational dimension to what Lisa Lowe has identified as the contradiction between the abstract equality of United States citizenship, in which all citizens are formally equal, and the actual material inequality of nonwhite immigrants: discourses of hemispheric citizenship highlight the fact that this inequality extends to the imperial subjects of the United States; see Lowe, *Immigrant Acts*, 2, 8–9.

41 United States neocolonialism took stronger hold in Cuba than it did in Mexico.

42 For an analysis of "dominance without hegemony" in the context of colonial India, see Ranajit Guha, *Dominance Without Hegemony*.

43 Hannah Arendt, "The Decline of the Nation-State and the End of the Rights of Man," 156. All further references to Arendt's essay are cited parenthetically in the text as "Decline."

44 "Letters from Dr. Du Bois," 1:167.

45 Etienne Balibar, *We, the People of Europe?* All further references to *We, the People* are cited parenthetically in the text as *WP*.

46 Doreen Massey, *Space, Place and Gender*, 3.

47 J. G. A. Pocock, "The Ideal of Citizenship Since Classical Times," 45–48.

48 "Denationalizing Citizenship," 241. Subsequent references will be paginated in the text as "Denationalizing."

49 Renato Rosaldo, "Cultural Citizenship," 402.

50 The plethora of terms for practices of citizenship that move beyond the nation emerges in response to the current predicament that "no idiom has yet emerged to capture the collective interest of many groups in translocal solidarities, cross-border mobilizations, and postnational identities" (Appadurai, "Patriotism," 418).

51 "The Ballot" (1918), 1:165.

52 Yasemin Nuhoglu Soysal, "Toward a Postnational Model of Citizenship," 190.

53 "The Pan-African Congresses: The Story of a Growing Movement," 2:484.

54 More specifically, Du Bois argues in 1921 that the world views any of the so-called experiments in full citizenship and self-determination by the darker races as a test of the viability of the others, so building an upward momentum is crucial for the success of all: "The experiment of making the Negro slave a free citizen in the United States is not a failure; . . . the experience of Spanish America does not prove that mulatto democracy will not eventually succeed there." ("To the World [Manifesto of the Second Pan-African Congress]"), 1:317.

55 "My Mission," 1:188.

56 "To the World [Manifesto of the Second Pan-African Congress]," 1:317–18.

57 "The Rise of the West Indian," 1:273.

58 "Peace on Earth," 2:435.

59 Du Bois goes on to express his hope that the United States would combine a respect for the sovereignty of Haiti with "a policy of honesty in Cuba and patience in Mexico" ("To the President," 1:211–12).

60 Du Bois, "An Open Letter to Warren Gamaliel Harding," 1:294.

61 Juan González, *Harvest of Empire*, 75.

62 I am indebted to George Lipsitz for this point.

63 Mary Renda, *Taking Haiti*, 188. Subsequent references will be cited in the text as *Taking*.

64 Plummer, "The Afro-American Response to the Occupation of Haiti, 1915–34," 131. Subsequent references will be cited in the text as "Response."

65 Saskia Sassen, *Globalization and Its Discontents*, xxviii.

66 Alonso Aguilar, *Pan-Americanism from Monroe to the Present*, 13.

67 Ardao, "Panamericanismo y Latinoamericanismo," 159.

68 Ronald L. Scheman, *The Inter-American Dilemma*, 1. I am grateful to Ana Patricia Rodríguez for this source. Martí, who attended the 1889 conference, famously warned Latin American attendees of the self-serving designs of the United States.

69 John Edwin Fagg, *Pan Americanism*, 26.

70 Ardao, "Panamericanismo y Latinoamericanismo," 159.

71 Gamio, *Forjando patria*, 30.

72 Pérez, *Cuba Under the Platt Amendment*, 252–53.

73 Miller, "Feminism and Social Motherhood, 1890–1938," 85–86.

74 Ibid., 150.

75 For a concise account of the processes leading to Wilson's Fourteen Points, see Joshua Freeman et al., *Who Built America?*, 2:248, 258.

76 Boas, "The Outlook for the American Negro," 310–16.

77 Spillers, "Introduction: Who Cuts the Border?" 1. In response, this project brings into view a powerful subcurrent within *latinoamericanismo* that has included certain subaltern segments of the United States population within its folds. Martí, for instance, translated Helen Hunt Jackson's *Ramona* and celebrated the title character as an "arrogant *mestiza*," a model for "Our America," because she is a character of mixed race who can pass for white but chooses to be Indian. Many years later, René Depestre constructed a Calibanic genealogy of "cimarronaje cultural" (cultural maroonage), which he defines as a "collective self-defense" running roughly along socialist and decolonizing lines. Depestre's genealogy begins by placing Du Bois alongside Martí and goes on to include Haitian, Mexican, and other Latin American intellectuals. See Rene Depestre, "Saludo y despedida a la negritud," in *Africa en América Latina*, 349.

78 Although scholars in African diasporic studies and Latin American studies have rightly criticized postcolonial studies for having displaced and ignored their fields, I find postcolonialism useful for its construction of a global comparative field and for its investigation of the contradictory political positions of colonized subjects. For one of many possible illustrations of such contradictions, in *The Squatter and the Don*, the Californios are oppressed by United States imperialism yet oppress those racialized as Indians and blacks.

ONE "WHITE SLAVES" AND THE "ARROGANT *MESTIZA*"

1 Tomás Almaguer, *Racial Fault Lines*, passim.

2 This second question will also shape the concerns of chapter 2, where I consider the ways in which sentimentalism is deployed in relation to Martí's Cuba and the diffuse geography claimed by Du Bois's Pan-Africanism.

3 On the class politics of domestic fiction, see Nancy Armstrong, *Desire and Domestic Fiction: A Political History of the Novel*, 8, 20.

4 Ann Douglas, *The Feminization of American Culture,* 65–66, 68. Branding sentimentalism as "fakery" and "anti-intellectual," Douglas pessimistically concludes, "Sentimentalism . . . never exists except in tandem with failed political consciousness" (12–13, 254).

5 José Martí, introduction to Helen Hunt Jackson, *Ramona: Novela Americana,* trans. José Martí. For a reprint, see his *Obras Completas* (Editorial Nacional de Cuba), 24:203–05. Martí was a celebrated poet, essayist, and Cuban independence leader who spent fifteen years in exile in New York before his death on the battlefield in Cuba in 1895.

6 Martí, "The Indians in the United States," 216. The tear is a defining trope of sentimentalism, writes Karen Sánchez-Eppler: "Reading sentimental fiction is . . . a bodily act, and the success of a story is gauged, in part, by its ability to translate words into heartbeats and sobs" (*Touching Liberty,* 26–27). I find Sánchez-Eppler's definition of sentimentalism useful here, even though I disagree with her overly pessimistic conclusions on white women's abolitionism.

7 The long-standing critical dismissal of the sentimental has worked to conceal an important inter-Americas cultural circuit: the antislavery and Indian sentimental reformism in Stowe and Jackson furnished Martí with a repertoire of sentimental rhetorical strategies for his revolutionary writings. See chapter 2 for a discussion of Martí's sentimentalism.

8 Martí, "Nuestra América," in *Sus mejores páginas,* 89. Martí's reading of *Ramona* in terms of "Our America" thus extends the term to include racialized groups in the United States.

9 For the easterner Albion Tourgée, like Martí a contemporary reviewer of *Ramona,* the novel's focus on Californio culture provokes a reflection on what constitutes "our Anglo-Saxon" culture. While Martí sees Ramona as the harbinger of an emerging civilization, Tourgée views her as embodying "two decaying civilizations," the Indian and the Spanish. Nevertheless, drawing on a study by the historian Hubert Bancroft, Tourgée argues that United States Indian policy was much more harsh than Spanish treatment of Indians and condemns the annexation of California. Tourgée, like Martí, reads *Ramona* as an anti-imperialist text: "Fiction and history have put in our hands the means of refuting error and rebuking wrong" ("A Study in Civilization," 261).

10 When Ruiz de Burton proclaims, "We . . . must wait and pray for a Redeemer who will emancipate the white slaves of California," she is drawing upon sentimentalism's rhetoric of Christian millennial commitment (372). Similarly, Jackson claims that writing *Ramona* fulfilled God's designs: "I did not write *Ramona.* It was written through me" (quoted in Antoinette May, *Helen Hunt Jackson,* 135). She says that she modeled her novel on Stowe's exemplar of sentimentalist reform novels: "If I could write a story that would do for the Indian a thousandth part of what *Uncle Tom's Cabin* did for the Negro, I would be thankful the rest of my life" (quoted in Michael T. Marsden, "Helen Hunt Jackson: Docudramatist of the American Indian," 17–18).

11 Lauren Berlant, "The Female Woman," 433, 435.

12 The widespread currency of the pairing between romantic racialism and romantic feminism can be seen in the multitude of antislavery advocates who also struggled on behalf of women's rights and in the widespread view that "the negro race is the feminine race of the world" (Theodore Tilton, "The Negro: A Speech at Cooper Institute, New York, May 12, 1863," quoted in George Fredrickson, "Uncle Tom and the Anglo-Saxons: Romantic Racialism in the North," 115).

13 Du Bois's famous formulation of the "*souls* of black folk" reveals his indebtedness to this tradition; see Fredrickson "Uncle Tom and the Anglo-Saxons," 97–129.

14 In the postbellum era of what Nina Silber terms the "romance of reunion," a strain of northern sentimental discourse took an about-face in extending sympathies to former slaveholders. Even Stowe herself reversed her earlier position on southern race relations by 1868, defending the former slaveholders as "poor, weak and defeated"; see Silber, *The Romance of Reunion*, 47–53.

15 Peter Brooks, *The Melodramatic Imagination*, ix. Jesús Martín Barbero argues that the melodrama consists of a narrative mixing of ethics and aesthetics that we are taught to ignore as popular and vulgar; see his *Communication, Culture, and Hegemony*, 112–19, 224–28. On the allegorical "national romance," see Doris Sommer, *Foundational Fictions*, 5–6. For an analysis of the melodrama as an allegorical narrative of United States racial conflicts, see Susan Gillman, "The Mulatto, Tragic or Triumphant? The Nineteenth-Century American Race Melodrama," 221–43.

16 Here I hope to contribute to a growing body of scholarship on whiteness from a wide range of disciplines. Especially relevant to my study is Alexander Saxton's historicization of whiteness in the nineteenth-century United States, *The Rise and Fall of the White Republic*. Saxton argues that white racism repeatedly served as a means of creating a cross-class alliance of whites who stood to benefit materially from the oppression and exploitation of nonwhites. Other studies of whiteness include Richard Dyer, "White," in his *The Matter of Images;* bell hooks, "Representing Whiteness in the Black Imagination"; George Lipsitz, "The Possessive Investment in Whiteness"; Eric Lott, "White Like Me: Racial Cross-Dressing and the Construction of American Whiteness"; Toni Morrison, *Playing in the Dark: Whiteness in the Literary Imagination;* and David Roediger, *Towards the Abolition of Whiteness*.

17 According to Almaguer, the integration of regions into a national economy, in part through the construction of a vast railway network, allowed the United States to move from semiperipheral to core status in the capitalist world system. Thus the very form of these two novels—whether viewed as "regional novels" or as allegorical melodramas—participates in the logic of capitalism by performing cultural work on behalf of national consolidation; see Almaguer, "Interpreting Chicano History: The World-System Approach to Nineteenth-Century California," 471, 491.

18 See Raymond Williams, *Keywords*.

19 Kinmont delivered a series of lectures outlining his views of Negroes in Cincinnati in 1837 and 1838. As George Fredrickson has argued, Stowe most likely came into contact with Kinmont's ideas while she was living in Cincinnati from 1832 to 1850. Moreover, Kinmont's ideas were widely circulated in a review of his book published in *The National Anti-Slavery Standard* in 1843, then edited by Lydia Maria Child (*The Black Image in the White Mind*, 104 106–07, 110).

20 Gregg Camfield, "The Moral Aesthetics of Sentimentality: A Missing Key to *Uncle Tom's Cabin*," 324. Child claims that a similar rejection of Locke's rationalism provided the impetus for the philosophical movement of transcendentalism ("Transcendentalism," 99). The moral philosophers and texts associated with the Scottish Enlightenment include Francis Hutcheson (1694–1746), a professor at the University of Glasgow who was best known for *An Inquiry Into the Original of Our Ideas of Beauty and Virtue* (1725) and *System of Moral Philosophy* (1755); Thomas Reid (1710–96), a professor at King's College, Aberdeen (1751–64) and author of *An Inquiry into the Human Mind on the Principles of Common Sense* (1764); David Hume (1711–76), the author of *Enquiry Concerning the Principles of Morals* (1751); and Adam Smith (1723–90), a professor at Glasgow beginning in 1751 and a friend of Hume's. Smith was the author of *The Theory of Moral Sentiments* (1759) and *The Wealth of Nations* (1776). Finally, Archibald Alison (1757–1839), the author of *Essays on the Nature and Principles of Taste* (1790), draws on the work of Hutcheson, Reid, Smith, and Shaftesbury.

21 Camfield, "The Moral Aesthetics of Sentimentality," 328.

22 Kinmont was born in Scotland in 1799, attended the University of Edinburgh, and then emigrated to the United States in 1823 (Fredrickson, *The Black Image in the White Mind*, 104n13). But as Alison's synthesis of a number of philosophers would indicate, Stowe also pieced together her own views from a variety of sources. Indeed, one could construct several intellectual lines leading from the Scottish Enlightenment to Stowe.

23 Linda Williams, *Playing the Race Card*, 49.

24 Ibid., 15, 28–40. According to the *Oxford English Dictionary*, the word *melodrama* has its origins in the late seventeenth-century Italian term *melodramma*, which denoted a type of opera. In one frequently mentioned early use of the term, Jean-Jacques Rousseau described his play *Pygmalion* (1762) as a *mèlodrame*. The term was also used to describe eighteenth-century Italian operas and English and Spanish plays. Peter Brooks has identified the formative period of the development of melodrama in the period of 1800 to 1830, particularly in the plays of Guilbert de Pixerècourt, then France's most popular playwright. In the 1830s, Victor Hugo's plays further developed the mode (*The Melodramatic Imagination*, 24, 87, 93).

25 June Howard, "What Is Sentimentality?" 70.

26 For a forcefully argued case that romantic racialism is at the center of the

racial politics of Stowe's sentimentalism, see Arthur Riis, "Racial Essentialism and Family Values in *Uncle Tom's Cabin*," 513–44.

27 The writings that reshaped the meanings of the keyword sentiment ranged from Roman republic plays of the late seventeenth century, such as those by Nathaniel Lee and John Dryden, to the eighteenth-century poetry of Phillis Wheatley, Hannah More, and Philip Freneau, English conduct books and novels of manners from 1760 to 1820, and domestic fiction written by men and women and periodicals in England and the United States in the first half of the nineteenth century. See Armstrong, *Desire and Domestic Fiction;* Julie Ellison, *Cato's Tears and the Making of Anglo-American Emotion;* Karen Halttunen, *Confidence Men and Painted Women.*

28 *Negro* and *Caucasian* are the terms Kinmont uses. See Kinmont, *Twelve Lectures on the Natural History of Man,* 173, 191. Subsequent references are cited parenthetically in the text.

29 Harriet Beecher Stowe, *A Key to Uncle Tom's Cabin,* 25.

30 Child similarly argues in 1843, "The African race are destined to a higher civilization than any the world has yet known; higher, because it will be more gentle and reverential" ("The African Race," 187). Continuing this line of thought nearly a decade later, in *Uncle Tom's Cabin,* George Harris claims the African side of his heritage, explaining, "I think that the African race has peculiarities, yet to be unfolded in the light of civilization and Christianity, which, if not the same with those of the Anglo-Saxon, may prove to be, morally, of even a higher type" (Stowe, *Uncle Tom's Cabin,* 610).

31 In a remarkable dialogue Kinmont stages between St. Augustine and Baron Cuvier, Cuvier summarizes Augustine's argument: "I understand you to say, that the infantile simplicity of primitive times must be combined with the stern philosophy of the present age" (112). For Kinmont, the presence of the Negro implicitly provides the Euro-American scientific culture of the nineteenth century with access to its earlier, simpler, and morally upright self.

32 More quoted in Gillian Silverman, "Sympathy and Its Vicissitudes," 9.

33 "The African Race," 187.

34 *The Souls of Black Folk,* 215.

35 Stowe, *Uncle Tom's Cabin,* 153. Subsequent references are cited parenthetically in the text.

36 Stowe, *Uncle Tom's Cabin,* 608. For a critique of Stowe's endorsement of African colonization, see, for just one example, Riis, "Racial Essentialism and Family Values in *Uncle Tom's Cabin.*"

37 Kimberlé Crenshaw and Gary Peller, "Reel Time/Real Justice," 59, 64. Marianne Noble has pointed out another danger of sentimental humanism's emphasis on bodily suffering: "The effort to provoke in readers an experience of intersubjective connectedness at the level of the body had the unanticipated effect of eroticizing the reading experience, and, in so doing, it undermined its own effort to humanize the slaves, who were positioned as erotic objects of sympathy rather than subjects in their own right" ("The Ecstasies of Sentimental Wounding in *Uncle Tom's Cabin,*" 296).

38 Berlant, "Poor Eliza," 646.

39 Elizabeth Barnes, *States of Sympathy*, 4.

40 In the concluding chapter of *Uncle Tom's Cabin*, Stowe writes, "Let the church of the north receive these poor sufferers in the spirit of Christ; receive them to the educating advantages of Christian republican society and schools, until they have attained to somewhat of a moral and intellectual maturity, and then assist them in their passage to those shores [Liberia], where they may put in practice the lessons they have learned in America" (*Uncle Tom's Cabin*, 626). Thus the cycle that links expressions of negrophobia to those of negrophilia in different texts of melodrama can also occur within a given text. On the tendency of melodrama's negrophilia to "mutate" into negrophobia, see Williams, *Playing the Race Card*, 46.

41 Leonard Pitt, *The Decline of the Californios*, 95. The breakup of the ranchos occurred more quickly in northern California than in southern California. Anglos controlled a great number of northern ranchos by 1856 but didn't make substantial inroads into southern ranchos until 1875.

42 Almaguer, "Interpreting Chicano History," 492.

43 For Ruiz de Burton's biography, on which my account is based, see Rosaura Sánchez and Beatrice Pita, Introduction, *The Squatter and the Don*, 8–10.

44 Agriculture in California actually took the course prescribed by Don Mariano, shifting from small-scale grain farming in the 1870s to large-scale capitalist cultivation of fruits and vegetables in the 1880s and 1890s (Almaguer, *Racial Fault Lines*, 31).

45 C. Vann Woodward, *Origins of the New South, 1877–1913*, 31. Scott has the dubious honor of having called for federal army suppression of the first general strike in U.S. history, the St. Louis General Strike of 1877; see Roediger, *Towards the Abolition of Whiteness*, 92.

46 Woodward, *Origins*, 48.

47 Following a depression in 1879, northeastern U.S. and English capital began investing heavily in the South and West; see Woodward, *Origins*, 113.

48 Although Ruiz de Burton presents capitalism in the context of the South in euphemistic terms, she criticizes the inequities of capitalism on a global scale: "In the meanwhile, the money earned in California (as Californians only know how) is taken to build roads in Guatemala. Towns are crushed and sacrificed in California to carry prosperity to other countries" (*S* 371).

49 See, Wallerstein, *The Capitalist World Economy*, 18–19, 29. After 1873, core zones (northern Europe) engaged primarily in manufacturing and were characterized by strong state systems and wage labor. By contrast, the primarily agricultural peripheral zones were characterized by slave labor or other forms of coerced labor.

50 Almaguer has shown that as early as the first decade of the 1800s California participated in the world system not only as a remote outpost during the Spanish (1769–1821) and Mexican (1821–48) periods, but as an important source of raw materials (furs, hides, cattle) for New England merchants; see "Interpreting Chicano History," 469–80.

51   Following the Civil War, white southerners seized on the image of the South as female—used by northerners to justify their control over the allegedly helpless South—to create a counterdiscourse of southern victimization by the North; see Silber, *The Romance of Reunion*, 4–7.

52   Later historians have found that the South underwent a swift recovery in manufacturing and transporation following the Civil War, contradicting southern claims of wholesale devastation. In addition, the slow growth of southern agriculture was owing primarily to blacks' withdrawal of labor following emancipation—their choice to work fewer days and fewer hours; see Roger Ransom and Richard Sutch, *One Kind of Freedom*, 41–51.

53   Quoted in Saxton, *The Rise and Fall of the White Republic*, 296.

54   One measure of mining's importance to the global economy is that "until 1887 more than half of the world's mercury supply came from California, the greater proportion from the New Almaden Quicksilver Mine near Santa Clara" (Pitt, *The Decline of the Californios*, 255).

55   Rawls, *Indians of California*, 81–82, 86.

56   Although northern California was pro-Union, as late as 1859 Los Angeles was a Democratic, proslavery town; see Pitt, *Decline of the Californios*, 194.

57   For a concise definition of allegory, see Fredric Jameson, *The Political Unconscious*, 30.

58   For Benedict Anderson fraternity is the key to national imaginings: "The nation is always conceived as a deep, horizontal comradeship" (*Imagined Communities*, 7). By contrast, in melodrama maternity and sexuality are also central.

59   David Montejano, *Anglos and Mexicans in the Making of Texas, 1836–1986*, 315.

60   Further complicating matters, C. Loyal can be read as encoding and concealing the loyalty to Mexico—it corresponds to the Spanish *ciudadano leal*, or loyal citizen, "a common letter-closing practice used in official government correspondence in Mexico during the nineteenth century" (Sánchez and Pita, Introduction, *The Squatter and the Don*, 11).

61   Ernest Renan, "What Is a Nation?" 11. See also Homi K. Bhabha, "DissemiNation," 291–322.

62   Williams, *Marxism and Literature*, 130–32.

63   Mikhail Bakhtin, *The Dialogic Imagination*, 271.

64   See Sommer, *Foundational Fictions*, passim.

65   See Rawls, *Indians of California*, 86, 29, 121, 130–33.

66   Burton's march to Temecula in 1856 occurred at a time of especially great hostility between whites and Indians; see George Harwood Phillips, *Chiefs and Challengers*, 132–34.

67   Disease, political-economic factors, and extreme racial antagonism all contributed to this decline: 60 percent of deaths were due to disease, 30 percent to malnutrition and starvation, and 10 percent to violent attacks by Anglos; see Almaguer, *Racial Fault Lines*, 130.

68   This brief biography of Jackson is based on Valerie Sherer Mathes, *Helen Hunt Jackson and Her Indian Reform Legacy,* introduction and chapter 2.

69   The intimate familial alliance that *Squatter* proposes between Anglos and Californios is not possible between *Ramona*'s Anglos and Indians, because even in romantic racialist, "noble-savage" ideology Indians were racialized as nonwhite. Since the Californios were deemed half-civilized, they were the only other cultural group whose members Euro-Americans would marry in late nineteenth-century California. By contrast, Native Americans were considered savage, so Indian women, or "squaws" as Anglos called them, were available only for illicit unions. The infrequency of formal marriage between Anglos and Indians meant that Jackson would be unlikely to win sympathy for the plight of Indians if she were to choose a white suitor for Ramona, so she paired her with an Indian; see Almaguer, *Racial Fault Lines,* 58, 108, 120.

70   Michele Moylan uses the concept of the "implied reader" from Wolfgang Iser's reader-response theory; see Moylan, "Reading the Indians: The Ramona Myth in American Culture," 155.

71   Stowe's description of St. Clare similarly posits a female core that is progressively hardened into manhood: "In childhood, he was remarkable for an extreme and marked sensitiveness of character, more akin to the softness of woman than the ordinary hardness of his own sex. Time, however, overgrew this softness with the rough bark of manhood, and but few knew how living and fresh it still lay at the core" (*Uncle Tom's Cabin,* 239).

72   For discussions of "romantic feminism," see my comments above and Fredrickson, *The Black Image in the White Mind,* 114–15.

73   "Imperialist nostalgia"—mourning what you have destroyed—is described by Renato Rosaldo in *Culture and Truth,* 68–90.

74   Kinmont, *Twelve Lectures on the Natural History of Man,* 191.

75   Moylan, "Reading the Indians," 154.

76   Martí, *Obras Completas,* 204.

77   Here "creole" refers not to black-Spanish and black-French mixtures in New Orleans, but rather to those American settlers who descended from the same European peoples who subjected them to colonial rule: Brazil and the colonies of Spain and the United States were all "creole states, formed and led by people who shared a common language and common descent with those against whom they fought" (Anderson, *Imagined Communities,* 47). Creole nationalists distinguished themselves from the *peninsulares,* or colonial loyalists to Spain, by developing ideologies contrasting the Americas with Europe.

78   Martí argues similarly, "Common cause must be made with the oppressed, so as to secure the system against the interests and customs of the oppressors" ("Our America," 90).

79   For his distinction between "centripetal" and "centrifugal" forces in the novel, see Bakhtin, *The Dialogic Imagination,* 271–73.

80   *Ramona* thus enacts the "myth of Latin American racial democracy," a myth in tension with her portrayal of Señora Moreno as a corrupt Spaniard in the tradition of the "black legend." On the ideology of Latin American racial democracy, see Aline Helg, *Our Rightful Share: The Afro-Cuban Struggle for Equality, 1886–1912*, 6–7 and passim; on the "black legend," see Michael Hunt, *Ideology and U.S. Foreign Policy*, 58.

81 Martí, "Nuestra América," 88.

82 Ibid., 90.

83 According to Stuart Hall, postcolonial analysis is valuable for its refusal to construct imperial conflicts along stark lines of opposition; see Hall, "When Was 'The Post-Colonial' "? 242–60.

84 I am indebted to Stuart Christie for this formulation.

85 On the emergent as the incipient crystalization of an alternative hegemony, see Williams, *Marxism and Literature*, 121–27; on "protopolitical impulses," see Jameson, *The Political Unconscious*, 287.

86 I have used whiteness as an analytical term rather than merely stressing the more abstract notion of the social construction of race because whiteness is more suited to describing hegemony, relations of power maintained by constituting and reconstituting "common sense," as Roediger has argued (*Towards the Abolition of Whiteness*, 4–5). Lipsitz has demonstrated the destructiveness of whiteness in its institutionalized form: government subsidies for racial suburbanization have constituted a massive "possessive investment" in whiteness, creating a systematic economic advantage for whites at the expense of people of color ("The Possessive Investment in Whiteness," passim). This investment in whiteness has fueled conservative and neoliberal attacks on public education, the universal health care plan, education, the inner city, and mass transportation.

TWO "THE COMING UNITIES" IN "OUR AMERICA"

1 José Martí, "A Vindication of Cuba," 262–64.

2 Martí, "With All, and for the Good of All," 139. Subsequent references will be cited in parentheses in the text as "WA."

3 W. E. B. Du Bois, *Darkwater*, 500. Subsequent references will be cited in parentheses in the text as *DW*.

4 Martí privileges national unity over racial grievances in famous phrases such as the following: "A Cuban is more than mulatto, black or white" (Martí, "My Race," 313).

5 Martí, Letter to Gonzalo de Quesada, 2:197–98.

6 Martí, "Congreso Internacional de Washington," 2:138; Said, *Culture and Imperialism*, 8.

7 Du Bois, "The Present Outlook for the Dark Races of Mankind," 53.

8 The Boxer Rebellion was a Chinese peasant movement that sought to do away with foreign control over Chinese society by expelling foreigners, especially Christian missionaries.

9 Du Bois, "Present Outlook," 48; "Letters from Dr. Du Bois," 167; "Italy and Abyssinia," 2:441–42; *Darkwater*, 504.

10 Alain Badiou, *Ethics*, 41. Subsequent references will be cited in the text as *Ethics*.

11 Slavoj Žižek, *The Ticklish Subject*, 135.

12 Badiou, *El ser y el acontecimiento*, 365. Subsequent references will be cited in the text as *El ser*.

13 Žižek, *The Ticklish Subject*, 131.

14 The process unleashed by an event epitomizes philosophy itself for Badiou: "Philosophy is, in the last instance, one resource among others for intervening in the real. . . . It tries to scorn what is in the name of what could be" (*El ser*, 6).

15 Joan Hedrick, *Harriet Beecher Stowe*, 202–03.

16 Harriet Beecher Stowe, "The Freeman's Dream: A Parable," 121.

17 *Uncle Tom's Cabin*, 624.

18 *A Key to Uncle Tom's Cabin*, 25.

19 Stowe's lack of commitment to equality becomes glaringly clear when one contrasts her treatment of the Fugitive Slave Act to that of Martin R. Delany, who argued that the act threatened the safety of all African Americans, including free blacks. As he memorably writes, "We know not the wretch who may grasp us by the throat" (*The Condition, Elevation, Emigration and Destiny of the Colored People of the United States*, 155). For Delany, freedom is a necessary though not sufficient political condition: he also insists on full citizenship rights for African Americans.

20 Maureen Ramsay, *What's Wrong With Liberalism?* 63.

21 Wendy Brown, "Injury, Identity, Politics," 163–64.

22 Mikhail Bakhtin, *The Dialogic Imagination*, 271–73.

23 Du Bois, *The Souls of Black Folk*, 215.

24 Martí, Letter to Gonzalo de Quesada, 2:192.

25 Du Bois, "The Present Outlook for the Darker Races of Mankind," 53.

26 On romantic racialism, see George Fredrickson, "Uncle Tom and the Anglo-Saxons: Romantic Racialism in the North," *The Black Image in the White Mind;* and for "racial messianism" as "the redemptive mission of the black race," see Wilson J. Moses, "The Concept of Messianism, Sacred and Secular," in *Black Messiahs and Uncle Toms,* 1 and passim. My definition of *anti-imperial messianism* differs from that of Moses in emphasizing its use as an ideology of alliance among colonized and racialized peoples.

27 Martí, "The Cutting Case," 182.

28 Du Bois, "Mexico," 78.

29 Du Bois, "The Present Outlook for the Darker Races of Mankind," 53.

30 Giorgio Agamben, "The Messiah and the Sovereign," 173. Subsequent references will be cited in parentheses as "Messiah."

31 Gershom Scholem quoted in Agamben, "The Messiah and the Sovereign," 166. Here Agamben is quoting from Scholem's "Towards an Understanding of the Messianic Idea in Judaism" (1959).

32 Agamben, *Il tempo che resta*, 99–104.

33 Agamben, *State of Exception*, 111–22.

34 Ibid., 3

35 Stuart Hall argues that postcolonialism differs from traditional historiography in viewing colonialism as both a system of rule and a system of knowledge and representation; see his "When Was the Postcolonial?" 242–60. Martí is quoted in Peter Turton, *José Martí*, 52. "Practical consciousness" is Raymond Williams's apt synonym for hegemony (*Marxism and Literature*, 130).

36 In "The African Roots of War" (1915), Du Bois writes, "The present world war is, then, the result of jeaousies engendered by the recent rise of armed national associations of labor and capital whose aim is the exploitation of the wealth of the world mainly outside the European circle of nations" ("The African Roots of War," 647).

37 Michel Foucault, "Nietzsche, Genealogy, History," 380.

38 See especially studies by Barnes, Berlant, Ellison, Hendler, Riis, and Silverman.

39 "El Terremoto de Charleston," 1:1742. Subsequent references are cited parenthetically in the text.

40 Lydia Maria Child, "The Different Races of Men," 122.

41 *The Souls of Black Folk, Three Negro Classics*, 220.

42 Alexander Kinmont, *Twelve Lectures on the Natural History of Man*, 192.

43 Gillian Silverman, "Sympathy and Its Vicissitudes," 7.

44 Julie Ellison, *Cato's Tears and the Making of Anglo-American Emotion*, 71. My list of English Roman republic plays is from Ellison.

45 Martí, *Abdala, José Martí: Obras Completas Edición Crítica*, 1:28. Subsequent references will be cited parenthetically in the text as *A*.

46 "Letters from Dr. Du Bois," *Selections from The Crisis*, 1:167.

47 On Martí's early life, see Roberto Fernández Retamar, "The Modernity of Martí," 3.

48 Rojo, como en el desierto,
　　salió el sol al horizonte:
　　y alumbró a un esclavo muerto,
　　colgado a un seibo del monte.
　　Un niño lo vio: tembló
　　de pasión por los que gimen:
　　¡y, al pie del muerto, juró
　　lavar con su vida el crimen!
　　(José Martí, Poema XXX, *Versos sencillos, Obra literaria*, 42).
Fernández Retamar associates the poem with Martí's childhood experience and includes the English translation.

49 Luis Toledo Sande, *Cesto de llamas*, 39–59. For an account in English, see John M. Kirk, *José Martí: Mentor of the Cuban Nation*, 26–33.

50 Toledo Sande, *Cesto de llamas*, 176.

51 Here I am relying on the work of Gerald Poyo; see his "José Martí," in *José Martí, Revolutionary Democrat*.

52 Following Martí's death, the Afro-Cuban activist Rafael Serra edited the newspaper *La doctrina de Martí* (The Doctrine of Martí) in New York, a newspaper that sought to sustain the momentum generated by Martí's insistence on linking the nationalist struggle to struggles of social justice and racial harmony (Poyo, "José Martí," 19, 28–29).

53 On *Modernismo* in *Amistad funesta*, see Carlos Javier Morales, "Introducción," *Lucía Jerez*; Manuel Pedro González, "Prefacio," *Lucía Jerez*; Angel Rama, "La Dialéctica de la Modernidad en José Martí"; Ivan Schulman, "Void and Renewal: José Martí's Modernity," 153–75. For approaches emphasizing gender or female figures, see Jacqueline Cruz, "'Esclava vencedora': la mujer en la obra literaria de José Martí"; Anibal González, "El intelectual y las metáforas: *Lucía Jerez* de José Martí," 136–57; Yolanda Martínez-San Miguel, "Sujetos Femininos en *Amistad Funesta* y *Blanca Sol*," 27–45; Nissa Torrents, "Passion and Order in *Amistad funesta.*" There is at least one notable exception to this gender split in Martí criticism. For an analysis of Martí's war diaries by a male critic who reveals the centrality of notions of gender in Martí's self-conception as an anti-imperialist poet/warrior, see Julio Ramos, "El Reposo de los Héroes."

54 Martí, *Lucía Jerez* in *Obra Literaria* 116. Subsequent references will be cited parenthetically in the text as *LJ*.

55 Fredric Jameson, *The Political Unconscious*, 30.

56 Indeed, in "Vindicación de Cuba" (1889), Martí refers to the proponents of U.S. imperialism as "elementos funestos" (4).

57 For an analysis of the melodrama as an allegorical narrative of U.S. race relations, see Susan Gillman, "The Mulatto, Tragic or Triumphant? The Nineteenth-Century American Race Melodrama," in *The Culture of Sentiment*, 221–43. On the melodrama more generally, see Peter Brooks, *The Melodramatic Imagination*, ix, 55, 205, and passim; Jesús Martín Barbero, *Communication, Culture, and Hegemony*, 112–19, 224–28; and Williams, *Playing the Race Card.*

58 On the allegorical "national romance," see Doris Sommer, 5–6.

59 Ibid., 50.

60 Cruz, "'Esclava vencedora,'" 35.

61 Sommer, *Foundational Fictions*, 50.

62 On the popularity of the "national romance" in Latin America, see Sommer, *Foundational Fictions*, 36.

63 Benedict Anderson, *Imagined Communities*, 7.

64 In 1867 Spain established a new tax in Cuba despite the opposition of Cubans, whose hopes for reform were dashed and hence began the Ten Years' War for Cuban Independence (1868–78). Martí himself was imprisoned and tortured for his youthful activism against Spanish colonial rule in 1870. See Philip Foner, Introduction, *Inside the Monster*, by José Martí, 18–21.

65 For instance, an 1884 cartoon that portrayed the World's International Cotton Centennial Exposition at New Orleans showed Cuba along with Mexico, Brazil, Chile, and other Latin American nations as attractive young women

about to board the train of progress at the invitation of a "southern Queen" accompanied by Uncle Sam with hat in hand (Jack J. Johnson, *Latin America in Caricature*, 78–79).

66 Martí, "Los Pinos Nuevos" (1891), in *Cuba, Nuestra América y los Estados Unidos*, 23.

67 Martí, "Nuestra América," in *Cuba, Nuestra América y los Estados Unidos*, 168; Martí, "Our America," *Our America*, 94.

68 Pointing out the influential essayist José Enrique Rodó's critique of Rubén Darío for the allegedly effeminate decadence of his poetry and Martí's discomfort with Oscar Wilde and with "unmanly" poetry in general, Sylvia Molloy argues that *fin-de-siglo* Latin America was marked by "the paranoid construction of gender and sexual norms" ("Too Wilde for Comfort," 187, 197). Elsewhere Molloy argues that Martí "cleanses" Whitman of the homosexuality evident in his "Calamus" poems ("His America, Our America: José Martí Reads Whitman," 87.

69 In "Concerning Violence," Frantz Fanon writes, "Decolonization is always a violent phenomenon" (*The Wretched of the Earth* [1961], 37).

70 "Domination has traditionally been semanticized in sexual terms and power has traditionally been associated with masculinity," as Jean Franco observes ("Beyond Ethnocentrism: Gender, Power, and the Third World Intelligentsia," 362).

71 In drawing a distinction between the direct rule (*dominio*) of military force and the indirect rule of hegemony, Gramsci's concept expands the concept of culture to include power relations. Hegemony produces consent to the status quo through interlocking cultural, political, and economic relations: "It is a whole body of practices and expectations, over the whole of living: our senses and assignments of energy, our shaping perceptions of ourselves and our world. It is a lived system of meanings and values. . . . It thus constitutes a sense of reality for most people in the society" (Williams, *Marxism and Literature*, 19, 110).

72 Juan, with his chaste male poetic sensibility, "en la mujer, veía más el símbolo de las hermosuras ideadas que un ser real" (saw in the woman, more the symbol of beautiful ideals than a real being) (115).

73 The phrase in Spanish is "hacer lo grande y amar lo puro."

74 Jacqueline Cruz finds "an intense misogynist current" evident in the figure of Lucía (Cruz, "'Esclava vencedora,'" 30). Similarly, Nissa Torrents argues that the text establishes a division between pure men and passionate women, an untenable point given that the female characters Sol and Ana are represented as being as pure as Juan (Torrents, "Passion and Order in *Amistad funesta*," 184).

75 Juan "tenía de su virtud idea tan exaltada como la mujer más puderosa."

76 See Javier Morales, "Introducción," *Lucía Jerez*, 35.

77 Ibid., 45. No critic of the novel has read *Lucía Jerez* as an allegorical figure of the greed of Spanish colonialism. Javier Morales situates Martí within the literary movement of Modernismo (1875–1918), which he defines as a broad aesthetic rather than a strict school. Like European Romanticism, Modernismo exalts the emotional and subjective over the rational but also adopts new emphases, including poetry as a vocation and even as "la ciencia transcendental," a science that is superior to the physical sciences and philosophy, which motivates Martí to poeticize his prose; the figure of the poet as a genius, prophet, and priest; the Americanization of Latin American literature by adopting subject matters unique to the continent; the adoption of French symbolism in such techniques as the association of one object with another without a natural resemblance—Martí describes Keleffy as "a wounded eagle"; the inextricability of Goodness and Beauty (Javier Morales, "Introducción," *Lucía Jerez*, 22–23, 33, 35, 89, 97).

78   Martí, "My Race," in *José Martí: Selected Writings*, 318–19. Subsequent references will be cited in parentheses as "MR."

79   Although my reading of Martí's racial politics in relation to the Cuban independence movement focuses on race in relation to institutional politics, there is much more work to be done on the topic of Martí and race. For a reading of Martí's ideology of race, see Rafael Rojas, *José Martí: la invención de Cuba*, 114–15. Examining Martí's notes (circa 1880–81) for his projected book *Mis negros* (My blacks), Rojas points to a racist emphasis in Martí that persists even in his later writings: "It is evident that in later texts, in the stage of revolutionary politics, such as 'Enough,' 'My Race,' and 'On Whites and Blacks,' Martí sought to liberate his discourse of those eugenic and racist enunciations. However, there is a principle from that brief discourse that persists [in Martí's later work]: the republican principle, that is, the emphasis that the black race does not comprise a 'unity' once the construction of a national civic community demands the disappearance of racial identities" (ibid., 115).

80   Ada Ferrer has argued that the leaders and official documents of the Cuban independence movement of the mid-1890s maintained a silence on race as a strategy of forging unity, but this silence failed to reflect the wishes of the majority of soldiers. See Ferrer, "The Silence of Patriots." My analysis of Martí's racial politics is deeply indebted to Ferrer's work.

81   On the so-called Morúa Amendment, see Aline Helg, *Our Rightful Share*, 165–69.

82   Du Bois, "The Conservation of Races" (1897), in *Classical Black Nationalism*, 236.

83   Du Bois, *The Souls of Black Folk*, 221. Subsequent references will be cited parenthetically in the text as *S*.

84   Du Bois, "Woman Suffrage" (1915), 298.

85   Gail Bederman has noted a split in ideologies of manhood in the late nineteenth-century United States: one emphasized the "rough" or "primitive" components of "masculinity" and the other called for a civilized and refined "manliness" (*Manliness and Civilization*, 12–13, 17–19).

86   As Wahneema Lubiano has noted, "Black nationalism is predicated on the notion of racial solidarity across class lines" ("Black Nationalism, Black Common Sense, and Popular Culture," n.p.).

87 Houston Baker has termed *Souls* a "singing book," as opposed to Booker T. Washington's "speaking manual" (*Modernism and the Harlem Renaissance,* 68).

88 Antonio Gramsci, *Selections from the Prison Notebooks,* 332–33.

89 This faith in national progress was exemplified by the generation of white historiographers in the early 1900s who told the story of Reconstruction so as to construct a racially euphemistic discourse of national reconciliation and unity, as Priscilla Wald has shown (*Constituting Americans,* 172–236).

90 In a reading of *Souls* that takes issue with the bevy of critiques of alleged racial essentialism in Du Bois, Nahum Chandler argues that Du Bois emphasized Negroes' "excessiveness" to discourses of racial purity: "Throughout his life, Du Bois privileged the theme of Negro capacity; a position construed such that it is radically excessive to any idea of a fixed or given essence in any simple sense" ("The Economy of Desedimentation," 84). Chandler's essay has helped me to clarify my own position regarding Du Bois's alleged racial essentialism.

91 Du Bois's discourse of racial mystery encompasses the Negro's "excessiveness" to racialist discourses in Chandler and Du Bois's modernist strategies of "vagueness" in Possnock. By citing the "grounds of meaning" I borrow a well-known critical move from Chandler's analysis of the early Du Bois; also see Ross Possnock, "How It Feels to Be a Problem," 343.

92 Du Bois, "Conservation of Races," 230–31.

93 "Master narrative" is Fredric Jameson's term (*The Political Unconscious,* 10).

94 Ethiopianist thought pervades the discourses of racial mystery because to diasporic African peoples Ethiopia was "an uncolonized territory of the spirit," in the words of Eric Sundquist (*To Wake the Nations,* 559).

95 See Kwame Anthony Appiah, *In My Father's House,* chapter 2.

96 Du Bois, "The Souls of White Folk," in *W. E. B. Du Bois: A Reader,* 453.

97 Du Bois, "The Negro Problem," 52.

98 See my introduction for a discussion of Du Bois's revisionist history of Reconstruction in *Souls.*

99 Du Bois, "Letters from Dr. Du Bois," *Selections from the Crisis,* 1:168–69.

100 The African American left criticized Du Bois for this decision to support the war; see, for instance, Claude McKay, *The Negroes in America,* 71. On the circumstances surrounding Du Bois's "Close Ranks" editorial endorsing the U.S. war effort, see David Levering Lewis, *W. E. B. Du Bois: Biography of a Race, 1868–1919,* 553–57.

101 Du Bois, "The Ballot," 1:165.

102 Du Bois, "Peace on Earth," 2:435.

103 Du Bois, "Mexico," 1:78.

104 In subsequent years, Du Bois would return to the topic of Mexico, arguing in 1927 that it was an important battleground for pacifists and anti-imperialists:

The land hogs and war profiteers are pushing us into war with Mexico just as fast as they can. . . . Now is the time for pacifists to act. Now and not later. Now is the time to say to America that not a gallon of oil nor a foot of land is worth the murder of a single human being, whether from Mexico or black or white America. Diaz and rich Americans cheated Mexico of her wealth while her people slept and we are asked to enforce these disgraceful contracts with blood and filth and war. Let us resolve never to do it. Let us face death, jail and poverty before war with Mexico on any pretext. We have stolen enough from that poor land. ("War," 2:457)

105 Ibid.

106 Herbert Aptheker, "Introduction," *Dark Princess*, 21, 22.

107 John Cawelti, *Adventure, Mystery and Romance*, 266.

108 Du Bois, *Dark Princess*, 312. This and subsequent references refer to the University of Mississippi edition and are cited in the text as *DP*.

109 Du Bois, "Criteria of Negro Art," 328. Subsequent references will be cited in the text as "CNA."

110 Rita Copeland quoted in Barbara Fuchs, *Romance*, 38.

111 Jameson, *Political Unconscious*, 112, 148.

112 Cawelti, *Adventure, Mystery and Romance*, 45; Williams, *Playing the Race Card*, 15. As Williams has persuasively argued, melodrama is the American narrative genre that has been most suited to expressing struggles for social justice: "Even as we note the limitations of the mode we need to recognize that it is in ever-modernizing forms of melodrama—not epic drama, not 'classical realism'—that American democratic culture has most powerfully articulated the moral structure of feeling animating its goals of justice" (*Playing the Race Card*, 26).

113 Claude McKay, *The Passion of Claude McKay*, 92, 93.

114 On the romance as a narrative "framework," see Williams, *Playing the Race Card*, 27.

115 Du Bois, "The African Roots of War," 650. Subsequent references will be cited parenthetically in the text as "ARW."

116 Here Kautilya sounds just like Du Bois's friend the Indian nationalist Lala Lajpat Rai, when he reported on the India to which he returned following his exile in New York City: "It is an entirely new India to which I have come back; it is an awakened, self-conscious and defiant India"; she could have been speaking of the Indian Student Union in London (quoted in Vijara Joshi, Introduction, *Lala Lajpat Rai*, 1:xliv); for a brief mention of the Indian Student Union as a model for the West African Student Union, see Adi, *West Africans in Britain*, 32.

117 Bill V. Mullen, "Du Bois, *Dark Princess*, and the Afro-Asian International," 221.

118 [Letter to the *People* (Lahore, India)] (1929), 386. Du Bois and Rai even lectured from the same podium in 1917 (Ahmad, "More than Romance," 788).

119   Karuna Kaushik, *Russian Revolution and Indian Nationalism*, 38.

120   Joshi, Introduction, *Lala Lajpat Rai*, xl.

121   Ibid., xliii.

122   For a more critical view of Rai, see Ahmad, "More than Romance," 788–91.

123   In "World War and the Color Line" (November 1914), Du Bois writes, "Undoubtedly, then, the triumph of the allies would at least leave the plight of the colored races no worse than now. Indeed, considering the fact that black Africans and brown Indians and yellow Japanese are fighting for France and England, it may be that they will come out of this frightful welter of blood with new ideas of the essential equality of all men" (1:84). And in his infamous "Close Ranks" editorial of 1918, Du Bois called on African Americans to back the U.S. war effort: "That which the German power represents today spells death to the aspirations of Negroes and all darker races for equality, freedom and democracy. . . . Let us, while this war lasts, forget our special grievances and close our ranks shoulder to shoulder with our own white fellow citizens and the allied nations that are fighting for democracy" (1:159).

124   In a bitter 1917 letter to the British prime minister David Lloyd George, Rai writes, "When the War came [Indians] deluded themselves with the hope that in your hour of need you might accord them a better treatment, but by this time they have found their mistake. . . . you have imposed fresh burdens on us" (Rai, *Lala Lajpat Rai*, 1:262). George would later incur the wrath of African exiles in London for using the term "nigger" in a campaign speech (Hakim Adi, *West Africans in Britain,* 41). Similarly, in "Returning Soldiers" (1919), Du Bois defiantly appropriates the "War to save democracy" slogan in arguing that black participation in the Great War must result in greater democracy in the United States: "Make way for Democracy! We saved it in France, and by the Great Jehovah, we will save it in the United States of America, or know the reason why" (Du Bois, "Returning Soldiers," 1:197).

125   Lewis, *W. E. B. Du Bois: The Fight for Equality and the American Century, 1919–1963*, 219.

126   As late as 1928, Rai called on Indian nationalists to strive for dominion status rather than full independence for pragmatic reasons: "The cry of Complete Political Independence leads people away from constructive political and social work," he argued ("Complete Political Independence Versus Dominion Status," *The People,* 11 October 1928, *Lala Lajpat Rai*, 2:441).

127   Rai, "Save India for the Empire—An Open Letter to David Lloyd George," 13 June 1917, *Lala Lajpat Rai*, 1:263.

128   Ibid., 1:280. Although Rai was interested in the Russian Revolution and the Communist International, he was no Bolshevist. In a speech in New York City in 1918, he praised the Russian Revolution for promoting democracy across the world: "For the first time in the political history of the world, the Russian Revolutionists have preached the brotherhood of nations" (quoted in Kaushik, *Russian Revolution and Indian Nationalism,* 44). In 1919 he wrote that Soviet Russia signified "that the world is for all and not for the few who happen to be in possession at this minute" (quoted ibid., 46). Influenced by the Fabian socialists Beatrice and Sidney Webb of England, he wanted not to abolish but to control capitalism (ibid., 59).

129   The race riots of 1919 in Britain took place in Liverpool, Manchester, South Shields, Glasgow, Hull, London, and other cities (Adi, *West Africans in Britain, 1900–1960,* 18).

130   This account of Rai's political life is based on Joshi, Introduction, *Lala Lajpat Rai.*

131   Ahmad has written a particularly perceptive critique of the politics of alliance and orientalism in *Dark Princess.* See her " 'More than Romance.' "

132   Rai, *Unhappy India,* xxii. Subsequent references will be cited parenthetically in the text as *UI.*

133   Rai writes, "White imperialism is the greatest world menace known to history, and its racial arrogance rests on the assumption that those who are not 'white' are 'less than men.' It has deprived vast populations of political and civic liberties, and is ruthlessly exploiting them for economic ends. . . . Unless it is promptly and effectively brought under check it promises not merely to bomb out non-white civilization, but even to end *all* civilization in a death dance—a death rehearsal of which we have had in the World War of 1914" (*UI* 140). Here Rai's argument on the "world menace" of imperialism's "racial arrogance" strikingly resembles Du Bois's analysis of the global color line.

134   Robin D. G. Kelley, " 'Afric's Sons with Banner Red,' " 37.

135   Mullen, "Du Bois, *Dark Princess,* and the Afro-Asian International," 231. Moreover, as early as 1913, Du Bois criticized U.S. socialism but also expressed keen interest in the movement: "The Negro Problem . . . is the great test of the American Socialist" ("Socialism and the Negro Problem," in *Writings by W. E. B. Du Bois in Periodicals Edited by Others,* 87).

136   Fredrickson, *Black Liberation,* 187.

137   Cedric Robinson, *Black Marxism,* 215–16.

138   Haywood, a member of the ABB in 1922 and of the Communist Party U.S.A. in 1925, was appointed to the Negro Commission for the Sixth Communist International in 1928 (Kelley, "'Afric's Sons with Banner Red,' " 38).

139   Mullen, "Du Bois, *Dark Princess,* and the Afro-Asian International," 220.

140   Du Bois, "A Second Journey to Pan-Africa," 2:159.

141   *The Oxford W. E. B. Du Bois Reader,* 625.

142   Fredrickson, *Black Liberation,* 151–52.

143   Blaise Diagne, for instance, a Senegalese member of the French national assembly and a minister in the French government, proclaimed that he was more French than Negro, and Pan-Africanists based in Paris condemned him for his defense of forced labor in the colonies (Fredrickson, *Black Liberation,* 151; Langley, "Pan-Africanism in Paris, 1924–36," 71, 75). Although at times Du Bois characterized French colonialism as more mild than other colonial-

isms, he was well aware of Diagne's complicity with French colonialism. Du Bois writes in July 1925, "France, following her special policy, has drawn no color line and . . . has admitted her black colonials to citizenship and even laid the foundation of an educational system which may yet prove the nucleus of a great mulatto empire in the heart of Africa" ("France's Black Citizens in West Africa," 262). However, in "A Second Journey to Pan-Africa" (December 1921), Du Bois criticizes the exploitative dimensions of France's alleged universalism: "France recognizes Negro equality not only in theory but in practice; she has for the most part enfranchised her civilized Negro citizens. But what she recognizes is the equal right of her citizens, black and white, to exploit by modern industrial methods her laboring classes, black and white" (161). In an article on his participation in the Pan-African Congress of 1921, Du Bois writes that Diagne strongly objected to the resolutions the Congress had adopted in London: "Diagne, the Senegalese Frenchman who presided, was beside himself with excitement after the resolutions were read; as an under-secretary of the French government, as ranking Negro of greater France, and perhaps as a successful investor in French colonial enterprises, he was undoubtedly in a difficult position. Possibly he was bound by actual promises to France and Belgium." Du Bois goes on to report that Diagne denounced the demand of the congress in London for "common ownership of the land" as "rank communism" ("A Second Journey to Pan-Africa," 159).

144 For a convincing argument on the "inherent difficulty of alliances" in *Dark Princess,* see Ahmad, " 'More than Romance,' " 798.

145 Geiss, *The Pan-African Movement,* 289.

146 Edwards, *The Practice of Diaspora,* 3.

147 Anticolonial organizing was prominent in London as well as in Paris. African student organizations in London included the African Association, founded in 1897 by Williams, the mastermind behind the first Pan-African Congress in London in 1900; the Ethiopian Association of Edinburgh, founded in 1904; the African Students' Union, founded in 1916; the African Races Association of Glasgow University and the African Union of Edinburgh University (both founded in 1917); the African Progress Union, founded in 1918, which included students from the West Indies, Honduras, British Guiana, and the U.S.; the Union of Students of African Descent, founded in 1921, which was the most prominent organization of African students in Britain during the early 1920s; and the West African Students' Union (WASU), which modeled itself after the Indian Student Union when it was founded in 1925. Although it was not explicitly a communist organization, WASU forged ties with the Communist Party of Great Britain and the International Trade Union Committee of Negro Workers (Adi, *West Africans in Britain,* chapters 1 and 2).

148 Geiss, *The Pan-African Movement,* 305–6; Langley "Pan-Africanism in Paris" 73.

149 J. Avo Langley, "Pan-Africanism in Paris" 75. On a trip to New York City in

August 1924, Houénou attended a UNIA congress meeting and spoke to the crowd (Langley, "Pan-Africanism in Paris" 76–77).

150 Langley, "Pan-Africanism in Paris," 79; for a fascinating analysis of Senghor's critique of French colonial racism see Brent Edwards, *The Practice of Diaspora*, 29–30.

151 Jean Jones, *The League Against Imperialism*, 7–8, 34–37; Langley, "Pan-Africanism in Paris," 81–82; Robinson, *Black Marxism*, 216–17.

152 Jones, *The League Against Imperialism*, 7.

153 Jones, *The League Against Imperialism*, 5, 9. The *Ligue de la defense de la race nègre* succeeded Senghor's *Comité* in late 1927. The *Ligue* was led by Tiémoho Garan Kouyaté and Abou Koité, both from Sudan. It associated with the French Communist Party and with radical labor unions. Kouyaté attended the second conference of the League Against Imperialism in July 1929 and was on the editorial staff of George Padmore's *The Negro Worker* (Langley, "Pan-Africanism in Paris," 86). Kouyaté wrote in a letter to Du Bois that was seized by French police that his aim was "winning back, by all honorable means, the national independence of the Negro peoples in the colonial territories of France, England, Belgium, Italy, Spain, Portugal etc. . . . and . . . setting up in Black Africa a great Negro State" (Kouyaté qtd. in Langley, "Pan-Africanism in Paris," 86).

154 Fredrickson, *Black Liberation*, 155.

155 Marcus Garvey argued, "Negroes [in Africa] have got to win their freedom just as the Russians and the Japanese have done—by revolution and bloody fighting. Negroes in the United States cannot do this. They would be hopelessly outnumbered and it would be foolish to attempt it" (Garvey quoted ibid.).

156 Ibid.

157 Ibid., 156.

158 The term *Pullman* comes from George Mortimer Pullman, whose company dominated the manufacture and operation of sleeping cars in the 1870s and 1880s (Eric Arnesen, *Brotherhoods of Color: Black Railroad Workers and the Struggle for Equality*, 16).

159 Ibid., 87.

160 Ibid., 59.

161 Ibid., 91.

162 Ibid., 92. White organizations such as the Women's Trade Union League and the American Federation of Labor provided organizational and financial assistance.

163 Ibid., 95.

164 Bakhtin, *The Dialogic Imagination*, 7.

165 Communist International, "The Black Question," in *Theses, Resolutions and Manifestoes*, 330.

166 McKay, "Report on the Negro Question," in *The Passion of Claude McKay*, 92; Communist International, "The Black Question," 330–31.

167 Communist International, "The Black Question," 330–31. One key result of

these theses was that the Communist Party U.S.A. found itself compelled to court black nationalists such as the Garveyites and "made a high priority of the recruitment of African-Americans into the party" (Kelley, " 'Afric's Sons with Banner Red,' " 38; Fredrickson, *Black Liberation*, 190).

168 Moses, *Black Messiahs and Uncle Toms*, 1.

169 Scholem quoted in Agamben, "Messiah," 166

170 Ibid., 161.

171 Agamben, *Il tempo che resta*, 18.

172 Ibid., 20.

173 Jameson, *The Political Unconscious*, 149.

174 Agamben, *Il tempo che resta*, 54–55.

175 Ibid., 39, 69.

176 Here I can't help but think about Hawthorne's description of the romance in the "Custom-House" essay that serves as a preface to *The Scarlet Letter* (1850). The narrator writes, "Moonlight, in a familiar room . . . is a medium the most suitable for a romance-writer to get acquainted with his illusive guests." As in Du Bois's description of the star's illumination, details "become things of intellect." The result is "a neutral territory, somewhere between the real world and fairy-land, where the Actual and Imaginary may meet and each imbue itself with the nature of the other" (65–66). Hawthorne's description of the operations and goals of the romance serve to clarify Du Bois's own aim of constructing a tension between the actual and imaginary or, in his own terms, between the "Pain of the Bone" and the "Dream of the Spirit."

177 Agamben, "Messiah," 168.

178 Agamben, *State of Exception*, 3, 11–22.

179 Agamben, *Il tempo che resta*, 91, 93. I have slightly altered the word order in my translation in order to make the sentence sound more idiomatic in English.

180 Ibid., 101.

181 Ibid., 109, 111.

182 Ibid., 74.

183 Ibid., 76.

184 On Ethiopianism, see Fredrickson, *Black Liberation*; Geiss, *The Pan-African Movement*; and Moses, *The Golden Age of Black Nationalism*.

185 Fredrickson, *Black Liberation*, 74–75. I suspect that these two strands often-times wound together.

186 Ibid., 63. The roster of the black intellectuals who used Ethiopianist discourses of the redemption of the black race in the nineteenth century reads like the index of an anthology of African American literature, ranging from Robert Alexander Young's *The Ethiopian Manifesto* (1829) and David Walker's *Appeal* (1829) and key texts by Martin R. Delany, Edward Blyden, and Alexander Crummel to the early work of Du Bois himself. In 1898 Bishop Henry Turner of the African Methodist Episcopal Church traveled to South Africa, where there had already existed an independent Ethiopian Church since 1893

(Fredrickson, *Black Liberation*, 83–84). Turner toured the country for six weeks, ordaining fifty-nine African ministers. He also delivered a speech at which he was later reported to have declared, "The black race is the race of the future, and one day the black man will wake up and shake off the white man's yoke" (Fredrickson, *Black Liberation*, 84). Although it is difficult to establish a causal relationship between the South African Ethiopianist church movement and developing struggles of black liberation, according to Fredrickson the Ethiopianist churches did assert black ownership of the land (Fredrickson, *Black Liberation*, 88–89).

187 Agamben, *Il tempo che resta*, 64.

188 Andre Shiek, "The Comintern Program and the Racial Problem," in *American Communism and Black Americans*, 164–65.

189 James Ford, [Untitled Speech to the Seventh Congress of the Third International], in *American Communism and Black Americans*, 181.

190 Robinson, "W. E. B. Du Bois and Black Sovereignty," 149.

191 Ibid., 153–54.

192 Lewis, *W.E.B. Du Bois: Biography of a Race, 1868–1919*, 555.

193 Ahmad, " 'More than Romance,' " 787. I would add that this orientalism is mixed with countervailing elements: the phrase "into the black womb of India the world shall creep to die" expresses Du Bois's cyclical view of history that plots a return to greatness by Africa and Asia; Du Bois emphasizes the importance of Indian history in the development of world civilization, underlines the human and animal diversity of India, and encapsulates India's position in the world economy by associating it with "toil." (*DP* 64, 227)

194 Martí, "Mother America," 78–79.

195 Ibid., 80–81.

196 "The After-Thought" of *Souls* engages in a more implicit messianism: Du Bois, addressing the reader as a "God" and God as a "Reader," expresses his hope that his book will give birth to "the righteousness which exalteth nations" through "vigor of thought and thoughtful deed" (388).

197 Benjamin, *Illuminations*, 261.

198 On "prophetic rebellions," see Michael Adas, *Prophets of Rebellion*. Many, if not most, decolonizing resistance movements in the late nineteenth century were messianic. Thousands of messianic rebellions took place during the two waves of decolonization across the globe featured in this book, including in Latin America, Asia, and Africa. To my knowledge, Du Bois and Martí made no direct reference to messianic rebellions. However, both participated in cultural currents that drew on messianic themes as part of a principled Christian resistance to oppression. Du Bois's brand of racial messianism stems from his immersion within nineteenth century Ethiopianist discourses. Martí's relationship to racial messianism is not as clear as Du Bois's. Although it is generally acknowledged that messianist movements were ubiquitous in Latin America during the nineteenth century, it is unknown to what extent Martí knew of such rebellions. But Martí had read his Stowe while in exile in

the United States and thus was familiar with the antislavery movement's fervent appeals to a coming reign of divine justice. An impassioned visionary himself, he knew how to harness Christian eschatology to the revolutionary cause, as we have seen in "Mother America." The religious rhetoric essential to messianism has been viewed as broadening the class base of nationalist movements in India, which is certainly the case for Du Bois and Martí as well. On messianism in India, see Guenter Lewy, *Religion and Revolution,* chapter 12; on Latin American messianism, see E. Bradford Burns, *The Poverty of Progress,* especially chapter 6; on messianism in Africa, see Lewy, *Religion and Revolution,* chapter 9.

199 For allusions to Urrea as "Reina de los Yaquis," see Brianda Domecq, *La insólita historia,* 86 and Paul Vanderwood, *The Power of God Against the Guns of Government,* 199.

200 The expansion of geographical focus and the questioning of conventional notions of authorship that allow for a consideration of Urrea's racial messianism alongside that of Martí and Du Bois provide a way of joining current efforts to add women to the existing canon of male writer-activists. Brianda Domecq, the author of a novelized biography of Teresa Urrea, has pointed to the exclusion of women from literary movements as an enduring problem: "Women have always been on the periphery of all great literary movements" (quoted in Kay S. García, "Part IV, Brianda Domecq," in *Broken Bars,* 183).

201 Racial messianism is a transnational cultural form with a high degree of "cultural transferability" that attempts to create a cross-class, intercultural alliance against racial oppression and colonialism. Millenarianism is on the increase rather than on the decline, argues Garry Trompf, "because the very 'exportability' or 'cultural transferability' of the millennial idea manifests itself *pari passu* with the growing global . . . awareness that all people share or are involved in common predicaments" (Introduction, *Cargo Cults and Millenarian Movements,* 4).

202 On Urrea's spiritual life, see Alex Nava "Teresa Urrea: Mexican Mystic," 504; Vanderwood, *The Power of God,* 168, 173.

203 Vanderwood, *The Power of God,* 168.

204 Carlos Larralde, "Santa Teresa, A Chicana Mystic," 51.

205 Domecq, "Teresa Urrea: La Santa de Cabora," 19.

206 This biographical sketch is based primarily on information provided by Larralde and Vanderwood. Where Larralde and Vanderwood differ, I have followed Vanderwood. See also Mario Gill, "Teresa Urrea, La Santa de Cabora."

207 On biopolitical power, see Foucault, *The History of Sexuality,* 139–41; on disciplinary power, see his *Discipline and Punish,* particularly 142; and on both, see and "Society Must Be Defended," esp. 242–50. Subsequent references to *The History of Sexuality* will be cited in the text in parentheses as *History,* while references to *"Society Must Be Defended"* will be cited as *"SMBD."*

208 Evelyn Hu-DeHart, *Yaqui Resistance,* 99.

209 As Miguel Tinker Salas has argued, "Sonoran elites viewed the Indians as a

retrograde force and the principal cause of the state's inability to develop" (*In the Shadow of the Eagles,* 12).

210   Edward Spicer, *Cycles of Conquest,* 67.

211   Here I am paraphrasing Tinker Salas, *In the Shadow of the Eagles,* 60.

212   Domecq, *La insólita historia,* 203.

213   Tinker Salas, *In the Shadow of the Eagles,* 4, 53.

214   Ibid., 56–57.

215   Spicer, "Highlights," 2–9.

216   Foucault, *The Order of Things,* xiv.

217   On these rebellions, see Spicer, *Cycles,* 75–76; Hu-DeHart, *Yaqui Resistance,* and "Peasant Rebellion"; Francisco Troncoso, *Las guerras con las tribus,* 181–82; Vanderwood, *The Power of God,* 195–211, 299–301.

218   Alan Knight, "Popular Culture and the Revolutionary State," 76.

219   Heriberto Frías, *Tomochic.* Larralde mentions the text by the same title co-authored by Urrea and Aguirre, but I have not been able to locate it or find its date of publication ("Santa Teresa, A Chicana Mystic," 73).

220   Knight, "Racism, Revolution and *Indigenismo,*" 73, 77–80; Guillermo Bonfil Batalla, *México profundo,* 155.

221   Martí, "Nuestra América," 159; Martí "Our America," 84.

222   Martí, "Nuestra América," 163.

223   The protestors demanded the release of other political prisoners along with Urrea, who was then held in confinement (Larralde, "Santa Teresa, A Chicana Mystic," 60–61).

224   Although Latin American historians more commonly associate neocolonialism with United States–installed regimes in the Caribbean during the first half of the twentieth century, Charles T. Hale has characterized nineteenth-century Latin America as neocolonial owing to its dependence on U.S. and European economic, cultural, and political formations, even though the nations were nominally independent ("Political and Social Ideas in Latin America, 1870–1930," 370).

225   Martí, Introduction, Helen Hunt Jackson, *Ramona: Novela Americana.* For a reprint see Martí, *Obras Completas,* 24:203–05. Urrea also briefly married a Yaqui miner (Larralde, "Santa Teresa, A Chicana Mystic," 80–81).

226   Domecq, *La insólita historia.* Subsequent references will be cited in the text in parentheses. This novel has been translated: see Domecq, *The Astonishing Story of the Saint of Cabora,* trans. Kay S. García. For a more recent novelized biography of Teresa Urrea, see Luis Alberto Urrea, *The Hummingbird's Daughter.* The cult of scientific progress in Porfirian Mexico was made possible by the ascendancy of positivism in Latin America. Coined and defined by Auguste Comte in his *Cours de philosophie positive* (1830–42), and subsequently developed by Herbert Spencer beginning in the 1850s, positivism was introduced to Mexico in 1858 (Martin S. Stabb, *In Quest of Identity,* 46). Positivism later came to dominate the intellectual scene in Latin America in the late nineteenth century and early 1900s. Positivism in Latin America emphasized secularism, scientific methods in intellectual and political life,

and technological innovation. The emphasis on scientific progress carried with it a distinctly Europhile and anti-indigenist cultural, social, and racial politics. The racial politics of positivism are evident in the evolutionary ranking of whites at the top of a social hierarchy, followed by mestizos and then Indians and blacks in the influential writings of the French social psychologist Gustave Le Bon and in the numerous "sick continent" theories. Among the latter are the Argentinian Carlos Bunge's *Nuestra América* (Our America, 1903) and the Bolivian Alcides Arguedas's *Pueblo enfermo* (Sick country, 1909), both of whom called for European immigration to bring about a *blanqueamiento* (whitening) of the population. Such positivist "sick continent" theorists found inspiration in the Mexico of Porfirio Díaz. On the "diagnosticians of the sick continent," see Stabb, *In Quest of Identity,* chapter 2. In Mexico, Justo Sierra called for an authoritarian government beginning in the 1870s. In the 1890s Sierra and his followers were labelled *los científicos* (the scientists) because they were thought to offer scientific leadership to the state. Díaz succeeded in coopting *los científicos*—he granted Sierra a position on the Supreme Court in 1894.

227 I am indebted to Norma Klahn for this point. The effort to revive Porfirio Díaz came at a time when the state increasingly broke with its populist traditions and colluded with the neoliberal agenda of business interests. Presidents de la Madrid and Salinas took a hard line toward labor—and even arrested its leadership—in stark contrast to the earlier policy of rewarding the political support of labor with better schools and hospitals (Judith Teichman, "Economic Restructuring, State-Labor Relations, and the Transformation of Mexican Corporatism," in *Neoliberalism Revisited,* 157).

228 Domecq compares him to a bull driven crazy by the darts of a bullfighter: "He arrived at home mortally wounded in his virility and rationalism. He was a *macho* who found himself cornered, a bull in a corral pierced by darts hurled by a bullfighter wearing a skirt who obliged him to lower his head, and driven crazy by the refrain of miracles with which a bullfighter saint assaulted him. When he encountered the growing invasion of his rancho, he saw red." (*IH* 188)

229 Benjamin, *Illuminations,* 263. What matters is not whether magic actually results in successful revolutions, but whether religious and magical beliefs serve to reconfigure conceptions of history, endowing the powerless with the sense that they can create social change.

230 Hu-DeHart, *Yaqui Resistance,* 7.

231 Ibid., 98.

232 Ibid.

233 Tinker Salas, *In the Shadow of the Eagles,* 26.

234 Domecq, *La insólita historia,* 20, 128; Vanderwood, *The Power of God,* 163.

235 Domecq, *La insólita historia,* 26; Vanderwood, *The Power of God,* 163–64.

236 Vanderwood, *The Power of God,* 166.

237 Troncoso, *Las guerras con las tribus,* 181.

238 Ibid., 182.

239 Vanderwood, *The Power of God,* 195.

240 Ibid., 211.

241 Ibid., 195.

242 "Mayos still celebrate the third of May as a saint's day dedicated to Teresa and also exalt her in their own cultural myths" (Vanderwood, *The Power of God,* 196).

243 Lauro Aguirre, "Tomóchic!!" *El Independiente,* 7 August 1896, 3.

244 *El Independiente,* 6 May, 1896, 1.

245 Ibid.

246 Agamben, *Il Tempo che Resta,* 64.

247 Agamben, "Messiah," 162–63. Indeed, as Aguirre writes, the messianic revolution must frame itself as fulfilling human and divine laws "for all": "Almost all revolutions have taken place as a result of the inability of the powers that govern to fulfill expectations. . . . And such revolutions are the inevitable and necessary struggles so that the laws will be completely followed, since it is absolutely necessary that societies and men are governed by fixed and equal laws for all and not for the capricious and variable will of those who govern." (*El Independiente,* 6 May 1896, 2)

248 *El Independiente,* 13 May 1896, 1.

249 *El Independiente,* 7 August 1896, 1.

250 Jameson, *Marxism and Form,* 416. Here I use "real" in both a philosophical sense to denote the positivist belief in an accessible, "objective" reality and in the literary sense of an aesthetic of the commonplace and everyday proposed by white, middle-class U.S. realists of the 1870s and 1880s, such as William Dean Howells. While scholars of realism have recently shown that it cannot be viewed as completely opposed to romance, my position is that Du Bois's awareness of the dialectical relationship between realism and romance allows for a politics that avoids the realist pitfall of scorning romance as a popular culture form. I by no means unequivocally endorse romance so as to make "realism by necessity a failure," in Amy Kaplan's words, but I do want to point out the provincialism of many realist practices, which, as she points out, tend to manage "the threats of social change" (Kaplan, "Introduction: Realism and 'Absent Things in American Life,'" in *The Social Construction of American Realism,* 1, 10, 13). On race and realism, see Kenneth Warren, *Black and White Strangers.*

251 Laura Corradi, lecture on the Zapatistas, University of California, Santa Cruz, 6 October, 1995.

THREE TRANSNATIONALISMS AGAINST THE STATE

1 *Survey Graphic* 52.1 (1924): 186.

2 Alain Locke, "Foreword," *The New Negro,* xxvii.

3 While the term *international* identifies a consortium of nationally based entities, the term *transnational,* which I adopt here, denotes modes of affiliation that elude national identities, such as Locke's terms "dark-peoples" and the "persecuted" ("The New Negro," *The New Negro,* 14). For contemporary scholars who have defined the term *transnational,* see the introduction.

4 Major studies on the Harlem Renaissance by Nathan Huggins, David Levering Lewis, and George Hutchinson have only mentioned in passing such transnational dimensions of the Harlem Renaissance. Nathan Huggins, for instance, argues that the post–World War I revaluation of the African as an antidote to the sterility of Western civilization meant that "the Harlem Renaissance was thus not isolated but part of a worldwide phenomenon" (*Voices from the Harlem Renaissance,* 8). But overlooking the evidence I have just cited, Huggins maintains that the discourse of the New Negro only "unconsciously" evoked this world context (6). Accordingly, Huggins does not include texts published outside the United States in his otherwise useful anthology. Likewise, Lewis restricts the Harlem Renaissance to the United States and even criticizes W. E. B. Du Bois's *Dark Princess* for transgressing national boundaries by allegedly esteeming other "darker peoples" more highly than African Americans (*When Harlem Was in Vogue,* 201). Scholars who have examined the renaissance in its transnational context, such as Michael Fabre and Paul Gilroy, usually focus exclusively on Europe. See Fabre and Gilroy, *The Black Atlantic.* Finally, scholars such as James De Jong have uncovered ample evidence of inter-Americas ties in the 1920s but have not provided an adequate historical and theoretical framework for understanding such ties. See De Jong, *Vicious Modernism;* Martha Cobb, *Harlem, Haiti, and Havana;* Edward J. Mullen, *Langston Hughes in the Hispanic World and Haiti;* and Guido A. Podestá, "An Ethnographic Reproach to the Theory of the Avant Garde."

5 Observers of the 1920s cultural scene in Mexico commonly referred to it as a renaissance. See Anita Brenner, "Revolution and Renascence"; "Editorials," *Survey Graphic* 52.1 (1924): 186; and Lucio Mendieta y Núñez, "El renacimiento del nacionalismo." For a broad historical survey of the Mexican renaissance in the context of U.S.–Mexico cultural relations, see Helen Delpar, *The Enormous Vogue of Things Mexican.*

   In a move that implicitly acknowledged his familiarity with the 1924 *Survey Graphic* special issue on Mexico, in 1925 Locke includes Mexico among an international array of movements that represent a "resurgence of a people," including that of "American Negroes" ("Foreword," *The New Negro,* xxvii). Similarly, the *New York Herald Tribune* viewed the *Opportunity* magazine literary awards ceremony of 1925 as evidence of a "Negro Renaissance" (Lewis, *When Harlem Was in Vogue,* 116). Quoting an article by Robert T. Kerlin, the Chicago School sociologist Robert E. Park refers to a "renaissance of the Negro soul" in the early 1920s ("Negro Race Consciousness as Reflected in Race Literature" [1923], 294).

6 The high degree of cross-fertilization among the Harlem Renaissance and cultural nationalist and decolonization movements in Europe, Africa, Asia, and Latin America (especially relevant to this chapter) consisted of migra-

tion, travel, activist collaboration, institutional interrelations, and shared publishing circles. Paulette Nardal's *La Revue du Monde Noir*, founded in 1931 in Paris, exemplifies the transnational cultural circuits operating at the time in its publication of African, African American, Afro-Caribbean, and French writers.

By adopting a hemispheric, inter-Americas approach to the Harlem Renaissance and by focusing on its relationships to Cuban *negrismo* and Mexican *indigenismo*, one can arrive at a fuller sense of the importance of the transnational dimensions of the New Negro Movement. First, these cultural nationalisms evolved in shared publishing circles, as in the way the *Survey Graphic* followed through on its issue on the "New Mexico" in 1924 with an issue on "The New Negro" in 1925. Similarly, the Afro-Cuban Gustavo Urrutia's "Ideales de una raza" section in the *Diario de la Marina* (1926–33) routinely published the writings of African Americans under the rubric of *negrismo* (On "Ideales de una raza," see Vera Kutzinski, *Sugar's Secrets*, 146–49).

Second, collaborative relationships developed among members of these groups. For instance, Miguel Covarrubias, a veteran of Mexican indigenismo, illustrated texts by Langston Hughes and Zora Neale Hurston. Like Hughes, Hurston, and Locke, Covarrubias was sponsored by the "godmother" of the Harlem Renaissance, Mrs. Rufus Osgood Mason (Adriana Williams, *Covarrubias*). Conversely, U.S. intellectuals associated with the Harlem Renaissance shaped Mexican indigenismo: Franz Boas taught anthropology in Mexico City as well as in New York and counted among his students both Hurston and Manuel Gamio, a prominent indigenista. In 1910 Boas, Edward Seller, and Gamio founded the International School of American Archeology and Ethnography in Mexico City (Arturo Warman, "Indigenist Thought," 75–96). On the collaboration between Boas and Gamio, see especially Guillermo de la Peña, "Nationals and Foreigners in the History of Mexican Anthropology," 276–303). Boas also trained the Mexican anthropologist Anita Brenner, the author of *Idols Behind Altars* (1929) and the translator of three of the most prominent Mexican novelists of the day: Mariano Azuela, Gregorio Lopez y Fuentes, and Mauricio Magdaleno (I am indebted to Norma Klahn for the de la Peña cite, and to Carlos Monsiváis for alerting me to Brenner's studies under Boas).

Third, these three cultural nationalist movements all emerged through an explosion in interest in what Locke terms "folk expression," as in Hurston's interest in "lies," or tall-tales, and Guillén's interest in the *son*.

7 Eric Sundquist, "Red, White, Black and Blue," 115.

8 In the historical uses of the term, *self-determination* has been bifurcated into two components: freedom from control by other nation-states and popular sovereignty. At times national self-determination has overridden subcultural grievances, as in the "race-blind" discourses of Cuban independence (Ada Ferrer, "The Silence of Patriots"). But when marginalized groups demand self-determination, they bind together the two sometimes antagonistic components of self-determination, insisting on independence at the national level and on the political enfranchisement at the level of ethnicity and class. Here I am working with Saskia Sassen's definition of "popular sovereignty" as "the will of the people as contained in the nation-state," but I am extending its analytical thrust in a different way (*Losing Control?* 2).

9   Henry Louis Gates Jr., "The Trope of a New Negro and the Reconstruction of the Image of the Black," 326; David Chinitz, "Rejuvenation through Joy," 76.

10   Elazar Barkan and Ronald Bush, Introduction, *Prehistories of the Future,* 13; Torgovnick, Introduction, *Primitive Passions,* 4.

11   Here I am adapting Raymond Williams's analysis of residual, dominant, and emergent forms of culture in *Marxism and Literature* (121–27).

12   Ramos is cited in Roger Bartra, *La jaula de la melancolía,* 109. Similarly, in 1927, Moisés Sáenz, the undersecretary of education of Mexico, wrote that the Revolution made the ruling class realize that "about two-thirds of the population are in a primitive stage of civilization" ("The Two Sides of Mexican Nationalism," 908). In the U.S. context, Madison Grant's *The Passing of the Great Race* (1916), a key source for "the resurgent racism of the early twenties," warned against the dangers of "mongrelization" created by the immigration and migration of nonwhites and Mediterranean peoples (John Higham, *Strangers in the Land,* 271).

13   Edward Sapir, "Culture, Genuine and Spurious," 318; Bartra, *La jaula de la melancolía,* 26.

14   Michael Taussig has coined the term "primitivist parody" to describe this technique (*Mimesis and Alterity,* 10).

15   Du Bois's comment occurs in the context of the following passage: "Primitive men are not following us afar, frantically waving and seeking our goals; primitive men are not behind us in some swift foot race. Primitive men have arrived. . . . They have used other paths and these paths have led them by scenes sometimes fairer, sometimes uglier than ours, but always towards the Pools of Happiness" (Du Bois, quoted in Adam Lively, "Continuity and Radicalism in American Black Nationalist Thought, 1914–1929," 228).

16   Doreen Massey, *Space, Place, and Gender,* 22.

17   Tulio Halperín Donghi, *The Contemporary History of Latin America,* 254.

18   Ibid., 185. In taking the somewhat idiosyncratic view of Mexico as a neocolonial state, I follow Guillermo Bonfil Batalla's lead in emphasizing the Mexican state's racist policies toward indigenous peoples; see Bonfil Batalla, *México profundo.*

19   Louis A. Pérez, Jr., *Cuba Under the Platt Amendment, 1902–1934,* 183. Subsequent references will be cited in the text as *Platt.*

20   See Jules Robert Benjamin, *The United States and Cuba,* passim.

21   See Paul Farmer, *The Uses of Haiti.*

22   Héctor Aguilar Camín and Lorenzo Meyer, *In the Shadow of the Mexican Revolution,* 80–81.

23 Movements that organized themselves in resistance to the postwar reconfiguration of neocolonial relations were also domestically based, of course.
For instance, the Cuban Partido Socialista Radical (Radical Socialist Party),
founded in 1920, created a broad-based social movement linking the rights of
women, the construction of public housing, and the socialization of property
within the nation (Pérez, *Cuba Under the Platt Amendment*, 239).

24 Antonio Cornejo Polar, "El indigenismo y las literaturas heterogéneas," 9.

25 Locke, *The New Negro*, xxvii, 14. The political spectrum of internationalism
in *The New Negro* was broad. At one end of the spectrum, a Lockean internationalism valuing self-determination runs at cross-purposes with its ideology
of black American vanguardism, the notion that the New Negro acts as "the
advance-guard of the African peoples" (14). At the other end of the spectrum,
a Du Boisian internationalism engaged in a socialist and Pan-Africanist opposition to "empire," understood as "the heavy hand of capital abroad"
(Du Bois, "The Negro Mind Reaches Out," 386).

26 Alexander Kinmont, *Twelve Lectures on the Natural History of Man*, 17. Subsequent references are cited parenthetically in the text as *TL*.

27 "Primitive, *a.* and *n.*," *Oxford English Dictionary*, 2d ed. 1989, *OED Online*.

28 John Winthrop, "Primitive," 218. Here I am paraphrasing Winthrop. Discourses of the primitive include the concepts of the golden age in Greek
thought, the fascination with prelapsarian society in Christianity, and the
romanticization of the noble savage, beginning with John Dryden in 1672
("noble savage, n.," *OED Online*). On these early forms of primitivism, see
Partha Mitter, "Primitivism," 1029–31.

29 Mitter, "Primitivism," 1029.

30 George Stocking, "Edward Burnett Tylor and the Mission of Primitive Man,"
in *Delimiting Anthropology*, 107.

31 Edward B. Tylor, *Primitive Culture*, 1:1. Subsequent references are cited parenthetically in the text as *PC*.

32 Claudio Lomnitz, *Deep Mexico, Silent Mexico*, 237.

33 George Fredrickson defines romantic racialism as the Herderian notion of
the special gifts of nations or cultural groups. As Fredrickson writes, "Those
who ascribed to the priority of feeling over intellect sanctioned both by
romanticism and evangelical religion could come up with a strikingly different concept of Negro 'differences.' Whereas scientists and other 'practical'
men saw only weakness, others discovered redeeming virtues and even evidences of black superiority" (Fredrickson, *The Black Image in the White
Mind*, 101).

34 Franz Boas, *The Mind of Primitive Man* (1911), 208. Subsequent references are
cited in the text in parentheses as *MPM*.

35 Boas, *The Mind of Primitive Man*, rev. ed. (1938) n.p.

36 On the *Volksgeist* theories of Herder and Humboldt, see Matti Bunzl, "Franz
Boas and the Humboldtian Tradition," 20–32.

37 Indeed, in a critical analysis of *The Mind of Primitive Man*, Charles Briggs and Richard Baumann have argued, "Here oppositions between tradition, myth, subjectivity, and emotion on the one hand and experimentation, science, rationality, and objectivity on the other equate two cartographies of difference—primitive versus civilized and 'the poor rural population . . . and . . . the lowest strata of the proletariat' versus 'the active minds representative of modern culture'" ("'The Foundation of All Future Researches,'" 518).

38 Gamio, *The Indian Basis of Mexican Civilization*, 171. According to Stocking, the "revolution in anthropology" was the long process of the critique of evolutionary theory ("Edward Burnett Tylor," 114).

39 Nevertheless, the new strains in the discourse of the primitive bore no necessary connection to decolonization.

40 Micaela Di Leonardo, "Wild Women Don't Have the Blues," 172, 187, 189.

41 Di Leonardo, "Margaret Mead and American Public Culture."

42 Lisa Yoneyama, "Habits of Knowing Cultural Differences," 75.

43 Ibid., 74.

44 John A. Britton, *Carleton Beals*, 55.

45 Langston Hughes, *The Big Sea*, 40.

46 This contrast between father and son distinguishes Langston Hughes as a "New Negro." Gates defines the New Negro movement as an explosion of writings from 1895 through the 1920s that attempted to distinguish the New Negroes, proud of their heritage and rebellious against the dominant culture, from the "Old Negro" associated with the stereotype of the compliant "Sambo" slave ("The Trope of a New Negro," 319–45).

47 In *Piedras de Sacrificio* (1924) and *Hora y Veinte* (1927) Pellicer glorifies pre-Columbian civilization (Edward Mullen, *Carlos Pellicer*).

48 Hughes, *The Big Sea*, 54.

49 Hughes, *The Collected Poems of Langston Hughes*, 23.

50 Appiah has criticized the homogenization of the diversity of Africa's populations in some U.S.-based versions of Pan-Africanism, particularly in Alexander Crummell and Du Bois; see Appiah, *In My Father's House*.

51 Hughes, *Collected Poems*, 25.

52 The complexities of oppression under capitalist imperialism "make 'color' useless as an emancipatory signifier," Gayatri Spivak writes ("Can the Subaltern Speak?" 294).

53 Hughes, *The Big Sea*, 50. In a landmark study on Mexican immigration to the United States, Gamio shows that the one-drop rule applied only to those brown people racialized as Negro, not those believed to be Mexican: "The darkest-skinned Mexican experiences almost the same restrictions as the Negro, while a person of medium-dark skin can enter a second-class lunchroom frequented also by Americans of the poorer class, but will not be admitted to a high-class restaurant. A Mexican of light-brown skin as a rule will not be admitted to a high-class hotel, while a white cultured Mexican will be freely admitted to the same hotel, especially if he speaks English fluently" (*Mexican Immigration to the United States*, 53).

54 One could object that Hughes is simply assuming a non-U.S. identity. But the fact that he was brown-skinned and spoke in Spanish meant he was claiming a more specific Latin American identity.

55 Hughes, "Poem" (1923), *Collected Poems*, 32.

56 Hughes, *Collected Poems*, 39.

57 Hughes, "White Shadows in a Black Land" (1932), in Mullen, *Langston Hughes*, 90. Subsequent references will be cited parenthetically in the text.

58 Brenda Plummer, "The Afro-American Response to the Occupation of Haiti, 1915–34," 125–43. See the introduction for a more thorough discussion of protests against the U.S. occupation of Haiti as constituting a practice of hemispheric citizenship.

59 Similarly, in "Merry Christmas" (1930), Hughes condemns imperialism in China, India, and Africa, and U.S. neocolonialism in Haiti and Cuba: "Ring Merry Christmas, Cuba!/(While Yankee domination/Keeps a nice fat president/In a little half-starved nation)" (Hughes, *Collected Poems*, 132).

60 For autobiographical information on Beals, see Britton.

61 Britton, *Carleton Beals*, 61.

62 Carleton Beals, "The Obregon Regime," 136–37.

63 Britton, *Carleton Beals*, 106.

64 See Aguilar Camín and Lorenzo Meyer, *Shadow of the Mexican Revolution*, 80–81.

65 Britton, *Carleton Beals*, 55, 59, 64.

66 Mella (1903–29) was a student activist who organized Cuba's first Marxist student movement, the Federation of University Students in 1922, and with Carlos Baliño founded Cuba's Communist party in 1925. For a brief biography of Mella, see Sheldon B. Liss, *Marxist Thought in Latin America*, 243–47.

67 Beals, *The Crime of Cuba*, 6–7. Subsequent references will be cited parenthetically in the text as *Crime*.

68 Benjamin, *The United States and Cuba*, 13.

69 Kutzinski, *Sugar's Secrets*, 135. Benjamin's estimate is 62 percent (*The United States and Cuba*, 17).

70 Benjamin, *The United States and Cuba*, 29.

71 On the Race War of 1912, see Aline Helg, *Our Rightful Share*.

72 In writing this paragraph, I have relied on Benjamin, *The United States and Cuba*, chapter 2.

73 Ibid., 50.

74 Alejo Carpentier, *¡Ecue-Yamba-O!* 123.

75 Roberto González Echevarría, *Alejo Carpentier: The Pilgrim at Home*, 47.

76 Carpentier, *¡Ecue-Yamba-O!* 125.

77 Beals, *The Crime of Cuba*, 38.

78 Such tourists, Beals claims, "would be shocked if told our Eighteenth Amendment had converted Havana into a gigantic saloon and brothel, or that American vested interests are ruling Cuba by fraud and murder" (*The Crime of Cuba*, 36).

79 An octoroon (preferred spelling) refers to a person who is descended from

seven white great-grandparents and one African or African American. For a history of racial classifications in the U.S. context, see F. James Davis, *Who Is Black?*, 75.

80 Torgovnick, *Primitive Passions*, 5.

81 Massey, *Space, Place and Gender*, 22.

82 The term "vaster reality" is Cornejo Polar's ("El indigenismo," 9).

83 Partha Chatterjee, *Nationalist Thought and the Colonial World*, 9.

84 In "El aspecto utilitario del folklore," Gamio argues that the study of folklore facilitates the "gradual forming of the Indian mentality until it is *molded* into the ways of modern thought" (emphasis added) (7).

85 For this definition of political liberalism see Chatterjee, *Nationalist Thought and the Colonial World*, 2.

86 Antonio Gramsci, *Selections from the Prison Notebooks*, 5.

87 Lewis, *When Harlem Was in Vogue*, 145–46.

88 Walter D. Mignolo, "Are Subaltern Studies Postmodern or Postcolonial?" 45–73.

89 In a letter to James Weldon Johnson, McKay wrote, "I consider *Home to Harlem* a real proletarian novel" (quoted in Cooper, *Claude McKay*, 247).

90 As Gilbert Osofsky has argued, "The most profound change that Harlem experienced in the 1920s was its emergence as a slum" (quoted in Cheryl Lynn Greenberg, *"Or Does It Explode?"* 31).

91 The depression reached Cuba in 1924 (Kutzinski, *Sugar's Secrets*, 136) and cropped up in Harlem in the high degree of unemployment and economic hardship among African Americans (Greenberg, *"Or Does It Explode?"* 39).

92 Greenberg, *"Or Does It Explode?"* 15.

93 Ibid., 21, 24.

94 Ibid., 28.

95 Ibid., 29.

96 Claude McKay, *The Negroes in America*, 18.

97 Wayne Cooper, *Claude McKay*, 77–78.

98 "Policing the Black Woman's Body in an Urban Context," 738–55.

99 Claude McKay, *Home to Harlem*, 40. Subsequent references will be cited parenthetically in the text as *Home*.

100 Moreover, at other points the narrative portrays the plight of women who are victimized by conventional standards of beauty, as in the case of Gin-head Susy and Lavinia Curdy, both of whom suffer at the hands of men because they aren't viewed as attractive (ibid., 60–61).

101 Adam Lively has similarly maintained, "The impulse behind his [McKay's] primitivism was political rather than aesthetic" ("Continuity and Radicalism in American Black Nationalist Thought, 1914–1929," 234).

102 McKay, "Speech to the Fourth Congress of the Third Communist International, Moscow," in *The Passion of Claude McKay*, 91–95. As William J. Maxwell has argued, black communism was more central to the Harlem Renaissance than is usually supposed—party members included Arna Bontemps,

Countee Cullen, Hughes, McKay, Paul Robeson, Louise Thompson, and Dorothy West, among others (*New Negro, Old Left,* chapters 1 and 2).

103 Cooper, *Claude McKay,* 116.

104 Ibid., 106.

105 Ibid., 104.

106 Farmer, *The Uses of Haiti,* 98–99.

107 Similarly, in *The Negroes in America* McKay writes, "The American Negro is the nightmare of American democracy. It never knows peace because the black spirit stands before its eyes day and night. The West Indies Negroes languish under the strain of unbearable exploitation by British landlords, and every year thousands are more ready to emigrate to South America, Central America, Cuba and the United States than to bear the . . . unbearable poverty to which they are doomed by the British form of government" (51).

108 Gates, "Critical Fanonism," 466.

109 Lewis, *When Harlem Was in Vogue,* 109.

110 Douglas, *Terrible Honesty,* 304, 312. "When African-Americans invaded Harlem in the 1900s and 1910s, they were, in a sense, retaking their own, reclaiming a strategic portion of the country that had enslaved them" (ibid., 312).

111 McKay, *The Negroes in America,* 58.

112 The "black Atlantic" is Paul Gilroy's term for the routes of oppression and resistance in relation to Africans and diasporic African Americans, Afro-Caribbeans, and black Britons.

113 Cary Nelson, *Repression and Recovery,* 234.

114 Knight, "Racism, Revolution and *Indigenismo,*" 79–80.

115 José Joaquín Blanco, *Se llamaba Vasconcelos,* 83, 91.

116 *Ladinos* include non-Indians and those who no longer identify as culturally Indian: acculturated Indians, *mestizos,* and whites.

117 For an overview of literary indigenismo in several countries, see René Prieto, "The Literature of *Indigenismo.*"

118 Desmond Rochfort, *Mexican Muralists: Orozco, Rivera, Siqueiros,* 21. Subsequent references will be cited in the text.

119 Martin Lienhard, "*La Noche de los Mayas:* Indigenous Mesoamericans in Cinema and Literature, 1917–1943," 35. Subsequent references will be cited in the text.

120 On indigenismo in Ecuador, see Marc Becker, "*Indigenismo* and Indian Movements in Twentieth-Century Ecuador."

121 On indigenismo in Peru, see especially Cornejo Polar, *Literatura y sociedad en el Perú: La novela indigenista.*

122 On the relationships between indigenismo, hispanismo, and latinoamericanismo as variants of nationalism, see Arturo Ardao, "Panamericanismo y Latinoamericanismo," 157–171; Ricardo Pérez Montfort, "Indigenismo, Hispanismo, y Panamericanismo en la Cultura Popular Mexicana de 1920 a 1940," 343–83.

123 Alexander Dawson, *Indian and Nation in Revolutionary Mexico,* 144.

124 Ricardo Pérez Montfort, *Estampas de nacionalismo popular mexicano,* 143.

125 As Knight writes, "The Indians themselves were the objects, not the authors of *indigenismo*" ("Racism, Revolution, and Indigenismo," 77).

126 Héctor Díaz-Polanco, "La teoría indigenista y la integración," *Indigenismo, modernización y marginalidad,* 41.

127 See Evelyn Hu-DeHart, "Peasant Rebellion in the Northwest: The Yaqui Indians of Sonora, 1740–1976," 141–75; and Heidi Zogbaum, *B. Traven,* 78.

128 José Vasconcelos called for "feminine society" to leave its "convents" and instead educate the humble: "Organicemos entonces al ejército de los educadores que substituya al ejército de los destructores" (Let us organize, therefore, the army of educators that will substitute for the army of destroyers) ("Discurso en la Universidad" [1920], 45).

129 Gamio, *The Indian Basis of Mexican Civilization,* 150. Further quotations will be cited parenthetically in the text as I B.

130 Gamio, "Nacionalismo e internacionalismo," 1.

131 Vasconcelos, *The Latin-American Basis of Mexican Civilization,* 5, 6, 8. Further quotations will be cited parenthetically in the text as *LAB.*

132 Richard Hofstadter, *Social Darwinism in American Thought, 1860–1915,* 148. For a description of the ways in which Gamio's practice of "applied anthropology" contradicted his ideological reliance on gradualist notions of progress, see chapter 4.

133 Guillermo Bonfil Batalla, *México profundo,* 42.

134 Plutarco Calles, "A Hundred Years of Revolution," *Survey Graphic* 52.1 (1924): 134–35.

135 Pérez Montfort, *Estampas de nacionalismo popular mexicano,* 118.

136 Ibid., 124.

137 Ibid., 162, 165.

138 Guillermo Sheridan, *Los Contemporáneos ayer,* 387.

139 On Mexican muralism, see Desmond Rochfort, *Mexican Muralists;* and Dawn Ades, "The Mexican Mural Movement," 153–76.

140 Bartra, *La jaula de la melancolía,* 52.

141 See Anna Macías, "Felipe Carrillo Puerto and Women's Liberation in Mexico," 286–301.

142 Aguilar Camín and Meyer, *Shadow of the Mexican Revolution,* 114; José Joaquín Blanco, *Se llamaba Vasconcelos,* 96; Gilbert Joseph, *Revolution from Without,* 185–227.

143 Joseph, *Revolution from Without,* 214. For Felipe Carrillo Puerto's own account of the *ligas,* see his "The New Yucatán," *Survey Graphic* 52.1 (1924): 141.

144 Knight, "Revolutionary Project, Recalcitrant People," 227.

145 Sheridan, *Los Contemporáneos ayer,* 386.

146 Francesca Miller, "Feminism and Social Motherhood, 1890–1938," 100.

147 Ibid., 86–87.

148 Ibid., 93.

149 Ibid., 100.

150 The only existing English translation is Miguel Angel Menéndez, *Nayar*, trans. Angel Flores.

151 Aguilar Camín and Meyer, *Shadow of the Mexican Revolution*, 132, 153. The nationalization of Mexican oil was "a measure . . . with few counterparts in world history" (ibid., 153).

152 Knight, "Revolutionary Project, Recalcitrant People," 229.

153 When the judge's son Gusano discovers Ramón in an attempt to see his own son, Ramón kills him with a machete (*Nayar*, 66).

154 The picaresque form engages in ethnographic discourse, reveals exploitative labor conditions, and also portrays the tragic consequences of the Cristero War, as when Indian women washing clothes at a river are massacred by the Cristeros.

155 Heidi Zogbaum, *B. Traven*, 50.

156 Vasconcelos, "Discurso en la Universidad," 45.

157 Bonfil Batalla, "Sobre la ideología del mestizaje," 404.

158 Kutzinski, *Sugar's Secrets*, 165.

159 Luis González, "El liberalismo triunfante," 918.

160 The passage reads as follows in the original: "Pero libertar a los indios es hacer que se vayan los blancos, que nos dejen solos, como cuando estábamos antes que vinieran. O matarlos si no quieren irse."

161 Here a typical problematic of the postcolonial arises in that Mexican national independence fails to produce independence for Indians, who in many cases did not view themselves as Mexican at all, and for good reason, given the Mexican government's protracted efforts to exterminate them. As we have seen, these extermination efforts are embodied by Cometa, the military chief of the Sierra who states, "The best Indian is the dead Indian" (155).

162 Even the limited goal of the assimilation of Indians is placed in doubt by the novel's use of environmental and biological determinism in describing locale: "Dense atmosphere, brutal sun, laboratory of the tropics in which life emerges from putrid waters, unredeemable" (16). Menéndez, then, takes a much more pessimistic view of the effects of tropical climes than does his contemporary José Vasconcelos, who served as minister of education from 1920 to 1924. In *La raza cósmica* (1925), Vasconcelos argues that the first great mestizo civilizations, such as Egypt, began in the tropics, and the final great mestizo civilization will return to the tropics (*La raza cósmica*, 32).

163 Bonfil Batalla, *México profundo*.

164 Luis Palés Matos, a white creole writer, has been celebrated as "the greatest poet in Puerto Rican literature" by Arcadio Díaz Quiñones ("Notas para el estudio del *Tun tun de Pasa y Grifería*," 117). Mercedes López-Baralt argues that *negrismo* in the Spanish Antilles begins with the publication of "Danzarina africana" (1917–18) by Palés Matos ("La tercera salida del *Tun tun de Pasa y Grifería*," 39). For other influential readings of Palés Matos, see José Luis González, "Literatura e identidad nacional en Puerto Rico," 82; and Díaz Quiñones, "La poesía negro de Luis Palés Matos." For an excellent overview

of the *negrismo* movement, see Kutzinski, *Sugar's Secrets*, chapters 5 and 6. On painting that focuses on Afro-Cuban themes, see Juan A. Martínez, *Cuban Art and National Identity;* and on musicians' participation in negrismo, see Robin Moore, *Nationalizing Blackness,* esp. chapter 5.

165 Alejo Carpentier, *¡Ecue-Yamba-O!* For a literary biography of Carpentier, see González Echevarría, *Alejo Carpentier. Negrismo* became a cultural force in Cuba with the publication of Guillén's poetry in *Motivos del Son* (1930), *Sóngoro Cosongo* (1931), and *West Indies, Ltd.* (1934). These are all included in Nicolás Guillén, *Obra Poética.* Regino Pedroso's early poetry, some of which has been translated into English by Langston Hughes, is collected in *Nosotros* (1933). Dedicated to "my exploited brothers," *Nosotros* epitomizes the collaboration between communists and Afro-Cubanists in the late 1920s and early 1930s; see Pedroso, *Orbita de Regino Pedroso.*

166 Kutzinski, *Sugar's Secrets,* 136; Alejandro de la Fuente, "Race, National Discourse and Politics in Cuba," 56.

167 Pérez, *Cuba Under the Platt Amendment,* 206–07.

168 Nicolás Guillén "El Camino de Harlem," quoted in Angel Augier, *Nicolás Guillén,* 89.

169 In addition, the growing Latin American interest in African populations evident in the Spanish translation of the West African Rene Marán's *Batouala* in 1921 suggests that the global vogue of primitivism created the space for tackling serious issues of race relations (ibid., 150).

170 Jesús Masdeu, *La raza triste,* 8. Subsequent references will be cited parenthetically in the text.

171 The frustrated promise of Afro-Cubans is also revealed in the contrast between the meeting places of Miguel and Gabriela: first they converse and read in the Estrada y Cespedes library, then, after Gabriela's father opposes their friendship, they meet clandestinely in the city cemetery.

172 Moore, *Nationalizing Blackness,* 35.

173 Benjamin, *The United States and Cuba,* 21; Alejandro de la Fuente, "Race, National Discourse and Politics in Cuba," 54.

174 Helg, "Race in Argentina and Cuba, 1880–1930," 55.

175 Afro-Cubans formed the PIC in 1909 to protest the fact that not a single black politician was elected to office that year. This event is alluded to in the incident in which Don Plutarco Hermosillo, the head of the Liberal party, recruits Miguel and other Afro-Cuban leaders, yet the assembly prevents their names from appearing on the ballot (*La raza triste,* 177).

176 On "the myth of Cuban racial equality" see Helg, *Our Rightful Share,* 6–7, 16, 106. For a persuasive critique of Helg's theory for failing to account for the agency of Afro-Cubans in appropriating dominant discourses of race for their own purposes, see de la Fuente, "Race, National Discourse and Politics in Cuba," 45.

177 Kutzinski, *Sugar's Secrets,* 181.

178 The fact that *El Demócrata* portrays Don Antonio's death as caused by Mi-

guel's strangling him reveals that the public discourse on race relations has the sole purpose of demonizing Afro-Cubans. Although by the end of the novel Miguel has in fact killed someone, the true crime was committed by those who cornered him with their racist discourses.

179   De la Fuente, "Race, National Discourse and Politics in Cuba," 45.

180   Ranajit Guha defines *subaltern* as "a name for the general attribute of sub-ordination . . . whether this is expressed in terms of class, caste, age, gender and office or in any other way" ("Preface," *Selected Subaltern Studies*, 35).

181   On "cognitive maps," see Fredric Jameson, "Cognitive Mapping," 347–60; on "stretched out" social relations, see Massey, *Space, Place and Gender*.

182   "Women, Literature and National Brotherhood," 51–52.

183   Pérez, *Cuba Under the Platt Amendment*, 182.

FOUR "RISING TIDES OF COLOR"

1   On Mexican *indigenismo* in relation to the Harlem Renaissance and *negrismo*, see chapter 3 of this book.

2   In an anthology of women's ethnographic writings, Ruth Behar includes Zora Neale Hurston with another lesser-known "daughter" of "Papa" Franz Boas: Ella Cara Deloria, the Native American author of a novel, *Waterlily*. These two joined Ruth Benedict, the Mexican Anita Brenner, Margaret Mead, Ruth Bunzel, Ruth Underhill, and Elsie Parson as Boas's "daughters" ("Intro-duction: Out of Exile," 1–29).

3   For mention of the "world melting pot," see Robert E. Park, "Our Racial Frontier on the Pacific" (1926), 149. For the "lady among the races" remark, see his "Education in its Relation to the Conflict and Fusion of Cultures" (1918), 280. The context for this remark follows: "The Negro is, by natural disposition, neither an intellectual nor an idealist, like the Jew; nor a brood-ing introspective, like the East African; nor a pioneer and frontiersman, like the Anglo-Saxon. He is primarily an artist, loving life for its own sake. His *métier* is expression rather than action. He is, so to speak, the lady among the races." At first this may sound like the Du Boisian thesis of racialist pluralism in *The Souls of Black Folk*: "The ideal of human brotherhood, gained through the unifying ideal of Race; the ideal of fostering and developing the traits and talents of the Negro, not in opposition to or contempt for other races, but rather in large conformity to the greater ideals of the American Republic, in order that some day on American soil two world-races may give each to each those characteristics both so sadly lack" (*The Souls of Black Folk* [1903], 220). However, contrary to the analysis of the "Sorrow Songs" by Du Bois, whom Park cites, Park argues, "The Negro is naturally sunny, cheerful, optimistic" ("Education," 278).

4   "The particular complex of inheritable characters which characterizes the individuals of a racial group constitutes the racial temperament" (Park, "Education," 282).

5 Cultural hybridity thus enables an appropriation of the forms but not the content of the dominant culture.

6 Park, "Our Racial Frontier on the Pacific," 151; Manuel Gamio, *The Mexican Immigrant: His Life-Story,* 45; Hurston, "Characteristics of Negro Expression," 59. In "Politics and 'The Man Farthest Down'" (1935), Park writes that Booker T. Washington coined the phrase during a trip to Europe in 1910, during which he visited the slums of London and the village peasants of Poland and Italy. According to Park, the phrase epitomizes "the optimism of other self-made Americans" in that Washington believed "that all men were predestined to rise" (167).

7 *La raza* ideologies, emerging out of transnational migration, depart from the prevailing postrevolutionary programs of *mestizaje* in Gamio and Vasconcelos, which were eugenicist in their construction of the ideal racial subject of the nation.

8 "I am arguing . . . that we distinguish theory from critical consciousness by saying that the latter is a sort of spatial sense, a sort of measuring faculty for locating or situating theory, and this means that theory has to be grasped in the place and the time out of which it emerges" (Edward Said, "Traveling Theory," 241).

9 Said argues that theory becomes an "ideological trap" when it fails to account for the historical specificities of its own emergence and the context of what it is used on ("Traveling Theory," 241). Gamio and Hurston gained access to theories that they used to understand participants in massive migrations by Mexicans and African Americans to and within the United States by themselves undergoing migration. From 1900 to 1930, 1.5 million Mexicans emigrated to the United States (many of whom returned to Mexico), and from 1910 to 1940, 1.5 million southern blacks migrated North in what is known as the Great Migration of African Americans. As a result of these migrations, by the 1920s "the political controversy over Mexican immigration reached fever pitch," and blacks were viewed as a menacing force, "like a silent, encroaching shadow," to quote the black Chicago School sociologist and Harlem Renaissance editor Charles S. Johnson (Mark Reisler, "Always the Laborer, Never the Citizen," 24; Johnson, "The New Frontage on American Life," 278). On the Great Migration of African Americans, see Nicholas Lemann, *The Promised Land.*

While most of these migrants traveled as menial laborers rather than as students, Gamio and Hurston shared experiences of racial oppression with them, if they differed in terms of their class trajectories. Like Franz Boas, Gamio and Hurston shared experiences of migration with the subjects of their ethnographies but were stigmatized by racial nationalism in the United States to a greater extent than was Boas, who as a Jew could pass more easily as an unhyphenated American. Even so, Boas left Germany partly because of the anti-Semitism he experienced there (Marshall Hyatt, *Franz Boas, Social Activist,* 84). Michael Rogin has argued that while 1920s "orientalist" discourses equated Asian Americans, African Americans, and Jews, Jews suffered a much lesser degree of anti-Semitism in the United States than in Europe, and so were less stigmatized by racial nationalism than African Americans (*Black-face, White Noise,* 63, 101). Nevertheless, Roger Rouse has suggested that I explore the ways in which Boas and his students were estranged from dominant U.S. culture—the Jewishness of Boas and Ruth Benedict's lesbianism being prime examples. This version of the story would emphasize the similarities in estrangement among the mainly white Boasian anthropologists, Chicago School sociologists, and Gamio and Hurston (Roger Rouse, personal communication, 19 January 1998). The alienation of Gamio and Hurston, if acute in the face of U.S. racism, was by no means unique among U.S. social scientists, many of whom participated in what George Stocking has described as the 1920s "counter-culture" of Boasian ethnographers and the Chicago School's focus on immigrants and racially and culturally marginalized populations. As the first generation of U.S. ethnographers traveling to such far-flung locales as Zuni Pueblo, Mexico, and Samoa, Boas's students Ruth Benedict, Margaret Mead, and Robert Redfield participated in a 1920s "counter-culture" that questioned the prevailing sex and gender norms and ethnocentrism of the dominant culture ("The Ethnographic Sensibility of the 1920s and the Dualism of the Anthropological Tradition," 218). Similarly, Chicago School sociology focused on immigrants, migrants, and populations marginalized by race and class in such texts as *The Polish Peasant in Europe and America* (1918–20) by W. I. Thomas and Florian Zanieki; *The Negro in Chicago* (1922), a text attributed to Charles S. Johnson (who served in 1923–28 as the editor of *Opportunity,* the organ of the National Urban League, which sponsored literary contests "to foster a market for Negro writers" beginning in 1925); Nels Anderson's *The Hobo* (1923); Louis Wirth's *The Ghetto* (1928); and E. Franklin Frazier's *The Negro Family in Chicago* (1931) (David Levering Lewis, *When Harlem Was in Vogue,* 97).

10 For instance, Martin Bulmer's *The Chicago School of Sociology* fails to even mention Gamio.

11 Hazel Carby has criticized Hurston for having constructed "an aesthetically purified form of blackness" confined to the rural South that places her writings "outside of the culture and history of contestation" of the black working class ("The Politics of Fiction, Anthropology and the Folk," 77). This charge has reached the level of accepted knowledge among critics like Ann Douglas. In a misreading of Sterling Brown's review of Hurston's *Their Eyes Were Watching God* (1937), Douglas has claimed that Brown detected a white-washing of the "bitterness" of black life: "The Negro poet Sterling Brown criticized Hurston's *Mules and Men* because it whitewashed the 'bitter[ness]' of 'the total truth'; in her account of the black South, there were no lynchings, no race riots, no trace of the world that prosecuted and imprisoned the Scottsboro Boys" (*Terrible Honesty,* 286). On the contrary, Brown wrote, "Here is bitterness, sometimes oblique . . . and sometimes forthright" and went on to provide examples of that "bitterness" in the novel ("Review of

Their Eyes Were Watching God," 20–21). Fatimah Rony has differed with the critique of Hurston as romanticizing the black South: "Hurston also broke from that romanticization in significant ways" (*The Third Eye,* 204).

12   Henry Louis Gates, Jr., "Afterword: Zora Neale Hurston, 'A Negro Way of Saying,'" *Mules and Men,* 293. Confining Gamio and Hurston within such highly circumscribed paradigms has obscured how they engaged in dialogues with U.S. social science that were intercultural and, in the case of Gamio, international. Gamio, for instance, was a frequent correspondent with Boas even after their close collaboration on Mexican archaeological projects ended (Angeles González Gamio, *Manuel Gamio,* passim).

13   Gamio and Hurston thus prefigure the radical revision of theories of acculturation by the Cuban anthropologist Fernando Ortiz. In coining the term *transculturación* in 1940, Ortiz refered to a tripartite process consisting of acculturation, that is, the acquisition of a distinct culture, deculturation, or the loss of a previous culture, and neoculturation, or "the creation of new cultural phenomena" (*Contrapunteo cubano del tabaco y el azúcar,* 141).

14   Chandler and the *New York Times* editorial are quoted in Mark Reisler, "Always the Laborer, Never the Citizen," 37–38.

15   Park, "Race Relations and Certain Frontiers," 123.

16   Boas, "The Problem of the American Negro," quoted in Hyatt, *Franz Boas, Social Activist,* 90.

17   In this essay, "hybridity" (Park speaks of a "cultural hybrid") marks a cultural and racial liminality, an in-between state made possible by the migration of oppressed groups such as Jews and African Americans into northern U.S. cities. For Park, the "mind of the marginal man," usually a person of mixed race or a European immigrant, reveals the processes of "contact and communication" leading to assimilation in the United States and abroad, making it possible for the social scientist to chart what elsewhere he calls a "miscegenation map of the world" ("Human Migration and the Marginal Man" [1928], 881–93). On the "miscegenation map of the world," see Park, "Race Relations and Certain Frontiers" (1934), 132.

18   Boas, "The Methods of Ethnology" (1920), 286.

19   Park, "Human Migration and the Marginal Man," 882.

20   Park, "Our Racial Frontier on the Pacific," 150.

21   This causal chain surreptitiously replays the evolutionary scenarios of a single path of development; see Boas's critique of evolutionary parallel development schemes in "The Methods of Ethnology," 282.

22   For Park's use of the term *racial group,* see Park, "Education in its Relation to the Conflict and Fusion of Cultures" (1918), 265.

23   Boas was becoming "the most important single force in shaping American anthropology" in the words of Stocking ("Introduction: The Basic Assumptions of Boasian Anthropology," 1). Having secured a lectureship in physical anthropology at Columbia in 1895, the man who had trained the country's first Ph.D. in anthropology began to train a bevy of doctoral students who

would eventually include Ruth Benedict, Melville Herskovits, Alfred Kroeber, Robert Lowie, Margaret Mead, and Edward Sapir. Similarly, the Chicago School, led by Park, a speechwriter for Booker T. Washington from 1905 until 1913, arguably became "the leading center of sociology in the world" from 1915 to 1940 (Bulmer, *The Chicago School of Sociology*, 1). In the 1920s the Chicago School was attracting a diverse group of students, including the African Americans W. O. Brown, E. Franklin Frazier, and Charles S. Johnson. Frazier and Johnson played important roles in the Harlem Renaissance.

24   Boas quotes Galton as having written, "In a mixture of types a new intermediate type will develop analogous to the appearance of the mule as a result of mixture between horse and donkey" ("Modern Populations of America," 22).

25   Stocking, *Race, Culture, and Evolution*, 205.

26   In "The Half-Blood Indian" (1894), Boas found that "half-breed" women bore taller children and more offspring than their racially pure counterparts, disputing claims that hybrid races were infertile (Stocking, *Race, Culture, and Evolution*, 172–73). Moreover, in a 1917 study of Puerto Ricans, Boas concluded, "Mulattoes excel in physical development the children of pure Spanish descent" ("Modern Populations of America," 21).

27   Stocking, *Race, Culture and Evolution*, 209.

28   Boas, *Race, Language and Culture*, 5.

29   Ibid., 3, 5–6. In Hurston's *Their Eyes Were Watching God*, Janie says, "We'se uh mingled people," referring to the intermingling of many racialized types included under the single heading of Negro in the United States (135).

30   Boas, "Race and Progress" (1931), in *Race, Language and Culture*, 5–6, 17.

31   Park, "Our Racial Frontier on the Pacific," 308–09.

32   This first notion of assimilation resembles what the Cuban anthropologist Fernando Ortiz would later term "transculturation," or the creation of new cultural materials out of the contact between groups. See note 13.

33   Park, "Racial Assimilation in Secondary Groups with Particular Reference to the Negro" (1913), 204, 220. Michel de Certeau makes a similar distinction between meanings of assimilation: "This misunderstanding assumes that 'assimilating' necessarily means 'becoming similar to' what one absorbs, and not 'making something similar' to what one is, making it one's own, appropriating or reappropriating it" (*The Practice of Everyday Life*, 166). In 1889, Boas similarly calls attention to the ways in which "foreign material taken up by a people [is] modified by preexisting ideas and customs" (Stocking, *Race, Culture and Evolution*, 207). As if to dramatize this process of modification in relation to her mentor's teaching, Hurston remarks, "The Negro, the world over, is famous as a mimic. But this in no way damages his standing as an original" (Hurston, "Characteristics of Negro Expression" [1934], 59).

34   Park, "Racial Assimilation in Secondary Groups with Particular Reference to the Negro," 220.

35   Park, "Our Racial Frontier on the Pacific," 150–51.

36 Park, "Education in its Relation to the Conflict and Fusion of Cultures," 280.

37 Park, "Negro Race Consciousness as Reflected in Race Literature," 297, 299.

38 Park, "Negro Race Consciousness," 297.

39 Park, "Our Racial Frontier on the Pacific," 144, 151.

40 Ibid., 149.

41 Park, "Racial Assimilation in Secondary Groups with Particular Reference to the Negro," 217.

42 Ibid., 220.

43 Park, "Politics and 'The Man Farthest Down,'" (1935), 172.

44 Park, "Human Migration and the Marginal Man," 888, 892.

45 Ibid., 893.

46 Hurston, *Their Eyes Were Watching God*, 125.

47 R. Fred Wacker argues that such criticisms miss the Chicago School's unusually "sophisticated" analysis of race relations in the United States (Introduction, *Ethnicity, Pluralism, and Race*, xii).

48 Stuart Hall has attacked Robert Young's argument in *Colonial Desire* that postcolonial critics are "complicit" with nineteenth-century racialism as "an inexplicably simplistic charge" ("When Was 'The Post Colonial'? Thinking at the Limit," 258).

49 Here I am paraphrasing Renato Rosaldo's insight about the ethical consequences of objectivity; see his *Culture and Truth*, 181.

50 David A. Brading, "Manuel Gamio and Official Indigenismo in Mexico."

51 Ibid., 78.

52 Juan Comas, "La Vida y la Obra de Manuel Gamio," 7.

53 Aurelio de los Reyes, *Manuel Gamio y el Cine*, 24.

54 González Gamio, *Manuel Gamio*, 47.

55 Gamio, *Forjando patria* (1916), 6. All subsequent references will be cited parenthetically in the text.

56 José Enrique Rodó, *Ariel*, 1. All subsequent references will be cited parenthetically in the text.

57 José Martí, "Nuestra América," in *Sus mejores páginas*, 89. For a discussion of the figure of Calibán, see Roberto Fernández Retamar, "Caliban: Notes Toward a Discussion of Culture in Our America," 14.

58 Guillermo Bonfil Batalla, *México profundo*, 13.

59 Gamio, "El Aspecto Utilitario del Folklore," 6–8.

60 Bonfil Batalla, *México profundo*, 172.

61 Devra Weber, Introducción, *El inmigrante mexicano—la historia de su vida: Entrevistas completas, 1926–1927*, 31–32; Alexander Dawson, *Indian and Nation in Revolutionary Mexico*, 149.

62 Salomón Nahmad Sittón and Thomas Weaver, "Manuel Gamio, el Primer Antropólogo Aplicado y Su Relación con la Antropología Norteamericana," 291–321.

63 In his subsequent anthropological, archaeological, and sociological study *The Population of the Valley of Teotihuacán* (1922), Gamio similarly calls for land distribution, a decent minimum wage, an eight-hour working day, rural mutualism, improved medical services, schools, and lower taxes on the valley residents; see *La población del Valle de Teotihuacán*. According to Claudio Lomnitz, Gamio achieved many of these ideals: "By his recommendation, the government raised the salary of the area's four hundred government employees . . . in order to nudge up the salaries that local hacendados paid their peons. Gamio had lands distributed to peasants. A new road, a railroad station, medical facilities, and educational facilities were built" (*Deep Mexico, Silent Mexico*, 252).

64 Nahmad Sittón and Weaver, "Manuel Gamio, el Primer Antropólogo," 300.

65 Brading, "Manuel Gamio and Official Indigenismo in Mexico," 88; Bonfil Batalla, *México profundo*, 52.

66 On Vasconcelos's neglect of contemporary Indians, see José Joaquín Blanco, *Se llamaba Vasconcelos*, 93.

67 Bonfil Batalla, *México profundo*, 176. However, the current "low intensity warfare" against the Zapatistas of Chiapas should serve as sufficient warning against viewing Mexico as having reformed its treatment of Indians.

68 Bulmer, *The Chicago School of Sociology*, 76.

69 Gamio, *Mexican Immigration to the United States*, 192; subsequent references will be cited parenthetically in the text. Gamio also suggests a reduction of the head tax on Mexican temporary laborers (185) and calls for the restrictionist American Federation of Labor to organize Mexican laborers (190–91).

70 Weber, Introducción, *El inmigrante mexicano*, 46–48.

71 Gamio, "Guía para los investigadores de campo usada en relación con este estudio preliminary," *El inmigrante mexicano*, 553–54.

72 Vasconcelos, *La raza cósmica*, 18.

73 As Roberto Schwarz has written in the context of Brazil, nationalists typically "condemn imperialism and hush up bourgeois oppression" (Schwarz, "Brazilian Culture: Nationalism by Elimination," 5).

74 Robert Redfield, "Conflict and Race Consciousness," in Gamio, *The Life Story of the Mexican Immigrant*, 140. Subsequent references to *The Life Story* will be cited parenthetically in the text.

75 On the Cristero War, see Alan Knight, "Revolutionary Project, Recalcitrant People: Mexico, 1910–1940," 229.

76 Said, "Traveling Theory," 241.

77 Gamio, *Mexican Immigration*, 53.

78 I am indebted to Roger Rouse for this point.

79 Ana Macías, *Against All Odds*, 143.

80 Gamio, "El Celibato y el Desarrollo de la Población en México," 67.

81 In *La raza cósmica* (1925) Vasconcelos similarly refers to a new, sexually liberated age of *mestizaje* in which "the laws of emotion, beauty, and happiness will regulate the election of pairs" (40).

82 Here I have emphasized subjects who have dissented from Gamio's narrative of gender relations, but it is equally possible to find subjects who also disagreed with his Mexican nationalist project, as José Limón has done in his analysis of Gamio. However, Limón overstates his case when he suggests that Gamio was naively optimistic about modernization in Mexico: "They [Gamio's Mexican immigrant subjects] still hold a certain patriotic pride and longing for Mexico, but unlike Gamio, they hold no easy and ultimately bourgeois illusions about the possibilities of fundamental political-economic change in that country, which they actually may know better than he at ground level" ("Nation, Love, and Labor Lost," 55). Contrary to this statement, by attempting to foment social change from the ground up, Gamio's projects of applied anthropology suggest that he knew the magnitude of the tasks before him.

83 Estimates of the Indian population in Mexico at the time of the Revolution vary between one-third and two-thirds of the population; see Knight, "Racism, Revolution and Indigenismo," 74.

84 Hughes and Hurston wrote *Mule Bone* in 1930 only to quarrel over the authorship and subsequently scrap the project. Hurston made several attempts to utilize her material on the New York stage in the early 1930s. In 1931 Hurston organized a concert of "Negro music" called "the Great Day." Hurston went into debt for the performance, which was a success but wasn't picked up by Broadway. Later the music was performed at Rollins College in Florida. After achieving great success, the show went on a travelling circuit. On Hurston as a playwright and on *Mule Bone,* see Robert E. Hemenway, *Zora Neale Hurston,* chapter 6.

85 Hurston, "High John De Conqueror" (1943), 78.

86 Wright argues, "Miss Hurston voluntarily continues . . . the minstrel technique that makes the 'white folks' laugh. Her characters eat and laugh and cry and work and kill; they swing like a pendulum eternally in that safe and narrow orbit in which America likes to see the Negro live: between laughter and tears. . . . The sensory sweep of her novel carries no theme, no message, no thought. In the main, her novel is not addressed to the Negro, but to a white audience whose chauvinistic tastes she knows how to satisfy. She exploits the phase of Negro life which is 'quaint,' the phase which evokes a piteous smile on the lips of the 'superior' race" (Review of *Their Eyes Were Watching God,* by Zora Neale Hurston, 17).

87 Carby, "The Politics of Fiction, Anthropology and the Folk," 79.

88 Hemenway, *Zora Neale Hurston,* 220.

89 Hurston, "The Characteristics of Negro Expression," 59. On the "reclaiming" of "borrowed characteristics" in the practice of hoodoo, see Hurston, *Mules and Men* (1935), 183. Subsequent references will be cited parenthetically in the text.

90 My comments here are particularly informed by Leys, Schwarz, and Taussig.

91 Homi Bhabha, "The Other Question," 66.

92 *The Slave Community,* 204. Another story that parodies the "Sambo" stereotype is "John Tells Fortunes," in which Old Massa claims that John "don't lie" right after John lies that he can tell fortunes (Hurston, *Mules and Men*, 81–83).

93 The tale "Ole Massa and John Who Wanted to Go to Heaven" plays on the white master's expectations that slaves are superstitious in their alleged literal-minded belief that God can appear on earth. John plays along with the scenario in order to trick Ole Massa (Hurston, *Mules and Men*, 70–72).

94 As Bhabha argues, "The display of hybridity—its particular 'replication'— terrorizes authority with the ruse of recognition, its mimicry, its mockery" ("Signs Taken for Wonders," 115).

95 Jane Tompkins, *Sensational Designs*, xi.

96 My reading of Hurston as a cosmopolitan migrant concurs with that of Benigno Sánchez-Eppler, who emphasizes Hurston's movement between metropolitan and rural sites as a shaping condition of *Mules and Men*. By comparing Hurston with the Brazilian Boasian anthropologist Gilberto Freyre, Sánchez-Eppler locates Hurston within the diasporic African "extended Caribbean," borrowing a phrase from Immanuel Wallerstein ("Telling Anthropology," 464).

97 Néstor García Canclini, *Culturas híbridas*, 288.

98 Ibid., 31.

99 E. Franklin Frazier, "Racial Self-Expression," 120. Although Frazier viewed black slave culture as a cipher, he spoke of the frequency with which a black person takes over "cultural forms about him" (120).

100 Frazier writes, " Any nationalistic program that made the Negro seek compensations in a barren racial tradition and thereby escape competition with the white man which was an inevitable accompaniment of full participation in American culture, would lead to intellectual, spiritual and material impoverishment such as one finds among southern mountain whites" (ibid., 121).

101 Melville Herskovits, *The Myth of the Negro Past*, 244–49.

102 Graciela Hernández similarly argues, "Hurston moves to destabilize her own interpretive authority" ("Multiple Subjectivities and Strategic Positionality," 161).

103 Hurston's passage reads as follows: "When I pitched headforemost into the world I landed in the crib of negroism. . . . But it was fitting me like a tight chemise. I couldn't see it for wearing it. It was only when I was off in college, away from my native surroundings, that I could see myself like somebody else and stand off and look at my garment. Then I had to have the spy-glass of Anthropology to look through at that" (1).

104 "Instead of participant observation, Hurston's methods may be characterized as observing participation" (Rony, *The Third Eye*, 206).

105 Redfield, *Tepoztlán, a Mexican Village*, 4.

106 José Rabasa and Javier Sanjinés have called for a similarly collaborative relationship between intellectuals and subalterns: "The fact that we do not constitute ourselves as intellectuals with a privileged access to subalterns defines

our group as one more entity in the contestatory movements" ("Introduction: The Politics of Subaltern Studies," viii).

107 Stocking, "The Ethnographic Sensibility of the 1920s," 213.

108 Even the swamp crew's axe-work counts as culture: "Not only do they chop rhythmically, but they do a beautiful double twirl above their heads with the ascending axe before it begins that accurate and bird-like descent" (66).

109 Stocking, *Race, Culture, and Evolution*, 233.

110 Boas, *Race, Language, and Culture*, 285.

111 Michel de Certeau, *The Practice of Everyday Life*, 13.

112 Houston Baker defines African American conjure practices as consisting of a combination of the definitions provided by the *OED*: conspiracy, the exercise of magical or occult influence, and playing tricks with words, or "narrative authority" ("Workings of the Spirit" 280, 299).

113 Certeau, *The Practice of Everyday Life*, 7. By taking hoodoo seriously, Hurston contests images of hoodoo as "ritualistic orgies" in representations produced by Broadway, popular fiction, and Hollywood. "Hoodoo is not drum beating and dancing," warns Hurston. Indeed, in the "pre-Code" Hollywood films *Kongo* (1932; William Cohen, director) and *Black Moon* (1933; Roy William, director) Africans or Afro-Caribbeans engage in wild ceremonies of drumming and dancing culminating in human sacrifice.

114 Hurston, "Characteristics of Negro Expression," 59. See this chapter's n. 6 above on "The Man Farthest Down."

115 Hurston, *Their Eyes*, 125. Subsequent quotations will be cited parenthetically in the text.

116 Ibid.

117 Paul Gilroy, *The Black Atlantic*, passim.

118 Hortense Spillers, "'All the Things You Could Be by Now,'" 88.

119 I am not falling into the trap of conflating race and class here: skin color denotes something quite different from race.

120 Gates, "*Their Eyes Were Watching God*: Hurston and the Speakerly Text," 154–99.

121 Carby, "The Politics of Fiction, Anthropology and the Folk," 77.

122 Hurston, *Mules and Men*, 8.

123 Hurston, *Tell My Horse*, 101–02.

124 Ibid., 93.

125 Plummer, "The Afro-American Response to the Occupation of Haiti, 1915–34," 133.

126 Ibid., 129. One scholar estimates that fifteen thousand Haitians were murdered in the suppression of a rebellion in 1920 (Farmer, *The Uses of Haiti*, 98).

127 Plummer, "The Afro-American Response," 138.

128 Spillers, "'All the Things You Could Be by Now,'" 106–07, 109.

129 "Two European Images of Non-European Rule," 114.

130 Francoise Lionnet, "Autoethnography," 166.

131 *Culture and Truth*, 181.

132   See Bhabha, "Signs Taken for Wonders," 115; and "Of Mimicry and Man," passim.

133   Stocking provides an exemplary mapping of "primitivistic longing" in 1920s anthropological texts by Ruth Benedict, Margaret Mead, Robert Redfield, and Edward Sapir at a time when cultural anthropology was expanding beyond the nation for the first time; see "The Ethnographic Sensibility of the 1920s."

134   For an exemplary model of the new transnational scholarship on the Harlem Renaissance, see Brent Hayes Edwards, *The Practice of Diaspora.*

135   Eric Sundquist, "Red, White, Black and Blue," 115.

136   Hurston quoted in Lionnet, "Autoethnography," 174. See Zora Neale Hurston, *Dust Tracks on a Road.* While I do not endorse Hurston's individualistic discourse here, the "individual" can be taken as standing for Said's notion of the "untidiness" that eludes a given theory.

CODA

1   Roberto Lovato, "Envisioning Another World: *Integración Desde Abajo,*" 24.

2   Ibid., 23.

3   Michael Blanding, "The World Social Forum: Protest or Celebration?" 2.

4   Jacques Ranciere, "Who Is the Subject of the Rights of Man?" 301.

Adas, Michael. *Prophets of Rebellion: Millenarian Protest Movements against the European Colonial Order.* Chapel Hill: University of North Carolina Press, 1979.

Ades, Dawn. "The Mexican Mural Movement." In *The Art of Latin America: The Modern Period, 1820–1980,* 153–76. New Haven: Yale University Press, 1989.

Adi, Hakim. *West Africans in Britain, 1900–1960: Nationalism, Pan-Africanism and Communism.* London: Lawrence and Wishart, 1998.

Adorno, Theodor. *Negative Dialectics.* Translated by E. B. Ashton. New York: Continuum, 1973.

Agamben, Giorgio. "The Messiah and the Sovereign: The Problem of Law in Walter Benjamin." In *Potentialities,* 160–74. Stanford: Stanford University Press, 1999.

——. *Il tempo che resta: Un commento alla Lettera ai Romani.* Torino: Bollati Boringhieri, 2000.

——. *State of Exception.* Translated by Kevin Attell. Chicago: University of Chicago Press, 2005.

Aguilar, Alonso. *Pan-Americanism from Monroe to the Present.* New York: Monthly Review, 1968.

Aguilar Camín, Héctor, and Lorenzo Meyer. *In the Shadow of the Mexican Revolution: Contemporary Mexican History, 1910–1989.* Translated by Luis Alberto Fierro. Austin: University of Texas Press, 1993.

Aguirre, Lauro. "Open Letter to the President of the United States/Carta Abierta al Presidente de los Estados Unidos." El Paso: Office of "The Social Reform," A News Paper of Independent Ideas, 1906.

Aguirre, Lauro, and Teresa Urrea, eds. *El Independiente: Periódico Universal* (El Paso). 6 May 1896, 13 May 1896, 7 August 1896.

Ahmad, Dohra. " 'More than Romance': Genre and Geography in Dark Princess." *ELH* 69 (2002): 775–803.

Almaguer, Tomás. "Interpreting Chicano History: The World-System Approach to Nineteenth-Century California." *Review* 4.3 (1981): 459–507.

——. *Racial Fault Lines*. Berkeley: University of California Press, 1994.

Alvarez, Sonia, Evelina Dagnino, and Arturo Escobar. "Introduction: The Cultural and the Political in Latin American Social Movements." In *Cultures of Politics, Politics of Cultures: Re-visioning Latin American Social Movements*, edited by Alvarez, Dagnino and Escobar, 1–29. Boulder: Westview Press, 1998.

Anderson, Benedict. *Imagined Communities*. New York: Verso, 1983.

——. *Under Three Flags: Anarchism and the Anti-Colonial Imagination*. New York: Verso, 2005.

Ansprenger, Franz. *The Dissolution of the Colonial Empires*. New York: Routledge, 1989.

Appadurai, Arjun. "Patriotism and Its Futures." *Public Culture* 5 (1993): 411–29.

Appiah, Anthony. *In My Father's House: Africa in the Philosophy of Culture*. New York: Oxford University Press, 1992.

Aptheker, Herbert. Introduction. *Dark Princess: A Romance* by W. E. B. Du Bois. Millwood, New York: Kraus-Thomson, 1974.

Ardao, Arturo. "Panamericanismo y Latinoamericanismo." In *América Latina en sus ideas*, edited by Leopoldo Zea, 157–71. Mexico City: Siglo Veintiuno, 1986.

Arendt, Hannah. "The Decline of the Nation-State and the End of the Rights of Man." In *Imperialism*. New York: Harcourt, Brace, Jovanovich, 1968.

Armstrong, Nancy. *Desire and Domestic Fiction: A Political History of the Novel*. New York: Oxford University Press, 1987.

Arnesen, Eric. *Brotherhoods of Color: Black Railroad Workers and the Struggle for Equality*. Cambridge: Harvard University Press, 2001.

Asad, Talal. "Two European Images of Non-European Rule." In *Anthropology and the Colonial Encounter*, 103–18. London: Ithaca Press, 1973.

Augier, Angel. "Prólogo: La Poesía de Nicolás Guillén." In *Obra Poetica*, 2d ed., by Nicolás Guillén. Havana: Editorial Letras Cubanas, 1980.

——. *Nicolás Guillén: Estudio Biográfico-Crítico*. Havana: Unión de Escritores y Artistas de Cuba, 1984.

Badiou, Alain. *El ser y el acontecimiento*. Translated by Raúl J. Cerdeiras, Alejandro A. Cerletti, Nilda Prados. Buenos Aires: Manantial, 1999.

——. *Ethics: An Essay on the Understanding of Evil*. Translated by Peter Hallward. New York: Verso, 2001.

——. "On Evil: An Interview with Alain Badiou." Christopher Cox and Molly Whalen. *Cabinet* 5 (2001): 69–74.

Baker, Jr., Houston. *Modernism and the Harlem Renaissance*. Chicago: University of Chicago Press, 1987.

——. "Workings of the Spirit: Conjure and the Space of Black Women's Creativity." In *Zora Neale Hurston: Critical Perspectives Past and Present*, edited by Henry Louis Gates Jr. and K. A. Appiah, 280–308. New York: Amistad, 1993.

Bakhtin, Mikhail. *The Dialogic Imagination*. Edited by Michael Holquist. Translated by Caryl Emerson and Michael Holquist. Austin: University of Texas Press, 1981.

Balibar, Etienne. *We, the People of Europe? Reflections on Transnational Citizenship.* Translated by James Swenson. Princeton: Princeton University Press, 2004.

Barkan, Elazar, and Ronald Bush. Introduction. *Prehistories of the Future: The Primitivist Project and the Culture of Modernism.* Edited by Barkan and Bush. Stanford: Stanford University Press, 1995.

Barnes, Elizabeth. *States of Sympathy: Seduction and Democracy in the American Novel.* New York: Columbia University Press, 1997.

Bartra, Roger. *La jaula de la melancolía: Identidad y metamorfosis del mexicano.* Mexico City: Grijalbo, 1987.

——. *The Cage of Melancholy: Identity and Metamorphosis in the Mexican Character.* Translated by Christopher J. Hall. New Brunswick: Rutgers University Press, 1992.

Baumgart, Winfried. *Imperialism: The Idea and Reality of British and French Colonial Expansion, 1880–1914.* New York: Oxford University Press, 1982.

Beals, Carleton. "The Obregon Regime." *Survey Graphic* 52.1 (1924): 136–37.

——. *The Crime of Cuba.* Philadelphia: J. B. Lippincott, 1933.

Becker, Marc. "*Indigenismo* and Indian Movements in Twentieth-Century Ecuador." Latin American Studies Association Conference, Washington D.C., 1995. *http://lanic.utexas.edu/project/lasa95/becker.html.* Accessed 10 June 2007.

Bederman, Gail. *Manliness and Civilization: A Cultural History of Gender and Race in the United States, 1890–1917.* Chicago: University of Chicago Press, 1995.

Behar, Ruth. "Introduction: Out of Exile." In *Women Writing Culture,* edited by Ruth Behar and Deborah Gordon, 1–29. Berkeley: University of California Press, 1996.

Benjamin, Jules Robert. *The United States and Cuba: Hegemony and Dependent Development, 1880–1934.* Pittsburgh: University of Pittsburgh Press, 1977.

Benjamin, Walter. "The Author as Producer." 1934. In *The Essential Frankfurt School Reader,* 254–69. New York: Continuum, 1982.

——. "Theses on the Philosophy of History." In *Illuminations,* 253–64. New York: Schocken, 1968.

Berlant, Lauren. "The Female Woman: Fanny Fern and the Form of Sentiment." *American Literary History* 3.3 (1991): 429–54.

——. "Poor Eliza." *American Literature* 70.3 (1998): 635–68.

Bhabha, Homi. "DissemiNation: Time, Narrative, and the Margins of the Modern Nation." In *Nation and Narration,* edited by Homi K. Bhabha, 291–322. New York: Routledge, 1990.

——. "Of Mimicry and Man: The Ambivalence of Colonial Discourse." In *The Location of Culture,* 85–92. New York: Routledge, 1994.

——. "Signs Taken for Wonders: Questions of Ambivalence and Authority Under a Tree Outside Dehli, May 1817." In *The Location of Culture,* 102–22. New York: Routledge, 1994.

Blanding, Michael. "The World Social Forum: Protest or Celebration?" *The Nation* (6 March 2006). /www.thenation.com/doc/20060306/blanding.

Blassingame, John. *The Slave Community: Plantation Life in the Antebellum South.* New York: Oxford University Press, 1979.

Boas, Franz. "The Half-Blood Indian." 1894. In *Race, Language and Culture*, 138–48. New York: Macmillan, 1940.

———. *The Mind of Primitive Man*. 1911. Revised edition. New York: Macmillan, 1938.

Bolton, Herbert. *The Spanish Borderlands: A Chronicle of Old Florida and the Southwest*. New Haven: Yale University Press, 1921.

———. "The Epic of Greater America." *American Historical Review* 38 (1933): 448–74.

Bonfil Batalla, Guillermo. *México profundo: una civilización negada*. Mexico City: Secretaría de Educación Pública, 1987.

———. *México profundo: Reclaiming a Civilization*. Translated by Philip A. Dennis. Austin: University of Texas Press, 1996.

———. "Sobre la ideología del mestizaje." In *Decadencia y auge de las identidades: Cultura nacional, identidad cultural, y modernización*, edited by José Manuel Valenzuela Arce, 35–45. Tijuana: El Colegio de la Frontera Norte, 1992.

Bosniak, Linda. "The Citizenship of Aliens." *Social Text* 56 (1998): 29–35.

———. "Denationalizing Citizenship." In *Citizenship Today: Global Perspectives and Practices*, edited by T. Alexander Aleinikoff and Douglas Klusmeyer, 237–52. Washington, D.C.: Carnegie Endowment for International Peace, 2001.

Brading, David A. "Manuel Gamio and Official Indigenismo in Mexico." *Bulletin of Latin American Research* 7.1 (1988): 75–89.

Brenner, Anita. "Revolution and Renascence." In *Idols Behind Altars: The Story of the Mexican Spirit*, 314–29. New York: Payson and Clarke, 1929.

Briggs, Charles, and Richard Baumann. "'The Foundation of All Future Researches': Franz Boas, George Hunt, Native American Texts and the Construction of Modernity." *American Quarterly* 51.3 (1999): 479–528.

Britton, John A. *Carleton Beals: A Radical Journalist in Latin America*. Albuquerque: University of New Mexico Press, 1987.

Brooks, Peter. *The Melodramatic Imagination*. New York: Columbia University Press, 1985.

Brown, Sterling. Review of *Their Eyes Were Watching God* by Zora Neale Hurston. In *Zora Neale Hurston: Critical Perspectives Past and Present*, edited by Henry Louis Gates, Jr. and K. A. Appiah, 20–21. New York: Amistad, 1993.

Brown, Wendy. "Injury, Identity, Politics." In *Mapping Multiculturalism*, edited by Avery F. Gordon and Christopher Newfield, 149–66. Minneapolis: University of Minnesota Press, 1996.

Brown, Wendy, Judith Butler, and Chris Connery. "Exchange: Epistemology and Vinegar." *The Nation* (11 May 1998): 2, 59.

Bulmer, Martin. *The Chicago School of Sociology*. Chicago: University of Chicago Press, 1984.

Bunzl, Matti. "Franz Boas and the Humboldtian Tradition: From *Volksgeist* and *Nationalcharakter* to an Anthropological Concept of Culture." In *Volksgeist as Method and Ethic*, edited by George Stocking, 17–78. Madison: University of Wisconsin Press, 1996.

Burns, E. Bradford. *The Poverty of Progress: Latin America in the Nineteenth Century*. Berkeley: University of California Press, 1980.

Calles, Plutarco. "A Hundred Years of Revolution." *Survey Graphic* 52.1 (May 1924): 134–35.

Camfield, Gregg. "The Moral Aesthetics of Sentimentality: A Missing Key to *Uncle Tom's Cabin.*" *Nineteenth-Century Literature* 43.3 (1988): 319–45.

Carby, Hazel V. "The Politics of Fiction, Anthropology and the Folk: Zora Neale Hurston." In *New Essays on Their Eyes Were Watching God,* edited by Michael Awkward, 71–93. New York: Cambridge University Press, 1990.

———. "Policing the Black Woman's Body in an Urban Context." *Critical Inquiry* 18.4 (1992): 738–55.

Carpentier, Alejo. *¡Ecue-Yamba-Ó!* 1933. Reprint Buenos Aires: Editorial Xanadú, 1968.

Carrillo Puerto, Felipe. "The New Yucatán." *Survey Graphic* 52.1 (1924): 138–42.

Cawelti, John. *Adventure, Mystery and Romance: Formula Stories as Art and Popular Culture.* Chicago: University of Chicago Press, 1976.

Certeau, Michel de. *The Practice of Everyday Life.* Berkeley: University of California Press, 1984.

Chamberlain, M. E. *Decolonization: The Fall of the European Empires.* Oxford: Basil Blackwell, 1985.

Chandler, Nahum Dimitri. "The Economy of Desedimentation: W. E. B. Du Bois and the Discourses of the Negro." *Callaloo* 19.1 (1996): 78–93.

———. "Reading Seminar: 'The Problem of the Twentieth Century is the Problem of the Color Line.'" Moravian College, Bethlehem, Pennsylvania. 19 November 2003.

Chatterjee, Partha. *Nationalist Thought and the Colonial World: A Derivative Discourse?* London: Zed, 1986.

Child, Lydia Maria. "Transcendentalism." *National Anti-Slavery Standard* (25 November 1841): 99.

———. "The Different Races of Men." *National Anti-Slavery Standard* (5 January 1842): 122.

———. "The African Race." *National Anti-Slavery Standard* (27 April 1843): 187.

Chinitz, David. "Rejuvenation through Joy: Langston Hughes, Primitivism, and Jazz." *American Literary History* 9.1 (1997): 60–78.

Chrisman, Laura, and Patrick Williams. Introduction. *Colonial Discourse and Post-Colonial Theory.* New York: Columbia University Press, 1994.

Clifford, James. *The Predicament of Culture: Twentieth-Century Ethnography, Literature, and Art.* Cambridge: Harvard University Press, 1988.

Cobb, Martha. *Harlem, Haiti, and Havana: A Comparative Critical Study of Langston Hughes, Jacques Roumain and Nicolás Guillén.* Washington, D. C.: Three Continents Press, 1979.

Comas, Juan. "La Vida y la Obra de Manuel Gamio." In *Estudios antropológicos publicados en homenaje al doctor Manuel Gamio,* 1–26. Mexico City: Dirección General de Publicaciones, 1956.

Communist International. "The Black Question." In *Theses, Resolutions and Mani-*

festos of the First Four Congresses of the Third International, 328–31. Atlantic Highlands, N.J.: Humanities Press, 1980.

Conferencias Internacionales Americanas, 1889–1936. Washington, D.C.: Dotación Carnegie para la Paz Internacional, 1938.

Cooper, Frederick. "Review Essay: Race, Ideology and the Perils of Comparative History." *American Historical Review* 101.4 (October 1996): 1122–38.

Cooper, Wayne. *Claude McKay: Rebel Sojourner in the Harlem Renaissance*. Baton Rouge: Louisiana State University Press, 1987.

Cornejo Polar, Antonio. "El indigenismo y las literaturas heterogéneas: su doble estatuto socio-cultural." *Revista de Crítica Literaria Latinoamericana* 7–8 (1978): 7–21.

———. "La novela indigenista: un género contradictorio." *Texto crítico* 14 (1979): 58–70.

———. *Literatura y sociedad en el Perú: La novela indigenista*. Lima (Peru): Lasontay, 1980.

Crenshaw, Kimberlé, and Gary Peller. "Reel Time/Real Justice." In *Reading Rodney King/Reading Urban Uprising*, edited by Robert Gooding-Williams, 56–70. New York: Routledge, 1993.

Cruz, Jacqueline. "'Esclava vencedora': la mujer en la obra literaria de José Martí." *Hispania* 75:1 (March 1992): 30–37.

Davis, F. James. *Who Is Black? One Nation's Definition*. University Park, Penn.: Pennsylvania State University Press, 1991.

Dawson, Alexander S. *Indian and Nation in Revolutionary Mexico*. Tucson: University of Arizona Press, 2004.

de Jong, James. *Vicious Modernism: Black Harlem and the Literary Imagination*. New York: Cambridge University Press, 1990.

de la Fuente, Alejandro. "Race, National Discourse, and Politics in Cuba: An Overview." *Latin American Perspectives* 100.25 (May 1998): 43–69.

de la Peña, Guillermo. "Nationals and Foreigners in the History of Mexican Anthropology." In *The Conditions of Reciprocal Understanding*, edited by James W. Fernández and Milton B. Singer, 276–303. Chicago: Center for International Studies, 1995.

Dekker, George. *The American Historical Romance*. New York: Cambridge University Press, 1990.

Delany, Martin Robinson. *The Condition, Elevation, Emigration, and Destiny of the Colored People of the United States, Politically Considered*. Philadelphia: Published by the Author, 1852.

Delpar, Helen. *The Enormous Vogue of Things Mexican: Cultural Relations between the United States and Mexico, 1920–1935*. Tuscaloosa: University of Alabama Press, 1992.

Depestre, Rene. "Saludo y despedida a la negritud." In *Africa en América Latina*, edited by Manuel Moreno Fraginals, 337–62. Mexico City: Siglo Veintiuno Editores, 1977.

———. "Hello and Goodbye to Negritud." In *Africa in Latin America*, edited by Manuel Moreno Fraginals, 251–72. New York: Holmes and Meier, 1984.

Desmond, Jane, and Virginia Domínguez. "Resituating American Studies in a Critical Internationalism." *American Quarterly* 48.3 (September 1996): 475–90.

Di Leonardo, Micaela. "Margaret Mead and American Public Culture: The Empire that Dared Not Speak its Name." American Studies Association Annual Conference. 31 October 1997.

——. "Wild Women Don't Have the Blues: The American Pragmatics of the Primitive Woman." In *Exotics at Home: Anthropologies, Others, American Modernity*, 145–98. Chicago: University of Chicago Press, 1998.

Diana, Goffredo, and John Beverly. "These Are the Times We Have to Live In: An Interview with Roberto Fernández Retamar." *Critical Inquiry* 21 (1995): 411–33.

Díaz-Polanco, Hector. "La teoría indigenista y la integración." Im *Indigenismo, modernización y marginalidad: Una revisión crítica*, edited by Hector Díaz-Polanco et al., 11–42. Mexico City: Centro de Investigación para la Integración Social, 1979.

Díaz Quiñones, Arcadio. *El almuerzo en la hierba.* Rio Piedras, Puerto Rico: Ediciones Huracán, 1982.

——. "1898." *Hispanic American Historical Review* 78.4 (1998): 577–81.

Domecq, Brianda. *La insólita historia de la Santa de Cabora.* Mexico City: Editorial Planeta, 1990.

——. "Teresa Urrea: La Santa de Cabora." In *Tomóchic: La revolución adelantada*, edited by Jesús Vargas Valdez, 2:15–47. Ciudad Juárez, Chihuahua: Universidad Autónoma de Ciudad Juárez, 1994.

——. *The Astonishing Story of the Saint of Cabora.* Tempe: Bilingual Press, 1998.

Dorris, Michael. Introduction. *Ramona* by Helen Hunt Jackson. New York: Signet Classics, 1988.

Douglas, Ann. *The Feminization of American Culture.* New York: Knopf, 1977.

——. *Terrible Honesty: Mongrel Manhattan in the 1920s.* New York: Farrar, Straus and Giroux, 1995.

Drake, St. Clair. *The Redemption of Africa and Black Religion.* Chicago: Third World Press, 1970.

——. "Diaspora Studies and Pan-Africanism." In *Global Dimensions of the African Diaspora*, 451–509. Washington D. C.: Howard University Press, 1993.

Duara, Prasenjit, ed. *Decolonization: Perspectives from Now and Then.* New York: Routledge, 2004.

Du Bois, W. E. B. "The Conservation of Races." 1897. In *Classical Black Nationalism*, edited by Wilson Jeremiah Moses, 228–40. New York: New York University Press, 1996.

——. "The Present Outlook for the Dark Races of Mankind." 1900. In *The Oxford W. E. B. Du Bois Reader*, edited by Eric J. Sundquist, 47–54. New York: Oxford University Press, 1996.

——. "To the Nations of the World." 1900. In *The Oxford W. E. B. Du Bois Reader*, edited by Eric J. Sundquist, 625–27. New York: Oxford University Press, 1996.

——. *The Souls of Black Folk.* 1903. In *Three Negro Classics*, edited by John Hope Franklin. New York: Avon, 1965.

——. "The Color Line Belts the World." 1906. In *W. E. B. Du Bois: A Reader*, edited by David Levering Lewis, 42–43. New York: Henry Holt, 1995.

——. *The Quest of the Silver Fleece*. 1911. Reprint New York: Kraus-Thompson, 1974.

——. "Socialism and the Negro Problem." *New Review* (New York), 1 February 1913. In *Writings by W. E. B. Du Bois in Periodicals Edited by Others*, edited by Herbert Aptheker, 2:85–87. Millwood, N.Y.: Kraus-Thomson, 1982.

——. "Mexico." *The Crisis* 8 (June 1914): 79. Reprint *Selections from The Crisis*, edited by Herbert Aptheker, 1:78. Millwood, N.Y.: Kraus-Thomson, 1983.

——. "World War and the Color Line." *The Crisis* 9 (November 1914): 28–30. Reprint *Selections from The Crisis*, edited by Herbert Aptheker, 1:83–85. Millwood, N.Y.: Kraus-Thomson, 1983.

——. "The African Roots of War." 1915. *W. E. B. Du Bois: A Reader*, 642–51.

——. "Woman Suffrage." 1915. *W. E. B. Du Bois: A Reader*, 297–98.

——. "To the President of the United States." 3 August 1915. *The Correspondence of W. E. B. Du Bois*, edited by Herbert Aptheker, 1:211–12. Amherst: University of Massachusetts Press, 1973.

——. "Close Ranks." *The Crisis* 16 (July 1918): 111. Reprint *Selections from The Crisis*, 1:159.

——. "The Ballot." *The Crisis* 17 (December 1918): 62. Reprint *Selections from The Crisis*, 1:165.

——. "Letters from Dr. Du Bois." *The Crisis* 17 (February 1919): 163–66. Reprint *Selections from The Crisis*, 1:166–69.

——. "My Mission." *The Crisis* 18 (May 1919): 7–9. Reprint *Selections from The Crisis*, 1:186–88.

——. "Returning Soldiers." *The Crisis* 18 (May 1919): 13–14. Reprint *Selections from The Crisis*, 1:197.

——. *Darkwater: Voices from within the Veil*. 1920. In *The Oxford W. E. B. Du Bois Reader*, 481–623.

——. "The Rise of the West Indian." *The Crisis* (September 1920): 214–15. Reprint *Selections from The Crisis*, 1:273.

——. "An Open Letter to Warren Gamaliel Harding." *The Crisis* 21 (March 1921): 197–98. Reprint *Selections from The Crisis*, 1:294–95.

——. "To the World [Manifesto of the Second Pan-African Congress]." *The Crisis* 23 (November 1921): 5–10. Reprint *Selections from The Crisis*, 1:317–21.

——. "A Second Journey to Pan-Africa." *New Republic* (7 December 1921): 39–42. Reprint *Writings by W. E. B. Du Bois in Periodicals Edited by Others*, 2:158–62.

——. "France's Black Citizens in West Africa." *Current History* (New York) (22 July 1925): 559–64. *Writings by W. E. B. Du Bois in Periodicals Edited by Others*, 2:262.

——. "The Negro Mind Reaches Out." In *The New Negro*, 385–414. 1925. Reprint New York: Atheneum, 1992.

——. "Peace on Earth." *The Crisis* 31 (March 1926): 215–16. Reprint *Selections from The Crisis*, 2:435–36.

——. "Criteria of Negro Art." *The Crisis* 32 (October 1926): 290–97. Reprint *The Oxford W. E. B. Du Bois Reader*, 324–28.

——. "Italy and Abyssinia." *The Crisis* 32 (June 1926): 62–63. Reprint *Selections from the Crisis*, 2:441–42.

——. "War." *The Crisis* 33 (February 1927): 179. Reprint *Selections from the Crisis*, 2:457.

——. "The Pan-African Congresses: The Story of a Growing Movement." *The Crisis* 34 (October 1927): 263–64. Reprint *Selections from The Crisis*, 2:480–84.

——. *Dark Princess: A Romance.* 1928. Reprint Jackson: University Press of Mississippi, 1995.

——. [Letter to the *People* (Lahore, India)]. 10 January 1929. In *The Correspondence of W. E. B. Du Bois*, 1:386.

Dyer, Richard. *The Matter of Images: Essays on Representations.* New York: Routledge, 1993.

Edwards, Brent Hayes. *The Practice of Diaspora: Literature, Translation, and the Rise of Black Internationalism.* Cambridge: Harvard University Press, 2003.

Ellison, Julie. *Cato's Tears and the Making of Anglo-American Emotion.* Chicago: University of Chicago Press, 1999.

Escobar, Arturo, and Sonia E. Alvarez, ed. *The Making of Social Movements in Latin America: Identity, Strategy, and Democracy.* Boulder: Westview Press, 1992.

Fagg, John Edwin. *Pan Americanism.* Malabar, Florida: Robert E. Krieger, 1982.

Farmer, Paul. *The Uses of Haiti.* Monroe, Me.: Common Courage Press, 1994.

Fernández Retamar, Roberto. "The Modernity of Martí." In *José Martí, Revolutionary Democrat*, edited by Christopher Abel and Nissa Torrents, 1–15. London: Athlone Press, 1986.

——. "Caliban: Notes Toward a Discussion of Culture in Our America." In *Caliban and Other Essays.* Minneapolis: University of Minnesota Press, 1989.

Ferrer, Ada. "The Silence of Patriots: Race and Independence in Cuba, 1868–1898." "Our America" and the Gilded Age: José Martí's Chronicles of Imperial Critique. University of California, Irvine, 27–28 January 1995.

Flores, William V. "New Citizens, New Rights: Undocumented Immigrants and Latino Cultural Citizenship." *Latin American Perspectives* 30.2 (2003): 295–308.

Foner, Philip S. Introduction. In *Inside the Monster: Writings on the United States and American Imperialism.* By José Martí. Translated by Elinor Randall. Edited by Foner. New York: Monthly Review Press, 1975.

Ford, James. [Untitled Speech to the Seventh Congress of the Third Comintern]. 1928. In *American Communism and Black Americans: A Documentary History, 1919–1929*, edited by Philip S. Foner and James S. Allen, 181–82. Philadelphia: Temple University Press, 1987.

Forgacs, David. "National-Popular: Genealogy of a Concept." In *Formations of Nation and People*, 83–95. London: Routledge and Kegan Paul, 1984.

Foucault, Michel. *The Order of Things.* New York: Vintage, 1970.

——. *Discipline and Punish.* Translated by Alan Sheridan. New York: Vintage, 1978.

——. *The History of Sexuality.* Volume 1. Translated by Robert Hurley. New York: Vintage, 1978.

——. "Nietzsche, Genealogy, History." In *Aesthetics, Method and Epistemology,* edited by James D. Faubion, translated by Donald Brouchard and Sherry Simon, 369–91. Volume 2 of *Essential Works of Foucault, 1954–1984*. New York: New Press, 1998.

——. *"Society Must Be Defended": Lectures at the Collège de France, 1975–1976.* Translated by David Macey. New York: Picador, 2003.

Franco, Jean. "Beyond Ethnocentrism." In *Marxism and the Interpretation of Literature*, 1–17. Urbana: University of Illinois Press, 1988.

——. "Beyond Ethnocentrism: Gender, Power, and the Third World Intelligentsia." In *Colonial Discourse and Post-Colonial Theory*, edited by Patrick Williams and Laura Chrisman, 359–70. New York: Columbia University Press, 1994.

Frazier, E. Franklin. "Racial Self-Expression." In *Ebony and Topaz: A Collectanea*, edited by Charles S. Johnson, 119–21. New York: National Urban League, 1927.

——. "Traditions and Patterns of Negro Family Life in the United States." In *Race and Culture Contacts*, edited by E. B. Reuter, 191–207. New York: McGraw-Hill, 1934.

Fredrickson, George. *The Black Image in the White Mind.* New York: Harper and Row, 1971.

——. *Black Liberation: A Comparative History of Black Ideologies in the United States and South Africa.* New York: Oxford University Press, 1995.

Freeman, Joshua, et al. *Who Built America? Working People and the Nation's Economy, Politics, Culture, and Society.* Volume 2. New York: Pantheon Books, 1992.

Frías, Heriberto. *Tomochic.* 1892. Reprint Mexico City: Editorial Porrúa, 1968.

Fuchs, Barbara. *Romance.* New York: Routledge, 2004.

Gamio, Manuel. *Forjando patria: Pronacionalismo.* 1916. Reprint Mexico City: Editorial Porrúa, 1960.

——. *La población del Valle de Teotihuacán.* Mexico City: Talleres Gráficos de la Nación, 1922.

——. "Nacionalismo e internacionalismo." *Ethnos: Revista dedicada al estudio y mejoría de la población indígena de México* 1.2 (1923): 1–3.

——. "El Celibato y el Desarrollo de la Población en México." *Ethnos* 1.2 (1923): 66–70.

——. "The New Conquest." *Survey Graphic* 52.1 (1924): 192–94.

——. "El Aspecto Utilitario del Folklore." *Mexican Folkways* 1.1 (1925): 6–8.

——. *The Indian Basis of Mexican Civilization: Aspects of Mexican Civilization.* With José Vasconcelos. Chicago: University of Chicago Press, 1926.

——. *Mexican Immigration to the United States.* Chicago: University of Chicago Press, 1930.

——. *The Mexican Immigrant: His Life-Story.* Edited by Robert Redfield. Chicago: University of Chicago Press, 1931.

——. *De vidas dolientes.* Mexico City: Ediciones Botas, 1937.

——. *El inmigrante mexicano—la historia de su vida: Entrevistas completas, 1926–1927.* Edited by Devra Weber, Roberto Melville, and Juan Vicente Palerm. Mexico City: University of California, Institute for Mexico and the United States, 2002.

García, Kay S. "Part IV: Brianda Domecq." In *Broken Bars: New Perspectives from Mexican Women Writers*, 157–204. Albuquerque: University of New Mexico Press, 1994.

García Canclini, Néstor. *Culturas híbridas: Estrategias para entrar y salir de la modernidad.* Mexico City: Editorial Grijalbo, 1990.

Gates, Henry Louis, Jr. "Afterword: Zora Neale Hurston, 'A Negro Way of Saying.'" In *Mules and Men* by Zora Neale Hurston, 287–97. New York: Harper Perennial, 1990.

———. "The Trope of a New Negro and the Reconstruction of the Image of the Black." In *The New American Studies,* edited by Phillip Fisher, 319–45. Berkeley: University of California Press, 1991.

———. "Critical Fanonism." *Critical Inquiry* 17.3 (1991): 457–70.

———. "*Their Eyes Were Watching God:* Hurston and the Speakerly Text." In *Zora Neale Hurston: Critical Perspectives Past and Present,* edited by Gates, Jr. and K. A. Appiah, 154–99. New York: Amistad, 1993.

Geiss, Immanuel. *The Pan-African Movement: A History of Pan-Africanism in America, Europe, and Africa.* New York: Africana, 1974.

Gill, Mario. "Teresa Urrea, La Santa de Cabora." *Historia Mexicana* 24 6:4 (April–June, 1957): 626–44.

Gillman, Susan. "The Mulatto, Tragic or Triumphant? The Nineteenth-Century American Race Melodrama." In *The Culture of Sentiment,* edited by Shirley Samuels, 221–43. New York: Oxford University Press, 1992.

Gilroy, Paul. *There Ain't No Black in the Union Jack.* Chicago: University of Chicago Press, 1991.

———. *The Black Atlantic: Modernity and Double Consciousness.* Cambridge: Harvard University Press, 1993.

———. "Bio-Politics and Black Solidarity." Center for Cultural Studies, University of California at Santa Cruz. 16 May 1996.

González, Aníbal. "El intelectual y las metáforas: *Lucía Jerez* de José Martí." *Texto Crítico* 12:34–35 (January–December 1986): 136–57.

González, Juan. *Harvest of Empire: A History of Latinos in America.* New York: Penguin, 2000.

González, Luis. "El liberalismo triunfante." *Historia General de México,* volume 2, edited by Daniel Cosío Villegas, 897–1015. Mexico City: El Colegio de México, 1976.

González Echevarría, Roberto. *Alejo Carpentier: The Pilgrim at Home.* New York: Cornell University Press, 1977.

———. *The Voice of the Masters.* Austin: University of Texas Press, 1985.

González Gamio, Angeles. *Manuel Gamio: Una lucha sin final.* Mexico City: Universidad Nacional Autónoma de México, 1987.

Gooding-Williams, Robert. "Outlaw, Appiah, and Du Bois' 'The Conservation of Races.'" In *W. E. B. Du Bois on Race and Culture,* edited by Bernard Bell et al. New York: Routledge, 1996.

Gramsci, Antonio. *Selections from the Prison Notebooks.* Translated by Quintin Hoare and Geoffrey Nowell Smith. New York: International Publishers, 1971.

Greenberg, Cheryl Lynn. "Depression in the Age of Prosperity." In *"Or Does it Explode?": Black Harlem in the Great Depression,* 13–41. New York: Oxford University Press, 1991.

Guillén, Nicolás. *Obra Poetica, 1922–1958*. 2d ed. Havana: Editorial Letras Cubanas, 1980.

Guha, Ranajit. "Preface." *Selected Subaltern Studies*, edited by Ranajit Guha and Gayatri Spivak. New York: Oxford University Press, 1988.

——. *Dominance Without Hegemony: History and Power in Colonial India*. Cambridge: Harvard University Press, 1997.

Gunn, Drewy Wayne. *Escritores Norteamericanos y Britanicos en México, 1556–1973*. Mexico City: Fondo de Cultura Económica, 1977.

Gupta, Akhil, and James Ferguson. "Discipline and Practice: 'The Field' as Site, Method, and Location in Anthropology." In *Anthropological Locations: Boundaries and Grounds of a Field Science*, edited by Akhil Gupta and James Ferguson, 1–46. Berkeley: University of California Press, 1997.

Gutiérrez, Ramon, and Genaro Padilla, eds. *Recovering the U.S. Hispanic Literary Heritage*. Houston: Arte Público Press, 1993.

Gutiérrez-Jones, Carl. *Rethinking the Borderlands: Between Chicano Culture and Legal Discourse*. Berkeley: University of California Press, 1995.

Hale, Charles T. "Political and Social Ideas in Latin America, 1870–1930." In *The Cambridge History of Latin America*, volume 4, edited by Leslie Bethell, 370–453. New York: Cambridge University Press, 1986.

Hall, Stuart. "On Postmodernism and Articulation: An Interview with Stuart Hall." *Journal of Communication Inquiry* 10:2 (1986): 52–55.

——. "Cultural Studies and Its Theoretical Legacies." In *Cultural Studies*, edited by Lawrence Grossberg, Cary Nelson, and Paula Treichler, 277–94. New York: Routledge, 1992.

——. "New Ethnicities." In *Black British Cultural Studies*, edited by Houston A. Baker, Manthia Diawara, and Ruth H. Lindeborg, 163–72. Chicago: University of Chicago Press, 1996.

——. "Cultural Studies and the Politics of Internationalization: An Interview with Stuart Hall by Kuan-Hsing Chen." In *Stuart Hall: Critical Dialogues in Cultural Studies*, edited by David Morley and Kuan-Hsing Chen, 392–408. New York: Routledge, 1996.

——. "When Was 'The Post Colonial'? Thinking at the Limit." In *The Post-Colonial Question: Common Skies, Divided Horizons*, edited by Ian Chambers and Lidia Curti, 242–60. New York: Routledge, 1996.

Hall, Stuart, Charles Critcher, Tony Jefferson, John Clarke, and Brian Roberts. *Policing the Crisis: Mugging, the State, and Law and Order*. London: Macmillan, 1978.

Halperín Donghi, Tulio. *The Contemporary History of Latin America*. Translated by John Charles Chasteen. Durham: Duke University Press, 1993.

Halttunen, Karen. *Confidence Men and Painted Women*. New Haven: Yale University Press, 1982.

Harris, Marvin. *The Rise of Anthropological Theory*. New York: Thomas Y. Crowell, 1968.

Harris, William H. *Keeping the Faith: A. Philip Randolph, Milton P. Webster, and the*

Brotherhood of Sleeping Car Porters, 1925–37. Urbana: University of Illinois Press, 1977.

Hawthorne, Nathaniel. *The Scarlet Letter: A Romance.* New York: Penguin, 1983.

Hedrick, Joan. *Harriet Beecher Stowe: A Life.* New York: Oxford University Press, 1994.

Helg, Aline. *Our Rightful Share: The Afro-Cuban Struggle for Equality, 1886–1912.* Chapel Hill: University of North Carolina Press, 1995.

Hemenway, Robert E. *Zora Neale Hurston: A Literary Biography.* Urbana: University of Illinois Press, 1977.

Hernández, Graciela. "Multiple Subjectivities and Strategic Positionality: Zora Neale Hurston's Experimental Ethnographies." In *Women Writing Culture,* edited by Ruth Behar and Deborah Gordon, 148–65. Berkeley: University of California Press, 1996.

Herskovits, Melville. *The Myth of the Negro Past.* Boston: Beacon Press, 1941.

Hesiod. *Theogony.* Translated by Norman O. Brown. Indianapolis: Bobbs-Merrill, 1953.

Higham, John. *Strangers in the Land: Patterns of American Nativism.* New York: Greenwood Press, 1981.

Hobsbawm, Eric. *Nations and Nationalism Since 1780: Programme, Myth, Reality.* New York: Cambridge University Press, 1990.

Hofstadter, Richard. *Social Darwinism in American Thought, 1860–1915.* Philadelphia: University of Pennsylvania Press, 1944.

Holland, R. F. *European Decolonization, 1918–1981: An Introductory Survey.* London: Macmillan, 1985.

Honig, Bonnie. "Immigrant America? How Foreignness 'Solves' Democracy's Problems." *Social Text* 56 (1998): 1–27.

hooks, bell. "Representing Whiteness in the Black Imagination." In *Cultural Studies,* edited by Lawrence Grossberg and Cary Nelson, 338–46. New York: Routledge, 1992.

Howard, June. "What Is Sentimentality?" *American Literary History* 11.1 (1999): 63–81.

Hu-DeHart, Evelyn. *Yaqui Resistance and Survival: The Struggle for Land and Autonomy, 1821–1910.* Madison: University of Wisconsin Press, 1984.

——. "Peasant Rebellion in the Northwest: The Yaqui Indians of Sonora, 1740–1976." In *Riot, Rebellion, and Revolution: Rural Social Conflict in Mexico,* 141–75. Princeton: Princeton University Press, 1988.

Huggins, Nathan. *Voices from the Harlem Renaissance.* New York: Oxford University Press, 1976.

Hughes, Langston. *The Big Sea.* New York: Thunder's Mouth Press, 1986.

——. *The Collected Poems of Langston Hughes.* Edited by Arnold Rampersad. New York: Vintage Books, 1994.

Hunt, Michael. *Ideology and U.S. Foreign Policy.* New Haven: Yale University Press, 1987.

Hurlburt, Laurance P. *The Mexican Muralists in the United States.* Albuquerque: University of New Mexico Press, 1989.

Hurston, Zora Neale. "Characteristics of Negro Expression." 1934. In *The Sanctified Church: The Folklore Writings of Zora Neale Hurston*, 41–78. Berkeley: Turtle Island, 1981.

———. *Mules and Men.* 1935. Reprint New York: Harper Perennial, 1990.

———. *Their Eyes Were Watching God.* 1937. Reprint New York: Harper Perennial, 1990.

———. *Tell My Horse.* Philadelphia: J. B. Lippincott, 1938.

———. *Dust Tracks on a Road.* 1942. Reprint Urbana: University of Illinois Press, 1984.

———. "High John De Conqueror." 1943. In *The Sanctified Church*, 69–78.

Hyatt, Marshall. *Franz Boas, Social Activist: The Dynamics of Ethnicity.* Westport, Conn.: Greenwood Press, 1990.

Jackson, Helen Hunt. *Ramona.* 1884. Reprint New York: Signet Classics, 1988.

Jameson, Fredric. *Marxism and Form.* Princeton: Princeton University Press, 1971.

———. *The Political Unconscious: Narrative as a Socially Symbolic Act.* Ithaca: Cornell University Press, 1981.

———. "Cognitive Mapping." In *Marxism and the Interpretation of Culture*, edited by Cary Nelson and Lawrence Grossberg, 347–60. Urbana: University of Illinois Press, 1988.

———. "On 'Cultural Studies.' " *Social Text* 34 (1993): 17–52.

Javier Morales, Carlos. Introduction. *Lucía Jerez.* Madrid: Ediciones Catedra, 1994.

Joaquín Blanco, José. *Se llamaba Vasconcelos: Una evocación crítica.* Mexico City: Fondo de Cultura Económica, 1977.

Johnson, Beverly J. "Africanisms and the Study of Folklore." In *Africanisms in American Culture*, edited by Joseph Holloway, 211–24. Bloomington: Indiana University Press, 1990.

Johnson, Charles S. "The New Frontage on American Life." In *The New Negro*, edited by Alain Locke, 278–98. New York: Atheneum, 1992.

Johnson, John J. *Latin America in Caricature.* Austin: University of Texas Press, 1980.

Jones, Jean. *The League Against Imperialism.* London: Socialist History Society, 1996.

Joseph, Gilbert M. *Revolution from Without: Yucatan, Mexico, and the United States, 1880–1924.* New York: Cambridge University Press, 1982.

Joshi, Vijaya Chandra. Introduction. *Lala Lajpat Rai: Writings and Speeches.* 2 volumes. Edited by Vijaya Chandra Joshi. Dehli: University Publishers, 1966.

Kaplan, Amy. *The Social Construction of American Realism.* Chicago: University of Chicago Press, 1988.

———. "Romancing the Empire: The Embodiment of American Masculinity in the Popular Historical Novel of the 1890s." *American Literary History* 2:4 (1990): 659–90.

Kaplan, Amy, and Donald Pease, eds. *Cultures of United States Imperialism.* Durham: Duke University Press, 1993.

Kaushik, Karuna. *Russian Revolution and Indian Nationalism: Studies of Lajpat Rai, Subhas Chandra Bose and Rammanohar Lohia.* Delhi: Chanakya Publications, 1984.

Kelley, Robin D. G. " 'Afric's Sons with Banner Red': African American Communists and the Politics of Culture, 1919–1934." In *Imagining Home: Class, Culture and Nationalism in the African Diaspora*, edited by Sidney Lemelle and Robin Kelley, 35–54. New York: Verso, 1994.

Kinmont, Alexander. *Twelve Lectures on the Natural History of Man, and the Rise and Progress of Philosophy*. Cincinnati: U. P. James, 1839.

Klor de Alva, J. Jorge. "The Postcolonization of the (Latin) American Experience: A Reconsideration of 'Colonialism,' 'Postcolonialism,' and 'Mestizaje.'" In *After Colonialism: Imperial Histories and Postcolonial Displacements*, edited by Gyan Prakash, 241–75. Princeton: Princeton University Press, 1995.

Knight, Alan. "Racism, Revolution and *Indigenismo*: Mexico, 1910–40." In *The Idea of Race in Latin America, 1870–1940*, edited by Richard Graham, 71–114. Austin: University of Texas Press, 1990.

——. "Revolutionary Project, Recalcitrant People: Mexico, 1910–1940." In *The Revolutionary Process in Mexico: Essays on Political and Social Change, 1880–1940*, edited by Jaime E. Rodríguez O., 227–64. Los Angeles: UCLA Latin American Center Publications, 1990.

——. "Popular Culture and the Revolutionary State in Mexico, 1910–1940." *Hispanic American Historical Review* 74.3 (August 1994): 393–444.

Kutzinski, Vera. *Against the American Grain: Myth and History in William Carlos Williams, Jay Wright, and Nicolás Guillén*. Baltimore: Johns Hopkins University Press, 1987.

——. "Commentary: American Literary History as Spatial Practice." *American Literary History* 4 (1992): 550–57.

——. *Sugar's Secrets: Race and the Erotics of Cuban Nationalism*. Charlottesville: University of Virginia Press, 1994.

Langley, J. Ayo. "Pan-Africanism in Paris, 1924–36." *Journal of Modern African Studies* 7.1 (1969): 69–94.

Langley, Lester D. *Struggle for the American Mediterranean: United States–European Rivalry in the Gulf-Caribbean, 1776–1904*. Athens: University of Georgia Press, 1976.

Larralde, Carlos. "Santa Teresa, A Chicana Mystic." *Grito del Sol* 3:2 (April–June 1978): 9–114.

Larsen, Neil. *Reading North by South: On Latin American Literature, Culture and Politics*. Minneapolis: University of Minnesota Press, 1995.

Latin American Subaltern Studies Group. "Founding Statement." *Dispositio/n* 19.46 (1994): 1–11.

Lazo, Rodrigo. "Filibustering an Empire: Transamerican Writing and U.S. Expansionism." Ph.D. diss., University of Maryland, 1998.

Lemann, Nicholas. *The Promised Land: The Great Migration and How It Changed America*. New York: Knopf, 1991.

Lemelle Sidney J., and Robin D. G. Kelley, eds. *Imagining Home: Class, Culture and Nationalism in the African Diaspora*. New York: Verso, 1994.

Lewis, David Levering. *When Harlem Was in Vogue*. New York: Oxford University Press, 1981.

——. *W. E. B. Du Bois: Biography of a Race, 1868–1919*. New York: Holt, 1993.

——, ed. *W. E. B. Du Bois: A Reader*. New York: Holt, 1995.

——. *W. E. B. Du Bois: The Fight for Equality and the American Century, 1919–1963.* New York: Henry Holt, 2000.

Lewis, Wyndham. *Paleface: The Philosophy of the 'Melting Pot.'* London: Chatto and Windus, 1929.

Lewy, Guenter. *Religion and Revolution.* New York: Oxford University Press, 1974.

Leys, Ruth. "The Real Miss Beauchamp: Gender and the Subject of Imitation." In *Feminists Theorize the Political,* 172–203. New York: Routledge, 1992.

Lienhard, Martin. "*La Noche de los Mayas:* Indigenous Mesoamericans in Cinema and Literature, 1917–1943." *Journal of Latin American Cultural Studies* 13:1 (2004): 35–62.

Limón, José. "Nation, Love and Labor Lost: Katherine Anne Porter and Manuel Gamio." In *American Encounters: Greater Mexico, the United States, and the Erotics of Culture,* 35–71. Boston: Beacon Press, 1998.

Lionnet, Françoise. "Autoethnography: The An-archic Style of *Dust Tracks on a Road.*" In *The Bounds of Race: Perspectives on Hegemony and Resistance,* edited by Dominick La Capra, 164–95. Ithaca: Cornell University Press, 1991.

Lipsitz, George. "The Possessive Investment in Whiteness." *American Quarterly* 47:3 (1995): 369–87.

Liss, Sheldon B. *Marxist Thought in Latin America.* Berkeley: University of California Press, 1984.

Lively, Adam. "Continuity and Radicalism in American Black Nationalist Thought, 1914–1929." *Journal of American Studies* 18.2 (1984): 207–35.

Locke, Alain, ed. *The New Negro.* New York: Atheneum, 1992.

Lomnitz, Claudio. *Deep Mexico, Silent Mexico: An Anthropology of Nationalism.* Minneapolis: University of Minnesota Press, 2001.

López-Baralt, Mercedes. "La tercera salida del *Tun tun de pasa y grifería.*" In *Tun tun de pasa y grifería* by Luis Palés Matos, 13–42. San Juan, Puerto Rico: Editorial de la Universidad de Puerto Rico, 1993.

Lott, Eric. "White Like Me: Racial Cross-Dressing and the Construction of American Whiteness." In *Cultures of United States Imperialism,* edited by Amy Kaplan and Donald E. Pease, 474–95. Durham: Duke University Press, 1993.

Lovato, Roberto. "Envisioning Another World: *Integración Desde Abajo.*" *The Nation* (6 March 2006): 22, 24, 26.

Lowe, Lisa. *Immigrant Acts: On Asian American Cultural Politics.* Durham: Duke University Press, 1996.

Lubiano, Wahneema. "Black Nationalism, Black Common Sense, and Popular Culture." University of California, Santa Cruz. 1 February 1996.

Macías, Anna. "Felipe Carrillo Puerto and Women's Liberation in Mexico." In *Latin American Women: Historical Perspectives,* edited by Asunción Lavrin, 286–301. Westport, Conn.: Greenwood Press, 1978.

——. *Against All Odds: The Feminist Movement in Mexico to 1940.* Westport, Conn.: Greenwood Press, 1982.

Maharaj, Sarat. "The Congo Is Flooding the Acropolis: Art in Britain of the Immigrations." *Third Text* 15 (1991): 77–90.

Marable, Manning. *W. E. B. Du Bois: Black Radical Democrat.* Boston: Twayne, 1986.

Mariátegui, José Carlos. *Siete Ensayos de Interpretación de la Realidad Peruana.* Caracas: Biblioteca Ayacucho, 1979.

Marsden, Michael T. "Helen Hunt Jackson: Docudramatist of the American Indian." *Markham Review* 10 (1980–81): 15–19.

Martí, José. *Abdala: Escrito expresamente para la patria.* 1869. In *José Martí: Obras Completas Edición Crítica*, 1: 22–33. Havana: Centro de Estudios Martianos, 2000.

——. *Abdala* [Selections]. In *José Martí: Selected Writings*, edited and translated by Esther Allen, 3–7. New York: Penguin, 2002.

——. "El Poema del Niágara." 1882. In *Obra Literaria*, edited by Cintio Vitier, 205–16. Caracas: Biblioteca Ayacucho, 1978.

———. "The Poem of Niagara." 1882. In *On Art and Literature*, edited by Philip S. Foner, translated by Elinor Randall et al., 308–27. New York: Monthly Review Press, 1982.

——. *Lucía Jerez.* 1885. In *Obra Literaria*, edited by Cintio Vitier, 107–73. Caracas: Biblioteca Ayacucho, 1978.

——. "The Indians in the United States." 1885. In *Inside the Monster by José Martí: Writings on the United States and American Imperialism*, edited by Philip S. Foner, translated by Elinor Randall et al., 215–25. New York: Monthly Review Press, 1975.

——. "Correspondencia." *El Partido Liberal* (Mexico City) 2 August 1886. In *Obras completas*, 7:36–45. Havana: Editorial de Ciencias Sociales, 1975.

——. "The Cutting Case." *El Partido Liberal*, 20 August 1886. In *José Martí: Selected Writings*, 176–82.

——. "El Terremoto de Charleston." 1886. In *Obras Completas*, 1: 1741–51. Havana: Editorial Lex, 1946.

——. "The Earthquake at Charleston." In *The Oxford Book of Latin American Essays*, edited by Ilan Stavans, translated by Jo Anne Engelbert, 37–47. New York: Oxford University Press, 1997.

——. "Fiestas de la Estatua de la Libertad." 1887. In *Obras completas*, 1: 1764–78.

——. "Dedication of the Statue of Liberty." In *Inside the Monster: Writings on the United States and American Imperialism*, edited by Philip Foner, translated by Luis A. Baralt, 133–57. New York: Monthly Review Press, 1975.

——. Introduction. 1888. *Ramona: Novela Americana* by Helen Hunt Jackson. Translated by José Martí. New York: José Martí, 1888. Reprint in *Obras Completas*, 24: 203–05. Havana: Editorial Nacional de Cuba, 1965.

——. "Vindicación de Cuba." 1889. In *Cuba, Nuestra América y los Estados Unidos*, edited by Roberto Fernández Retamar, 3–9. Mexico City: Siglo Veintiuno Editores, 1973.

——. "A Vindication of Cuba." In *José Martí: Selected Writings*, edited and translated by Esther Allen, 261–67. New York: Penguin Books, 2002.

——. "Conferencia Internacional Americana." *La Nación* [Buenos Aires] 8 November 1889. In *Obras Completas*, 2:118–125.

———. Letters to Gonzalo de Quesada. October–December 1889. In *Obras Completas*, 2:189–98.

———. "El Congreso de Washington." *La Nación* [Buenos Aires] 19 December 1889. In *Obras Completas*, 2:125–29.

———. "Congreso Internacional de Washington. *La Nación* [Buenos Aires] 20 December, 1889. In *Obras Completas*, 2:137–44.

———. "La Conferencia Americana." *La Nación* [Buenos Aires] 24 January 1890. In *Obras Completas*, 2:145–51.

———. "La Política Internacional de los Estados Unidos." *La Nación* [Buenos Aires] 3 February 1890. In *Obras Completas*, 2:151–53.

———. "El Ferrocarril Interamericano y la Conferencia Pan-Americana." *El Partido Liberal* [Mexico City] 18 December 1890. In *Obras Completas*, 2:153–55.

———. "La Conferencia de Washington." *La Nación* [Buenos Aires] 9 May 1890. In *Obras Completas*, 2:156–61.

———. "La Conferencia de Washington." *La Nación* [Buenos Aires] 31 May 1890. In *Obras Completas*, 2:161–175.

———. "El Congreso de Washington." *La Nación* [Buenos Aires] 15 June 1890. In *Obras Completas*, 2: 176–180.

———. "Madre América." 1889. In *Cuba, Nuestra América, y los Estados Unidos*, 121–29.

———. "Mother America." In *Our America*, edited by Philip Foner, 69–83. New York: Monthly Review Press, 1977.

———. "Nuestra América." 1891. In *Cuba, Nuestra América, y los Estados Unidos*, 111–20.

———. "Nuestra América." In *Sus mejores páginas*, 87–93. Mexico City: Editorial Porrúa, 1970.

———. "Our America." *Our America*, edited by Philip Foner, 84–94. New York: Monthly Review Press, 1977.

———. "Poema XXX." *Versos sencillos*. 1891. In *Obra literaria*, edited by Cintio Vitier, 41–42.

———. "With All, for the Good of All." 1891. In *José Martí Reader: Writings on the Americas*, edited by Deborah Shnookal and Mirta Muñiz, 132–44. New York: Ocean Press, 1999.

———. "My Race." 1893. In *José Martí: Selected Writings*. 318–21.

———. "Los cubanos de Jamaica y los revolucionarios de Haití." 1894. In *Obras Completas*, 1:494–96.

Martin, Ronald E. *The Languages of Difference: American Writers and Anthropologists Reconfigure the Primitive, 1878–1940*. Newark: University of Delaware Press, 2005.

Martín Bárbero, Jesús. *Communication, Culture, and Hegemony*. London: Sage, 1993.

Martínez, Juan A. *Cuban Art and National Identity: The Vanguardia Painters, 1927–1950*. Gainesville: University Press of Florida, 1994.

Masdeu, Jesús. *La Raza Triste*. Havana: Rambla, Bouza, 1924.

Masiello, Francine. "Rethinking Neocolonial Aesthetics: Literature, Politics and Intellectual Community in Cuba's *Revista de Avance.*" *Latin American Research Review* 28.2 (1993): 3–32.

Massey, Doreen. *Space, Place, and Gender.* Cambridge, England: Polity Press, 1994.

Mathes, Valerie Sherer. *Helen Hunt Jackson and Her Indian Reform Legacy.* Norman: University of Oklahoma Press, 1990.

Maxwell, William J. *New Negro, Old Left: African American Writing and Communism Between the Wars.* New York: Columbia University Press, 1999.

May, Antoinette. *Helen Hunt Jackson: A Lonely Voice of Conscience.* San Francisco: Chronicle Books, 1987.

McCole, John. *Walter Benjamin and the Antinomies of Tradition.* Ithaca: Cornell University Press, 1993.

McKay, Claude. "Speech to the Fourth Congress of the Third Communist International, Moscow." 1922. In *The Passion of Claude McKay: Selected Poetry and Prose, 1912–1948,* edited by Wayne F. Cooper, 91–95. New York: Schocken Books, 1973.

———. *The Negroes in America.* 1923. Edited by Alan L. McLeod. Translated by Robert J. Winter. Port Washington, N.Y.: National University Publications, 1979.

———. *Home to Harlem.* 1928. Reprint Boston: Northeastern University Press, 1987.

McLellan, David, ed. "Antonio Gramsci." In *Marxism: Essential Writings,* 264–82. New York: Oxford University Press, 1988.

Meléndez, Concha. *La novela indianista en Hispanoamérica.* Madrid: Hernando, 1934.

Mendieta y Núñez, Lucio. "El renacimiento del nacionalismo." *Ethnos: Revista dedicada al estudio y mejoría de la población indígena de México* 1.1 & 2 (1925): 3–5.

Menéndez, Miguel Angel. *Nayar.* Mexico City: Editorial Porrúa, 1978.

———. *Nayar.* Translated by Angel Flores. New York: Farrar and Rinehart, 1942.

Mignolo, Walter D. "Afterward: From Colonial Discourse to Colonial Semiosis." *Dispositio* 14.36–38 (1989): 333–37.

———. "Colonial and Postcolonial Discourse: Cultural Critique or Academic Colonialism?" *Latin American Research Review* 28.3 (1993): 120–33.

———. "Are Subaltern Studies Postmodern or Postcolonial? The Politics and Sensibilities of Geo-Cultural Locations." *Dispositio/n* 19.46 (1994): 45–73.

———. "Coloniality at Large." Latin American Studies Association International Congress, Chicago, 24–26 September 1998.

———. *Local Histories/Global Designs: Coloniality, Subaltern Knowledges, and Border Thinking.* Princeton: Princeton University Press, 2000.

Miller, Francesca. "Feminism and Social Motherhood, 1890–1938." In *Latin American Women and the Search for Social Justice,* 68–109. Hanover, N.H.: University of New England Press, 1991.

———. "Feminisms and Transnationalism." Unpublished essay, 1998.

Mitter, Partha. "Primitivism." In *Encyclopedia of Cultural Anthropology.* Volume 3, edited by David Lewinson and Melvin Ember, 1029–32. New York: Henry Holt, 1996.

Molloy, Sylvia. "Too Wilde for Comfort." *Social Text* 31/32 10.2–3 (1992): 187–201.

——. "His America, Our America: José Martí Reads Whitman." In *Breaking Bounds: Whitman and American Cultural Studies,* edited by Betsy Erkkila and Jay Grossman, 83–91. New York: Oxford University Press, 1996.

Monsiváis, Carlos. "Los milenarismos." In *Las culturas de fin de siglo,* edited by Josefina Ludmer, 164–83. Buenos Aires: Beatriz Viterbo Editora, 1994.

——. "Millenarianisms in Mexico: From Cabora to Chiapas." In *Mexican Postcards,* 129–47. New York: Verso, 1997.

Montejano, David. *Anglos and Mexicans in the Making of Texas, 1836–1986.* Austin: University of Texas Press, 1987.

Montero, Oscar. "Pan-Americanism's Empty Train." In *José Martí: An Introduction,* 85–104. New York: Palgrave, 2004.

Moore, Robin D. *Nationalizing Blackness: Afrocubanismo and Artistic Revolution in Havana, 1920–1940.* Pittsburgh: University of Pittsburgh Press, 1997.

Morrison, Toni. *Playing in the Dark: Whiteness in the Literary Imagination.* Cambridge: Harvard University Press, 1992.

Moses, Wilson. *The Golden Age of Black Nationalism, 1850–1925.* New York: Oxford University Press, 1978.

——. "The Concept of Messianism, Sacred and Secular." In *Black Messiahs and Uncle Toms,* 1–16. University Park: Pennsylvania State University Press, 1982.

Moylan, Michelle. "Reading the Indians: The Ramona Myth in American Culture." *Prospects* 18 (1993): 153–87.

Mullen, Bill V. "Du Bois, *Dark Princess,* and the Afro-Asian International." *Positions* 11.1 (2003): 217–39.

Mullen, Edward J. *Langston Hughes in the Hispanic World and Haiti.* Hamden, Conn.: Archon, 1977.

——. *Carlos Pellicer.* Boston: Twayne, 1977.

Nahmad Sittón, Salomón, and Thomas Weaver. "Manuel Gamio, el Primer Antropólogo Aplicado y Su Relación con la Antropología Norteamericana." *América Indígena* 50.4 (1990): 291–321.

Nava, Alex. "Teresa Urrea: Mexican Mystic, Healer and Apocalyptic Revolutionary." *Journal of the American Academy of Religion* 73.2 (2005): 497–519.

Nelson, Cary. *Repression and Recovery: Modern American Poetry and the Politics of Cultural Memory.* Madison: University of Wisconsin Press, 1989.

Noble, Marianne. "The Ecstasies of Sentimental Wounding in *Uncle Tom's Cabin.*" *Yale Journal of Criticism* 10.2 (1997): 295–320.

Ong, Aihwa. "Cultural Citizenship as Subject-Making: Immigrants Negotiate Racial and Cultural Boundaries in the United States." *Current Anthropology* 37.5 (1996): 737–62.

——. *Flexible Citizenship: The Cultural Logics of Transnationality.* Durham: Duke University Press, 1999.

Ortiz, Fernando. *Contrapunteo cubano del tabaco y el azúcar.* Havana: Jesús Montero, 1940.

Outlaw, Lucius. " 'Conserve' Races? In Defense of W. E. B. Du Bois." In *W. E. B.*

Du Bois on Race and Culture, edited by Bernard Bell et al., 15–37. New York: Routledge, 1996.

Palés Matos, Luis. *Tun tun de pasa y grifería.* 1925–37. Reprint San Juan, Puerto Rico: Editorial de la Universidad de Puerto Rico, 1993.

Park, Robert E. *Race and Culture.* Glencoe, Ill.: Free Press, 1950.

——. "Human Migration and the Marginal Man." *American Journal of Sociology* 33.6 (1928): 881–93.

Parry, Benita. "Resistance Theory/Theorizing Resistance, or Two Cheers for Nativism." In *Colonial Discourse/Postcolonial Theory,* edited by Francis Barker, Peter Hulme, and Margaret Iversen, 172–96. Manchester: Manchester University Press, 1994.

Pedroso, Regino. *Orbita de Regino Pedroso.* Havana: Unión de Escritores y Artistas de Cuba, 1975.

Pérez, Jr., Louis A. *Cuba Under the Platt Amendment, 1902–1934.* Pittsburgh: University of Pittsburgh Press, 1986.

——. "Between Meanings and Memories of 1898." *Orbis* 42.4 (1998): 501–17.

Pérez Montfort, Ricardo. "Indigenismo, Hispanismo, y Panamericanismo en la Cultura Popular Mexicana de 1920 a 1940." In *Cultura e identidad nacional,* 343–83. Mexico City: Fondo de Cultura Económica, 1994.

——. *Estampas de nacionalismo popular mexicano: Ensayos sobre cultura popular y nacionalismo.* Mexico City: CIESAS, 1994.

Perus, Françoise. "Martí y el modernismo." *Manatí* 11 (1977): 8–19.

Phillips, George Harwood. *Chiefs and Challengers: Indian Resistance and Cooperation in Southern California.* Berkeley: University of California Press, 1975.

Pieterse, Jan Nederveen, and Bhikhu Parekh. "Shifting Imaginaries: Decolonization, Internal Decolonization, Postcoloniality." In *The Decolonization of Imagination,* edited by Jan Nederveen Pieterse and Bhikhu Parekh, 1–19. London: Zed, 1995.

Pitt, Leonard. *The Decline of the Californios.* Berkeley: University of California Press, 1965.

Plummer, Brenda Gayle. "The Afro-American Response to the Occupation of Haiti, 1915–34." *Phylon* 43.2 (1982): 125–43.

——. "Firmin and Martí at the Intersection of Pan Americanism and Pan Africanism." "Our America" and the Gilded Age: José Martí's Chronicles of Imperial Critique. U. C. Irvine, 27–28 January 1995.

Pocock, J. G. A. "The Ideal of Citizenship Since Classical Times." *Queen's Quarterly* 99.1 (1992): 33–55.

Podestá, Guido A. "An Ethnographic Reproach to the Theory of the Avant Garde: Modernity and Modernism in Latin America and the Harlem Renaissance." *MLN* 106.2 (1991): 395–422.

Porter, Carolyn. "What We Know That We Don't Know: Remapping American Literary Studies." *American Literary History* 6:3 (1994): 467–526.

Posnock, Ross. "How It Feels to Be a Problem: Du Bois, Fanon, and the 'Impossible Life' of the Black Intellectual." *Critical Inquiry* 23 (1997): 323–49.

Poyo, Gerald E. "José Martí, Architect of Social Unity in the Emigré Communities of the United States." In *José Martí, Revolutionary Democrat*, edited by Christopher Abel and Nissa Torrents, 16–31. London: Athlone Press, 1986.

Pratt, Mary Louise. "Women, Literature and National Brotherhood." In *Women, Culture and Politics in Latin America: Seminar on Feminism and Culture in Latin America*, 48–73. Berkeley: University of California Press, 1990.

———. *Imperial Eyes: Travel Writing and Transculturation*. New York: Routledge, 1992.

———. "Edward Said's *Culture and Imperialism:* A Symposium." *Social Text* 40 (1994): 2–10.

———. " 'Don't Interrupt Me': The Gender Essay as Conversation and Countercanon." In *Reinterpreting the Spanish American Essay,* edited by Doris Meyer, 10–26. Austin: University of Texas Press, 1995.

Prieto, René. "The Literature of *Indigenismo.*" In *The Cambridge History of Latin American Literature.* Volume 2: *The Twentieth Century,* 138–63. New York: Cambridge University Press, 1996.

Rabasa, José, and Javier Sanjinés. "Introduction: The Politics of Subaltern Studies." *Dispositio/n* 19.46 (1994): v–xi.

Rai, Lala Lajpat. *Lala Lajpat Rai: Writings and Speeches.* Edited by Vijaya Chandra Joshi. 2 vols. Dehli: University Publishers, 1966.

———. *Unhappy India.* 1928. Reprint New York: AMS Press, 1972.

Rama, Angel. "La Dialéctica de la Modernidad en José Martí." In *Estudios Martianos,* 129–97. Puerto Rico: Editorial Universitaria, 1974.

———. *La ciudad letrada.* Hanover, N.H.: Ediciones del Norte, 1984.

———. *The Lettered City.* Translated by John Charles Chasteen. Durham: Duke University Press, 1996.

Ramos, Julio. *Desencuentros de la modernidad en América Latina.* Mexico City: Secretaría de Educación Pública, 1989.

———. "El Reposo de los Héroes." *Apuntes Posmodernos /Postmodern Notes* 5:2 (1995): 14–19.

Ramsay, Maureen. *What's Wrong With Liberalism? A Radical Critique of Liberal Political Philosophy.* London: Leicester University Press, 1997.

Ransom, Roger, and Richard Sutch. *One Kind of Freedom: The Economic Consequences of Emancipation.* New York: Cambridge University Press, 1977.

Rawls, James J. *Indians of California.* Norman: University of Oklahoma Press, 1984.

Redfield, Robert. *Tepoztlán, a Mexican Village: A Study of Folk Life.* Chicago: University of Chicago Press, 1930.

———, ed. *The Life Story of the Mexican Immigrant.* New York: Dover Publications, 1971.

Reisler, Mark. "Always the Laborer, Never the Citizen: Anglo Perceptions of the Mexican Immigrant During the 1920s." In *Between Two Worlds: Mexican Immigrants in the United States,* edited by David G. Gutiérrez, 23–44. Wilmington, Del.: Scholarly Resources, 1996.

Renan, Ernest. "What Is a Nation?" In *Nation and Narration,* edited by Homi K. Bhabha, 8–22. New York: Routledge, 1990.

Renda, Mary A. *Taking Haiti: Military Occupation and the Culture of U.S. Imperialism, 1915–1940.* Chapel Hill: University of North Carolina Press, 2001.

Reyes, Aurelio de los. *Manuel Gamio y el cine.* Mexico City: Universidad Nacional Autónoma de México, 1991.

Ricoeur, Paul. "Towards a Hermeneutics of Historical Consciousness." In *Time and Narrative,* volume 3, translated by Kathleen Blamey and David Pellauer, 207–40. Chicago: University of Chicago Press, 1988.

Riis, Arthur. "Racial Essentialism and Family Values in *Uncle Tom's Cabin.*" *American Quarterly* 46.4 (1994): 513–44.

Robinson, Cedric J. "W. E. B. Du Bois and Black Sovereignty." In *Imagining Home: Class, Culture and Nationalism in the African Diaspora,* 145–57. New York: Verso, 1994.

——. *Black Marxism: The Making of the Black Radical Tradition.* 1983. Reprint Chapel Hill: University of North Carolina Press, 2000.

Rochfort, Desmond. *Mexican Muralists: Orozco, Rivera, Siqueiros.* New York: Universe Publishing, 1994.

Rodó, José Enrique. *Ariel.* Mexico City: Editorial Porrúa, 1968.

Roediger, David. *Towards the Abolition of Whiteness.* New York: Verso, 1994.

Rogin, Michael. *Blackface, White Noise: Jewish Immigrants in the Hollywood Melting Pot.* Berkeley: University of California Press, 1996.

Rojas, Rafael. *José Martí: la invención de Cuba.* Madrid: Editorial Colibrí, 2000.

Rony, Fatimah Tobing. *The Third Eye: Race, Cinema and Ethnographic Spectacle.* Durham: Duke University Press, 1996.

Rosaldo, Renato. *Culture and Truth: The Remaking of Social Analysis.* Boston: Beacon Press, 1989.

——. "Cultural Citizenship and Educational Democracy." *Cultural Anthropology* 9.3 (1994): 402–11.

Ross, Kristin. "The World Literature and Cultural Studies Program." *Critical Inquiry* (1993): 666–76.

Rotker, Susana. *The American Chronicles of José Martí: Journalism and Modernity in Spanish America.* Translated by Jennifer French and Katherine Semler. Hanover, N.H.: University Press of New England, 2000.

Rouse, Roger. "Thinking Through Transnationalism: Notes on the Cultural Politics of Class Relations in the Contemporary United States." *Public Culture* 7.2 (1995): 353–402.

Ruiz de Burton, María Amparo. *The Squatter and the Don.* 1885. Reprint Houston: Arte Público Press, 1992.

Saénz, Moisés. "The Two Sides of Mexican Nationalism." *Current History* (September 1927): 908–12.

Said, Edward. "Traveling Theory." In *The World, the Text, and the Critic,* 226–47. Cambridge: Harvard University Press, 1983.

Saldívar, José. *The Dialectics of Our America.* Durham: Duke University Press, 1991.

——. *Border Matters: Remapping American Cultural Studies.* Berkeley: University of California Press, 1997.

Sánchez, Rosaura, and Beatrice Pita. Introduction. *The Squatter and the Don* by María Amparo Ruiz de Burton. Houston: Arte Público Press, 1992.

Sánchez-Eppler, Benigno. "Telling Anthropology: Zora Neale Hurston and Gilberto Freyre Disciplined in Their Field Home-Work." *American Literary History* 4.3 (1992): 464–88.

Sánchez-Eppler, Karen. *Touching Liberty: Abolition, Feminism, and the Politics of the Body.* Berkeley: University of California Press, 1993.

Sand, Patrick. "Left Conservatism?" *The Nation* (9 March 1998): 6–7.

Sanjinés C., Javier. *Mestizaje Upside-Down: Aesthetic Politics in Modern Bolivia.* Pittsburgh: University of Pittsburgh Press, 2004.

Sapir, Edward. "Culture, Genuine and Spurious." In *Selected Writings of Edward Sapir in Language, Culture, and Personality,* edited by David Mandelbaum, 308–31. Berkeley: University of California Press, 1958.

Sassen, Saskia. *Losing Control? Sovereignty in an Age of Globalization.* New York: Columbia University Press, 1995.

——. *Globalization and Its Discontents.* New York: New Press, 1998.

Saxton, Alexander. *The Rise and Fall of the White Republic.* New York: Verso, 1991.

Scheman, Ronald L. *The Inter-American Dilemma: The Search for Inter-American Cooperation at the Centennial of the Inter-American System.* New York: Praeger, 1988.

Schulman, Ivan. "Void and Renewal: José Martí's Modernity." In *José Martí, Revolutionary Democrat,* edited by Christopher Abel and Nissa Torrents, 153–75. London: Athlone Press, 1986.

Schulyer, George S. "The Negro-Art Hokum." 1926. In *Voices from the Harlem Renaissance,* edited by Nathan Irvin Huggins, 309–12. New York: Oxford University Press, 1976.

Schwarz, Roberto. "Brazilian Culture: Nationalism by Elimination." In *Misplaced Ideas: Essays on Brazilian Culture,* 1–18. New York: Verso, 1992.

Seed, Patricia. "Colonial and Postcolonial Discourse." *Latin American Research Review* 26.3 (1991): 181–200.

——. "More Colonial and Postcolonial Discourses." *Latin American Research Review* 28.3 (1993): 146–52.

Sheridan, Guillermo. *Los Contemporáneos ayer.* Mexico City: Fondo de Cultura Económica, 1985.

Shiek, Andre. "The Comintern Program and the Racial Problem." In *The Communist International,* 15 August 1928. Reprint *American Communism and Black Americans: A Documentary History, 1919–1929,* edited by Philip S. Foner and James S. Allen, 164–66. Philadelphia: Temple University Press, 1987.

Silber, Nina. *The Romance of Reunion: Northerners and the South, 1865–1900.* Chapel Hill: University of North Carolina Press, 1993.

Silverman, Gillian. "Sympathy and Its Vicissitudes." *American Studies* 43.3 (2002): 5–28.

Sklair, Leslie. *Sociology of the Global System*, 2d ed. Baltimore: Johns Hopkins University Press, 1995.

Sommer, Doris. *Foundational Fictions: The National Romances of Latin America*. Berkeley: University of California Press, 1991.

Soysal, Yasemin Nuhoglu. "Toward a Postnational Model of Citizenship." In *The Citizenship Debates: A Reader*, edited by Gershon Shafir, 189–220. Minneapolis: University of Minnesota Press, 1998.

Spicer, Edward. *Cycles of Conquest: The Impact of Spain, Mexico and the United States on the Indians of the Southwest, 1533–1960*. Tucson: University of Arizona Press, 1962.

——. "Highlights of Yaqui History." *Indian Historian* 7.2 (1974): 2–9.

Spillers, Hortense. "Introduction: Who Cuts the Border? Some Readings on 'America.'" In *Comparative American Identities: Race, Sex and Nationality in the Modern Text*, 1–25. New York: Routledge, 1991.

——. "'All the Things You Could Be by Now, If Sigmund Freud's Wife Was Your Mother': Psychoanalysis and Race." *boundary 2* 23.3 (1996): 75–141.

Spivak, Gayatri. "Can the Subaltern Speak?" In *Marxism and the Interpretation of Culture*, edited by Lawrence Grossberg and Cary Nelson, 271–313. Urbana: University of Illinois Press, 1988.

Stabb, Martin S. *In Quest of Identity: Patterns in the Spanish American Essay of Ideas, 1890–1960*. Chapel Hill: University of North Carolina Press, 1967.

Stepan, Nancy. "Race and Gender: The Role of Analogy in Science." In *Anatomy of Racism*, edited by David Theo Goldberg, 38–57. Minneapolis: University of Minnesota Press, 1990.

Stocking, George. *Race, Culture, and Evolution: Essays in the History of Anthropology*. Chicago: University of Chicago Press, 1982.

——. "Introduction: The Basic Assumptions of Boasian Anthropology." In *A Franz Boas Reader: The Shaping of American Anthropology, 1883–1911*, edited by George Stocking, 1–20. Chicago: University of Chicago Press, 1982.

——. "The Ethnographic Sensibility of the 1920s and the Dualism of the Anthropological Tradition." In *Romantic Motives*, edited by George Stocking, 208–60. Madison: University of Wisconsin Press, 1989.

——. "Edward Burnett Tylor and the Mission of Primitive Man." In *Delimiting Anthropology: Occasional Essays and Reflections*, 103–15. Madison: University of Wisconsin Press, 2001.

Stowe, Harriet Beecher. "The Freeman's Dream: A Parable." *National Era* (1 August 1850): 121.

——. *Uncle Tom's Cabin, or Life Among the Lowly*. 1852. Reprint New York: Penguin, 1981.

——. *A Key to Uncle Tom's Cabin*. Boston: John P. Jewett, 1853.

Streeby, Shelley. *American Sensations: Class, Empire and the Production of Popular Culture*. Berkeley: University of California Press, 2002.

Sundquist, Eric. *To Wake the Nations: Race in the Making of American Literature*. Cambridge: Harvard University Press, 1993.

——. "Red, White, Black and Blue: The Color of American Modernism." *Transition* 70 (1996): 94–115.

Tate, Claudia. *Domestic Allegories of Political Desire: The Black Heroine's Text at the Turn of the Century.* New York: Oxford University Press, 1992.

——. Introduction. *Dark Princess* by W. E. B. Du Bois. Jackson: University of Mississippi Press, 1995.

Taussig, Michael. *Mimesis and Alterity: A Particular History of the Senses.* New York: Routledge, 1993.

Teichman, Judith. "Economic Restructuring, State-Labor Relations, and the Transformation of Mexican Corporatism." In *Neoliberalism Revisited: Economic Restructuring and Mexico's Political Future,* edited by Gerardo Otero, 149–66. Boulder: Westview Press, 1996.

Tinker Salas, Miguel. *In the Shadow of the Eagles: Sonora and the Transformation of the Border during the Porfiriato.* Berkeley: University of California Press, 1997.

Toledo Sande, Luis. *Cesto de llamas: Biografía de José Martí.* 1996. Reprint Seville: Ediciones Alfar, 1998.

Tompkins, Jane. *Sensational Designs: The Cultural Work of American Fiction.* New York: Oxford University Press, 1985.

Torgovnick, Marianna. Introduction. *Primitive Passions: Men, Women and the Quest for Ecstasy.* New York: Knopf, 1997.

Torrents, Nissa. "Passion and Order in *Amistad Funesta.*" In *José Martí, Revolutionary Democrat,* edited by Christopher Abel and Nissa Torrents, 176–91. London: Athlone Press, 1986.

Tourgée, Albion. "A Study in Civilization." *North American Review* 143:3 (September 1886): 246–61.

Trompf, Garry. Introduction. *Cargo Cults and Millenarian Movements: Transoceanic Comparisons of New Religious Movements.* Berlin: Mouton de Gruyter, 1990.

Troncoso, Francisco P. *Las guerras con las tribus yaqui y mayo.* Mexico City: Instituto Nacional Indigenista, 1977.

Turton, Peter. *José Martí: Architect of Cuba's Freedom.* London: Zed Books, 1986.

Tylor, Edward B. *Primitive Culture: Researches into the Development of Mythology, Philosophy, Religion, Language, Art and Custom* (1871). 2 volumes. London: John Murray, 1920.

Vanderwood, Paul J. *The Power of God Against the Guns of Government: Religious Upheaval in Mexico at the Turn of the Nineteenth Century.* Stanford: Stanford University Press, 1998.

Vasconcelos, José. "Discurso en la Universidad." 1920. In *Obra selecta,* 41–45. Caracas: Biblioteca Ayacucho, 1992.

——. *La raza cósmica.* 1925. Reprint Mexico City: Colección Austral, 1990.

——. *The Latin-American Basis of Mexican Civilization: Aspects of Mexican Civilization.* Chicago: University of Chicago Press, 1926.

Vidal, Hernán. "The Concept of Colonial and Postcolonial Discourse." *Latin American Research Review* 28.3 (1993): 113–19.

Wacker, R. Fred. *Ethnicity, Pluralism, and Race: Race Relations in America Before Myrdal.* Westport, Conn.: Greenwood Press, 1983.

Wald, Priscilla. "Minefields and Meeting Grounds: Transnational Analyses and American Studies." *American Literary History* 10:1 (1998): 199–218.

Wallerstein, Immanuel. *The Capitalist World Economy.* New York: Cambridge University Press, 1979.

Warman, Arturo. "Indigenist Thought." In *Indigenous Anthropology in Non-Western Countries,* edited by Hussein Fahim, 75–96. Durham: Carolina Academic Press, 1982.

Warren, Kenneth W. "Troubled Black Humanity in *The Souls of Black Folk* and *The Autobiography of an Ex-Colored Man.*" In *The Cambridge Companion to American Realism and Naturalism,* edited by Donald Pizer, 263–77. New York: Cambridge University Press, 1995.

Weber, Devra. Introduction. *El inmigrante mexicano—la historia de su vida: Entrevistas completas, 1926–1927.* Edited by Devra Weber, Roberto Melville and Juan Vicente Palerm. Mexico City: University of California, Institute for Mexico and the United States, 2002.

Williams, Adriana. *Covarrubias.* Austin: University of Texas Press, 1994.

Williams, Linda. *Playing the Race Card: Melodramas of Black and White from Uncle Tom to O.J. Simpson.* Princeton: Princeton University Press, 2001.

Williams, Patrick, and Laura Chrisman, eds. *Colonial Discourse and Post-Colonial Theory.* New York: Columbia University Press, 1994.

Williams, Raymond. *Marxism and Literature.* New York: Oxford University Press, 1977.

———. *Keywords.* New York: Oxford University Press, 1983.

Winthrop, Robert H. "Primitive." In *Dictionary of Concepts in Cultural Anthropology,* 217–22. Westport, Conn.: Greenwood Press, 1991.

Woodward, C. Vann. *Origins of the New South, 1877–1913.* Baton Rouge: Louisiana State University Press, 1951.

Wright, Richard. Review of *Their Eyes Were Watching God* by Zora Neale Hurston. In *New Masses* (4 October 1937). Reprint in *Zora Neale Hurston: Critical Perspectives Past and Present,* edited by Henry Louis Gates, Jr. and K. A. Appiah, 16–17. New York: Amistad, 1993.

Yoneyama, Lisa. "Habits of Knowing Cultural Differences: Chrysanthemum and the Sword in the U.S. Liberal Multiculturalism." *Topoi* 18 (1999): 71–80.

Young, Robert. *Colonial Desire: Hybridity in Theory, Culture and Race.* New York: Routledge, 1995.

Yúdice, George. "Comparative Cultural Studies Traditions: Latin America and the U.S." Paper delivered at Mexico City, Spring 1993.

Zinn, Howard. *A People's History of the United States.* New York: Harper Perennial, 1980.

Žižek, Slavoj. "The Spectre of Ideology." In *Mapping Ideology,* edited by Žižek, 1–30. New York: Verso, 1994.

———. *The Ticklish Subject: The Absent Center of Political Ontology.* New York: Verso, 1999.

Zogbaum, Heidi. *B. Traven: A Vision of Mexico.* Wilmington, Del.: Scholarly Resources, 1992.

DAVID LUIS-BROWN is an assistant professor of English at the University of Miami.

Library of Congress Cataloging-in-Publication Data

Luis-Brown, David
Waves of decolonization : discourses of race and hemispheric citizenship in Cuba, Mexico, and the United States / David Luis-Brown.
p. cm. — (New Americanists)
Includes bibliographical references and index.
ISBN 978-0-8223-4365-3 (cloth : alk. paper)
ISBN 978-0-8223-4366-0 (pbk. : alk. paper)
1. Racism—Cuba—History.
2. Racism—Mexico—History.
3. Racism—United States—History.
4. Cuba—Race relations—History.
5. Mexico—Race relations—History.
6. United States—Race relations—History.
7. Decolonization—Cuba—History.
8. Decolonization—Mexico—History.
9. Decolonization—United States—History.
I. Title.
F1789.A1L85 2008
305.800972—dc22
2008013871